ATLANTIC FAMILIES

Atlantic Families

Lives and Letters in the Later Eighteenth Century

SARAH M. S. PEARSALL

OXFORD
UNIVERSITY PRESS

Great Clarendon Street, Oxford OX2 6DP

Oxford University Press is a department of the University of Oxford.
It furthers the University's objective of excellence in research, scholarship,
and education by publishing worldwide in

Oxford New York

Auckland Cape Town Dar es Salaam Hong Kong Karachi
Kuala Lumpur Madrid Melbourne Mexico City Nairobi
New Delhi Shanghai Taipei Toronto

With offices in

Argentina Austria Brazil Chile Czech Republic France Greece
Guatemala Hungary Italy Japan Poland Portugal Singapore
South Korea Switzerland Thailand Turkey Ukraine Vietnam

Oxford is a registered trade mark of Oxford University Press
in the UK and in certain other countries

Published in the United States
by Oxford University Press Inc., New York

© Sarah M. S. Pearsall 2008

The moral rights of the author have been asserted
Database right Oxford University Press (maker)

First published 2008
First published in paperback 2010

All rights reserved. No part of this publication may be reproduced,
stored in a retrieval system, or transmitted, in any form or by any means,
without the prior permission in writing of Oxford University Press,
or as expressly permitted by law, or under terms agreed with the appropriate
reprographics rights organization. Enquiries concerning reproduction
outside the scope of the above should be sent to the Rights Department,
Oxford University Press, at the address above

You must not circulate this book in any other binding or cover
and you must impose the same condition on any acquirer

British Library Cataloguing in Publication Data
Data available

Library of Congress Cataloging in Publication Data
Data available

Typeset by SPI Publisher Services, Pondicherry, India
Digitally printed and bound in Great Britain by
CPI Antony Rowe, Chippenham and Eastbourne

ISBN 978–0–19–953299–5 (Hbk)
ISBN 978–0–19–960044–1 (Pbk)

For Peter,
'whether on this or the other side the Atlantick'.

Acknowledgements

This book has been transatlantic from the outset. Like many in the eighteenth century, therefore, I have contracted debts on both sides of the Atlantic. Although I cannot begin to repay them, I am pleased to acknowledge my many feeling creditors.

I am thankful to the following libraries for their collections, and their helpful staff for assistance over the years. In the United States these include Harvard University libraries (especially Widener), the American Antiquarian Society, the Massachusetts Historical Society, Yale University Libraries (especially Sterling), the Newport Historical Society, the New-York Historical Society, the New York Public Library, Columbia University Library (especially the Rare Books and Manuscript Division), the Historical Society of Pennsylvania, the Library Company of Philadelphia, the Library of Congress, the Virginia Historical Society, the Library of Virginia, Alderman Library at the University of Virginia, the Rockefeller Library at Colonial Williamsburg, Duke University Library (especially the Rare Book, Manuscript, and Special Collections Library), the University of North Carolina, Chapel Hill Library (especially the Manuscripts Department), Northwestern University Library, the Newberry Library (and the Consortium of Academic and Research Libraries in Illinois), and the Huntington Library. In Great Britain these include the British Library, National Archives (at Kew), the Institute of Commonwealth Studies, University of London, Cambridge University Library, the Cambridgeshire County Record Office, Oxford University libraries (including the Bodleian, the Vere Harmsworth Library, the Sackler, and Rhodes House), the Liverpool Libraries and Record Office, St Andrews University Library, and the National Library of Scotland.

Without funding, there would have been few, if any, trips to these collections; funding also paid for the time to make sense of what I found on these travels. While conducting the initial research, I was supported by the Jacob K. Javits Fellowship, as well as the CBS Bicentennial Narrators' Scholarship, History Department Research Grants, Charles Warren Center Research Grants, the Packard Fellowship, and the Artemis Ward Fellowship, all at Harvard University, and the Mellon Fellowship in American History, Cambridge University. The Robert Middlekauff Fellowship at the Huntington Library, the Virginia Historical Society Mellon Fellowship, the Duke University Women's Studies Research Grant, the Kraus Grant from the American Historical Association, the Gilder Lehrman Fellowship, and Research Grants from St Andrews University afforded me the opportunity to travel to collections. Northwestern University generously funded further research; the University Research Grants Committee at the Graduate School kindly paid for the images used in the book. I was also fortunate enough to receive a year-long Mellon Foundation/National Endowment for the Humanities Fellowship at the Newberry Library, which made a tremendous difference. Jim Grossman, Sara Austin, Erin Lucido, and Katie McMahon, as well as my fellow Fellows, were especially important in making the Newberry the wonderful place to work that it is.

Other voyages brought me not to collections but to conferences and seminars. Over many years, commentators and audiences at numerous conferences, on both sides of the Atlantic, offered helpful criticisms. I am especially grateful for invitations to present work at seminars, for my hosts who energetically entered into the project with me, and for the audiences who offered good questions and comments. In the United States these included the Fellows' Seminar and the Early American Seminars at the Newberry Library; the Colloquium at the Omohundro Institute of Early American History and Culture (and a special session the next day with Institute staff and Rhys Isaac); the History Seminar at Johns Hopkins University; and the Colonies Seminar at the University of Iowa. In Europe these included the Oxford University Atlantic World Seminar; L'Association pour l'Étude de la Colonisation Européenne at l'Université Paris Sorbonne—Paris IV; the Cambridge University American History Seminar; the History Seminar at the University of Dundee; and the American Studies Seminar, University of East Anglia.

I am grateful to *The William and Mary Quarterly* for permission to reproduce, in Chapter 7, a version of my article, '"The late flagrant instance of depravity in my Family": The Story of an Anglo-Jamaican Cuckold', *William and Mary Quarterly*, 60: 3 (July 2003). I am also grateful to the British Library, Cambridge University Library, the Bodleian Library, Oxford, and the Guildhall Library, City of London, for permission to reproduce images held in their collections.

I have had the pleasure of teaching, conducting research, and conversing with stimulating colleagues at a number of fine ports along the way: Harvard University, Cambridge University (especially Clare College), St Andrews University, and Northwestern University. Thanks, too, to the deans, chairs, and administrators at those institutions for help, financial and otherwise, to complete this project. I also appreciate my students, both undergraduates and graduates, from whom I have learned much about the craft of history.

Various mentors have been kind enough 'to guide [me] from running on the . . . Shoals, by persuading [me] to aim at the Dissipation of the Fogs of *Ignorance* by the Sunshine of Learning.'[1] Laurel Thatcher Ulrich has been a wise guide, as well as a sunny presence, from the genesis of this project (and even before), tireless in her enthusiasm, challenging in her criticisms, and patient in her readings. An extraordinary dissertation advisor, she has also been an inspiration in making history in all kinds of ways. Joyce Chaplin helped considerably with the

---

[1] Wyndham Beawes, *Lex Mercatoria Rediviva: Or, the Merchant's Directory. Being a Complete Guide to all Men in Business* (London, 1771), 486.

dissertation upon which this book is based, and has been a great support ever since. Betty Wood has been a fine ally in things early American (and otherwise). Hamish Scott exemplifies intellectual rigor and personal kindness, and our conversations at St Andrews in particular were lifelines. Jan Lewis has been a warm and witty mentor over the years. Phil Morgan early offered encouragement, which meant a lot. Ron Hoffman and Sally Mason have consistently shown confidence in this project and its author; this faith, and insightful questions and observations, have made a great deal of difference. The sage counsel of Al Young, a true *mensch*, has been a gift. Mark Peterson gave excellent advice on many matters. With his amazing intelligence and energy, Tim Breen has taught me much in our time together at Northwestern.

A number of other colleagues have also made me feel part of a community of scholars: David Armitage, Michael Braddick, Holly Brewer, Chris Brown, Trevor Burnard, Emily Clark, Elaine Forman Crane, Jim Epstein, Sylvia Frey, Adele Hast, Linda Kerber, Sarah Knott, Simon Middleton, Louis Nelson, Marie-Jeanne Rossignol, Eric Slauter, Kirsten Sword, Betsy Wright, and Kariann Yokota. I am also thankful for the early American writing group at Harvard, whose members offered critiques and moral support over the years. I have also had many useful conversations about this project with various colleagues at Northwestern, including Betsy Erkkila, Mark Bradley, Nancy MacLean, Kate Masur, Sarah Maza, Susan Pearson, Dylan Penningroth, Claire Priest, David Schoenbrun, Ethan Shagan, Julia Stern, and Butch Ware.

Ruth Parr's enthusiasm for this project brought it to Oxford University Press, where Rupert Cousens has tended it admirably. I am grateful for the good efforts of Seth Cayley, Kate Hind, Jeff New, and Tony Williams, as well as the rest of the staff at OUP. I have also been glad for Susan Ferber's involvement. The astute critiques of Ned Landsman and two anonymous readers for OUP improved the book. Jan Lewis, Elaine Crane, and Alfred Young also turned their critical acumen to sections of the book. A few hardy and generous souls waded through the whole unedited thing and improved it greatly: Laurel Ulrich, as well as several Northwestern colleagues: Tim Breen, Kate Masur, Sarah Maza, and Susan Pearson. The faults that remain are, of course, my own.

Many friends have provided happy havens from work and worry. They include: Frances Andrews, Sara Austin, Louise Bourdua, Peter Carroll, Carlo Caruso, Annalisa Cipollone, Emily Clark, Miryam Conesa, Deborah Cunningham, Elisabetta Frontoni, Michael Green, Emma Griffin, Dan Hamilton, Katherine Hawley, Jon Hesk, Ron Hoffman, Nikos Kakalis, Mike Kramer, Lisa Laskin, Sally Mason, Kate Masur, Beth Nichols, Dasha Nicholls, Susan Pearson, Lori Schuyler, Hamish Scott, Julia Smith, Kirsten Sword, Alessio Vaccari, Frank Valadez, Russell Viner, Mary-Ann Winkelmes, Betty Wood, Betsy Wright, and Kariann Yokota.

My many English (and Welsh and Scottish) in-laws have welcomed me, for which I am grateful. Amy Gambrill has become family since our first meeting nearly twenty years ago (for which I'll always pay homage to the gods of roommate matching). Ira and Ella Meyer provided an education in all kinds of ways. I first learned about the tumultuous joys of family life, as well as its enduring affections, from my mother, Marilyn Pearsall, my brother, Anthony Pearsall, and my sister, Cornelia Pearsall. Remarkable individuals and brilliant scholars all, they have also inspired with their own books. John Rogers and Pauline Stone willingly entered in, and, in typical fashion, have made it all so much better over the years. My nieces, Adeline, Lily, Marina, and Christina, and my god-daughter Zoe, delight in all sorts of ways. Our Scottish cat, Edmund, provided excellent company for many years; he is much missed.

My English husband, Peter Kail, was not the inspiration for this project, but he has nevertheless given me deeper insight into the ways that love can survive Atlantic distance. He has given me much else besides. It has been an abiding pleasure to share the eighteenth (and twentieth and twenty-first) centuries with him. As I finished the book, we were joined by our son, Edward, who appropriately began crossing the Atlantic before he was even born. These two wonderful traveling companions will always have my loving thanks for accompanying me on all kinds of journeys, transatlantic and otherwise.

Contents

List of Figures	xii
List of Abbreviations	xiii
Prologue. 'This Silent Art': Reading Other People's Letters	1
Introduction	4

I. 'DEALING BY INK ALTOGETHER': MECHANISMS OF CONNECTION AND DISCONNECTION

Introduction	23
1. Fractured Families: The Perils and Possibilities of Atlantic Distance	26
2. Familiarity in Life and Letters	56
3. Sensibility in Life and Letters	80
4. Credit in Life and Letters	111

II. 'WHAT MAY BE OUR LOT': STORIES OF CONNECTION AND DISCONNECTION

Introduction	145
5. The Repentant Son and the Unforgiving Father: Making a Man of Feeling, a Man of Credit	149
6. The Farewell Between Husband and Wife: The Politics of Family Feeling	179
7. The Old Husband and the Young Wife: Scandal, Feeling, and Distance	210
Conclusion	240
Epilogue	244
Bibliography	248
Index	283

List of Figures

1.1. Frontispiece to *The Court Letter Writer* (London, 1773). Bodleian Library, University of Oxford, Vet.A.f.1860, frontispiece. — 27

1.2. Frontispiece to George Brown, *The English Letter-Writer; Or, The Whole Art of General Correspondence* (London, 1785?). © British Library Board. All Rights Reserved, 10920.aaa.5. — 40

1.3. Frontispiece to [Dorothea DuBois], *The Lady's Polite Secretary, or New Female Letter Writer* (London, 1771). © British Library Board. All Rights Reserved, 10920.aa.11. — 41

1.4. Anonymous, 'The Middle Temple Macaroni', *c.*1772. Guildhall Library, City of London. — 51

5.1. 'The Penitent Son', to accompany 'The Repentant Son: A Moral Tale', *Town and Country Magazine*, 8 (Mar. 1776), 137–41. Cambridge University Library, T900.c.38.8. — 150

6.1. 'The Farewell', to accompany 'The Farewel: or, the History of Horatius and Flavilla', *Town and Country Magazine* (July 1781), 376–8. Bodleian Library, University of Oxford, Per. 2705 e.674, pp. 376–7, vol. 13. — 180

7.1. Thomas Rowlandson, 'The Old Husband' (*c.*1800), reprinted from Peter Wagner, *Eros Revived: Erotica of the Enlightenment in England and America* (London: Secker & Warburg, 1988). Bodleian Library, University of Oxford, M00.E 10035, p. 146. — 211

List of Abbreviations

BL	British Library, London
CCRO	Cambridgeshire County Record Office, Cambridge
CURB	Columbia University Rare Books and Manuscripts Collection, New York
DUL	Duke University Library, Special Collections, Durham, NC
HL	Huntington Library, Art Collections, and Botanical Gardens, San Marino, Calif.
HSP	Historical Society of Pennsylvania
ICS	Institute of Commonwealth Studies, University of London
LoC	Library of Congress, Washington, DC
LRO	Liverpool Record Office, Liverpool City Library
LV	Library of Virginia, Richmond
MHS	Massachusetts Historical Society
NA	National Archives (of England), Kew
NHS	Newport Historical Society
NLS	National Library of Scotland, Edinburgh
NYHS	New-York Historical Society
NYPL	New York Public Library
SHC	Southern Historical Collection, Manuscripts Department, University of North Carolina, Chapel Hill, NC
VHS	Virginia Historical Society

Prologue
'This Silent Art': Reading Other People's Letters

'This silent art of speaking by letters, remedies the inconvenience arising from distance of time, as well as place... This preserves the works of the immortal part of man, so as to make the dead still useful to the living.'[1] So remarked the *New Complete General Letter Writer* in 1803. This book aims to reach the dead through their letters. When literate family members found themselves, by dint of choice or chance, divided into multiple households, the connections that remained were occasionally literary. For the families that are the focus of this book, their households were divided by the Atlantic Ocean, in a rapidly changing eighteenth-century world. There are certain universals in family communications: claims of enduring love, news shared, carping, bickering, requests for money. But there are also aspects of letters particular to their times. This book considers the conventions of letter-writing, connecting them with larger changes and movements of the eighteenth century. It does so in order to reveal more about not only letters, but also families and their Atlantic worlds.

Family letters from the eighteenth century bear many similarities to letters or even emails of today. They were sent privately to avoid prying eyes; they included salutations and signatures; they contained all kinds of information, from the trivial to the monumental. Eighteenth-century letters look like letters we know, but they are also different, carrying subtle messages about their time and place that might elude the casual observer. Such is true of their contents, as we shall see, but it is also true of their physical form. The way letters were sealed, with family crests or images imprinted into wax, could indicate identities, rank, even significant personal events. Black wax, as opposed to red, alerted the recipient that some great catastrophe or death had befallen the family. The quality of the whitish paper spoke to access and privilege, while the occasional black border could, again, signify mourning. Blots on the page, as well as the handwriting, could indicate the inexperience, carelessness, or hurry of the writer. These letters

---

[1] *The New Complete General Letter-Writer, And Universal Correspondent* (London, 1803), introduction.

do not carry postage stamps, though they will sometimes have a figure written on them, to indicate the cost of postage (a cost generally borne by the recipient, not the sender). The lack of such notations can reveal that someone carried them personally. Sometimes an ink stamp can indicate a route (especially if it went through a British port, when it might be stamped as a SHIP LETTER). It is possible to match dates, to learn that it took in general six to eight weeks to go from one side of the Atlantic to the other.

Families from the eighteenth century bear many similarities to families of today. Families then, as now, include love, rivalries, economics, and complicated dynamics of authority, expectation, and affection. Like letters, eighteenth-century families look like families we know, but they are also different. Laws placed far more power in the hands of the master of the house. Household subordinates worked within much more constrained circumstances. Nevertheless, all kinds of individuals within that household were able to negotiate and make sense of their positions. One of the ways they did so was through the use of certain kinds of expressions and persuasive tools, of which letters were one form. Bearing in mind these differences can help to make sense of the past.

This book is about families and their worlds, not simply their letters, but in this case, the medium is part of the message. Letters are one of the best ways to reach families and their histories, but they are also an excellent way of reaching larger changes in societies and cultures. Their production, circulation, and reception allow us to witness families and individuals at various stages and various situations. The increased circulation of letters, and shifts in their forms and tones, provide a useful means of entry into larger cultural and social changes. As one historian has rightly noted, 'the study of "the feelings" [in the history of the family] is necessarily the study of *expressions* of feeling, and so must begin with conventions, genres, and languages'.[2]

To enter into family life, even through letters, is to be confronted with longing affections, clinging desires, deep chasms of misunderstanding. 'Somewhere between a hug and a chokehold', is how a friend described a daughter's grip on her little sister; this is an apt description for much family life. There are too many competing claims, too many perspectives, too many justifications, for narratives about families to be entirely straightforward. Myths, claims and counter-claims, the heavy weight of expectations: all these contribute to family histories. Historians sometimes eschew this mess; perhaps it disturbs them. They have instead sought typologies of sorts of families, in a laudable, if ultimately rather futile, attempt to impose order on this teeming chaos. Alas, such typologies tend to crumble in the face of the idiosyncratic testimony of individual families.

---

[2] Rhys Isaac, 'Communication and Control: Authority Metaphors and Power Contests on Colonel Landon Carter's Virginia Plantation, 1752–1778', in Sean Wilentz (ed.), *Rites of Power: Symbolism, Ritual, and Politics Since the Middle Ages* (Philadelphia: University of Pennsylvania Press, 1985), 275–302: at 299.

The very multiplicity of perspectives provides a means of understanding how people negotiated with each other, how they loved and protected each other, how they sometimes failed each other. This project embraces the mess as well as the multiplicity of perspectives, the chokeholds as well as the hugs. At the same time, family letters do form patterns, and these patterns tell us both about individual lives and the larger cultures in which they were immersed.

With little hint of irony, *Town and Country Magazine*, a periodical known more for its titillating divorce cases than its stern morality, declared in 1776 that the 'essential characteristics' of a historian were 'scrupulous honour and strict integrity'.[3] To that end, I announce here that, in using these letters and other sources, I have transcribed quotations as faithfully as possible, leaving idiosyncrasies and anachronisms in spelling, capitalization, and punctuation. I have only added punctuation or spelled out abbreviations where I feared the original meaning would be obscured. I have also generally referred to individuals by their first names. I am not implying that these people are my pals. It is simply that family members often shared the same family name, and it could prove confusing otherwise. *Town and Country Magazine* further cautioned that it was necessary for a historian to be 'grave and honest,' for 'How much soever we might be entertained with the wit of a sprightly debauchee, we should give but little credit to his relation of facts'.[4] I concede I might be a little sprightly. Still, I hope, along with Samuel Richardson, that the reader will be equally so, and that this work, like *Pamela*, 'will not fail to engage the Attention of the gay and more sprightly Readers'.[5]

---

[3] 'Thoughts on Historians', *Town and Country Magazine* (Dec. 1776), 624.   [4] Ibid.
[5] Samuel Richardson, 'To the Editor of *Pamela*', *Pamela; or, Virtue Rewarded*, 2 vols., 2nd edn. (London, 1741), i. p. viii.

Introduction

'Remember the Ladies', Abigail Adams wrote to her husband in Philadelphia from their home in Massachusetts in 1776, in what must be the most famous early American domestic letter, as well as the most well-known statement by an early American woman. Abigail entreated her husband to remember married women's need for legal protection against possibly tyrannical husbands. Abigail continued: 'Remember, all Men would be tyrants if they could. If perticuliar care and attention is not paid to the Ladies we are determined to foment a Rebelion.' She further declared of men: 'That your Sex are Naturally Tyrannical is a Truth so thoroughly established as to admit of no dispute but such of you as wish to be happy willingly give up the harsh title of Master for the more tender and endearing one of Friend.'[1] In his reply, John refused to take Abigail's desire seriously: 'As to your extraordinary Code of Laws, I cannot but laugh. We have been told that our Struggle has loosened the bands of Government every where.' He continued: 'We know better than to repeal our Masculine systems. Altho they are in full Force, you know they are little more than Theory... We are obliged to go fair, and softly... We have only the Name of Masters.'[2]

Numerous textbooks have used this epistolary episode (or at least Abigail's part in it) to demonstrate the way that women such as Abigail Adams imported the ideas of the American Revolution into domestic struggles. In the usual reading, the American Revolution provided the inspiration for her threats, jocular or not, that women might start their own rebellion, just as they did her claims that women, like Americans more generally, might well refuse to accept a lack of representation. This reading further implies that she gained notions about tyranny from political writings of the American Revolution that denounced British tyranny. One historian has argued that this letter shows 'her manipulation of Revolutionary rhetoric in ways that were unanticipated and unintended by American Revolutionaries'.[3] John's reply, less oft-reprinted, is generally deployed to show both that he did not take her seriously and

---

[1] Abigail Adams to John Adams, 'Braintree March 31–April 5 1776', L. H. Butterfield, Wendell D. Garrett, and Marjorie E. Sprague (eds.), *Adams Family Correspondence*, 6 vols. (Cambridge, Mass.: Harvard University Press, 1963), i. 369–371.
[2] John Adams to Abigail Adams, 'Ap 14, 1776', ibid. i. 381–3.
[3] Elaine Forman Crane, 'Political Dialogue and the Spring of Abigail's Discontent', *William and Mary Quarterly*, 56 (1999), 745–74: 760–1.

to demonstrate the anxieties that the leaders of the American Revolution had about the possibility of revolutionary principles extending to those who were not elite white men. These interpretations are persuasive, but they also miss something vital in this exchange: its larger domestic, epistolary, and ultimately Atlantic context.

This book opens up the briny Atlantic oyster that produced the Adams' American pearls of wisdom, and offers, in so doing, a new way of thinking about their world. This book is about how families nurtured ties, sentimental and otherwise, in an Atlantic beset with considerable disruption, of which the American Revolution was one source among many. The letters of Abigail and John Adams, even when sent only between Massachusetts and Pennsylvania, were products not just of an American but of an Atlantic culture concerned with feelings, attachments, and domestic behavior and its relationship to politics. Later, their own letters, as for many letter-writers in this era, became transatlantic, and this aspect signals one of the sources of disorder and reordering of families and societies through letters. Whether due to economic shifts, political dislocation, imperial ambitions, or even simply personal tragedy, many families in the later eighteenth century found themselves divided and disoriented by the growth and later fissure of a larger Atlantic world.

Letters and other stories about affectionate connections offered a way to reconstitute families and societies so upended. 'Is there no Way for two friendly Souls, to converse together, altho the Bodies are 400 Miles off?—Yes by Letter.'[4] So announced John in another letter of this period. Letters allowed many, including Abigail and John, to surmount the distance between bodies, even as they wished for closer contact. In so doing, literate families who experienced such separations left a valuable source by which to track both their ideas about family, and also to witness the upheavals of their worlds. This book thus focuses on such letters, looking at the ways that families enduring transatlantic distance used letters to make sense of chaos and to maintain a burgeoning Atlantic world. The 'Atlantic families', as I term them, at the center of this study are those in which members were divided by the Atlantic, in general between American colonies, Caribbean ones, and Britain.

Beyond the Adams clan, many families of their time and place survived distances, even as they similarly emphasized the unceasing feelings cementing their relations. Turning from individual letters to the larger culture in which they were immersed, we can begin to discern a larger pattern of developments occurring in parallel that can confound. How extraordinary for a culture to celebrate families so frequently, in all kinds of texts, as a source of love and comfort, a necessity of life, at the same time that so many families endured separations and reconfigurations, or inflicted such separations on other families.

---

[4] John Adams to Abigail Adams, 'April 28. 1776', *Adams Family Correspondence*, i. 398–401: 400.

One historian has asked: 'Why is the loving family so vivid, overblown, and ubiquitous in the culture of the West in the eighteenth century?'[5] Why, we might also ask, was this true even as unloving, or at least disordered, families were equally vivid, overblown, and ubiquitous in this same period?

In the eighteenth century, these endless visions of loving families occurred simultaneously with endless visions of fractured ones. The Adams letters are a good example of this phenomenon: the fact of distance and disorder married to constant invocations of affectionate relations. This seeming contradiction is apparent in many areas: in domestic letters, to be sure, but also in literature, art, and philosophy circulating throughout an Atlantic world. Magazines told stories of prodigal sons who ran through inheritances far from home, but were received back by kindly fathers, of wives who withstood the many temptations of adultery while their husbands were away, of husbands who endured the hell of war only to return to the loving arms of wives. Novels recounted tales of daughters and sons navigating the dangers of seduction and misadventure in uncertain new worlds, away from the family who might protect or advise them. As one literary scholar has observed, 'being cast out of a family or taken into a family *is* the adventure in eighteenth-century novels'.[6] Portraits of the time celebrated in warm and radiant tones the domestic harmony between family members who were dead or separated by the time the portraits were painted.[7] Philosophers who never married or had children lauded marriage and family as sources of moral benevolence.[8]

---

[5] Sarah Maza, 'Only Connect: Family Values in the Age of Sentiment: Introduction', Special Issue on the Family, *Eighteenth-Century Studies*, 30 (1997), 207–12: 208. Jan Lewis has made a similar point about the letters of Thomas Jefferson and his daughters: 'Only recently had men and women begun to sentimentalize the family, to think of it in almost religious terms as a sanctuary or haven. We need think only of Shakespeare's families—the warring Montagues and Capulets, the conflict-ridden Lears, the scheming Macbeths—to realize how remarkable, how revolutionary was the notion that a family might be any source of pleasure at all, let alone the source of *everything* pleasurable', as Thomas Jefferson claimed in his letters. Jan Ellen Lewis, 'The White Jeffersons', in Jan Ellen Lewis and Peter S. Onuf (eds.), *Sally Hemings & Thomas Jefferson: History, Memory, and Civic Culture* (Charlottesville, Va.: University Press of Virginia, 1999), 127–60: 130–1.

[6] Ruth Perry, *Novel Relations: The Transformation of Kinship in English Literature and Culture, 1748–1818* (Cambridge: Cambridge University Press, 2004), 8.

[7] Consider John Singleton Copley's 1778 *Sir William Pepperrell and his Family*, which shows a happy family, bathed in the sensible glow attending so many family portrayals of this time. However, it depicts a family that no longer existed, if it ever had. By the time the painting was completed, the Loyalist Pepperrell family had been exiled from Boston to London and had most of their property confiscated. The serene mother at its center had died in 1775. This picture served to memorialize her, if silently, even as it also represented a celebration of joyful domesticity in the face of profound upheaval. John Singleton Copley, *Sir William Pepperrell (1746–1816) and His Family, 1778*, held at the North Carolina Museum of Art. See Margaretta M. Lovell, *Art in a Season of Revolution: Painters, Artisans, and Patrons in Early America* (Philadelphia: University of Pennsylvania Press, 2005), 153–83. The painting also receives attention in Kate Retford, *The Art of Domestic Life: Family Portraiture in Eighteenth-Century England* (New Haven: Yale University Press, 2006).

[8] Neither David Hume nor Adam Smith, for instance, married or apparently had children. Nevertheless, Hume lauded the Platonic ideal of a loving marriage in his essay, 'Of Love and Marriage'. He also discussed the domestic origins of moral feeling in 'Of Moral Prejudices'. See

At one level, these phenomena make little sense; at another level, they make a great deal of sense. Invoking happy families did a great deal of cultural, as well as social, political, and economic work. The grim reality of family disorder, married with the exalted visions of sentimental domesticity, suggests that something was changing. One of the things changing, this book argues, was the pressure that Atlantic ventures, among others, put upon family members in the anglophone world. As the Adams letters imply, family members themselves were uneasily aware of the possibility that separations, in their case occasioned by the American Revolution and Atlantic distance, might cause problems in the smooth running of life. The incessant claims to the enduring power of family affections were symptomatic of the concerns swirling around the maintenance of family life in such circumstances. They were also symptomatic of new abilities to remain connected over distance, and a sense that stories about families could keep them whole despite apparent fracture.

In short, sentimentalizing families was one way of coping with the dislocations of the eighteenth century. Glowing images of domestic life, whether forwarded in personal letters or in other texts, were less a signal of something shifting in the nature of family life than a signal of deeper anxieties about the ways that social, economic, and political situations were shifting, as well as the increasing resonance and circulation of such images. One of the chief ways by which people nurtured ties in the face of disruption was through their invocations of 'family feeling' (a phrase which denotes the linkage of familial relations with claims to sentiment). Projecting the family as unified and happy, as a sentimental as much as a political or economic entity, provided a means of surmounting concerns over societies fractured by imperial distance, global wars, urban growth, and increasing social stratification.

Transatlantic anglophone families were not novel in the eighteenth century; after all, the seventeenth century witnessed considerable outward migration from Britain to colonies in Ireland and North America. Nevertheless, such disruptions gained momentum as continued migration, colonial population increases, transatlantic economic growth, and global wars gave rise to increased concerns about imperial movements. At the same time, increased literacy and circulation of texts (including letters) around that Atlantic world meant that those disruptions were more widely broadcast, and also meant that more individuals could contribute to trying to bridge distances, between families and between colonies and nations. Letters and other texts about affectionate families allowed a society increasingly stratified and divided geographically to exorcize demons of distance and dislocation. Invoking the family also became an increasingly popular method of justifying difficult decisions surrounding empire and war, for both individuals and also

---

David Hume, *Essays Moral, Political, and Literary*, ed. Eugene F. Miller, rev. edn. (Indianapolis: Liberty Fund, 1987), 557–62 and 538–44. Smith, too, connected families and moral sentiment in his *The Theory of Moral Sentiments* (London and Edinburgh, 1759). See my discussion in Ch. 3.

societies as a whole. In transatlantic family letters and lives, the greatest appeals to tenderness, affection, and 'family feeling' tended to occur when situations were at their most strained, and relations at their most vulnerable. The imperial and colonial rise of the British Atlantic created significant challenges for families, as well as significant opportunities, and these challenges were one reason for the increasingly frantic attempts at generating cheery domesticity in fiction, art, and life. There were of course many other strains on families in this period, but Atlantic distance and imperial growth were significant ones. They are the focus of this book.

There have been many names for what happened to British and American families in the eighteenth century, but historians, art historians, and literary critics can more or less agree on one thing: something changed in the portrayal of household life in roughly the middle of the eighteenth century (even if its roots were older, and the basic affections, and significant inequalities, underpinning family life remained largely unchanged).[9] Most have generally agreed that this period saw a rise in what has been termed 'companionate marriage' as well as gentler methods of child-rearing, with an emphasis placed on feeling. This transition has been connected with a shift from patriarchy to paternalism. As literary scholars in particular have been at pains to demonstrate, this shift was accompanied by considerable concern about the family, expressed in the literature of the day.[10] This change was also not unrelated to the rise of a culture of sensibility, in which it became important for individuals to demonstrate their lively sensations. Historians of the family have gestured toward the rise of sensibility, while historians of sensibility have gestured toward the family.[11] Yet

---

[9] The classic formulations focus on the rise of 'companionate marriage' as well as gentler methods of child-rearing. See Lawrence Stone, *The Family, Sex and Marriage in England, 1500–1800* (New York: Harper & Row, 1977). Historians of colonial America echoed this line, with some modifications. See e.g. Jan Lewis, *The Pursuit of Happiness: Family and Values in Jefferson's Virginia* (Cambridge: Cambridge University Press, 1983), and Daniel Blake Smith, *Inside the Great House: Planter Family Life in Eighteenth-Century Chesapeake Society* (Ithaca, NY: Cornell University Press, 1980). Historians of slavery, looking at the wider household, have similarly presumed the change to be a shift from brutal patriarchy to warmer paternalism. This has been most clearly and recently articulated in Philip D. Morgan, *Slave Counterpoint: Black Culture in the Eighteenth-Century Chesapeake and Lowcountry* (Chapel Hill, NC: University of North Carolina Press for the Omohundro Institute of Early American History and Culture, 1998). Art historians have concentrated on the images of sentimental families that became *the* popular way for elite members of society to represent themselves. See, e.g. Retford, *The Art of Domestic Life*, and Lovell, *Art in a Season of Revolution*, ch. 5. Literary critics have also drawn attention to this shifting representation in literature. See, e.g. Eve Tavor Bannet, *The Domestic Revolution: Enlightenment Feminisms and the Novel* (Baltimore, Md.: Johns Hopkins University Press, 2000); Christopher Flint, *Family Fictions: Narrative and Domestic Relations in Britain, 1688–1798* (Stanford, Calif.: Stanford University Press, 1998); and Perry, *Novel Relations*.

[10] Christopher Flint summarizes: 'The creation of the sentimentalized nuclear household was both a conscious tactical maneuver and a means of making the family seem healthy [and] whole.' Flint, *Family Fictions*, 77.

[11] One historian of the family in Virginia alludes to the importance of a British-imported 'cult of sensibility' in reshaping family relations, a line found elsewhere in the history of the family. Lewis, *Pursuits of Happiness*, 217–19. See also Stone, *The Family, Sex and Marriage*, Smith, *Inside the Great*

the connections between these changes remain as yet unclear. In part, families created and sustained cultures of sensibility, so that 'family feeling' became an ideal as well as a cultural, social, and political tool. This book contends that one of the principal reasons for the constant mentions of loving attachments was their seemingly imperiled status as a result of the many and frequent dislocations of an Atlantic world. It also posits that literary forms such as letters allowed many to invoke family feeling as a means of bridging distance and quelling disorder.

To return to the well-known Adams' dispute, for instance, these invocations of attachments, amid disorienting distance, resonate powerfully in the rest of Abigail's famous letter. Her letter began, as so many of her time did, with conventional complaints, not radical notions: chiding her husband for not writing her as much as she wished. Much of the rest of the letter, again like so many from this era, was concerned with households, their own in Boston included, disrupted and devastated, in this case by the Revolutionary War. Her letter also invoked her heart: 'I feel a gaieti de Coar [gladness of heart] to which before I was a stranger... and Nature puts on a more chearfull countanance.' Here, she connected her own emotional state to the environment around her, thus exhibiting the sensibility so prized in her era. She rejoiced that many who had fled their homes because of war were able to return even while fretting over those who feared their own homes might be destroyed: 'we sympathize with those who was trembling least the Lot of Boston should be theirs.' She thus connected political and domestic orders. It was at this point that she entreated her husband to 'Remember the Ladies'. Her syntax, which linked household disorder and the need for new laws to protect women, indicated her sense that these topics were related. Both were about the need for improved domestic and political orders. After the signature, written a few days later, she noted that her gaiety has dissipated: 'I have been attending the sick chamber of our Neighbour Trot whose affliction I most sensibly feel but cannot discribe, striped of two lovely children in one week... Our own little flock are yet well. My Heart trembles with anxiety for them.' Exhibiting again her sensible heart, she also informed her husband that their own family was well, although she worried deeply over them. Children were central to her concerns, and, even as she acknowledged the disruptions of war and death, she emphasized her continued affection for her own family. Her signature stressed her enduring loyalty: 'I need not say how much I am Your ever faithfull Friend.' She need not say it, but she did.

John's letter, too, in his mention of 'loosening the bands of government', raised concerns about connections, and what might happen when they were loosened. This point also epitomizes a general eighteenth-century Atlantic one. His claim

House, and Jay Fliegelman, *Prodigals and Pilgrims: The American Revolution Against Patriarchal Authority, 1750–1800*, (Cambridge: Cambridge University Press, 1982). A noted historian of sensibility, on the other hand, has attributed the rise of a culture of sensibility in part to 'a newer ideal' of affectionate family relations. G. J. Barker-Benfield, *The Culture of Sensibility: Sex and Society in Eighteenth-Century Britain* (Chicago: University of Chicago Press, 1992), 101–2.

that good husbands 'had only the Names of Masters' was again typical of its times. John's point here, of the need even for husbands 'to go fair, and softly', is generally seen as bad faith, when, as Abigail pointed out, laws were stacked entirely in their favor. There are delusional and sidestepping aspects to this claim (just as in Abigail's March 1776 hopes for domestic peace), but they also indicate something else. John Adams shared with many similar men of his time a sense that there was a need for a man to treat at least some household subordinates, especially wives, with what others termed 'tenderness'. Even when they did not do so, they inhabited a transatlantic culture that increasingly privileged certain kinds of elite masculine behavior, and condemned others. John's reply further expressed his pleasure at the preservation of their Boston house. In his letter, as in many of his time, he also worried over the future of their children. Family and home were as much a part of his letter as were his political ruminations.

Beyond the Adams, many other letter-writers under consideration here linked domestic and political orders. Also like John and Abigail, many were eventually separated by the Atlantic ocean. As such, they represent what one scholar has termed 'the normal exception'.[12] They were unusual, but not wildly so. They are more unusual in their wealth and education, their ability to exchange letters, than in their Atlantic crossings. The individuals under focus here were divided by the Atlantic for years at a time, whether because of lengthy sojourns or permanent migrations.[13] They reveal most clearly and most eloquently the dislocations that they and many others faced in this period, many of which were related to the triumphs and terrors of the development of a global empire. Just as these families were not tied to a single national location, this project is also not tied to a single national historiography.[14] I am using 'Atlantic' as a means of approach as well as a category of analysis, although I do not mean to imply either that these same trends did not affect national trajectories, or that these families represent the entire Atlantic world.[15] Concentrating on an Atlantic arena is a way of circumventing national boundaries, of correcting exceptionalist narratives (which have in particular plagued American families), and of placing the Atlantic at the center of family history.[16]

---

[12] See Edward Muir's discussion of this term, from Edoardo Grendi in his 'Introduction', in Edward Muir and Guido Ruggiero (eds.), *Microhistory and the Lost Peoples of Europe* (Baltimore, Md.: Johns Hopkins University Press, 1991), p. xiv, and Jacques Revel (ed.), *Jeux d'échelles: la micro-analyse à l'expérience* (Paris: Gallimard/Le Seuil, 1996).

[13] It is true that many individuals in this period did not travel the Atlantic at all. However, many did, and even those who did not relied on links of travel, trade, and transport forged by many of the individuals considered here.

[14] It is my hope that they may be fruitfully compared with other Atlantic families.

[15] This was a deeply varied, complicated, and ever-shifting place, with a variety of languages, cultures, politics, and imperatives. The choice of focusing on certain kinds of Atlantic families is also one made in the full knowledge that other kinds of distances separated anglophone families in this era. This is also far from the whole Atlantic world.

[16] Another book that combines empire and family is Elizabeth Buettner, *Empire Families: Britons and Late Imperial India* (Oxford: Oxford University Press, 2004).

Family letters helped to make empire possible, bearable, justifiable, and profitable for many. The families here experienced dislocations of profound sorts: revolutions, political defeat, cuckoldry, economic loss, bastardy, separations never remedied. They were the lucky ones. They could write and read soothing stories of family life, remaining connected by letter. Letters were also tangible measures of the power they commanded. One historian has rightly declared: 'Ultimately the English Atlantic was a literate empire, a paper empire.'[17] Family letters, while not always considered as important to this empire as other forms of communication, were nevertheless integral to its development. Writing sensible familiar letters in this period was one way to signal and even to reinforce status, wealth, and authority in this world. Letters made Atlantic family life possible and even desirable for many, and the emphasis on sentiment made distances bearable and even worthwhile.

Many families were separated by the Atlantic, but plenty of other families experienced other kinds of divisions. Indeed, almost any analysis of families in the eighteenth century makes use of their letters. They are such a rich means of entry into family dynamics. It is much harder to access domestic life when there are no letters and no movement. It is in part difficult because it is not easy to find any family in the eighteenth century that did not have some members who traveled, or who at least heard about or read stories of those who did. Distance and its concomitant emphasis on 'family feeling' affected even those who experienced little by way of separation. Families who did experience major fracturing emphasized feeling perhaps more than others, but it is not that others did not do so. These kinds of representations of domestic bliss came to affect many such families, even if the most intense emphasis on representing feeling stemmed from those families who experienced the greatest dislocations.

'Family feeling' was a story people told themselves to make sense of a world in flux and to obscure the agonizing and grim realities of that world. The family remained an entity painfully riven with tense hierarchies, rivalries over economic resources, and ambitions dynastic and multi-generational in scope. Necessary for the social order, the family was nevertheless constantly in peril from these rivalries and inequalities, as well as from other social, economic, and political pressures. Such did not change in this period; what changed was how people wrote about and represented private life. They did this in order to serve both their individual ends and larger societal ones. Families did not get happier in the eighteenth century; they just emphasized claims of domestic harmony more, in order to serve various ends. Shifting languages could, for certain individuals in certain situations, provide a kind of limited leverage, as will be detailed here. Yet in this period it more often served to cut against the harsh realities of household life, and the difficult vectors of political and economic disruptions that also underlay

---

[17] Ian K. Steele, *The English Atlantic, 1675–1740: An Exploration of Communication and Community* (Oxford: Oxford University Press, 1986), 265.

it—the ways individuals fought over decisions and resources as well as the ways they suffered necessary distances. It was a way to perform feeling in its possible absence. By juxtaposing the letters of individuals with the larger cultural images, this book aims to show how both individuals and larger societies benefited from and made use of these widespread sentimentalizing impulses, as well as the ways in which larger disconnections and Atlantic realities underlay them.

It is my hope that this study will illuminate the history of the Atlantic, the history of the family, and the history of letter-writing. So much recent work has paid lip-service to the Atlantic that many are already beginning to grow Atlantic World-weary.[18] Still, for all the cascade of scholarship, much remains obscure. The relationship of households to the Atlantic growth of the eighteenth century is one case in point. Atlantic history has seemed distinct from, or even antithetical to, the history of families; these tend to be viewed as separate worlds (often coded as public and private spheres).[19] One scholar has helpfully defined 'the new Atlantic history' as 'the history . . . of the creation, destruction, and re-creation of communities as a result of the movement, across and around the Atlantic basin, of people, commodities, cultural practices, and ideas'.[20] Such movement created, destroyed, and re-created not only communities, but also families. This project demonstrates that families were not incidental to the growth and maintenance of at least some Atlantic cultures; they were central to its development and its maintenance.

This study also illuminates the history of the family—or, at least, of some families. Despite many voices, historical and more recent, placing them somehow

---

[18] For a few of the recent considerations of Atlantic history, and its rise and possible impending decline, see Bernard Bailyn, 'The Idea of Atlantic History', *Itinerario*, 20 (1996), 19–44; Nicholas Canny, 'Writing Atlantic History; or, Reconfiguring the History of Colonial British America', *Journal of American History*, 86 (1999), 1093–114; Peter A. Coclanis, '*Drang Nach Osten*: Bernard Bailyn, the World-Island, and the Idea of Atlantic History', *Journal of World History*, 13 (2002), 169–82, David Armitage and Michael J. Braddick, (eds.), *The British Atlantic World, 1500–1800* (Basingstoke: Palgrave/Macmillan, 2002); Bernard Bailyn, *Atlantic History: Concept and Contours* (Cambridge, Mass.: Harvard University Press, 2005); Elizabeth Mancke and Carole Shammas (eds.), *The Creation of the British Atlantic World* (Baltimore, Ma.: Johns Hopkins University Press, 2005); Alison Games, 'Atlantic History: Definitions, Challenges, Opportunities', *American Historical Review*, 111 (2006); and Alison Games, Philip J. Stern, Paul W. Mapp, and Peter A. Coclanis, 'Forum: Beyond the Atlantic', *William and Mary Quarterly*, 63 (2006), 675–742.

[19] There are a few notable exceptions, including David Cressy, *Coming Over: Migration and Communication Between England and New England in the Seventeenth Century* (Cambridge: Cambridge University Press, 1987), esp. ch. 9; Richard D. Brown, *Knowledge is Power: The Diffusion of Information in Early America, 1700–1865* (Oxford: Oxford University Press, 1989); Ronald Hoffman with Sally D. Mason, *Princes of Ireland, Planters of Maryland: A Carroll Saga* (Chapel Hill, NC: University of North Carolina Press for the Omohundro Institute of Early American History and Culture, 2000); Peter Mathias, 'Risk, Credit and Kinship in Early Modern Enterprise', in John J. McCusker and Kenneth Morgan (eds.), *The Early Modern Atlantic Economy* (Cambridge: Cambridge University Press, 2000), 15–35; and S. D. Smith, *Slavery, Family, and Gentry Capitalism in the British Atlantic: The World of the Lascelles, 1648–1834* (Cambridge: Cambridge University Press, 2006).

[20] J. H. Elliott, 'Afterword: Atlantic History: A Circumnavigation', in Armitage and Braddick, (eds.), *The British Atlantic World, 1500–1800*, 233–49, at 239.

in opposition to the rise of an Atlantic culture and economy (or ignoring them altogether), many individuals used family lines, family credit, and family feeling to make their ways in these Atlantic worlds. Just as this project argues for the agency of Atlantic worlds in shaping family lives, so too does it argue for the agency of families in shaping Atlantic worlds.[21] Few historians have considered families on the move, across the ocean, and the effects of these motions on ideas and representations of the family. By and the large, historians of the family have focused on a single nation (England) or even region (the Chesapeake). In general, when members move away from each other, and outside the household of origin, many historians no longer consider them family in the same way. A recent and in many respects helpful trend, to speak of the wider household-family which includes blood relations as well as apprentices, servants, and slaves, has helped to reorient much of the history of the eighteenth-century family.[22] Nonetheless, this tendency has reinforced the notion that families are the same as households, and thus at their core stable and grounded in a single locale. For many such was true, and this was the ideal by which family life was measured. On the other hand, rare was the family in the eighteenth century that did not send a child outside of this originating household-family. This mobility and movement inspired concerns about the nature of domestic life.

As we have seen from the Adams letters, such concerns proliferated in family letters. This study contributes to a burgeoning historical interest in letters, and letter-writing.[23] Despite ongoing work, especially by literary scholars, too many

---

[21] In exploring the historiography of the early modern British family, Keith Wrightson has argued that historians should focus less on the ways in which the family *was affected* by broader political and cultural changes and more on the ways in which the family itself had agency in altering cultural values. Keith Wrightson, 'The Family in Early Modern England: Continuity and Change', in Stephen Taylor, Richard Connors, and Clyve Jones (eds.), *Hanoverian Britain and Empire: Essays in Memory of Philip Lawson* (London: Boydell Press, 1998), 1–22.

[22] See Naomi Tadmor, *Family and Friends in Eighteenth-Century England: Household, Kinship, and Patronage* (Cambridge: Cambridge University Press, 2001).

[23] Various collections have addressed letter-writing: Rebecca Earle, (ed.), *Epistolary Selves: Letters and Letter-Writers, 1600–1945*, (Aldershot: Ashgate, 1999); David Barton and Nigel Hall (eds.), *Letter Writing as a Social Practice* (Amsterdam: John Benjamins Publishing Co., 2000); and Jane Couchman and Ann Crabb (eds.), *Women's Letters Across Europe, 1400–1700: Form and Persuasion* (Aldershot: Ashgate, 2005). For useful discussions on the American side, see Jan Lewis, *The Pursuit of Happiness: Family and Values in Jefferson's Virginia* (Cambridge: Cambridge University Press, 1983), introduction; Steven M. Stowe, 'The Rhetoric of Authority: The Making of Social Values in Planter Family Correspondence', *Journal of American History*, 73 (1987), 916–33; Andrew Burstein, 'Jefferson and the Familiar Letter', *Journal of the Early Republic*, 14 (1994), 195–220; Elisabeth B. Nichols, ' "Pray Don't Tell Anybody That I Write Politics": Private Expressions and Public Admonitions in the Early Republic', Ph.D, University of New Hampshire (1997); Virginia Elsie Radatz Stewart, 'The Intercourse of Letters: Familiar Correspondence and the Transformation of American Identity in the Eighteenth Century', Ph.D, Northwestern University (1997); William Merrill Decker, *Epistolary Practices: Letter Writing in America Before Telecommunications* (Chapel Hill, NC: University of North Carolina Press, 1998); Toby L. Ditz, 'Shipwrecked; or, Masculinity Imperiled: Mercantile Representations of Failure and the Gendered Self in Eighteenth-Century Philadelphia', *Journal of American History*, 81 (1994), 51–80; 'Formative Ventures: Eighteenth-Century Commercial Letters and the Articulation of Experience', in Rebecca Earle (ed.), *Epistolary*

historians continue to use letters as indicators of 'real' or 'private' feelings. Letters play to a particular audience, and are at their core about a dialogue. At the same time, a tendency to view letters simply as a form of 'self-fashioning' is equally problematic. 'Self-fashioning', a notion originating with literary critics, has become the dominant means of addressing life-writing, whether diaries or epistles. It has an honorific gloss: to fashion a self out of paper and quill was potentially to liberate, to participate in broader cultures, to gain agency through language, especially for those who suffered legal and economic disadvantages. Still, when people wrote letters, they may have fashioned a self, but they were generally at least as interested in fashioning others. Had this not been the case,

Selves: Letters and Letter-Writers, 1600–1945 (Aldershot: Ashgate, 1999), 59–78, and 'Secret Selves, Credible Personas: The Problematics of Trust and Public Display in the Writing of Eighteenth-Century Philadelphia Merchants', in Robert Blair St. George (ed.), *Possible Pasts: Becoming Colonial in Early America* (Ithaca, NY: Cornell University Press, 2000), 219–42; as well as several works by Konstantin Dierks, including 'Letter Writing, Gender, and Class in America, 1750–1800', Ph.D, Brown University (1999); '"Let Me Chat a Little": Letter Writing in Rhode Island Before the Revolution', *Rhode Island History*, 53: 4 (1995), 120–33; 'Letter Writing, Masculinity, and American Men of Science, 1750–1800', *Pennsylvania History*, 65 (1998), 167–198; 'Letter Manuals, Literary Innovation, and the Problem of Defining Genre in Anglo-American Epistolary Instruction, 1568–1800', *Papers of the Bibliographical Society of America*, 94 (2000), 541–50; and 'Letter Writing, Stationery Supplies, and Consumer Modernity in the Eighteenth-Century Atlantic World', *Early American Literature*, 41 (2006), 473–94. For the British side, see Bruce Redford, *The Converse of the Pen: Acts of Intimacy in the Eighteenth-Century Familiar Letter* (Chicago: University of Chicago Press, 1986); Susan E. Whyman, *Sociability and Power in Late-Stuart England: The Cultural Worlds of the Verneys, 1660–1720* (Oxford: Oxford University Press, 1999), introduction; James Daybell (ed.), *Early Modern Women's Letter Writing* (Basingstoke: Palgrave, 2001); id., *Women Letter-Writers in Tudor England* (Oxford: Oxford University Press, 2006); James How, *Epistolary Spaces: English Letter Writing from the Foundation of the Post Office to Richardson's 'Clarissa'* (Aldershot: Ashgate, 2003); and Clare Brant, *Eighteenth-Century Letters and British Culture* (Basingstoke: Palgrave/Macmillan, 2006). British-Atlantic letter models receive attention in Eve Tavor Bannet, *Empire of Letters: Letter Manuals and Transatlantic Correspondence, 1680–1820* (Cambridge: Cambridge University Press, 2005). Anglo-American elite women's epistolary circles are considered in Kate Davies, *Catherine Macaulay and Mercy Otis Warren: The Revolutionary Atlantic and the Politics of Gender* (Oxford: Oxford University Press, 2005). Some of the most interesting work has been done on French letter-writing: Roger Chartier, Alain Boureau, and Cécile Dauphin (eds.), *Correspondence: Models of Letter-Writing from the Middle Ages to the Nineteenth Century*, trans. Christopher Woodall (Oxford: Polity Press, 1997), as well as several articles on letter-writing manuals by Janet Gurkin Altman, including: 'The Letter Book as a Literary Institution 1539–1789: Toward a Cultural History of Published Correspondence in France', *Yale French Studies*, 71 (1986), 17–62; 'Political Ideology in the Letter Manual (France, England, New England)', *Studies in Eighteenth-Century Culture*, 18 (1988), 105–22; 'Teaching the "People" to Write: The Formation of a Popular Civic Identity in the French Letter Manuals', *Studies in Eighteenth-Century Culture*, 22 (1992), 147–80; and 'Epistolary Conduct: The Evolution of the Letter Manual in France in the Eighteenth Century', *Studies on Voltaire and the Eighteenth Century*, 304 (1992), 866–70. The most extensive work done on letter-writing desks is by Dena Goodman, working on France: 'Furnishing Discourses: Readings of a Writing Desk in Eighteenth-Century France', in Maxine Berg and Elizabeth Eger (eds.), *Luxury in the Eighteenth Century: Debates, Desires, and Delectable Goods* (Basingstoke: Palgrave, 2003), 71–88; 'The *Secrétaire* and the Integration of the Eighteenth-Century Self', in Dena Goodman and Kathryn Norberg, (eds.), *Furnishing the Eighteenth Century: What Furniture Can Tell Us About the European and American Past* (New York: Routledge, 2007), 183–204; and 'Letter Writing and the Emergence of Gendered Subjectivity in Eighteenth-Century France', *Journal of Women's History*, 17 (2005), 9–37.

they would not have sent the missive at all. This dialogic quality of letters has too often been missing in the use of letters as sources. Letters follow conventions, but the shifting nature of those conventions, and the metaphors used in them, makes them an especially rich source by which to witness family life. Conventions in the later eighteenth century began to dictate that seemingly natural and spontaneous expressions of sentiment should fill personal letters.

Atlantic family letters, then, allow us to see a number of vexed debates differently. John Adams's claim that men of his time had 'only the Name of Masters' resonates with a transition many historians of the household, gender, and slavery have identified as one from patriarchy to paternalism. In this reading, the colder, more formal relations of patriarchy, which had informed household relations of all kinds, softened in the later eighteenth century into paternalism, a milder, if no less hierarchical, version of masculine authority. This book posits that this transition represents less a genuine shift than novel ways of speaking and writing about family relations. This change was in part related to the rise of a culture of sensibility, or the ability to demonstrate and display feeling, and the emphasis placed on going 'fair, and softly'. In fact, as this book will demonstrate, explanations that have relied on patriarchy, paternalism, or a transition from one to the other have less explanatory force than those that attend to shifting ideals of masculinity in this period. This book thus surveys the power of those changing conventions, as well as the ways that individual men navigated within them. The book also demonstrates the power that women wielded, or in some cases tried to wield, in influencing the course of masculine behavior. Choices were made on the basis of a complicated nexus of domestic, political, and economic considerations.

In so exploring these decisions, this book thus also offers a reconsideration of distinctions between public and private; these were deeply integrated worlds, in ways not always appreciated, either at the time or subsequently. John Adams, for instance, lamented in a letter to Abigail: 'Instead of domestic Felicity, I am destined to public Contentions... In the Place of private Peace, I must be distracted with the... Vexation of developing the deep Intrigues of Politicians.'[24] This self-serving statement, justifying his absence and his short letters, sketched domestic happiness and public good as opposing forces; many historians have agreed. It is true that they did sometimes clash, but far more often they did not. In point of fact, John's letters, as well as his activities, indicate a profound interest in the public good as well as in domestic harmony and prosperity; these were integrated desires. There was no public Atlantic world separate from the private world of household-families, even though different historiographies have tended to separate them from each other. For many, these worlds were one and the same, as wives wrote to their husbands about households and new laws

---

[24] John Adams to Abigail Adams, 'April 28. 1776', *Adams Family Correspondence*, i. 398–401, at 399.

in Congress, as generals in war marched into houses and threw wives out on the street, and as slave-traders split children and parents up for life.

Indeed, appeals to family relations provided social, cultural, economic, and political capital for many, among them wives, generals, slaves, and masters. Families provided a significant means of justification in the face of a number of difficult situations. As John Adams did, fathers could cite the future of their children as a reason for their economic, political, and domestic decisions; politicians could do the same when they argued for certain kinds of political settlements. Appeals to the proper treatment of families, and the ways that they should be honored, provided a means of leverage for those seeking political and economic changes. The usual line of argument in this area is that political changes influenced family life, so that the American Revolution, for instance, unleashed larger calls for recasting family life.[25] Still, this process did not only move in one direction; domestic strategies and languages also influenced more broadly political ones.

This perspective thus helps us to see the American Revolution, or at least some aspects of it, in a new light. Calls for liberty, rights, and independence—all focused on what a self could expect—were important political languages in this period, but they were not the only ones. Indeed, the emphasis on the American Revolution and its more obvious rhetoric (as in the Declaration of Independence) may have obscured our vision. Had there been no American Revolution, we might have noticed sooner other powerful kinds of expressions being invoked by people on both sides of the Atlantic: appeals to family and feeling. Although many have tended to associate rhetoric invoking families with conservative values, in contrast to notions of individualism and independence, in fact, in this era, such claims to 'family feeling' had radical potential. This book posits that, although scholars have understandably pressed letters like Abigail's into arguments about how Americans of various sorts translated the political language of the American Revolution into domestic concerns, in fact what many texts of this era, including Abigail's famous letter, demonstrate is a reverse trajectory: domestic images were put in service of political arguments. In many cases, as in Abigail's, rhetoric did move from the revolutionary realm into the familial one. But in just as many cases, including hers, rhetoric also moved from the familial realm into the revolutionary one. To question tyranny and to emphasize attachments was a typical move in a transatlantic culture of sensibility and 'family feeling'.

The domestic and sensible languages of family members, men and women, fed into and helped to shape political languages of revolution and reform;

---

[25] Carole Shammas has noted: 'The belief that the Revolutionary era had a withering effect on a father's authority over his children seems widely held. Notions about the antipatriarchal tendencies of republicanism become fused with modernization of the family arguments to produce one big theoretical stone of intergenerational affectivity rolling down a 1750–1850 hill.' Carole Shammas, 'Anglo-American Household Government in Comparative Perspective', *William and Mary Quarterly*, 52 (1995), 104–44, at 132.

indeed, they were themselves a political language. One scholar has argued that 'the problems of family government addressed in the fiction and pedagogy of the period... were the larger political problems of the age translated into the terms of daily life'.[26] In fact, it was often the terms of daily life—the relations between family members, the concerns about disrupted households, and a desire for new kinds of behavior—that were translated into the larger political realm. It was not simply novels and other texts that forwarded these languages, although they helped. In fact, individuals themselves helped to broker new rhetorical styles in their daily lives.

The emphasis on 'family feeling' had resonance in political disputes both within and beyond the household itself. Wives pushed husbands to remember the ladies, and so to treat them differently. Enslaved members of households argued for freedom by invoking their own familiar attachments. This is not rights talk, but it had an equally powerful potential. A standard line of argument contends that Abigail and others borrowed the claims to liberty and rights first articulated by Revolutionaries (themselves elite white men protesting British imperial policy), and then made them their own (so that ladies could threaten to become rebels themselves).[27] Such an argument risks giving credit first to white male Revolutionaries, and presuming that others—from women like Abigail to enslaved men and women seeking freedom—learned how to be political from the very white men to whom they were subordinate. This book suggests that other influences were at work, and that many of those who were legally and economically subordinate developed their own ideas about feeling that could sometimes then feed into more explicitly political disputes. Many of these notions were developed first in familiar letters of all kinds. Women like Abigail could adopt the language of Revolutionaries because they were already primed by the circulation in this Atlantic world of countless other kinds of texts, including their own letters, to question tyranny and to emphasize that men needed to be not masters, but tender and endearing friends.[28]

That the most famous line of political protest by an early American woman was uttered in the context of a domestic and sensible familiar letter exchange is part of its significance, though most have dismissed this as the only avenue a learned woman of the era could find. The assumption has been that, had Abigail

---

[26] Fliegelman, *Prodigals and Pilgrims*, 5.

[27] The most well-known articulation of this kind of argument can be found in Gordon S. Wood, *The Radicalism of the American Revolution* (New York: Knopf, 1990). See also Michael McGiffert, et al., 'Forum: How Revolutionary was the Revolution? A Discussion of Gordon S. Wood's *The Radicalism of the American Revolution*', *William and Mary Quarterly*, 51 (1994), 677–716.

[28] This argument is thus broadly consonant with those of Rhys Isaac in his recent treatment of the world of Landon Carter. Isaac has argued: 'the sentimental and subversive language of the new novels—the anti-authoritarian sensibility they sustained—was in the air by the 1770s.' I would say that this sensibility was not just in the air, but firmly in the household (as Isaac himself notes). Rhys Isaac, *Landon Carter's Uneasy Kingdom: Revolution and Rebellion on a Virginia Plantation* (Oxford: Oxford University Press, 2004), 47.

been able to berate Congress or to publish such a claim in a newspaper, she would have done so. The presumption is that she settled for the more private letter in order not to upset her husband or the larger social order, or because she had little choice. 'Letters', as Virginia Woolf observed in relation to women's writings, 'did not count.'[29] Abigail might well have chosen other avenues, but the assumption that she surely would have done so carries other, more pernicious, ones along with it. Thinking of familiar letters as somehow inferior, less political, or less significant texts is an assumption we need to reject. Such letters registered complex dynamics and made a number of important political, cultural, social, and economic claims. Many families, most far more obscure than the Adams family, used familiar letters to question tyranny, to lament domestic and political disorder, to connect households with larger social and political landscapes, to keep bands from loosening in times and places when they seemed most in peril of doing so. Along the way, they reshaped their lives and made sense of a world in flux. Letters did count.

Such letters, then, form the central focus of this book, which uncovers epistles from a number of different family members—women and men, adults and children—divided by the Atlantic in a period of revolution and war (roughly 1760 to 1815). The letter collections represented here cover areas from Massachusetts, Rhode Island, Connecticut, New York, New Jersey, Pennsylvania, Virginia, North Carolina, South Carolina, and Georgia; to Scotland, England, and Ireland; to Jamaica, the Bahamas, Grenada, and Barbados. An educated, Anglo-American elite, many of whom belonged to merchant and planter families, produced nearly all of these letters. They thus necessarily provide the greatest information about this limited stratum of society. In part, in fact, they demonstrate how an educated elite maintained itself and defined itself against other groups; refinement was part of this story.[30] The book uses other letters, including those from slaves, where possible. Research for it has included collections ranging from a few letters to hundreds, located at numerous depositories both in Great Britain and in the United States. Occasionally, it has also been possible to reunite families separated in archives, so that records for the Parker family in Virginia, Scotland, and England are reunited into one story. Even as it takes family letters as its main focus, this study also spans other kinds of sources. So that the conventions of letter-writing in this period are better understood, it delves into printed literature in which letters appeared, including novels, magazines, letter-writing manuals, and letter collections. To make sense of critical cultural imperatives in letters, the book also surveys medical treatises, philosophical accounts, economic tracts, polemics and petitions, newspaper articles, novels, frontispiece drawings, and other forms

---

[29] Virginia Woolf, *A Room of One's Own* [1929], ed. Jennifer Smith (Cambridge: Cambridge University Press, 1995), 69.
[30] Konstantin Dierks provides many insights into this process. Dierks, 'Letter Writing, Gender, and Class in America, 1750–1800', *passim*.

of printed material. In order to reconstruct some of the family stories found in these letters, the book also deploys more conventional social-historical sources, such as wills, deeds, diaries, probate inventories, parish registers, lists of tithables, legal records, school lists, newspaper articles and advertisements, even gravestones.

Throughout the book, the concatenation of printed literature, stock images, and set languages with far more obscure manuscript letters and lives, many of which also make use of the same vocabularies, is a central focus. It is not a simple relationship; the claim is not that individuals read these stories and then acted in a certain way. Rather, it is to underline that certain themes preoccupied all kinds of writers, from well-known and oft-published ones, to far more obscure letter-writers playing to smaller audiences.[31] Letters from such people deserve close attention, even to their 'literary' qualities (such as tone, diction, metaphor, and syntax), as they reveal points of both historical and literary importance. There is also much untapped eloquence in such letters, even when their authors were worrying about a thousand other tasks. As Virginia Woolf described a woman's epistolary output: 'A woman might write letters while she was sitting by her father's sick-bed. She could write them by the fire whilst the men talked without disturbing them. The strange thing is... what a gift that untaught and solitary girl had for the framing of a sentence, for the fashioning of a scene.'[32] Letters were written in between real life; for some, they also became real life. Investigating those sentences, those scenes, can not only illuminate these lives, but can also demonstrate the ways that individuals of all sorts expressed the themes of their age.

It is the unity of epistolary practices and conventions, across many people and places, which is more striking than the differences. There were distinctions between colonies, regions, religions, cities, and country, as well as divisions by rank, age, ethnicity, race, and gender. Still, on the whole, a remarkably coherent set of Atlantic values emerges from these letters. It is this shared set of ideals that forms the focus of Chapters 2–4. The first four chapters here attend to the 'longue durée' of transatlantic family histories. In a sense, they are maps of currents and winds, slow, subtle movements in the way that families and their letters functioned over Atlantic distance. By contrast, the next three chapters are about moments of raging and sudden storms, crises in individual families that caused a recasting of the situation, and which have at their core both the perils and the opportunities of Atlantic distance for families.

---

[31] Some of the complications of the relationship between reading and then writing letters can be seen in the shared epistolary readings of Samuel Richardson's *Pamela* and *Clarissa* by Esther Edwards Burr and Sarah Prince. They receive attention in Carol F. Karlsen and Laurie Crumpacker (eds.), *The Journal of Esther Edwards Burr, 1754–1757* (New Haven: Yale University Press, 1984), introduction; Ned C. Landsman, *From Colonials to Provincials: American Thought and Culture, 1680–1760* (New York: Twayne, 1997), 47–52; and his 'Presbyterians, Evangelicals, and the Education Culture of the Middle Colonies', *Pennsylvania History*, 64 (1997), 168–82, at 176–80.
[32] Woolf, *A Room of One's Own*, 69.

All of these chapters provide glimpses of families working under the strain of Atlantic distance. Yet they also provide insights into how such separations could benefit families, how they could and did exploit it. They also demonstrate the deep and abiding connection between the private lives of individuals, and their larger political contexts. West Indian planters came under fire for problematic domestic arrangements at a time when their political clout was challenged. Women writing intimate letters as well as politicians speaking in Parliament exploited similar forms of language, and claims to family feeling. Credit in domestic epistolary exchanges could be as critical as credit in the economy. This book faces head-on, as few have, at least one of the many challenging truths of Abigail Adams's letter to John in March 1776: that households were at the center of life in this period, whether in one place, or two, or three. This book remembers the ladies, but it remembers other things, too, including the integration of worlds now gone. Facing this Atlantic world, and its disruptions, families made their thoughts heard on both sides of the Atlantic. And so we turn to those words, and the strange and troubling worlds that produced them.

PART I

'DEALING BY INK ALTOGETHER': MECHANISMS OF CONNECTION AND DISCONNECTION

Introduction

You men of Europe think nothing of a voyage by sea. With us of China, a man who has been from sight of land is regarded upon his return with admiration. I have known some provinces where there is not even a name for the ocean. What a strange people therefore am I got amongst, who have founded an empire on this unstable element, who build cities upon billows that rise higher than the mountains of Tipartala, and make the deep more formidable than the wildest tempest.

(Oliver Goldsmith, 1762)[1]

But a change has now come over the affairs of mankind. Walled cities and empires have become unfashionable. The arm of commerce has borne away the gates of the strong city... Oceans no longer divide, but link nations together. From Boston to London is now a holiday excursion. Space is comparatively annihilated. Thoughts expressed on one side of the Atlantic are distinctly heard on the other.

(Frederick Douglass, 1852)[2]

Only a 'strange people' found an empire on uncertain seas, even as their communication networks allowed thoughts to be heard on the other side of the ocean. This instability informed family correspondences of the era, as well as countless other texts. In the eighteenth century all sorts of concerns surrounded 'connexions,' and how they might be nurtured. Mobility in part generated these concerns. The first chapter here provides general background for the many reasons families experienced Atlantic distance in this century. Families had long endured separations for a variety of reasons, but the eighteenth century accelerated this trend. There were many reasons for such separations, including colonial growth, migration, slavery, war, and revolution. These all broke apart families and caused concerns, not simply for the families involved but for the culture as a whole. Anxieties about the family in this period in part reflect these larger societal and

---

[1] 'Lien Chi Altangi to ——, Merchant in Amsterdam', Letter II, 'Lond.', in Oliver Goldsmith, *The Citizen of the World; or Letters from a Chinese Philosopher*, 2 vols. (London, 1762), i. 3–4.
[2] 'What to the Slave is the Fourth of July?: An Address Delivered in Rochester, New York, on 5 July 1852', in John W. Blassingame (ed.), *The Frederick Douglass Papers, Series 1: Speeches, Debates, and Interviews*, 5 vols. (New Haven: Yale University Press, 1982), *II (1847–1852)*, 359–88, at 387.

economic shifts. It is necessary to understand this context, to comprehend how family letters emerged from, and helped to bridge, these distances.

The next three chapters address the ways family letters functioned to surmount some of these anxieties, as individuals sought to keep taut ties between family members. Chapter 2 considers the concept of familiarity, a means by which even individuals not related by family could achieve family-like relationships. Such familiarity, distinguished from either politeness or intimacy, allowed individuals adrift to join other circles, and enjoy the support this implied. Letters carved out a space of familiarity, even when family members found themselves on different sides of the ocean, thus forcing them to rely on non-family members. Another way of keeping families and societies together was by emphasizing the bonds of affection that held them close. Chapter 3 investigates the domestic origins of sensibility, or the ability to display a feeling heart. In many respects, sensibility originated in families, while also, like familiarity, moving beyond the immediate household-family. To write with feeling in familiar letters was one way to demonstrate the feeling, and to ensure the continuation of the connections. All kinds of epistolary manuals, as well as novels and stories, conveyed this message, and many family members took it to heart. This chapter thus traces a shift as this language of feeling became a dominant domestic one, one that also resonated in ever wider circles, including political circles aiming to end slavery or to foment the American Revolution. Feeling was one form of connection, but credit was, too. Chapter 4 examines the ways that credit was a value also inculcated by families. Credit was critical to this Atlantic economy, and fathers in particular were uncomfortably aware of this fact. They thus sought to create 'men of credit' out of sons especially. The profound loss of credit, in the form of ruin, was a specter that haunted families, communities, and nations. Letter-writers, men and women, measured each other's credit, in domestic and economic terms, as much through their letters as through their behavior.

In remarking on the increasing use of bills of credit in lieu of cash, one English newspaper author declared in 1730: 'we deal by Ink altogether.'[3] For many families, 'dealing by Ink' was also what they did. Writing letters allowed individuals to communicate with each other across the ocean, and it also signaled participation in and maintenance of networks of connections. Nevertheless, 'dealing by Ink' was a risky prospect. Bills of credit could be protested or stopped, and letters could lie. Familiarity, sensibility, and credit were ways to ensure sincerity in the face of possible dissimulation, but still, anxieties swirled around these inky representations. Those who received letters scrutinized them for their authenticity. Those who wrote letters, paradoxically, often resorted to artifice and convention in order to capture the natural truth of their experience. Many pedagogical texts about letter-writing claimed the authenticity, freshness,

---

[3] *London Journal*, 11 July 1730, as quoted in Julian Hoppit, *Risk and Failure in English Business, 1700–1800* (Cambridge: Cambridge University Press, 1987), 163.

and honesty of letters, even while they gave very precise instructions on how to be fresh and spontaneous. Epistolary novels and stories often revolved around the dissimulations of protagonists, as well as their letters. The possible distance between the appearance of a letter and the reality behind it often weighed heavily on those involved in these correspondences. While these concerns surrounded letters of all kinds, they were especially pointed when the distance was the Atlantic, and when it was even more difficult to check the veracity of what a particular letter-writer wrote. When an ocean separated a creditor and a debtor, or a husband and wife, their letters needed to do even more work to surmount the instability inherent in sending letters over tempestuous seas.

1
Fractured Families: The Perils and Possibilities of Atlantic Distance

Behind the happy family lies the ocean (see Fig. 1.1). Kissed by sea breezes, at once indoors and out, the family members—father, mother, daughter—write their letters in a pseudo-classical setting, in the frontispiece of the 1773 *The Court Letter-Writer*.[1] The productive epistolary efforts of this prosperous group occur under the watchful gaze of Hermes, messenger god. While both the title and its frontispiece were designed to appeal to those with pretensions to refinement, the illustration, like most of the book, portrayed not the formal elegance of the court but the efforts of a well-heeled but not notably royal family. That the picture idealized that setting is clear not just from the harmonious activity of the family, but also from the presence of gods and cherubs. This image, designed to sell a book of model familiar letters, glorified the world of domestic letter-writing. Yet something—or someone—was missing. There is no son here, and the implication is that the mother, father, and sister may well be writing to him. While this family apparently enjoys the services of Hermes, the more usual method of transport for trans-oceanic letters, a great-masted ship, rides in the distance. Is that the ship that carries a beloved man away? It seems that this imagined family wrote and sent their letters in an attempt to reintegrate its missing member across the sea.

This romanticizing frontispiece captures a critical aspect of letter-writing, and of life, in the eighteenth-century Atlantic world. That sense of the domestic world fronting a world of long-distance trade, travel, and colonization is a fundamental, yet all too often unremarked, feature of life in this era. This picture brings together the domestic and the distant, and, in this, it was hardly alone. These worlds were profoundly integrated, even as many other texts of the era, and subsequent historians, have stressed their separation, sometimes drawing that distinction as one between public and private. For better or worse, such trips helped to forge an Atlantic world. They thus have usually been coded as public

---

[1] In general, oceans appeared as a backdrop mainly in the case of portraits of naval officers, rather than such family scenes. See e.g. John Singleton Copley, *Admiral Clark Gayton* (1779). In the domestic activity of the family placed in an outdoor setting, though, this drawing paralleled portraits like John Hamilton Mortimer, *William Powell and his wife, Elizabeth, and his Daughters, Ann and Elizabeth Mary* (1768): see cover.

Fig. 1.1. Frontispiece to *The Court Letter Writer* (London, 1773). Bodleian Library, University of Oxford, Vet.A.f.1860, frontispiece.

choices, associated with the circulation of goods, peoples, polities, policies, and ideas. While not incorrect, this treatment is insufficient, since each voyage across the Atlantic implied a separation from a family and a household. These trips affected those left behind, as well as those who left. These were personal, painful decisions, sometimes inflicted by others, that responded both to individual, intimate circumstances and to collective, public ones.

The effect of Atlantic mobility on families is the focus of this chapter, which provides background for understanding the reasons for the separation and re-creation of families in this era, as well as the effects of these distances on views of family life. As this frontispiece promised, letters could allow at least some families to surmount those separations, and to remain families even across the oceans. There were other reasons for concern about family, but this chapter argues that Atlantic distance was an important one. It is therefore necessary to assess the sources of transatlantic distance in the eighteenth century in order to comprehend their effects on families, and ideas about families. It is also important to understand how literacy and letters worked for such families, and helped both to generate and to counteract concerns about the effect of separations on families.

In his 1755 *Dictionary*, Samuel Johnson defined 'family' first as follows: 'those who live in the same house; household.'[2] This definition points to the fact that family might include those beyond the blood or legal family in this period, but it obscures something else.[3] Many family members, such as those featured in this study, did not live in the same house. The point is not that Johnson got it wrong somehow; rather, the failure of his definition to work for so many families of his own time flags a point of entry into this culture. For a considerable number of families, distance, including transatlantic distance, was a condition of life in the eighteenth century (as it had been, and would continue to be, and for places well beyond the Atlantic world). Defining families is a vexed issue, since families can be forged by birth, marriage, cohabitation, obligation, inheritance, sex, or sentiment. The fact that many in the eighteenth century tended to use the word 'Friend' where we might use 'family' further complicates the issue, since these were relationships of sentiment and obligation, which might imply a blood or marital relationship, but might not. For the purposes of this study, I have defined family as those individuals related by blood, marriage, inheritance, or cohabitation who either had shared a household, or who might, in the normal course of events, expect to share one. Furthermore, such relationships—or friendships—also implied a sense of reciprocal obligation, either in economic or sentimental terms, or both.

---

[2] Definition: 'Family', Samuel Johnson, *A Dictionary of the English Language*, 2 vols. (London, 1755).

[3] Naomi Tadmor, *Family and Friends in Eighteenth-Century England*, ch. 1, and her 'The Concept of the Household-Family in Eighteenth-Century England,' *Past & Present*, 151 (1996), 110–40.

Johnson's *Dictionary* definition also demonstrates the ways that texts of the day sought to standardize and even idealize the family, much as the frontispiece to *The Court Letter-Writer* did. Both of these texts, along with myriad others, worked to render agreeable and orderly a set of relationships that could be anything but. Letter-writers of this era did the same. Finding themselves on opposite sides of the ocean, often in situations of considerable anxiety and uncertainty, these individuals had to forge family out of factors other than simple co-residence or lineage. One of the means individuals used to find familial connection in its apparent absence was to normalize and render sentimental its workings, even (indeed especially) in the face of evident familial disarray at both the individual and the societal level. They could thus forge family through domestic letters, using the tools of the quill, paper, and imagination. For families to look like families—with all the legal, economic, and social privileges such a status afforded—was one way for those in the British-Atlantic world to emphasize order even amid imperial disorder, at both a personal and a general level.

Creating and maintaining family was, then, both a personal and a political act. Nevertheless, mobility and separation had also long characterized anglophone families.[4] 'These fidgeting mortals! always whisking about from place to place!', was how one character in a 1771 epistolary novel phrased it.[5] The economy and society of Britain and its colonies depended on the separation of families, since the standard routes to many careers, from law to weaving to housekeeping, demanded lengthy apprenticeships, instigated at an early age, outside the house of birth. Rich sons were sent early to school; even from the colonies, they were often sent off to school in Britain itself. Less well-off sons were often put to trades, living for years in the family of a master craftsman. Or they might enter service in a household. Daughters, too, went into other households: either as servants or as students or as helpers. The world of all kinds of individuals, from Nehemiah Wallington in early seventeenth-century London to Martha Ballard in late eighteenth-century Maine, demonstrate how commonplace it was for a household-family to comprise servants, helpers, apprentices.[6] There were variations in terms of status and gender in such apprenticeships, but on the whole, it was more likely than not that a child would be put at a fairly young age into the household of individuals who were not his or her parents of birth.

In earlier times, and in smaller communities, even those young people who left their own family often remained part of the same larger community. Their parents might not be far away, and might be able to watch over them. Where parents could or would not monitor, larger community norms, supported by

---

[4] Alison Games, 'Migration,' in Armitage and Braddick (eds.), *The British Atlantic*, 31–50, at 31.
[5] 'A Lady', *Fatal Friendship. A Novel* (Dublin, 1771), 15.
[6] Paul S. Seaver, *Wallington's World: A Puritan Artisan in Seventeenth-Century London* (Stanford, Calif.: Stanford University Press, 1985), and Laurel Thatcher Ulrich, *A Midwife's Tale: The Life of Martha Ballard, Based on Her Diary, 1785–1812* (New York: Knopf, 1990).

complex informal networks of surveillance and communication, often acted to maintain checks on behavior, or at least provided a sense that they might do so. However, the eighteenth century accelerated trends in both internal and external migration, exacerbating an unease that these networks were imperiled. As literacy rates increased, however, letters became a central means of remedying some of these absences. This concern over disconnection from larger parental and communal networks informed all kinds of letters of the day, especially letter-writing manuals and well-known epistolary novels such as Samuel Richardson's *Pamela*, a fictional series of letters from a servant to her family back home.

Internal migration, both within the countryside and from country to town, had been a major feature of British society for centuries. Most historians now recognize that emigration to the colonies was 'an extension of internal mobility'.[7] As one historian of eighteenth-century England has pointed out, 'the social ideal was of a fixed, immobile, and ordered society, the reality was something else altogether'.[8] Indeed, not only had British families long encountered separation between members, but they had often endured separation by bodies of water. This is, after all, an island-nation. The Irish Sea, the North Sea, and the English Channel, among others, had all been important seas for the British. In the seventeenth century, for instance, the number of English migrants to Ireland was comparable to the number of English migrants to America, while from 1650 to 1700 the number of Scottish migrants to Ireland massively exceeded the number of Scots heading to American colonies.[9] Later, especially from the 1760s on, the Indian and the Pacific Oceans would loom equally large in the consciousness of Britons.[10]

Still, in the eighteenth century the Atlantic Ocean and the Caribbean Sea were of vital importance, for the economy and culture of Britain and its overseas possessions. As one historian has noted: 'Any informed adult living within the English Atlantic empire in 1739 knew that the Atlantic Ocean was traversed regularly, whether or not that person had crossed it.'[11] The distance of the Atlantic fuelled anxieties about maintaining families, even as its infrastructure, including mail-carrying, meant that many more individuals could remain connected across its vast waves. Such families used their letters to cross the ocean and to forge family even when they did not live in the same household. In so doing, they

---

[7] Ian D. Whyte, *Migration and Society in Britain, 1550–1830*, ed. Jeremy Black, Social History in Perspective (Basingstoke: Macmillan, 2000), 105. See also Nicholas Canny (ed.), *Europeans on the Move: Studies on European Migration, 1500–1800* (Oxford: Clarendon Press, 1994).

[8] Julian Hoppit, *A Land of Liberty? England, 1689–1727* (Oxford: Oxford University Press, 2000), 67.

[9] Whyte, *Migration and Society in Britain*, 108, 114–15. Following Nicholas Canny's work, Whyte calculates that of the 2,450 annual Scottish migrants between 1650 and 1700, some 140 went to America, while 2,000 went to Ireland. Ibid. 115.

[10] See P. J. Marshall (ed.), *The Oxford History of the British Empire*, Vol. 2: *The Eighteenth Century* (Oxford: Oxford University Press, 1998).

[11] Steele, *The English Atlantic*, 273.

both made sense of, and in some cases ameliorated, their particular individual circumstances. Yet they did more than this. They participated in the construction of an Atlantic world and culture, one in which writing a letter to a family member was both a personal and a political act.

Let us get our sea-legs, then. There were many causes for Atlantic separations and movements in the eighteenth century, and it is useful to trace them out, albeit briefly. 'Those who would go to sea for pleasure would go to hell for pastime', was how one contemporary proverb had it.[12] If the Atlantic was not a source of pleasure, it was nevertheless a source of treasure for many, as great-masted ships carried rich loads to make a family a fortune. For many, it was worth the risks attendant on such crossings. It was also in many cases considered worth it to make others take those risks, as a transatlantic trade, in slaves as well as in goods, brought prosperity to many in the anglophone Atlantic world. As one scholar has put it: 'Britain's overseas expansion was a multi-faceted, kaleidoscopic swirl of enterprise, a huge lumbering machine of related parts, a trading process for the transfer and exchange of people, a generator of hope, and a terrible perpetrator of bloodshed and despair.'[13] Intimately related to the hope, as well as the despair, was the way the Atlantic separated families for many reasons in the eighteenth century. The Atlantic was both a source of separation and trauma and of cohesion and growth, as colonies became important players in the growth of a British-Atlantic world. These colonies took on additional importance, in terms of population, economy, and cultural output, in this same century, and thus contributed not just to a sense that Atlantic separations between family members were vital to the growth of these colonies, but also to a sense that the Atlantic was a critical space for anglophone inhabitants on either side. Although these developments are well known, they have yet to be linked to families and images of families.

Britons had been on the move for centuries, but the character of that mobility took a new shape in this era. The eighteenth century witnessed a considerable rise in population and wealth for the British colonies as a whole.[14] In 1700 the American and West Indian colonies represented only 3 per cent of the population size that England itself did (so England contained 5,058,000 people, while the mainland and Caribbean anglophone colonies had only 167,000 settlers). By 1770 the population of these colonies represented 43 per cent of the English home population (so the English population of 6,448,000 compared with 2,762,000 in

---

[12] As quoted in Marcus Rediker, *Between the Devil and the Deep Blue Sea: Merchant Seamen, Pirates, and the Anglo-American Maritime World, 1700–1750* (Cambridge: Cambridge University Press, 1987), 12.

[13] Bernard Bailyn, 'Introduction: Europeans on the Move, 1500–1800', in Canny (ed.), *Europeans on the Move: Studies on European Migration, 1500–1800*, 1–8, at 2.

[14] Indeed, Ned Landsman persuasively argues for the increased integration of Americans into Britain, and a transformation from colonials to provincials, in the first several decades of the eighteenth century. See Landsman, *From Colonials to Provincials*.

the British colonies).[15] The colonies had much more claim to figure prominently in this anglophone Atlantic world. Eighteenth-century war and revolution only reinforced this sense.

These population statistics reduce into orderly lines the household disorder and familial disconnection attendant on that circulation of peoples. Immigrant letters from the eighteenth century witness both the hope and the despair that accompanied major changes with familial effects, even for English migrants who chose to make the journey. Take the example of John and Eliza Ambler, Dissenters who emigrated from Halifax, Yorkshire, to the Philadelphia area in the 1790s. Only a handful of their letters, some in fragments, remain, but these letters can stand in for many similar voyages of this century. The aptly-named Amblers chose to relocate to the new United States, and sent home letters praising the opportunities for business, and the religious freedoms, they enjoyed.[16] Despite their approval of their new land, their sense of loss and disconnection from their old home is made clear in one vignette by Eliza Ambler. She related in one letter to her parents how: 'I had almost begun to despair hearing from you, and was sitting by my self musing and fretting about you.' Such musings were broken by the arrival of a neighbor, who informed her that he had recently seen people at the wharf from her own home, with a letter from her family. When she finally found them, Eliza greeted the newcomers: 'welcome, says I, to the land of liberty but have you got letters for me?'[17] This salutation summarizes neatly both the promise and the poignancy of the voluntary immigrant experience: her praise of her new country of religious and economic liberty, but also her desire to have letters from her old home, to reconnect with family across the ocean.

The Amblers crossed the Atlantic in part for financial reasons; many others did the same, as transatlantic ships carried goods, as well as people. The considerable rise of these North Atlantic populations, one dependent on the displacement of many native populations, accompanied economic development for the British Atlantic. Overall, economic growth in both the mainland and Caribbean colonies was strong throughout the century. The colonies became much more significant sources for the production of goods and also as consumer markets. In the period from 1700 to 1780 transatlantic trade, which had earlier been peripheral to Britain's international economy, became instead its core.[18] From 1700 to 1798, the annual average of imports from North America and the West Indies to England (and later also Scotland) rose from £1,157,000 to £7,678,000. A

---

[15] These figures are calculations based on table 3.3 in Nuala Zahedieh, 'Economy', in David Armitage and Michael J. Braddick (eds.), *The British Atlantic World, 1500–1800* (Basingstoke: Palgrave/Macmillan, 2002), 51–68, at 62.

[16] John Ambler to Mr and Mrs John Aked, 'Philadelphia 12th Novr 1794', Ambler Family Papers, DUL.

[17] Eliza Ambler to Mr and Mrs John Aked, 'Philadelphia Oct. 21r 179[4]', ibid.

[18] R. C. Nash, 'The Organization of Trade and Finance in the British Atlantic Economy, 1600–1830', in Coclanis (ed.), *The Atlantic Economy During the Seventeenth and Eighteenth Centuries*, 95–151, at 95.

similar, if even more dramatic, trend emerges in terms of exports, as there was a tenfold growth of annual exports, from £461,000 to £4,985,000, from 1700 to 1790.[19] Put another way, although mainland and Caribbean colonies accounted for a mere 11 per cent of exports from Britain in 1700, by the 1770s the number was more like 38 per cent.[20] Such integration led to considerable growth in the colonies and also in Britain itself, resulting in the development of what one historian has termed 'a unified, coherent, and increasingly cohesive Atlantic economy'.[21] This Atlantic economy was the foundation for the subsequent growth of the Atlantic world, since it was economic incentives that drove many to colonize, settle, displace, fight, enslave, and ship. A core of merchants, traders, and backers, in the colonies and in Britain, devoted themselves to building up this economy, for their own individual desire for enrichment, for themselves and their families. Many of the people in this study endured Atlantic separation in order to exploit Atlantic financial opportunity, but so did many others.[22] In the process of pursuing their personal and familial objectives, however, they also forged a much larger collectivity based around the Atlantic. As a result of these processes, the rise of imports from and exports to the colonies from Britain rose dramatically in the eighteenth century, as the British empire became truly 'an empire of goods'.[23]

For all the public and national importance of this integrated Atlantic economy, it was also critically dependent on the lines of connection drawn between families and friends. The infrastructure of the Atlantic economy, in an era before the full institutionalization of banks and other financial institutions, depended greatly on personal credit and connections, a point to be taken up at much greater length in Chapter 4. Nevertheless, it is worth pointing out that this Atlantic economy would not have grown as it did had it not been for the strength of many intimate personal connections between members of families. Some of these were blood or legal families, others were extended families forged by kinship and community links, still others were created by common ethnic or religious identities (notable examples include Jews, Quakers, and Scots).[24] As the success of these groups

---

[19] These figures are based on calculations of Jacob Price, esp. tables 4.3 and 4.4 in Jacob M. Price, 'The Imperial Economy, 1700–1776', in P. J. Marshall (ed.), *The Oxford History of the British Empire*, Vol. 2: *The Eighteenth Century* (Oxford: Oxford University Press, 1998), 78–104, at 101.

[20] These figures are from table 3.4 in Nuala Zahedieh, 'Economy', in Armitage and Braddick (eds.), *The British Atlantic World, 1500–1800*, 51–68, at 62.

[21] Coclanis (ed.), *The Atlantic Economy During the Seventeenth and Eighteenth Centuries*, p. xii. Similar claims are made in John J. McCusker and Kenneth Morgan (eds.), *The Early Modern Atlantic Economy* (Cambridge: Cambridge University Press, 2000), esp. introduction.

[22] One such group is ably discussed by David Hancock, *Citizens of the World: London Merchants and the Integration of the British Atlantic Community, 1735–1785* (Cambridge: Cambridge University Press, 1995).

[23] T. H. Breen, *The Marketplace of Revolution: How Consumer Politics Shaped American Independence* (Oxford: Oxford University Press, 2004), esp. introduction and Part 1.

[24] For Jews, see Holly Snyder, 'A Sense of Place: Jews, Identity, and Social Status in Colonial British America, 1654–1831', Ph.D, Brandeis University (2000); for Quakers, see Thomas A.

demonstrates, friendship was as vital a resource in business as it was in any other area in this period. As one eighteenth-century merchant in the Madeira trade pointed out, 'early attachments are always the most lasting... [they] often reap much happiness in point of society, business or advancement of life'.[25]

The economic growth afforded by these Atlantic developments influenced families themselves, and their dynamics, in the colonies as well as in Britain. While the exact contributions of this Atlantic growth to British domestic economic development remains a matter of some debate, it is clear that it had an impact on the British economy, especially since a relatively small population growth was far outpaced by economic growth.[26] The effects of this growth were highly visible. Still, the increased availability of goods—whether manufactured goods in the colonies or colonial products in Britain—brought with it anxiety (a point considered further later in this chapter). This Atlantic economy meant that elite individuals in both Britain and the colonies could purchase, for instance, a silver sugar-pot and the sugar to go inside it. These purchases depended on the labor of many, from enslaved Africans sweating in Jamaican sugar-works, to sailors who steered that sugar across the Atlantic, to merchants who extended credit to sugar-planters in return for their sugar, to artisans who crafted sugar-bowls. All of these laborers and more were required to put that sugar in a sugar-bowl on a family's table inside a house. This example, among others, shows the profound interpenetration of domesticity and the Atlantic economy.

Along with this economic growth came a development of communications infrastructures. Although literacy is difficult to measure, there was an increase in literacy in the early modern period and, in particular, in the eighteenth century,

---

Doerflinger, *A Vigorous Spirit of Enterprise: Merchants and Economic Development in Revolutionary Philadelphia* (Chapel Hill, NC: University of North Carolina Press for the Institute of Early American History and Culture, 1986); Elaine Forman Crane, *A Dependent People: Newport, Rhode Island in the Revolutionary Era* (New York: Fordham University Press, 1985); Leonore Davidoff and Catherine Hall, *Family Fortunes: Men and Women of the English Middle Class, 1780–1850*, ed. Catharine R. Simpson, Women in Culture and Society (Chicago: University of Chicago Press, 1987), and Barry Levy, *Quakers and the American Family: British Settlement in the Delaware Valley* (Oxford: Oxford University Press, 1988); for Scots, see Alan L. Karras, *Sojourners in the Sun: Scottish Migrants in Jamaica and the Chesapeake, 1740–1800* (Ithaca, NY: Cornell University Press, 1992), T. C. Smout, N. C. Landsman, and T. M. Devine, 'Scottish Emigration in the Seventeenth and Eighteenth Centuries', in Canny (ed.), *Europeans on the Move*, 76–112, and Douglas J. Hamilton, *Scotland, the Caribbean and the Atlantic World, 1750–1820*, ed. John M. Mackenzie, Studies in Imperialism (Manchester: Manchester University Press, 2005).

[25] John Corrie to Thomas Gordon, Jan 7. 1771, box 5, bundle 1770–1771, Cossart & Gordon Papers, Liverpool University Archives, as quoted in David Hancock, 'Self-Organized Complexity and the Emergence of an Atlantic Market Economy, 1651–1815', in Coclanis (ed.), *The Atlantic Economy During the Seventeenth and Eighteenth Centuries*, 30–71, at 35.

[26] There is a discussion of this debate in Patrick K. O'Brien, 'Inseparable Connections: Trade, Economy, Fiscal State, and the Expansion of Empire, 1688–1815', in P. J. Marshall (ed.), *The Oxford History of the British Empire*, Vol. 2: *The Eighteenth Century* (Oxford: Oxford University Press, 1998), 53–77, at 75. See also Simon Smith, 'British Exports to Colonial North America and the Mercantilist Fallacy', *Business History*, 37 (1995), 45–63.

especially for women.[27] Overall, more and more individuals could read and write, and more were able to purchase books. The popularity of books such as *The Court Letter-Writer* indicates that letter-writing was one skill that many sought to master. Distances between family members increased, but so too did methods of surmounting them. Both Britain and its colonies enjoyed increased rates of literacy and also of book and newspaper production, although the dissemination of literacy and books varied significantly by status, wealth, gender, and age.[28] For instance, for the sixty-eight anglophone imprints produced in mainland North America in 1700, there were 798 in 1789. If newspapers are added, then the total exceeds 8,000.[29] Despite this growth in colonial output, imports of books and periodicals from Britain continued to increase. There was an especially 'steep rise' in books exported from England in the second half of the eighteenth century.[30]

Indeed, literacy, letters, and other papers were critical to the development of the Anglophone Atlantic world. For the Atlantic economy to prosper, it was vital for communication networks to improve, which they did over the eighteenth century.[31] Most transatlantic voyages took six to eight weeks—slow by modern standards, but efficient for the times. A general rise in ship traffic, because of a rise in trade, provided more opportunities for sending papers of all kinds by private ships. Also, packet services—regular postal ships that left on a reliable monthly basis, cutting the voyage time to just over four weeks—were instituted in 1755, so that letters could move more easily between England and the ports of New York, Charleston, and Kingston.[32] Postal services internally also

---

[27] See R. A. Houston, *Literacy in Early Modern Europe: Culture and Education, 1500–1800*, 2nd edn. (Harlow: Longman, 2002). Two historians of Atlantic literacy have claimed: 'Unmistakably, the rate of literacy...increased in the course of the eighteenth century.' Ross W. Beales and E. Jennifer Monaghan, 'Practices of Reading, Part 1: Literacy and Schoolbooks', in Hugh Amory and David D. Hall (eds.), *The History of the Book in America*, Vol. 1: *The Colonial Book in the Atlantic World* (Cambridge: Cambridge University Press, 2000), 380–7, at 380. Richard D. Brown, writing of white populations in the mainland American colonies, has posited: 'the gap between male and female literacy... in 1700 was considerable throughout the colonies. This gender gap, manifest in writing skills, all but vanished during the course of the eighteenth century.' Brown, *Knowledge is Power*, 12.

[28] David D. Hall has found that 'for the history of the book, the story is one of rising production and consumption'. David D. Hall, 'The Atlantic World, Part 1: The Atlantic Economy in the Eighteenth Century,' in Amory and Hall (eds.), *The History of the Book in America*, i. 152–62, at 153.

[29] Production accelerated particularly following the Seven Years War, especially in terms of newspaper production. In 1750 there were twelve American newspapers; by 1790 there were ninety-nine. Ibid. i. 153–4.

[30] James Raven, 'The Atlantic World, Part 3: The Importation of Books in the Eighteenth Century', in Amory and Hall (eds.), *The History of the Book in America*, i. 183–97, at 183.

[31] This circulation of information receives useful attention in Brown, *Knowledge is Power*.

[32] The first packet service went from New York to England; later services were instituted between England and Charleston, South Carolina, and Kingston, Jamaica. On packets, see J. C. Arnell, *Transatlantic Mail to and from British North America from Early Days to U.P.U.*, Transatlantic Mail Study Group Handbook no. 4, (Oyama, British Columbia: British North America Philatelic Society, 1996), 1, and Richard R. John, *Spreading the News: The American Postal System from Franklin to Morse* (Cambridge, Mass.: Harvard University Press, 1995), 26.

improved.³³ All of these shipping methods made it possible not only for books, newspapers, and people to move more efficiently across the Atlantic, but also for letters to do so. The ability to transmit familiar letters depended on increases in trade, transport, and communication links.

All of these developments combined to separate families, but also allowed their members to remain in regular contact. They also helped to create a thriving transatlantic culture of letter-writing in this century. Since Atlantic family letters are both the chief sources as well as subjects in themselves, it is necessary to understand a little more about the ways that people sent and received, as well as read and wrote, letters in this period.³⁴ It is therefore helpful to peer over the shoulders of a few eighteenth-century letter-writers, at those moments when the fluster of getting a letter to a ship, or the worry of not having received a reply, imprinted the missive itself. People read letters carefully; they even read not receiving them carefully. Epistles from family members on the other side of the Atlantic were generally anxiously awaited, and eagerly received. When one husband had not heard from his wife, he counted the ships that might have carried her letters, as well as detailing those carriers who had taken his letters to her. He concluded: 'So much about Letters, and no Letters.'³⁵ This wry comment approaches a point made by a recent scholar, who has claimed: 'The real subject matter of letter-writing is the writing of the letters.'³⁶

It was not only the addressee who may have been eager to pounce on the newly arrived letters. As one Virginia planter noted in a letter: 'Our lives are uniform without any great variety, til the seasons bring in the ships, then we tear open the letters they bring us from freinds [sic], as eagerly as a greedy heir tears open a rich fathers will.'³⁷ Letters were often read aloud to a family or group of friends, passed around to other friends, and were generally in circulation within a small group of people.³⁸ Salutations to others often fill the concluding remarks of a

---

33 Howard Robinson, *The British Post-Office: A History* (Princeton: Princeton University Press, 1948), and Kenneth Ellis, *The Post Office in the Eighteenth Century* (Oxford: Oxford University Press, 1958).

34 Eighteenth-century letters do not look like today's letters and emails, nor were they necessarily read and written in the same ways. As Robert Darnton has written of books: 'Books as physical objects were very different in the eighteenth century from what they are today, and their readers perceived them differently.' Robert Darnton, *The Great Cat Massacre and Other Episodes in French Cultural History* (New York: Basic Books, 1984), 222.

35 Charles Dudley to Catherine Dudley, 'London 27 May 1785', Folder 6 (41–226), Box 41, Dudley Family Papers, NHS.

36 Roger Chartier, 'Introduction: An Ordinary Kind of Writing—Model Letters and Letter-Writing in Ancien Régime France', in Roger Chartier, Alain Boureau, and Cécile Dauphin (eds.), *Correspondence: Models of Letter-Writing from the Middle Ages to the Nineteenth Century*, trans. Christopher Woodall (Oxford: Polity Press, 1997), 1–23, at 19.

37 William Byrd to Ann Taylor Otway, 30 June 1736, as quoted in Brown, *Knowledge is Power*, 45.

38 A good example of this are those letters moving in the circles of Mercy Otis Warren, Abigail Adams, and other elite New England women in the period of the American Revolution, adroitly discussed in Davies, *Catharine Macaulay and Mercy Otis Warren*, ch. 4, esp. pp. 201–19.

missive. We also know that letters were usually considered group property, from those moments when the occasional letter-writer begged that their letters *not* be shown to anyone else. One estranged wife in England directed her correspondent in Jamaica always to burn her letters, 'in Case of their getting in the hands of any other of his [her husband's] friends'.[39] A sister wrote from London to Barbados in a secret language, marked later as 'in short hand respecting confidential correspondence'.[40] Still, by the later eighteenth century the assumption was that a familiar letter would be revealed to a small group on its arrival, but that sealing-wax and courtesy would protect it from prying eyes on its journey. This presumption comes through most clearly in its absence during wartime, when people did feel unusually constrained by the possibility of outside readers.[41] One 1780 letter-writer from the West Indies to New England noted: 'I shall make no apology for the laconic Epistle—the reason must be Obvious to you.'[42] The Galloway family, divided between England and America, sent some letters on tiny scraps of paper, to be carried secretly across enemy lines. Nevertheless, the daughter Elizabeth complained: 'When I write to my dear Mamma, I am like a spider spinning its web from Nothing, for as there is no subject that I can write freely upon I may almost be said to write without any.'[43] Elizabeth was justified in her fear of 'impertinent inspection', for this letter is found in a bundle which bears the following label by her mother: 'other Letters sent me By this Packet... now burnt Near the lines by ye bearer', apparently in order to escape inspection of possibly hazardous material.[44]

In general, the recipient was the reader who provoked the most worry. Some readers inspected letters minutely for slips of spelling, grammar, and penmanship, signs not only of rudeness but of possible larger educational and even moral failings. Words mattered a great deal in letter exchanges; so did silences. Enormous, stomach-churning anxiety surrounded the *non*-receipt of letters. One son in England fretted over not receiving a letter from his father for more than two years: 'Though I have wrote to you by every opportunity... yet I have not been fortunate enough to receive any from you... A thousand conjectures start up in my imagination.'[45] Some would-be recipients attributed silence to the letters miscarrying, but others imputed it to neglect in writing, anger at some

---

[39] Ann Tharp to William Green, undated but postmarked 6 May 1803, R55.7.128(a), Tharp Family Papers, CCRO.
[40] Abigail Barrell to Theodore Barrell, undated, Barrell Family Papers, CURB.
[41] On the issue of intercepted letters during the American Revolution, see Julie M. Flavell, 'Government Interception of Letters from America and the Quest for Colonial Opinion in 1775', *William and Mary Quarterly*, 58 (2001), 403–30.
[42] Abigail Redwood to Francis Brinley, 'June 30-[17]80', Series I, Folder I, Box 173, Malbone–Brinley Papers, NHS.
[43] Elizabeth Galloway to Grace Galloway, 'February 2th 1780', Betsey Galloway—Correspondance of [to mother and others]', Joseph Galloway Papers, LoC.
[44] Envelope of letters, File: Joseph Galloway to Grace Growden Galloway, 1776–81, Joseph Galloway Papers, LoC.
[45] Thomas Ruston to Job Ruston, 'Exeter July 4th: 1782', Ruston Family Papers, LoC.

perceived fault, or sudden tragedy. One man in Ireland wrote home to North Carolina: 'I have rec[eive]d no letter from you which makes me apprehend that my letter miscarried or that there has been something in my conduct which has displeased you if the Later is the case nothing in this world would give me more concern.'[46] An ill-tempered husband in England castigated his wife in Georgia: 'I thought you would have been a more attentive correspondent... it is really cruel & unkind that no one would write a single line.'[47] It turned out that it was not inattention, but an epidemic and the sudden death of his oldest son, that had prevented his wife from writing. The receipt of letters, or the non-receipt, signified all kinds of life-altering events.

Given how carefully letters and silences were read, it is hardly surprising that they were also often written with great care. All kinds of printed materials combined to teach letter-writers how to write letters, although they also learned from each other. They needed not just the knowledge of how to write letters, but also the tools of writing. It was only when quills were sharpened, inks mixed, and paper purchased that people could sit down to write their letters.[48] Some complained about the challenges of scratchy quills or frozen ink.[49] Many wrote at desks or tables; the better-off had secretaries or bureaus at which to write.[50] Others, especially those involved in business, wrote from desks in counting-houses or offices of various kinds. Some letter-writers were forced into less peaceful settings, such as ships or coffee-houses. One such harried writer recorded his frustration in trying to write his letter: 'I have stept int[o] the Pennsyl[vania] coffee House, & am now writing there in a Corner Box—I can hardly collect together my Thoughts, for the confused Noice of the Company.'[51]

For some, there were regular rhythms to letter-writing. A number of correspondents seem to have written their letters all at one time, or at least used this

---

[46] John Brownrigg to Lewis Knight, 'Dublin 20 Fey 92', typescript, Brownrigg Family Papers, SHC.

[47] Robert Mackay to Eliza Mackay, 'London 20th October 1804', in Walter Charlton Hartridge (ed.), *The Letters of Robert Mackay to His Wife, Written from Ports in America and England, 1795–1816* (Athens, Ga.: University of Georgia Press Under the Auspices of the Georgia Society of Colonial Dames, 1949), 151.

[48] These issues are compellingly addressed in Dierks, 'Letter Writing, Stationery Supplies, and Consumer Modernity'.

[49] Thomas Coombe grumbled about his 'horrid pen... aching head & a hand trembling with the intenseness of the weather'. Thomas Coombe to Sally Coombe, 'Philadelphia Augst 21, 1776', Thomas Coombe Papers, HSP. Patrick Parker complained: 'We have had Dreadfull Cold weather Lately—the ink I am now writing with I was Obliged to melt', Patrick Parker to James Parker, 'Norfolk Virginia January 10th 1783 [1784]', Parker Family Papers, LRO.

[50] The surviving papers of Thomas Coombe, which include many familiar letters, also include a receipt for a 'Mohogany writing Table'. See Receipt for Goods for Thomas Coombe 'Bot of Robt Jewell', 'August 7 1774', Thomas Coombe Papers, HSP. The most extensive work done on letter-writing desks is by Dena Goodman, working on France.

[51] Thomas Coombe to Thomas Coombe [sr], 'Pennsyla. Coffee-House London Jany 4th 1769', Thomas Coombe Papers, HSP.

as an excuse for not writing more; one man apologized to his mother: 'Excuse my hurry as it is late Sunday night & I have written two letters already.'[52] Some correspondents seem to have written their letters at a regular time (for instance, every Sunday).[53] Others wrote in advance, in case they heard of a ship ready to sail. In 1769 one son, far from home in London, heard of a ship about to sail from Gravesend to Philadelphia: 'When I heard it, I was dining... above two Miles from my Lodgings, but as soon as I could disengage myself, I hurried Home, sealed my Letters which had been wrote several Days before, & dispatched them by the Post to Gravesend And in the Day or two after, had the Mortification to have them all returned with the News that the Ship had sailed.'[54] Others wrote because they heard of the opportunity of a ship sailing: 'Dadda tells me there's a Vessel bound for London, that will sail tommorrow, I thought I'd write if it was but a few lines.'[55] A sleepy nephew, writing in 1812, apologized for his messy handwriting and meandering style: 'I have heard only at the moment of this opportunity & have been obliged to write at 12 O Clock at night... which must apologize for this scrawl... for I am half asleep.'[56]

Half-asleep or not, by the later eighteenth century most people wrote their familiar letters themselves. This marked a significant shift from earlier periods, when secretaries and scribes did most of the writing. Frontispiece drawings to letter-writing manuals show idealized visions of how people wrote their letters: some in a family production line, as in the drawing at the front of *The English Letter-Writer* (Fig. 1.2), or on their own, as in the frontispiece to the *Lady's Polite Secretary* (Fig. 1.3).

Still, these idealized visions reflect the fact that, increasingly, familiar letters were written personally by those who sent them. Some clerks did still draft and copy some letters, especially in more obviously business-related settings. It is not always possible to tell when clerks or others were interceding in letters, but occasionally one can. For instance, a Jamaican correspondent, Simon Taylor, copied over his own familiar letters as well as writing them himself, until the end of life when his health failed and clerks' handwriting intercedes.[57] Similarly, one woman noted that her letter 'must (from the badness of my eyes) be copied by one of my girls before you can read it'.[58] Some family members wrote letters together;

---

[52] John M. Forbes to Dorothy Forbes, 'Novr. 8th 1789', Forbes Family Papers, MHS.
[53] See the dates on Pierce Butler's letters to his son, Thomas. Pierce Butler Letter Collection, Add. Mss. 16603, BL.
[54] Thomas Coombe to Thomas Coombe (sr.), 'London Ocr 3d. 1769', Thomas Coombe Papers, HSP.
[55] Elizabeth (Betsey) Hadwen to Mrs Bragg, 'New Port 3d Mo: 7th—1774', copied by John Bragg, '2d Mo: 1778', Hadwen–Bragg Family Papers, LoC. Originals in Whitehaven Public Library, Cumberland.
[56] Bennet Forbes to Mrs Eliza Robbins, 'Marseilles 21 Octr 1812', Forbes Family Papers, MHS.
[57] See Simon Taylor Papers, ICS.
[58] Mary Story to Hannah Hobart, 'London July 31st–1789', Hannah Hobart Papers, LoC.

Fig. 1.2. Frontispiece to George Brown, *The English Letter-Writer; Or, The Whole Art of General Correspondence* (London, 1785?). © British Library Board. All Rights Reserved, 10920.aaa.5.

Fig. 1.3. Frontispiece to [Dorothea DuBois], *The Lady's Polite Secretary, or New Female Letter Writer* (London, 1771). © British Library Board. All Rights Reserved, 10920.aa.11.

the letters from Edward and Ann Chandler to her brother, for instance, include two signatures, as well as two styles of handwriting.[59] Some correspondents kept copies of their correspondence or sent more than one copy in order to be sure the letter reached its recipient.[60] Some also drafted a rough version, and then copied a final one to be sent. Often, the only surviving copies are either the draft versions or the letter-book copies.[61] Many senders looked over letters before they sent them, even if they did not keep copies, making corrections or even noting: 'Upon Reading over this Im afraid youll Complain that it is rather upon a Melancholly Strain, I acknowledge it, but I know My Dear Billy has a heart that Can feel for a friend, and will forgive my dull Reflections.'[62] Even when letters were filled with 'dull Reflections', they were written, read, received, and even not received with considerable attention, anxiety, and self-consciousness. Some writers dashed off letters in a hurry, but even these pressed writers demonstrated their quiet knowledge of the conventions of such letters, their salutations and closings, the acknowledged forms.

The sending of letters had other kinds of meanings; those in a position to exploit the technologies of literacy were disproportionately advantaged in terms of their ability to prosper. The circulation of letters, like that of books and newspapers, indicated increased access to literate resources, but they also indicated widened gaps between those who could use them and those who could not. Eliza Ambler's ability to reconnect with her family by letter was a measure of her privilege, a privilege that by the 1790s was more likely to be enjoyed by a woman of a middling status. As one historian has observed, this access to postal services and letters 'represented very real economic, political and social power for those with the literacy, the resources, and the time to maintain correspondence with kin, friends, partners, agents, patrons, and clients who were similarly blessed and living elsewhere within the progressively more integrated English Atlantic'.[63] Those without such resources were increasingly disadvantaged. Chief among those so deprived were the largest group of eighteenth-century migrants to North America: Africans. Behind the poignant letters of anglophone families separated by the Atlantic in the eighteenth century resonate the far more poignant silences of African families. These African Atlantic silences shaped the words of the elite anglophone families, in part because to have access to letters also indicated one of the forms of power they commanded.

---

[59] See Chandler Letters, American Loyalists Box, NYPL.

[60] For instance, there are letter-books such as Simon Taylor's, although these are more common in business-related collections (though of course many family letter collections revolve around business). Taylor not only kept copies; he also sometimes sent multiple copies to recipients. Draft copies exist in various collections, such as the Brown Family Papers, NYHS.

[61] See e.g. the many letter-books that form the basis for the Lee Family Papers and Jenings Family Papers at VHS.

[62] Elizabeth Robertson to William Robertson, 'April 21 1768', Robertson Family Papers, Chicago Historical Society, microfilm at VHS.

[63] Steele, *English Atlantic*, 131.

In the British-Atlantic world of the eighteenth century, it is worth stressing, maintaining family connections over Atlantic distance was a luxury, not a right. Free men who wanted to be with their families were called loving; enslaved men who wanted to be with theirs were called, in ads for runaway slaves, 'lurking'.[64] Even as British-Atlantic culture celebrated the family as a source of benevolence, and lauded the silken ties binding family members together, it was also a culture that condoned, if implicitly, the permanent rending of other families and the binding of others with ties that were anything but silken. The same masters who wrote affectionate letters to their own family members casually noted in advertisements that husbands and wives had fled in order to join their own families. That these elite individuals understood such motives is clear. That they behaved differently as a result of them (or against what they perceived as their own economic self-interest) is much less clear.

Writing letters, and reading reports, was also a way to connect even in war and revolution, another reason for the separation of families in this century. It is in part for this reason that these wars helped to increase Atlantic consciousness. British periodicals reported on events in North America and the Caribbean, as the costs of these devastating conflicts were brought home. Individuals in America and the Caribbean had to follow events in Europe, as they watched dynastic and territorial ambitions turn into deadly battles and captivities at home. It also meant that travel across the Atlantic became even more widespread, for ever larger populations. Sailors, soldiers stationed across the Atlantic, sojourners, refugees, exiles, revolutionaries, and anti-revolutionaries, and their families all found themselves divided from loved ones by the Atlantic, and some were able to send letters to ameliorate their situation. Sailors and their families suffered Atlantic distance, though a few were able to keep in contact. Recognizing the domestic disruption of the sailor's life, the sailors' lament, a particular genre of ballad, was a song that bemoaned separation from family, friends, and home.[65] Those left at home felt those dislocations just as strongly, as recent work on women and seafaring has also pointed out.[66]

---

[64] There are numerous examples, such as John B. Forse, who informed readers of the *Virginia Gazette* in 1771 that his slave Ned had run away: 'as he has a Wife...in Shockoe, it is most probable he may be lurking about the Falls of James River.' Runaway Advertisement for Ned placed by John B. Forse, *Virginia Gazette*, Williamsburg, 18 April 18 1771, from Virginia Center for Digital History at *http://www.vcdh.virginia.edu/gos/* (consulted 10 May 2005).

[65] Rediker, *Between the Devil and the Deep Blue Sea*, 189.

[66] See esp. Lisa Norling, *Captain Ahab Had a Wife: New England Women and the Whalefishery, 1720–1870*, ed. Thadious M. Davis and Linda K. Kerber, Gender and American Culture (Chapel Hill, NC: University of North Carolina Press, 2000); Elaine Forman Crane, *Ebb Tide in New England: Women, Seaports, and Social Change, 1630–1800* (Boston: Northeastern University Press, 1998); Ruth Wallis Herndon, 'The Domestic Cost of Seafaring: Town Leaders and Seamen's Families in Eighteenth-Century Rhode Island', in Margaret S. Creighton and Lisa Norling (eds.), *Iron Men, Wooden Women: Gender and Seafaring in the Atlantic World, 1700–1920* (Baltimore, Md.: Johns Hopkins University Press, 1996), 55–69; and Paul A. Gilje, *Liberty on the Waterfront: American Maritime Culture in the Age of Revolution* (Philadelphia: University of Pennsylvania Press, 2004), ch. 2.

War badly disordered family life, in particular by taking men away from their households, sometimes for good. One sea-song lamented that, 'when once the din of war's begun... Friends from dear friends are sunder'd'.[67] The effects of these wartime constraints and separations—in both specific individual terms and in general demographic ones—were suffered both by those who left and by those who were left. In the eighteenth century Britons became heavily involved in wars that were increasingly Atlantic in their reach. The eighteenth century saw wars involving both sides of the Atlantic, including the War of the League of Augsburg/King William's War (1689–97), the War of Spanish Succession/Queen Anne's War (1702–13), the War of Austrian Succession/King George's War (1739–48), and, most notably, the Seven Years War/French and Indian War (1754–63).[68] This last conflict began not in Europe but in North America, an indication of the growing importance of the colonies to European calculations.[69] The American Revolutionary War (1775–82) was as profoundly Atlantic in its orientation. Like the other wars, this one also separated families. Indeed, one English magazine in 1779 declared: 'What mournful scenes in private families have these flames already occasioned! How many more such scenes may justly be apprehended!'[70] These scenes were repeated even after that war had ended, sending a flood of exiles around the globe.[71] After a scant ten years of peace, the British became embroiled in wars with the French, from 1793 to 1815, which again clustered conflict around the Atlantic and also the Caribbean. In the meantime, in addition to numerous battles in the Caribbean, revolution of a profound sort had gripped the former French colony of San-Domingue, which became the independent nation of Haiti.[72] This revolution upended life in the Caribbean, and sent shock-waves to the United States and also to Europe. The Haitian Revolution also triggered a cascade of further Atlantic displacement

---

[67] 'Magnanimity', in Charles Dibdin, *Sea Songs and Ballads* (London, 1863), 84.

[68] King George's War in particular brought many soldiers to the West Indies: Stephen Conway, *The British Isles and the War of American Independence* (Oxford: Oxford University Press, 2000), 29.

[69] Fred Anderson, *Crucible of War: The Seven Years' War and the Fate of Empire in British North America, 1754–1766* (New York: Knopf, 2000), 11. See also Bruce P. Lenman, 'Colonial Wars and Imperial Instability, 1688–1793', in P. J. Marshall (ed.), *The Oxford History of the British Empire*, Vol. 2: *The Eighteenth Century* (Oxford: Oxford University Press, 1998), 151–68, at 159.

[70] 'The Fatal Separation: A Moral Tale', *Town and Country Magazine* (Jan. 1779), 133–5, at 133.

[71] For information on Loyalist exiles, see Mary Beth Norton, *The British-Americans: The Loyalist Exiles in England, 1774–1789* (Boston: Little, Brown & Co., 1972); Janice Potter-MacKinnon, *While the Women Only Wept: Loyalist Refugee Women* (Montreal: McGill-Queen's University Press, 1993); Wallace Brown, *The Good Americans: The Loyalists in the American Revolution* (New York: William Morrow, 1969); Gail Saunders, *Bahamian Loyalists and their Slaves* (London: Macmillan Caribbean, 1983); James W. St G. Walker, *The Black Loyalists: The Search for the Promised Land in Nova Scotia and Sierra Leone, 1783–1870* (Halifax, Nova Scotia: Dalhousie University Press, 1976); and Cassandra Pybus, *Epic Journeys of Freedom: Runaway Slaves of the American Revolution and their Global Quest for Liberty* (Boston: Beacon Press, 2004).

[72] Laurent Dubois, *Avengers of the New World: The Story of the Haitian Revolution* (Cambridge, Mass.: Belknap Press of Harvard University Press, 2004).

and more refugees.⁷³ While the revolution had intoxicating effects for some in the Anglophone Atlantic, it also had profoundly unsettling implications for many others. Its ideas—of the overthrow of slavery, of the right of African-Americans to self-rule—were as simultaneously enthralling and horrifying to many contemporary witnesses as were its events.

This Shiva-like quality of the Atlantic world, its ability to destroy as well as to build, should be apparent. All of these features both fractured and created an Atlantic world. The destructive consequences of slavery, war, and other developments are all too clear. These were events with enormous human costs, paid disproportionately by certain populations. These destructive elements also contributed to the integration and growth of an Atlantic economy and culture, one with the power to unite distant populations. Transport and communication links improved in this era, and offered a means of ameliorating the pain of separation by vast geographic distances, at least for some. They also created connections across the Atlantic, as people came to feel a greater investment, for all kinds of reasons, on events on the other side of the Atlantic, whether the winning of a battle, the selling of goods, or the arrival of a letter.

This sense of anxiety over these distances, combined with new access to literacy and communication, meant that letter-writers could repeatedly stress their continued affections, even while recognizing the terrors of Atlantic distance. One wife of a ship's captain in Newport, Rhode Island, bemoaned the departure of both her brother and her husband, remarking how dreadful it was that: 'Friends seperate in this World, some from almost avaritious principle And others O how reluctantly they go . . . I am ever uneasy when your at Sea & think it a Miserable Life for a Man that can enjoy a Wife, & too [two] pretty Children.'⁷⁴ Others also lamented circumstances that could take an individual away from family and across the ocean. One correspondent reported on a woman who had just left: 'How much resolution & fortitude must she possess to leave freinds, Connections & Country, & cross the Ocean, alone, unprotected, & unknown to every body in the country where she was going.'⁷⁵ It was not only the act of crossing the ocean but also the sense of leaving 'freinds, Connections & Country' that was so disturbing. However, correspondents emphasized that love was not affected by distance, even as they exhibited a fear that it might be. A mother promised her son that: 'my affection is not abated since we parted. Notwithstanding we are separated by an immense distance & boundless ocean, yet I am often, very often with you in mind.'⁷⁶ At the end of the American Revolution one friend informed another: 'so far from forgetting my friend & her dearest connections through an absence of between five & six

---

⁷³ See David P. Geggus (ed.), *The Impact of the Haitian Revolution in the Atlantic World* (Columbia, SC: University of South Carolina Press, 2001), esp. Part 4, 'Refugees'.
⁷⁴ Mary Ellery to Christopher Ellery, 'Newport Febr 14 1765', Ellery Family Papers, Folder 2, Box 62, NHS.
⁷⁵ Rebecca Shoemaker to Samuel Shoemaker, '1 July 1784', Shoemaker Family Papers, HSP.
⁷⁶ Rebecca Shoemaker to Edward Shoemaker, '19 Sept. [17]84', Shoemaker Family Papers, HSP.

years I have continually sympathized with them in distresses.'[77] A son lamented to his father, mother, and sister: 'my Happiness will be incomplete, whilst a broad Ocean rolls between us.'[78] One man assured the recipient of his letter that 'neither time, distance, nor the unhappy Revolutions that have taken place can make me forget my friends'.[79] One father in South Carolina fretted over his son in England: 'I have my apprehensions that so long a separation may weaken His affection for His Mother and myself—filial affection is not only the surest but most pleasing tie to hold him by—to direct and influence his Actions hereafter.'[80] This same father informed his son's tutor: 'No Change—No time—no distance—no length of Separation can Weaken those impressions of high Esteem and warm regard.'[81] Such disconnections inspired all sorts of reassurances, but also all sorts of anxieties.

The way ocean voyages created an enduring sense of disconnection is captured by a particular oceanic metaphor of this era. While such metaphors pre-dated the eighteenth century, they nevertheless appeared sufficiently frequently in that century to merit some explanation. In 1799 Dr Daniel Robert, about to depart from New York City for Dominica in the West Indies, wrote to his wife: 'I embark once more on the wide ocean of the World, leaving behind me all I hold dear.'[82] Daniel's statement was both metaphor and reality, and it thus neatly conflated larger preoccupations of the age. He was literally about to get on a ship, but he was also metaphorically launching himself into a world separate from his family and friends. One Loyalist Anglican minister, Thomas Coombe, about to leave his position in Pennsylvania, assured his congregation of the anguish he felt that he had 'to quit a decent Competency among a People whom I affectionately respect & Love, and launch out upon the Ocean of the World'.[83] Like Daniel, Thomas deployed this as both metaphor and reality.

Other uses of this metaphor of 'launching into the ocean' indicated not the conflation of a genuine voyage with a sense of distance, but rather a sense of danger and dispossession in a new environment. One Loyalist exile living in London after the Revolution declared: 'Never was Mortal more completely set afloat, and where I shall land again, Heaven only knows.'[84] One imagined business correspondent, in a guide for young tradesmen, informed his correspondents

---

[77] Hannah Hobart to Mary Story, draft, '[Philadelphia] Novr 29th. 1783', Hannah Hobart Papers, LoC.

[78] Thomas Coombe to father, et al., 'Wednesday Evening Jany 3d, 1770', Thomas Coombe Papers, HSP.

[79] John Johnson to Robert Watts, 'Montreal 26th Novr, 1785', Robert Watts Papers, Box II, NYHS.

[80] Pierce Butler to Weeden Butler, 'N York September ye. 1st. 1790', Pierce Butler Letter Collection, Add. Mss. 16603, BL.

[81] Pierce Butler to Weeden Butler, 'Philad. January ye 2d 1798', ibid.

[82] Daniel Robert to Mary Smith Robert, undated [New York City June 1799], Daniel Robert Letters, NYHS.

[83] Thomas Coombe to 'Gentlemen', 'July 7. 1778', Thomas Coombe Papers, HSP.

[84] Isaac Low to Nicholas Low, 'London March 2d. 1785', Nicholas Low Papers, Box 1, File: 'Low, Isaac 1785', LoC.

that he had 'launch'd forth into the great ocean of business.'[85] This metaphor conveyed not only his sense of having entered a new and unsettling territory, but also that he had entered it alone, without the ties that would support him. In a letter to a tutor, one father referred to a son's eventual placement at Oxford University: 'then indeed He will be launched into a troubled Sea without Your just pilotage—it is then my breast will bleed for Him.'[86] Another father warned a son about to arrive alone in London: 'If this meets you in London, it will meet you in an open & wide Ocean of danger: hitherto you have had friends to advise with, & good Example constantly before you, now you can only rely on Gods grace, yr: own prudence & the good principles, instilled into you by a virtuous Education.'[87] Launching into the ocean of the world was both to enter an unknown and fearsome world, but also to be set afloat alone, without the friends and family who might help, advise, and support. It was also to give up the authority that came from the ties already established by one's family.

Transatlantic distance, a common feature of eighteenth-century life, was a source of comment and concern for family members. The ability of transatlantic distance to fracture families made individuals worry about how the ties of friends and family could be maintained in such circumstances. But there were many other reasons for family members to feel adrift in the eighteenth century. While change and even crisis in the family occurs in every century, perhaps even every generation, its particular shape in the eighteenth century bears further scrutiny. There were genuine changes in the configurations of families, some of them the result of Atlantic changes (such as slavery) and some the result of other, more nebulous factors. The tremendous economic growth, Atlantic reorientations, mobility, population-growth, urbanization, and increasing status stratification in both British and colonial locales brought with them attendant anxieties that the moral foundations of society were giving way, that what seemed fantastic prosperity might turn quickly and alarmingly into luxury and corruption. The rot would begin at home. Many features of family life in this era contributed to this sense. It is useful to sketch them out, albeit briefly, to gain a sense of how individuals might have felt adrift in this age in terms of the family.

Marriage, illegitimacy, and bridal pregnancy were major subjects of discussion. From critical essays on marriage, to many narratives of marriages in popular stories and novels, to legislative reform, marriage was taking new shapes in this

---

[85] Daniel Defoe, *The Complete English Tradesman, in Familiar Letters. Directing him in all the several Parts and Progressions of Trade* (London, 1726), 23.

[86] Pierce Butler to Weeden Butler, 'Mary-Ville So Carolina November ye 16th 1788', Pierce Butler Letter Collection, Add. Mss. 16603, BL.

[87] Charles Carroll to Charley Carroll, 'Octr 6th 1759,' Ronald Hoffman, Sally D. Mason, and Eleanor S. Darcy (eds.), *Dear Papa, Dear Charley: The Peregrinations of a Revolutionary Aristocrat, as told by Charles Carroll of Carrollton and his Father, Charles Carroll of Annapolis*, 3 vols. (Chapel Hill: University of North Carolina Press for the Omohundro Institute of Early American History and Culture, 2001), i. 128.

century. Of considerable importance in England especially was the 1753 passage of Lord Hardwicke's Marriage Act, which sought to regulate marriages so that they could not be contracted informally. This Act was not only an indication of the anxieties surrounding marriage in this era, but it was also the source of further concern, as it regulated against elopements and other forms of clandestine marriage. Even as regulations for marriage were becoming stricter, there was a rise in both bridal pregnancy and illegitimacy rates, across a large part of the British-Atlantic world.[88] This growth may have been related in part to changing senses of what constituted marriage and proper arenas for sexual activity. Still, they led many to fear for a society with such perceived sexual dissipation.

Just as illegitimacy and bridal pregnancy rates increased, so, it seemed, did adultery, although this perception may have stemmed from an increase in publications, not incidents. One scholar has contended that 'lamentations at the exceptional sexual turpitude of the age are a common theme at all times and places, but they recurred with peculiar intensity between 1660 and 1820'.[89] Publications of major divorce proceedings contributed to a sense of moral and sexual decline, as did discussions of prostitution. From 1770 there was a marked increase in English 'criminal conversation' cases, in which the wronged husband sued his wife's lover for damages. Such cases also attracted much more attention from the press. The anonymous author of a collection of adultery trials published in 1790 noted: 'The great Desire which readers of every Description entertain for well-reported Cases of ADULTERY, FORNICATION, SEDUCTION, and all Kinds of CRIMINAL CONVERSATION.'[90] Periodicals such as the *Town and Country Magazine* and the *Bon Ton Magazine* specialized in reporting incidents of adultery, and enjoyed considerable popularity in the 1770s and 1780s (for the former) and the 1790s (for the latter).[91] The increased circulation of news, as today, often brought with it a sense of doom, as story after story appeared about adultery, fops, ruined families, and other indicators of domestic and national disorder. These developments accelerated in the 1790s, in light of the French Revolutions and its attendant upsets, in an atmosphere that one historian has termed 'a moral panic'.[92]

---

[88] See Ulrich, *A Midwife's Tale*, ch. 4; Cornelia Hughes Dayton, *Women Before the Bar: Gender, Law, and Society in Connecticut, 1639–1789* (Chapel Hill, NC: University of North Carolina for the Institute of Early American History and Culture, 1995), ch. 4; E. A. Wrigley and R. S. Schofield, *The Population History of England, 1541–1871: A Reconstruction*, ed. Peter Laslett, R. S. Schofield, and E. A. Wrigley, Studies in Social and Demographic History (Cambridge, Mass.: Harvard University Press, 1981), 266 ff.; and Stone, *The Family, Sex and Marriage in England*, 607–15. Stone notes a considerable eighteenth-century rise in both pre-nuptial pregnancy and illegitimacy: 'The rate of recorded pre-nuptial pregnancies shot up, reaching over forty per cent in the last half of the century in many places on both sides of the Atlantic.' Stone, *Family, Sex and Marriage*, 609. The figures for illegitimacy in the British West Indies would doubtless be even higher.

[89] Lawrence Stone, *Road to Divorce: England, 1530–1987* (Oxford: Oxford University Press, 1990), 256.

[90] *Trials for Adultery* (London, 1790), preface, A2.   [91] Stone, *Road to Divorce*, 252.
[92] Ibid. 255, 248–9, 273–7.

These domestic concerns seemed to indicate the chaos loosed upon a society where older forms of punishment and control—such as skimmingtons and church court suits—had all but disappeared. As one tract from the early 1770s fretted, 'virtue has dropped, so vice has reared its head... Where luxury has gained ground, there effeminacy has done the same... Where lasciviousness reigns, there flows in a torrent of debauchery, to the destruction of private families and to the insult of public laws.'[93] A 1792 exposition similarly condemned adultery: 'No vice can prove more fatal to dissolve the ties of society, to bring distrust and distress into families; no vice can be more infectious, and have a more dreadful influence on the rising population.'[94] This dissolution of 'the ties of society' demonstrated the presumed fragility of such links. The sense that such vices might prove 'infectious' meant they could hardly be contained within a single family, but would instead move outward, to wreak havoc in society at large.

Similar worries revolved around other kinds of marital failures elsewhere in the British-Atlantic world. One particular form of non-marriage and illegitimacy that increasingly dismayed at least some commentators was that between Britons and their descendants and non-Europeans. In particular, the unions of Anglo-Americans with African-Americans, the vast majority of which were not recognized by legal marriage, troubled many. In his 1794 history of the West Indies, Bryan Edwards observed that: 'no White man of decent appearance... will condescend to give his hand in marriage to a Mulatto!'[95] The failure of British men to marry and form British-style households in the West Indies also worried Edward Long, a notorious commentator on Jamaica: 'it might be much better for Britain, and Jamaica, too, if the white men in that colony would abate of their infatuated attachments to black women, and, instead... perform the duty incumbent on every good citizen, by raising in honourable wedlock a race of unadulterated beings.'[96] The apparent inability or unwillingness of Anglo-Jamaicans, both women and men, to replicate metropolitan ideals and familial models was an especially problematic form of family disorder and illegitimacy, but such issues sounded more generally throughout the British-Atlantic world. These were not simply domestic issues, but indeed political ones, since maintaining orderly household-families was 'the duty incumbent on every good citizen'.

Whether in the British colonies or Britain itself, children were also a source of concern, since there was a worry that imperial ventures were slowly poisoning the

---

[93] T. Pollen, *The Fatal Consequences of Adultery to Monarchies as well as Families* (London, 1772), as quoted in ibid. 277.

[94] *The Evils of Adultery and Prostitution; with an Inquiry into the Causes of their Present Alarming Increase* (London, 1792), 3, as quoted in David M. Turner, *Fashioning Adultery: Gender, Sex and Civility in England, 1660–1740*, ed. Lyndal Roper, Past & Present Publications (Cambridge: Cambridge University Press, 2002), 201.

[95] Bryan Edwards, *The History, Civil and Commercial, of the British Colonies in the West Indies*, 2 vols., 2nd edn. (London, 1794), ii. 22.

[96] Edward Long, *The History of Jamaica* (London, 1774), 327.

British, both at home and abroad. This poison might appear first in the midst of the happy family, seeping outward from the emptied cup of each drunken son, the stained bedclothes of each debauched daughter. Beyond the issue of legitimacy lay the vexed issue of the behavior of the next generation. As prosperity rose, so did the massive consumer growth of the eighteenth century, with ever more goods and indeed luxuries in circulation. Much of this prosperity rested on the sustained efforts of individuals who risked much in this Atlantic world, but who then fretted that their children would simply take advantage of this wealth, and become idle and dissipated. Their domestic decisions would resonate more generally in the commonwealth, which would then crumble. This theme haunted innumerable texts, from novels to newspapers, from magazines to sermons. One author in the *Town and Country Magazine* summarized what might be said to be one of the great anxieties of the age: 'The refinements of dissipation have arisen to such a pitch, that what was luxury to our fore-fathers does not now even comprize the necessaries of life. Every quarter of the globe is ransacked for shortening their lives.'[97] This sense that the entire globe was pillaged for the selfish desires of a short-sighted and luxury-loving generation, an apprehension disconcertingly contemporary in its orientation, implies the fear that the major economic and political changes wrought by the increase in imperialism and colonialism might effect cultural and social changes in the domestic population. The article also lamented the way that both rich and poor were turning to extravagance and also to 'intrigue and cuckoldom'.[98]

Individuals wondered if the love of luxury and travel was causing debauchery and even effeminacy. 'The macaroni', the late eighteenth-century extravagant male type so ridiculed by the metropolitan press, highlights such issues. The very origin of the epithet 'macaroni' came from the pretentious love of Italy shown by those young men who had taken the Grand Tour.[99] While not a specifically Atlantic issue, it does demonstrate the fears that swirled around the luxuries brought by travel and mobility of varying kinds. Macaronis could also reflect Atlantic concerns, as in the vain effeminacy of the young man training for the law in the 1772 'Middle Temple Macaroni' (Fig. 1.4). Using a quotation from Richard Cumberland's 1771 play, *The West Indian*, the caption read: 'In short I am a West Indian.' The caption implied that overseas money was producing ruffled and furbelowed degeneracy in the heart of London and the English law. Here was an image of rich, overweening Atlantic masculinity to strike worries into the heart of a nation now looking uneasily across the Atlantic to colonies that both buoyed up and threatened the very heart of the metropolis itself.

Some articles also explicitly linked Atlantic distance and family disorder, as in a lawsuit reported in *The Times* in 1797, that of *Esten v. the Duke of Hamilton*.

---

[97] 'The Man of Pleasure, No III', *Town and Country Magazine* (Aug. 1771), 425.   [98] Ibid.
[99] 'Character of a Macaroni', *Town and Country Magazine* (May 1772), 242–3.

Fig. 1.4. Anonymous, 'The Middle Temple Macaroni', c.1772. Guildhall Library, City of London.

In many ways an entirely typical adultery suit, it involved the classic cast of a cuckolded husband, a seducing duke, and an actress-wife. Esten sued the Duke of Hamilton for 'criminal conversation' with his wife. Thomas Erskine, later Lord Chancellor, and one of the most successful litigants of the era, defended Hamilton.[100] Esten was a ship's purser who, in 1784, married Harriot Bennet, with whom he had a daughter. Upon determining, however, that 'he was incapable of furnishing a sufficient provision for his wife and daughter', Esten went back to sea. A report of the trial notes that: 'If Mr. Esten had been left to his own choice, it would have given him great pleasure to have lived with his family, but his circumstances rendered it impossible. It was necessary that a temporary separation should take place, and that he should get into a better situation than he then possessed.'[101] Accordingly, he shipped out in His Majesty's Navy in 1789, going first to Jamaica and later to St Domingo. In this, as we have already seen, he was doing what many had already done, and would continue to do. Nevertheless, in a rather startling turnaround, the defense argued that Esten's decision amounted to nothing less than the shirking of his marital duty.

The defense claimed that the main source of blame for Mrs Esten's undeniable and ongoing infidelity (she was by this point living with the divorced Duke of Hamilton) lay not with her, or with the duke, but instead with Esten himself. According to Erskine, Esten had 'withdrawn all protection, patronage, and care from his wife... [and committed] a breach of moral duty... by forsaking his station. By withdrawing his protection, which was the only guard of female virtue, the husband threw out a lure and temptation to the adulterer; and therefore, he being the cause of the commission of the crime, was justly considered as the object of blame.' To make such an argument, the defense apparently declared further that there was no evidence that Esten had been especially sorry to leave his wife, nor that he had hurried to return to her:

If Mr. E. had occasion to go to the West-Indies, or to any other part beyond the seas, in consequence of not being able to maintain his wife, why should he not separate from her like any other man? Why could he not leave his wife in tears, lamenting that the urgency of his affairs reduced him to the necessity of withdrawing his protection from her. He [Erskine] saw nothing of that pathetic language here. If that had been the condition and feeling of the husband, if he had not been living with a determination never to see her again, would he not have seized the first favourable opportunity of returning home to his family [?].[102]

Erskine used Esten's alleged failure to act as a man of feeling on parting from his wife, as well as his lengthy stay at sea, as proof of his intention never to return

---

[100] According to Lawrence Stone, Thomas Erskine was a notably eloquent pleader in court. He was more often the prosecutor in crim. con. cases, but in this case he acted for the defense. Stone, *Road to Divorce*, 253–4, 257, 264–6, 273–7. More recently, John Barrell has termed Erskine 'the great liberal advocate'. John Barrell, *The Spirit of Despotism: Invasions of Privacy in the 1790s* (Oxford: Oxford University Press, 2006), 83.
[101] *The Times*, 23 Feb. 1797, 3.   [102] Ibid. 3.

to her, a claim that depends on the vitality of the culture of sensibility. For this argument to gain ascendancy would also have set quite a precedent, since, as we have seen already, such separations were fairly commonplace in this era.

Nevertheless, Erskine was not finished with his defense. His earlier mention of Esten's having thrown out a 'lure' was only the beginning of an extended analogy, which one historian has rightly termed 'extraordinary':[103]

> The custom with regard to Greenland Whales is the law in this case. As long as the line is fast to the fish, the fish is yours, though the line should reach from Greenland to St. Domingo or Nova Zembla; but the moment she is a loose fish, any body may strike her; and I maintain, *meo periculo*, that the Law of Greenland Fish, is the Law of England with regard to Women, I shall show you Mrs. E was a loose fish.[104]

This scholar has persuasively suggested that this image, equating women and fish and treating them both as so much property to be 'struck' by men, refutes notions of the rise of 'companionate marriage' underpinned by ideas of gender equality and friendship.[105] Yet it does much more than this. This analogy highlighted the concerns about maintaining connections in moments of disconnection, of keeping 'lines' up between two spouses. Its imagery was undeniably both misogynistic (being a 'loose fish' was no compliment) and violent (in that such lines kill fish, as is made clear by the use of the word 'strike').

This image also clarified, however, precisely the problem with which so many others had to grapple in this era: how could connections, and the lines of authority, 'patronage, protection, and care' they implied, be kept up when the Atlantic divided family members? At the same time, these place references could not have been accidental. Esten had been stationed in Jamaica and St Domingo, among other places, but the invocation of a locale that sent shivers down the spines of many in the anglophone Atlantic by this time underscored the kind of Atlantic disorder against which 'lines' had to be drawn. The reference to Nova Zembla, an Arctic island, implied that these lines could stretch as far as the most distant and mysterious place that could be imagined; other contemporary writers also used Nova Zembla in precisely this way.[106] This analogy also critically implied that such lines were forged by feeling between family members, and that such feeling proved family ties, to the missing spouse and to a court and reading public. Had Esten been able to produce loving letters to his wife, then it

---

[103] Donna T. Andrew, ' "Adultery à-la-Mode": Privilege, the Law and Attitudes to Adultery 1770–1809,' *History (The Journal of the Historical Association)*, 82 (1997), 5–23, at 19.

[104] *The Times*, 23 Feb. 1797, 3.

[105] Andrew, 'Adultery à-la-Mode', 19–20.

[106] One daughter of a Loyalist exile reassured her mother, then across the Atlantic, that she would live anywhere on earth as long as she could live with her mother and have enough money there: 'Where ever I could get the most to live on with you, there I would go whether at Nova Zembla or Otaheite.' Elizabeth Galloway to Grace Growden Galloway, 'High Street Mary Le bone No 24 July 17th 1779', Folder: 'Betsey Galloway—Correspondence of [to mother and others]', Galloway Papers, LoC.

would have put paid to this line of defense. It was this 'feeling', which could be sustained by affectionate letters, that would keep that line attached to that fish, no matter how far away, a point to be revisited in much greater detail in the next two chapters.

While this lawsuit and the arguments used were unusual, they articulated and broadcast more general, if usually more implied, concerns about the possible dislocating effects of split households. For a society underpinned by households, divided households created all kinds of worries. It might mean that some individuals, whether wives or sons or servants, would not be governed at home as they ought to be. It also meant that the chief cornerstone of stability in this world would itself be imperiled by its own fracturing. At the same time, outside forces—whether expensive tours of Italy or luxury or mobility—might 'strike' at these individuals, further rupturing the bonds of society. Such separations, then, created liminal moments in the sense invoked some time ago by the anthropologist Victor Turner. He has written that 'liminal entities are neither here nor there; they are betwixt and between'. In much the same way, Atlantic families were 'neither here nor there', were both and yet neither, in between what became nation-states but also in between the most usual forms of household formation, continuity, and authority. Turner further posited that liminality often generates powerful cultural metaphors: 'liminality is frequently likened to death, to being in the womb, to invisibility, to darkness.'[107] Or, we might add for these populations, it could be likened to being a 'loose fish' in the 'ocean of the world'.

To return to the image with which this chapter began, the odd setting of the family in the frontispiece of *The Court Letter-Writer*—both indoors and out on the ocean—was itself a liminal setting, on the threshold between the domestic, the interior, and what has been called the 'private', and the distant, the exterior, and the 'public.' Neither inside nor out, but also neither of one part or another (since one member was clearly far away), this family was thus itself liminal, placed in a liminal setting. Part of the resonance of this image lay not only in its invocation of many other portraits of the era, but also in the fact that letters themselves were liminal, crossing the threshold between households and linking the domestic and the distant. They were neither private nor public, circulating within families and households but necessarily traveling outside of them, on that very world of great-masted ships shown in the image itself. They thus served as 'lines' themselves, maintaining family feeling even in situations in which it was at risk, as the next chapters will demonstrate. Letters allowed family life to continue, even across the Atlantic.

The Atlantic currents of this century altered permanently domestic landscapes, for all of those lands that bordered it. In some places they contributed to booming

---

[107] Victor W. Turner, *The Ritual Process: Structure and Anti-Structure* (Hawthorne, NY: Aldine Publishing Co., 1969), 95.

economic growth, growth to pay for a macaroni to primp, for a slave to hoe, and for a nation to go to war. One ballad issued a siren song of paradoxes calling men to sea: 'where men lose their lives, a sure fortune to gain.'[108] The Atlantic brought fortunes as surely as it also took away lives. While some made a fortune, others simply made a living. They did so at a high cost, and others suffered lost fortunes and lost livings as a result of these changes. The individuals in this Atlantic created an integrated economy and integrated cultural worlds enjoyed by many, some through family letters. Letters allowed many to bridge distance, and to remain families. Yet the costs were undeniably, horrifically high, both for those who chose to take the risks and for those who had no such choice. One woman lamented to her brother, in a letter that kept them attached: 'What a great loss it is for me, that Such a worthy Friend as you are at such a distance.'[109] This Atlantic world put distance between many friends and created a lot of 'loose fish', launched in the ocean of the world. At the same time, its cultures of communication allowed many to maintain lines of affection and continuity. Behind a lot of happy families lay the Atlantic Ocean; that same Atlantic lay behind a lot of unhappy families, too.

[108] 'Tight Lads of the Ocean', in Dibdin, *Sea Songs and Ballads*, 156.
[109] Cicilia Steuart Ruddach to Charles Steuart, 'Kirkll 30th Sepr 1768', MS. 5025 fo. 92, Charles Steuart Papers, NLS.

2

Familiarity in Life and Letters

'Dear Father and Mother, I Have great Trouble', began the letters of *Pamela*, both book and heroine.[1] Great trouble indeed: so started the tale of one of the most famous 'loose fish' of the eighteenth century. The opening of this novel encapsulates both Pamela's distance from her family of birth, and also the trouble and chaos that could come from this separation and lack of familial protection. The world was a hazardous place for both men and women, away from friends and family. Prey to the 'strikes' of her master, Pamela embodied both the worrisome effects of making one's own way and the ways in which letters helped to alleviate those anxieties and maintain those imperiled connections. One scholar has claimed that 'the early novel takes its life from motion'.[2] The early novel also took its life from the disconnection wrought by that motion, and the new connections forged by mobility. No wonder that so many early novels were epistolary in form. In the destruction and re-creation of families across the Atlantic world, lines forged by letters could also help to ameliorate the trouble of divided families. For Pamela, as for many others, letters to her family, after a separation from them, provided a set of lines connecting her to a world left behind. Such family letters did more than provide emotional support in difficult times. They carved out a social world and a set of relations. They also defined the bounds of familiarity. Lines of connection, especially letters, offered emotional and financial support, and they also provided links to a family and a community. Without such lines, it was nearly impossible to succeed in increasingly stratified, mobile, and especially Atlantic worlds.

Familiarity was a central virtue, in life and letters. It was an ideal that allowed non-family members to become integrated in family-like worlds. Beyond politeness, familiarity helped to broker connections between individuals who were on the move. Familiar letters helped to create critical 'fictive families', carving out a familiar social space, and so reinforcing the connections that existed between familiar individuals. Letters could provide immediate links to families and friends (so a son remained connected to his father, a wife to her husband). But they

---

[1] Pamela to Father and Mother, Letter I, in Richardson, *Pamela*, i. 1.
[2] Christopher Hill also notes, 'perhaps the expansion of overseas trade added to this sense of mobility'. Christopher Hill, *A Tinker and a Poor Man: John Bunyan and His Church, 1628–1688* (New York: Norton, 1988), 361, 362.

also smoothed a path to familiarity in new circles (to provide a family to take care of a son at school, to help that son enter into a business concern). In new situations and new lands, such letters smoothed a path to civility, inclusion, and even prosperity.

This chapter argues that familiarity, like civility, politeness, and sensibility, was a key eighteenth-century ideal. In a wide world, familiarity carved out a particular social space, one in which certain freedoms were permitted. In 1755 Samuel Johnson defined 'familiar' both as 'domestick; relating to a family' and as 'affable; not formal... unceremonious; free... unconstrained'.[3] This concatenation, being both domestic and also free, is a vital one (the word 'familial' only came into use in the twentieth century). Achieving familiarity was a critical goal of these letter-writers, and letters themselves helped to define relationships not only as 'domestick' but also as affable, informal, and free. They were allowed only to certain people, though, and this meant that familiarity excluded as much and as many as it included. Familiarity originated in the domestic setting, but it did not remain exclusively there. It was thus an exceptionally useful way for lines to be forged and maintained between individuals who relied upon each other. Stemming from the family setting, but moving outward into other realms, familiarity thus cut across the public and the private. But familiarity, precisely because it cut across boundaries of varying kinds, also provoked considerable worry. Many texts of the age, but most centrally letters, offered ways both of expressing and of ameliorating these anxieties surrounding familiarity.

The Atlantic world was created as much through these familiar connections as through unfamiliar encounters. There has been an assumption that going to a new place spelled the end of kin and family relations. In point of fact, these strange new locations could force some to cling ever more resolutely to older ties, or at least those old ties enabled some to make a life in strange and unfamiliar places. Making the circle of familiarity narrow and manageable, but also, crucially, mobile, meant that its power could reach across the ocean. In fact, these ties often helped to forge imperial and colonial power. A son could go to the colonies and join a business on the basis of familiar ties. Those who controlled those ties, and who used letters to maintain them, disproportionately gained access to imperial power. Familiarity was a way to forge connections in their apparent absence. In this sense, it made possible much by way of political and territorial and economic expansion. The family, then, had agency on influencing the course of empire. They created worlds of trust and allowed for even long distances to be surmounted.

Samuel Johnson was clear about what he meant by familiarity (undeniably a virtue in the author of a dictionary), but how can historians make sense of this concept? It is best to begin with what familiarity was *not*. Familiarity was neither simple physical intimacy nor politeness. The distinction between familiarity and

---

[3] Definition: 'Familiar', Johnson, *A Dictionary of the English Language*.

intimacy is clear when considered in relation to slaves and servants in elite households, who were expected to maintain their distance. Servants like Pamela, as well as slaves, could routinely be deeply and physically intimate with their masters and mistresses. After all, they pulled off boots, laced up stays, emptied chamber-pots, and sometimes even nursed babies who might one day be their masters. Still, while such individuals shared considerable intimacies, they did not necessarily share familiarity. Extreme physical intimacy (even of a sexual nature) did not ensure familiarity, startling as that may seem. Thomas Thistlewood in Jamaica had sex with numerous slaves, but only Phibbah, his long-term partner and mother of his son, could enjoy the privileges of familiarity with him.[4] Familiar relationships depended on a degree of equality between actors, and also implied ease and freedom. In most cases, servants and slaves did not enjoy these privileges.[5] This fact explains why one eighteenth-century writer could declare servants to be aliens in the house: 'A servant... lives as a kind of foreigner under the same roof; a *domestick*, and yet a stranger too.'[6] Household-families may have included servants and slaves, but such household members did not have the privilege of equal and familiar footing with other family members.

Familiarity was also not politeness or civility, though it often worked in tandem with these ideals.[7] To be sure, there were similarities between politeness and familiarity. Familiarity and politeness involved both men and women, in mixed company, and allowed an individual to make his or her way in a setting filled with strangers, thus affording an opportunity to demonstrate both

---

[4] See Douglas Hall, *In Miserable Slavery: Thomas Thistlewood in Jamaica, 1750–1786* (Basingstoke: Macmillan, 1989), as well as Trevor Burnard, *Mastery, Tyranny, and Desire: Thomas Thistlewood and his Slaves in the Anglo-Jamaican World* (Chapel Hill, NC: University of North Carolina Press, 2004).

[5] This point echoes contentions made by Elizabeth Foyster about the work of Naomi Tadmor, whose emphasis on the household-family underplayed differences between members of that household. Foyster points out that servants 'continued to be defined and described differently from family and kin'. Elizabeth Foyster, *Marital Violence: An English Family History, 1660–1857* (Cambridge: Cambridge University Press, 2005), 184.

[6] 'South's Sermons', as quoted in Samuel Johnson, *Dictionary*, s.v. 'domestick' (italics in original).

[7] Coverage includes: Anna Bryson, *From Courtesy to Civility: Changing Codes of Conduct in Early Modern England* (Oxford: Clarendon Press, 1998); Paul Langford, *A Polite and Commercial People, England, 1727–1783* (Oxford: Oxford University Press, 1989); John Brewer, *The Pleasures of the Imagination: English Culture in the Eighteenth Century* (London: HarperCollins, 1997); Lawrence E. Klein, *Shaftesbury and the Culture of Politeness: Moral Discourse and Cultural Politics in Early Eighteenth-Century England* (Cambridge: Cambridge University Press, 1994); Amanda Vickery, *The Gentleman's Daughter: Women's Lives in Georgian England* (New Haven: Yale University Press, 1998); and Philip Carter, *Men and the Emergence of Polite Society, Britain, 1660–1800* (Harlow: Longman, 2001). For America, see Richard L. Bushman, *The Refinement of America: Persons, Houses, Cities* (New York: Knopf, 1992); Kathleen M. Brown, *Good Wives, Nasty Wenches, and Anxious Patriarchs: Gender, Race, and Power in Colonial Virginia* (Chapel Hill, NC: University of North Carolina Press for the Institute of Early American History and Culture, 1996); David S. Shields, *Civil Tongues and Polite Letters in British America* (Chapel Hill, NC: University of North Carolina Press for the Institute of Early American History and Culture, 1997); C. Dallett Hemphill, *Bowing to Necessities: A History of Manners in America, 1620–1860* (Oxford: Oxford University Press, 1999).

inclusion (of some) and exclusion (of others). Both politeness and familiarity provided a guide to behavior in unfamiliar worlds. Still, for all their similarities, politeness and familiarity were not the same thing. Familiarity was a degree of easy informality beyond politeness. For elite individuals, politeness was the basic expectation, the approach that an individual should bring to a room full of new people. Familiarity was a level of access and involvement beyond this basic politeness, one that depended on something other than either simply status or other such markers. So, one father in Virginia warned his son in London: 'Avoid in general your countrymen in London... be civil and polite to all—familiar with none.'[8] Politeness implied an effort, a ceremony of manners that brought strangers together. Still, they might remain only polite strangers. In fact, many commentators feared that being too polite could work against familiarity, ease, and feeling. One American woman in London in the 1780s complained that 'the People here are... too polite... to feel for others'.[9] She also rejoiced when she could go to one London friend's home 'without ceremony', thus bypassing the high politeness that often accompanied such meetings.[10] Another woman remarked on having tea 'sans ceremonie'.[11] Ceremonial politeness might lead to the ease of familiarity, but it might not, leaving only the more formal relationship between individuals.

Familiarity, then, was a mode of interaction that stemmed from the family setting and that implied degrees of knowledge and easy affability. It was both a tone, and a space for relations. Familiarity was not incompatible with inequalities of status, and yet, in a sense, it could help to ameliorate those inequalities by conferring the privilege of familiarity on individuals of inferior legal and social standing. This is what might happen in the family itself, as well as beyond it. The very imprecision in the means by which familiarity might be achieved was precisely what made it so valuable. Therefore, withholding familiarity could be a potent form of exclusion, as can be seen in advice from parents to children about how to behave with various non-familiar individuals. One father, Michael Keane, cautioned his son not to be too familiar with the Gregs, individuals who were looking after the son at Cambridge University, and with whom the father had business dealings in St Vincent in the West Indies. This relationship of care would normally have implied familiarity between members of these two families, since there were obligations being filled on both sides. Taking care of children, as we shall see, was a relationship that usually resulted in familiarity. It was, therefore, unusual for Keane to warn his son, echoing the words of

---

[8] Ralph Wormeley to Warner Lewis Wormely, 'Rosegill 8th: Septr: 1803', Mss1/W8945/a-8, Wormeley Family Papers, 1791–1952, VHS.
[9] Elizabeth Galloway to Grace Galloway, 'High Street Mary Le bone No 24 July 17th 1779', File: Betsey Galloway (correspondence to mother and others), Joseph Galloway Papers, LoC.
[10] Elizabeth Galloway to Grace Galloway, 'February 2th 1780', ibid.
[11] Margaret Cowper to Eliza McQueen Mackay, 'Kensington 25th. June Saturday [n.y.]', Mackay–Stiles Papers, SHC.

the Virginia father: 'Take care to be polite & civil to Mr. & Mrs. Greg but avoid any familiarity or freedom, he has behaved rather shabbily to me.'[12] This comment makes clearer than most precisely what was at stake here. For the son to instigate familiarity with the Gregs was, for this father, not what the 'shabby behavior' of Mr Greg deserved. Familiarity was a privilege, one that could be withheld as necessary. Another anxious American father informed his son in London: 'Polite attention to a Country Man is one thing, and intimacy another.'[13]

Throughout the early modern period, especially the eighteenth century, the boundaries of familiarity within the family itself were shifting. An earlier familial ideal had held that even family relationships—as between husband and wives or parents and children—should involve a certain degree of formality. If a wife in 1484 addressed her husband in letters as 'Ryght [re]u*er*[en]d *and* worchupfull Ser', then it was the case that in earlier eras this familiarity was not always privileged even in these familial relationships.[14] Part of this had to do as much with the nature of letter-writing as with the nature of the family: if a clerk was writing a letter for a wife, then familiarity was less likely to be the tone adopted. Nevertheless, it also speaks of the cultural ideal of formality in even close family relationships. This ideal of formality shifted into one of familiarity in this period. A 1739 article about the relations between husband and wife approved of the familiarity of marital relations: 'the Matrimonial intimacies between a Man and his Wife may discharge them of much of the bondage of ceremony in the circumstances', although this should not translate into 'rudeness and indecency'.[15] There was a happy medium to familiarity: it allowed freedom and ease, but not indecencies.

As in marital relations, so too was there a transformation in ideals of parent–child relations. Prior to the later eighteenth century, the kind of language children were supposed to use to their parents was the language of reverential affections, not a familiar one. This emphasis was especially clear in Puritan writings, which stressed the honor children owed their parents. Even parents were expected to keep their distance. That ordinary behavior often diverged from these ideals is clear, and admonitions not to be too familiar imply that some were being exactly that. But they also indicate a particular cultural ideal. Thomas Cobbet, a New England minister whose works were published in seventeenth-century London, warned parents: 'By being too fond of your children, or

---

[12] Michael Keane to Hugh Keane, 'St. Vincent, 16 March 1788', Michael Keane Letterbook, Keane Family Papers, Box 1, VHS, 52.

[13] Pierce Butler to Thomas Butler, 'Philadelphia November ye 19th 1792', Pierce Butler Letter Collection, Add Mss. 16603, BL.

[14] Margaret Cely to her husband (1484), as quoted in Daybell (ed.), *Early Modern Women's Letter Writing*, 6–7.

[15] *Universal Spy or London Weekly Magazine*, 26 (5 Oct. 1739), 252–4, as quoted in Turner, *Fashioning Adultery*, 81.

too familiar with them... & not keeping constantly your due distance; such fondness and familiarity breeds and causes contempt & irreverence.'[16] One dutiful preacher's daughter in the early eighteenth century apologized to her father for being too free and familiar in her letters to him. He replied that it was right for her to apologize: 'even when you say your Thoughts of Reverence and Esteem to your Father, or to your Spouse... it is easy to be lavish... I think you have done well to correct yourself.'[17] The editor of her posthumously published letters commended her: 'No Child had a greater Love to and Reverence for her Parents, she even exceeded in Fear and Reverence of her Father.'[18] In later eras familiarity became a far more prevalent ideal in a full range of private and public relationships. What had been a fault—being too fond—became instead a virtue. Familiarity also extended beyond the immediate nuclear family, especially since families had to let unfamiliar individuals (such as in-laws) into their ranks. The boundaries had to be porous, especially in an era in which families experienced physical distance for all kinds of reasons.

There were several ways to move beyond politeness and to establish familiarity. Most obviously, it could stem from the family itself: from being born into it. Yet familiarity, while increasingly presumed between parents and children, did not always translate into slightly more distant relations: aunts and uncles, or cousins, for instance. In these cases, either proximity or letters were necessary to establish the familiarity of members who already had such a relationship. In other words, being a family member outside of the nuclear family could help ensure familiarity, but did not guarantee it. The lines of familiarity could be extended by friendship. Friends, whether family or not, could be familiar with each other; this was the privilege of friendship.

Familiarity outside the immediate bounds of the nuclear family could be established by helping to raise a child. Even where there was no family relationship, the care of a child could result in familiarity. As Michael Keane's letter to his son about avoiding familiarity with the Gregs implied, taking responsibility for children of another family was in general a route to familiarity, or a way of cementing it. Few historians have remarked on the fact that all kinds of elite children, boys and girls, ended up in the care of families other than their own, a process which was accelerated by imperial movements. They also existed more often in cases where the death of one or both parents meant that extra care, from a wider community

---

[16] Thomas Cobbet, *A Fruitfull and Usefull Discourse Touching the Honour Due from Children* (London, 1656), 96.

[17] Benjamin Colman to Jane Colman [Turrell], 'Boston August 10th. 1725', in Ebenezer Turell (ed.), *Memoirs of the Life and Death of the Pious and Ingenious Mrs. Jane Turell* (London, 1741), 16.

[18] Ibid. 75. Rhys Isaac, citing the work of sociolinguistic scholar Basil Bernstine, has argued that patriarchal systems, in which roles were clear, made use of 'positional' forms of communications. Isaac argues that with the shift into more paternal modes, more 'elaborated' styles, in which 'personal needs are articulated and the anticipated or desired feelings of the recipient are addressed', came into being as part of the 'cult of "sensibility"'. Isaac, 'Communication and Control', in Wilentz (ed.), *Rites of Power*, 298.

of what were termed 'Friends', was deemed necessary. In an age of high mortality, and imperial movement and migration, family functions were often filled by people who were not family. Familiarity helped to secure such relationships.

Highly conventional statements about 'performing a parents duty' or 'acting the part of a parent' demonstrate the foundational nature of the household. Individual children, even when sent abroad to school or left in care of others, were to remain in a household setting. There are numerous examples of this type of familiarity. One woman praised another woman for 'how she had performed a parents duty' to two sisters.[19] When, after the Revolutionary War, the Virginia-born, English-educated son of John Martin of Virginia returned to England, his aunt informed his father of the safe arrival: 'I used to Look upon him as one of my own Childern [sic], and retain the same affection for him as Ever.'[20] A nephew from North Carolina who had been in the care of his uncle in Dublin declared: 'he looks upon me as his son.'[21] One woman, disconnected from her family in the Bahamas and recently recovered from illness in the family, commended new friends in Perth Amboy, New Jersey: 'had they been my sisters they could not have been more tender & attentive.'[22] An uncle, where the father was dead, sought to ensure that his nephew 'be boarded with some decent Family, the Master of which . . . would act the Part of a Parent over him, overlook his Studies, and keep a strict Eye over his Companions and Moralls.'[23]

This last example indicates that boys sent to school, as from the colonies to Britain, could forge familiarity in their host families. Boys were rarely lodged in the school itself, especially in holidays. They often boarded with other families. The son of Ralph Wormeley, Warner, lived with a tutor, Mr Reeves, in England. Ralph reminded his son that Mr Reeves could offer the best advice since he was far closer: 'I have no objection to your paying [Mr Beverly] a visit provided Mr: Reeves should approve of it, to him you are to look for advice, by him you are to be controled, in short, to his judgement I submit you; far better than mine at the distance of three thousand miles, and fully equal to it, if we were equally proximate.'[24] Much the same occurred in the integration of Thomas Butler into the household of his English tutor.[25] Thomas's father, Pierce, informed the Revd

---

[19] Eliza Ambler Brent Carrington to 'Mildred', 'Williamsburg January 10th 1786', Ambler–Brown Family Papers, DUL. Also in Eliza Jaquelin Ambler Brent Carrington Papers, LoC.

[20] Elizabeth Phelps to John Martin, 'Critchill Octobr: ye 4, 1784', Martin Family Papers, LoC.

[21] John Brownrigg to Mary Blackstock, 'Dublin Febry 16th [17]88', Brownrigg Family Papers, SHC.

[22] Sophia W Brown to Susanna Brown, 'Perth Amboy April 21st 1796', Brown Family Papers, NYHS.

[23] Simon Taylor to Lady Taylor, 'Kingston Jamaica October 30. 1798', I/B/28, Simon Taylor Papers, ICS.

[24] Ralph Wormeley to Warner Lewis Wormely, 'Rosegill 24 April 1802', Mss1/W8945/a-3, Wormeley Family Papers, 1791–1952, VHS.

[25] Pierce Butler Letter Collection, Add. Mss. 16603, British Library, London. For further information on this family, see Malcolm Bell, Jr., *Major Butler's Legacy: Five Generations of a Slaveholding Family* (Athens, Ga.: University of Georgia Press, 1987), esp. ch. 4.

Weeden Butler, not a relation but his son's tutor, 'my little fellow is fixed with You to Manhood. You have received only the raw Materials, the formation is entirely with Yourself... and I [have] the inexpressible happiness of Knowing that before He leaves You, or is launched into this World of vice and dissipation, He will have imbibed such pure principles of true religion and morality.'[26] Elsewhere, he fretted: 'I have my apprehensions that so long a Separation may weaken His affection for His Mother and myself—filial affection is not only the surest but most pleasing tie to influence his Actions hereafter... I place all my Confidence in Your keeping the Spark alive.'[27] Ties and sparks could keep a son connected to his family elsewhere, as well as keeping him on the straight and narrow path of virtue. Pierce considered the familiarity with the tutor to be reciprocal. In one letter, before thanking the tutor for 'Your Parental Attention to Our dear Boy', he also noted that 'my family... are as well acquainted with you... & talk as familiarly about You, as if they had been under the same roof with you'.[28] Familiarity usually came from being 'under the same roof', but other circumstances, and letters, could make it a reality for those separated across several households.

Women in particular were expected to live always under someone else's roof.[29] One man, whose unmarried, orphaned cousin lived with another family, worried that she had no relations nearby. He argued that she should leave London, because 'I conceive that to be a very improper Place for any single Woman who has no Relations about her to protect her. and being among perfect Strangers to her & her Family.'[30] A dependant needed someone on whom to depend. When a husband and wife were divided by the American Revolution, the father, left with the daughter, similarly fretted over what to do with the daughter when he left America for Britain, as he wrote to her mother: 'It was at first my resolution to leave her. It was also her Inclination to stay. But with whom could I leave her, in a Strange Place destitute of either father or Mother. I have Sought a proper place, but none has been offerd.'[31] A 'proper place' would be one where a friend might offer the protection of a household. In the end, the daughter accompanied her father to London.

---

[26] Pierce Butler to Weeden Butler, 'Bath February ye 22d. 1785', Pierce Butler Letter Collection, Add. Mss. 16603, BL.
[27] Pierce Butler to Weeden Butler, 'Nyork September ye 1st. 1790', ibid.
[28] Pierce Butler to Weeden Butler, 'New York August ye 1st 1787', ibid.
[29] Even in colonial Philadelphia, a city in which nearly 20% of households were headed by women, 'Incorporation into the household of another family was the most common arrangement for single women' who 'seldom lived alone.' In other areas, such as the rural areas surrounding Philadelphia, 'virtually all women lived in male-headed households.' Karin Wulf, *'Not All Wives': Women of Colonial Philadelphia* (Ithaca, New York: Cornell University Press, 2000), 87, 106, 92. Of England, Amy Froide notes: 'Contemporaries expected never-married women to live as dependants in the households of their fathers, male relatives, or masters.' Amy M. Froide, *Never Married: Singlewomen in Early Modern England* (Oxford: Oxford University Press, 2005), 19.
[30] Simon Taylor to Martha Graham Spiers, 'Kingston Jamaica July 28. 1800', I/D/27, Simon Taylor papers, ICS.
[31] Joseph Galloway to Grace Galloway, undated, File: Joseph Galloway to Grace Growden Galloway, 1776–1781, Galloway Family papers, LoC.

One extended example demonstrates that daughters were a particular point of concern as well as a means of reinforcing ties between households. The extended family of Charles Steuart, the head of Customs in America before the Revolution, was a classic example of a Scottish imperial family of the late eighteenth century; familiarity made his long-distance family life, and successes, possible.[32] He was a widower with one daughter, and many nephews. He had lived in Virginia prior to the Revolution, and his daughter, Jennie (or Jeannie), remained with a local Virginia family, the Parkers, when he returned to Britain at the start of the Revolutionary period. There was no family relationship between them; Charles Steuart had been involved in business with James Parker, and was his friend. The decision to leave Jennie with his friends allowed Charles to pursue an imperial career while still offering a household to his daughter. Margaret Parker sent letters to Charles Steuart, as did Jennie herself, in order to maintain this family connection. After the war, when Margaret was to leave America for Britain, Charles asked that Jennie remain in America, with Margaret's sister, Rebecca Aitchison. Margaret was unhappy with this arrangement, and initially argued that she be permitted to take Jennie with her. She informed him: 'indeed I look on her as one of my children... I sincerely love her, & it would be a great shock to me to part with her.'[33] Eventually, Margaret capitulated, and left Jennie with her own sister, who herself later declared, when Jennie married: 'I know no difference between parting with her & my own Children [because of] her dear feeling heart... indeed my Children are as fond of her as they are of one another.'[34] When Jennie died, her epitaph read: 'Her Remains rest here/In the Ground dedicated to the last Repose/of the much honoured Friends/Under whose Protection/She lived from early Youth.'[35] Such familiar connections were immortalized in her very gravestone. While Charles Steuart entrusted his daughter to other families across the seas, he also helped broker such placements for his nephews, one of whom was sent to Tobago, another to Jamaica. This level of involvement in family, as well as the extent of their imperial ambitions, was typical of Scots in this period, but it was hardly absent from English, American, and West Indian families.[36] Other family letter collections from this period reveal the extent to which distant family members, or even simply friends, might

---

[32] Douglas Hamilton argues persuasively that kinship networks were critical to Scottish imperial success in the eighteenth-century Caribbean. See Hamilton, *Scotland, the Caribbean and the Atlantic World*.

[33] Margaret Parker to Charles Steuart, 'Eastwood March 8th 1784', MS. 5033, fos. 178–9, Charles Steuart Papers, NLS.

[34] Rebecca Aitchison to Charles Steuart, 'Eastwood Princess anne Virginia Feby 20 1788', MS. 5035, fo. 106–7, ibid.

[35] 'Epitaph of Jeannie [Jane] Steuart Cringan', died 26 April 1789, MS. 5035, fos. 230–231, ibid.

[36] See e.g. Karras, *Sojourners in the Sun*; T. M. Devine, *Scotland's Empire and the Shaping of the Americas, 1600–1815* (Washington, DC: Smithsonian Institute Press, 2004); and esp. Hamilton, *Scotland, the Caribbean and the Atlantic World*.

be integrated into a different family. The bounds of the family, then, could be extended by care of children, even sometimes children grown into adults.

Courtship and marriage was another route to familiarity. It was the very imprecision of the bounds of familiarity that made courtship such a fraught time. Families exhibited concern that the person with whom a son or especially a daughter was being familiar deserved that closeness. A mistake could last a lifetime, and even ruin a family. There were various ways by which a lover might become familiar, and all were potentially hazardous. These included physical intimacy (such as kissing, or lingering over a hand), sharing of food, sharing of jokes, and the giving of gifts.[37] They also included writing letters: many a dramatic narrative of the period hung on the secret correspondence carried out between a man and woman. Books of model letters often included letters apologizing for their own existence: 'I doubt not but you will be astonished at receiving a letter from a stranger, and I have no excuse to offer, for my boldness but the warmth of my affection.'[38] Gift-giving, like letter-writing, in courtship could be a sign of burgeoning affection, or it could be a taking of 'liberty'. So, when a suitor sent a gift, he generally enquired whether such a gift would be acceptable, or he obtained permission from a father before sending it. Model letter-books often included letters to accompany such a gift, as in this one from a 'Gentleman to a Lady': 'Your acceptance of the trifle, herewith enclosed, will confer upon the donor . . . satisfaction . . . Let no delicate punctilio raise an objection to this humble offer.'[39] One fiancé, who had in courtship sent several books to his beloved, sent along a few more gifts, as his fiancée was about to depart: 'I beg your acceptance of a few Books . . . I also take the liberty of requesting you receive as a trifling remembrance at your departure a watch . . . I trust you will not think me forward in using this freedom—in the situation we now are, surely there can be no impropriety in the offer or in your receiving it—.'[40] Freedom only allowed so much.

Familiarity was a vexed social space. One of the chief troubles Richardson's Pamela and many others—both fictional and historical—faced was how to navigate the boundaries of familiarity. In his pursuit of Pamela, her master sought to become familiar with her. She had to discern whether he meant truly to 'be a Friend' or whether he had baser intentions. So did many others. Both

---

[37] All of these receive useful attention in David Turner's discussions of adultery. Turner, *Fashioning Adultery*, 79, 101, 165–7.

[38] Anon, *The Complete American Letter-Writer, Containing Letters on Trade & merchandize. Also, Letters on Familiar & Interesting Subjects* (Otsego, NY, 1807), letter LXXIV.

[39] Anon, *[Scott's Cheap and Elegant Edition of] The Complete American Letter-Writer, and Best Companion for the Young Man of Business* (New York: 1807), letter XX, p. 62.

[40] Robert Mackay to Eliza McQueen, '31st July 1799—', Hartridge, *Letters of Robert Mackay*, 7. Previously, Robert Mackay had sent Eliza McQueen, whose father had moved to Spanish East Florida, 'Spanish Grammars' as well as 'the Exploits of Don Quixote'. Robert Mackay to Eliza McQueen, 'April? 1795? Wednesday', Hartridge, letters, 3 and Robert Mackay to Eliza McQueen, 'Tuesday 21st March 96', ibid. 4.

women and men could be seduced into ruin. A worry that the friend might turn out to be merely a seducer haunted innumerable correspondences, fictional and factual. Familiarity might take place with the wrong person, or might go too far. It is this concern that fills family letters of this era, but it also pervades novels, magazines, and tracts of all sorts. Adultery was generally described in terms of over-familiarity.[41] The legal action launched against adultery was a suit of 'criminal conversation', a phrase that also resonates with the illicit overstepping of the bounds of sociability.[42]

It was the prerogative, as well as the responsibility, of the head of the household, usually male, to monitor the precise bounds of familiarity. Wives and children were not supposed to make their own choices in terms of who might be familiar with them. While wives and daughters could be familiar with other women, for them to be so with men outside of the family was a potential problem. One of the disturbing aspects of adultery was that it indicated that it had been the wife who had chosen the terms of familiarity, presumably under the enthralling power of her seducer. The husband was supposed to be the one to guard the bounds of familiarity. The father had the privilege of supervising the choices his children made in terms of friends, but especially in terms of spouses. Many stories told in the eighteenth century held the following message: trouble might ensue when household subordinates—wives, sons, or daughters—determined for themselves the bounds of familiarity.

Still, as we have seen, many individuals in the same family did not always live in the same household. How, then, could the bounds of familiarity be monitored? One way was by replicating households, or offering a substitute one. So if Charles Steuart could not offer his daughter the immediate authority, guidance, and affection of her own family, then the Parkers could fill in for him. Another way, though, of monitoring familiarity was by letter. This was by no means as satisfactory as personal and direct attention, but it provided the lines of authority and affection that could keep family members familiar. It could help to maintain the lines that connected the loose fish of Atlantic families. But it often added a frenetic quality to monitoring letters, because it was so easy for such letters to be subverted, and for a child out in the world to run amok into 'great Trouble'.

Letters supported familiarity in two chief ways. First, they allowed for individuals far away to maintain familiar connections, to keep up family and friendship in new environments. But they also helped to forge the tone of familiarity. In the anglophone Atlantic world, the rising importance of familiarity and the rising importance of familiar letter-writing went hand-in-hand, helping

---

[41] One historian of adultery in eighteenth-century Britain has pointed out that 'adulterous behaviour was characterised as behaving "very familiarly" or as taking a "criminal familiarity", or was described as a "farther familiarity"'. Turner, *Fashioning Adultery*, 46.
[42] Turner helpfully parses this phrase, among others: ibid. 48.

each other along. Letters helped both to create and to make claims of familiarity, not only in their subjects and their writers, but in their very style.

FAMILIAR LETTERS

Familiar letters could bridge geographical distances such as the Atlantic, but they could also bridge distances of status within and outside the household. There was a radical leveling potential here, but it was cut into by the exclusivity of familiarity, its limited range. To learn to write with familiarity was an important lesson for many. Many didactic books of letter-writing taught as much about how to write familiar letters as how to write formal ones.[43] One declared its intentions: 'For the express purpose of instructing the youthful and uninformed mind in the art of easy and familiar correspondence.'[44] The introductory sections of books such as this one, or the most popular of them, *The Complete Letter-Writer* (the most widely reprinted of any of these books of model letters), generally advised its readers that a familiar letter should 'wear an honest chearful Countenance, like one who truely esteems, and is glad to see his Friend; and not like a Fop, admiring his own Dress, and seemingly pleased with nothing but himself.'[45] Friends, not fops, were supposed to populate the world of the familiar letter, with letters standing in for their writers.[46] The introduction of *The Complete Letter-Writer* instructed its readers that 'a fine Letter does not consist in saying fine Things, but in expressing ordinary ones with Elegance and Propriety'.[47] It was the very ordinariness of the familiar letter, like familiarity itself, that could make it so difficult to master.

Many of these guides tried to help the would-be letter-writer along by noting the way that letters should replicate the ease of polite, familiar conversation. This is an ancient trope for letters, but it took on a peculiar force in a century consumed with ideals of polite conversation. For example, John Tavernier exhorted his readers in 1759: 'Letter-writing is but a sort of literary conversation,

---

[43] Katherine Gee Hornbeak, 'The Complete Letter Writer in English, 1568–1800', *Smith College Studies in Modern Languages*, 15 (1934), pp. iii–150; Jean Robertson, *The Art of Letter Writing: An Essay on the Handbooks Published in England during the Sixteenth and Seventeenth Centuries* (Liverpool: University Press of Liverpool, 1942); Harry Weiss, *American Letter-Writers, 1698–1943* (New York: New York Public Library, 1945); Dierks, 'Letter Writing, Gender, and Class in America', ch. 1, and his 'Letter Manuals, Literary Innovation, and the Problem of Defining Genre'; Bannet, *Empire of Letters*, and Brant, *Eighteenth-Century Letters and British Culture*.

[44] *The Universal Letter-Writer* (Philadelphia, 1810), 25.

[45] *The Complete Letter-Writer: Or, Polite English Secretary*, 11th edn. (London, 1767). I have chosen this edition as a fairly representative one; it was reprinted in similar ways before and after this date; ibid. 32.

[46] There were many such manuals, and many editions of a few of them (such as *The Complete Letter-Writer*). See the Bibliography. For a discussion of the practices of these manuals, see Bannet, *Empire of Letters*.

[47] *The Complete Letter-Writer*, 11th edn. (1767), 32.

and that you are to write to the person absent, in the manner you would speak to him, if present.'⁴⁸ According to these guides, a letter-writer must write as he or she speaks: 'When you sit down to write a Letter, remember that this Sort of Writing should be like Conversation.'⁴⁹ In ways that sometimes seem contradictory, these guides advised ease and naturalness while at the same time exhorting that particular care and formality be taken to make the letters easy and natural. So, one declared: 'But, though lofty Phrases are here improper, the Stile should not be low and mean; and to avoid it, let an easy Complaisance, an open Sincerity, and unaffected Good-nature appear in all you say. . . . ' This precisely summarizes familiarity: neither 'low and mean' nor oppressively polite and formal. In a section on writing letters to superiors or inferiors, the manual advised that the writer should not appear 'too familiar'. To be so to a superior would show 'Ignorance and Impudence', while to be so to an inferior would be 'contemptible'.⁵⁰ Elsewhere, this manual commanded: 'Write freely, but not hastily; let your Words drop from your Pen, as they would from your Tongue when speaking deliberately on a Subject of which you are Master, and to a Person with whom you are intimate.' Intimacy could smooth the writing of the letter. This would help to avoid being affected in tone: 'before you begin a Sentence, have the Whole of it in your Head, and make Use of the first Words that offer themselves to express your Meaning.'⁵¹ This immediacy of style was critical.

Part of the shift in tone can be attributed to the nature of the writing and sending of letters. In earlier centuries the use of scribes and clerks was common. In such circumstances the tone was more formal, and familiarity was to be avoided. This situation changed as people became their own letter-writers, to echo the title of one such manual.⁵² Easy sincerity was to replace the ceremony of the courtly letter, while avoiding becoming too informal and thus inelegant. It was to be the happy mean of the letter:

But there is still something requisite beyond all this, towards the writing a polite and agreeable Letter, and that is, an Air of good Breeding . . . By this I would not be supposed to mean, overstrained or affected Compliments, or any Thing that Way tending, but and [*sic*] easy, genteel, and obliging Manner of Address, in a Choice of Words that bears the most civil Meanings, with a thorough generous and good-natured Disposition.⁵³

Politeness and civility were indeed fundamental to this endeavor, but they were not quite enough.

---

⁴⁸ John Tavernier, *The Entertaining Correspondent; Or, Newest and Most Compleat Polite Letter Writer* (Berwick, 1759), 4.
⁴⁹ *The Complete Letter-Writer*, 11th edn. (1767), 32.
⁵⁰ *The Complete Letter-Writer*, 8th edn. (London, 1762), 37–8.
⁵¹ *The Complete Letter-Writer*, 11th edn. (1767), 32–3.
⁵² Wallace and Townshend, *Every Man His Own Letter-Writer*.
⁵³ *The Complete Letter-Writer*, 11th edn. (1767), 32–3.

A plain style showed a friend, not a fop. It was vital to avoid 'overstrained or affected' styles in favor of 'easy, genteel, and obliging' ones. It needed to be 'easy' even in its very construction: 'Express your Meaning as freely as possible; long Periods may please the Ear, but they perplex the Understanding; a short Stile and plain, strikes the Mind, and fixes an Impression; a tedious one is seldom clearly understood, and never long remembered.'[54] One manual advised readers: 'When you write to a friend, your letter should be a picture of your heart, the style loose and irregular; the thoughts themselves should appear naked, and not dressed in the borrowed robes of rhetoric; for a friend will be more pleased with that part of a letter which flows from the heart, than that which is the product of the mind.'[55]

Many of the frontispieces of these guides showed domestic scenes, thus reinforcing familiarity in style and setting. As we have seen in Chapter 1, there were often scenes of domestic epistolarity shared by the family. A similar scene, though in a library, opened *The English Letter-Writer* (see Fig. 1.2). In this image, the father seems to be checking over the daughter's letter, while the mother and son sit and compose their letters with the help of *The English Letter-Writer*. The accompanying poem exulted in this domestic production:

> Father, Daughter, Youth & blooming Fair;
> Make our NEW WORK the object of their care;
> From these Plain Rules in every Form they know,
> To make their style with ease and freedom flow.[56]

Familiar plainness was the goal, and it was expected that such manuals could teach the plain and familiar style as much as a courtly and formal one. Other images portrayed children learning to write letters. In another domestic library scene, a girl and boy, presumably sister and brother, write their letters with the help, it is suggested, of the book next to them: *Newberry's Familiar Letters*.[57] This same book announced its goal: 'To furnish every class of readers, whether parents or children, masters or servants, with letters written in the most plain and familiar manner, and adapted to all occasions and circumstances, is the intentions [*sic*] of this little work.'[58] A 'plain and familiar' style became the ideal upheld by these books of model letters, an echoing, most likely, of countless Protestant sermons on the same theme.

This familiar style corresponded to the familiar scenes often depicted in these guides. Many of the letters they modeled were family letters, as, for instance, between children away at school or work, distant relations, husbands away at

---

[54] ibid.
[55] H. W. Dilworth, *The Complete Letter-Writer: Or, Young Secretary's Instructor* (Glasgow, 1783), 3.
[56] George Brown, *The English Letter-Writer; Or, The Whole Art of General Correspondence* (London, 1785?), frontispiece.
[57] *Newberry's Familiar Letter Writer* (London: E. Newbery, 1788). [58] ibid., preface.

sea. In some instances they described these as letters 'on the most useful and common Occasions'.⁵⁹ Letters in these model books whizzed back and forth between youths, apprentices, sons, and daughters in school or service to mothers and fathers, uncles and aunts, sisters and brothers. Husbands and wives, lovers and beloved, and others also feverishly penned letters in these model books. A few examples, plucked from countless domestic scenarios portrayed therein, include: *'From a Mother, in Town, to her Daughter at a Boarding School in the Country, recommending the practice of Virtue.'* Or *'From a young Woman, just gone to service in London, to her Mother in the Country'*.⁶⁰ There was also: 'A Letter from a Niece to her Aunt', 'A Letter from a Nephew to an Uncle, who wrote him a Letter of Rebuke', and a 'Letter from a Youth at School to his Parents', among many others.⁶¹ They also modeled the ways of keeping familiarity, and cautioned against familiarity with the wrong sort, as in letters, oft repeated, 'to a young Lady, Cautioning her against Keeping Company with a Gentleman of bad Character', or one 'From a Father to his Son just beginning in the World'. Many of these letters indicate that a lot of these books were targeted at children, to teach them how to write letters in a polite, familiar style. Familiarity was a learned style, one inculcated through and by family letters.

This shared culture of letter-writing crossed the British Atlantic.⁶² Although many of these books were British in origin, they circulated throughout the British-Atlantic world. Such manuals were also printed in the American colonies, and later states. Some of the printings were exact replicas of British manuals. For instance, when William Durrell undertook to publish *The Complete Letter-Writer* in New York in 1793, there was no attempt to alter the original text to produce a more American version. Place-names that had been British remained so in this American edition. Some texts included a mélange of British and American geographical referents.⁶³ Other, later American editions did change the place-names to American ones.'⁶⁴ *The Complete American Letter-Writer* (1807), for instance, even included a specific preface denouncing 'the ridiculous trash which would disgrace the pen of a chambermaid, [which] has been imported and sold to the young Americans'. *The Complete American Letter-Writer* smugly continued

---

⁵⁹ *The Complete Letter-Writer: Or, Polite English Secretary*, 16th edn. (London, 1778.), pt. I, p. 50.
⁶⁰ *The New Letter Writer; Or, The Art of Correspondence* (Whitehaven, 1775), 9.
⁶¹ *The Complete Letter-Writer: Or, Polite English Secretary*, 4th edn. (London, 1757), letters XX–XXII, pp. 82–83.
⁶² This is a point that historians and literary critics have increasingly noted. I discussed this point in Pearsall, *'After All These Revolutions'*, ch. 1, and it has recently received far more detailed treatment in Bannet, *Empire of Letters*.
⁶³ Thomas Cook, *The New Universal Letter Writer* (Hallowell, Maine, 1812). London is mentioned on p. 47, while 'New-York' is mentioned on p. 62.
⁶⁴ *The New Complete Letter Writer*, for instance, included place-names from the United States. See *The New Complete Letter Writer* (Albany, NY, 1802).

that its letter models 'are not taken from the English books of forms, nor are they copied from the ignorant productions, of which we have already spoken; but are obtained from the best American authorities'.[65] The printers of these new American versions positioned their books as the patriotic choice, especially in a period—the first decade of the nineteenth century—which saw the renewal of hostile relations between the United States and Great Britain. Still, despite these attempts to differentiate the American texts from their British antecedents, the letters in these manuals bore remarkable similarities to those in equivalent British books. Indeed, even the frontispiece that adorned [*Scott's Cheap and Elegant Edition of*] *The Complete American Letter-Writer* was borrowed from older British books of letters.

The precise pathways of these manuals remain elusive. Nonetheless, they were clearly popular and in wide circulation on both sides of the Atlantic. Between 1755 and 1768 alone, for example, twelve editions of *The Complete Letter-Writer; or, Polite English Secretary* appeared in Great Britain. The 'General Utility' of these books is partially underlined by a survey of the signatures found in extant copies. A much-marked copy of a 1759 edition of *The Complete Letter-Writer* gives at least a little insight into the ownership and circulation of such books. The book seems first to have been in the possession of John Ruscoe in the early 1760s: 'John Ruscoe 1762.' It seems that the book was passed on from one JR to another, as there is also the following signature: 'Joseph Ruscoe His Booke Joseph Ruscoe 1771.' This JR seems to have grown up or else passed it along to another Joseph Ruscoe, perhaps his son, who signed it: 'Joseph Ruscoe His Book 1799.' While it is difficult to discern precisely what lessons John and the two Joseph Ruscoes drew from their reading, it does seem clear that such books were owned and read with some degree of care.[66] The inscriptions in extant copies further reveal that both men and women owned these books. A survey of the surviving manuals held by the British Library and the American Antiquarian Society indicates that those with extant signatures were fairly evenly split between male and female names (with the occasional book revealing both, where it had been shared or passed between a boy and a girl).[67] One 1778 copy of *The Complete Letter-Writer* has signatures from several readers, one of whom has marked the following letter, a borrowing from Lord Chesterfield's *Letters*, '*From a Gentleman to his Son just arrived from* Paris; *against servile Complaisance and Talkativeness; with some Directions for behaving politely in Company*', as 'a

---

[65] The statement above is found in: *The Complete American Letter-Writer* and [*Scott's Cheap and Elegant Edition of*] *The Complete American Letter-Writer, and Best Companion for the Young Man of Business* (New York, 1807), preface.

[66] *The Complete Letter-Writer*, 6th edn. (London, 1759), BL copy.

[67] Of 59 remaining manuals at the BL, 21 have signatures. Nine have female ones, 10 have males ones, and two have both. At the American Antiquarian Society, out of 23 manuals, 11 have inscriptions. Of these, four are male and five are female, while two of them have both male and female names inscribed.

very good letter'.[68] Quite why this particular letter struck such a chord is hard to know, but it does indicate that these books were read, at least occasionally, with some care.

These manuals had a variety of uses. They taught adults and children how to write letters. They seem to have been especially popular as pedagogical tools, judging by the advertisements in them aimed at schoolmasters, and by their emphasis on letters to and from children. They fit nicely into the vogue for conduct literature. They also seem to have served a similar function to epistolary novels, or at least fed a similar appetite. Many of their letters read as brief narratives, including courtship ones.[69] These stories sometimes had clear morals (for example, a woman writes against convention to declare her love for a man and ends up a laughing-stock, thus teaching young women not to be forward in their courtships). But throughout, they modeled familiarity. One letter from a French woman noted, rather saucily, her hope that her letter 'may please you as well without the Formalities of Stile, as a pretty Woman, without Stays, may some of your Acquaintance'.[70] This is the kind of sentiment that, in British manuals, could only be expressed by a French woman. However, plenty of other writers in these manuals emphasized the plain, familiar style, and how it demonstrated friendship and affection. Whatever the precise form of the individual letters, familiarity was both a style to be emulated and a concern displayed in them. A later edition of *The Complete Letter-Writer* was even entitled: *The Complete Letter-Writer, Containing a Great Variety of Plain, Easy, Entertaining and Familiar Letters*.[71]

These epistolary manuals often included, and are not unrelated to, another major form of familiar epistolary publication in this period: collections of letters, especially those by well-known authors. Letter-writing manuals usually began with fictional letters, and then contained a section of letters by writers, politicians, and others, to teach by model. These might include letters from authors such as Alexander Pope, or they might be letters from dramatic or historical occasions, such as '*Mrs.* Penruddock's *last Epistle to her Husband*', executed in the English Civil War.[72] One letter from Bishop Atterbury to his son at school especially noted that: 'Time and Use will teach you to write readily afterwards; not but that too much Care may give a Stiffness to your Style, which ought in all Letters, by all means, to be avoided. The Turn of them should be always natural and easy,

---

[68] Anon., *The Complete Letter-Writer: Or, Polite English Secretary*, 16th edn. (London, 1778), BL copy.
[69] See the courtship narrative of Mr Smith and Polly in *The Universal Letter-Writer; Or, Whole Art of Polite Correspondence* (Philadelphia, 1808), 79–85.
[70] 'Mrs *Centlivre* to Mr B____', *The Complete Letter-Writer: Or, Polite English Secretary*, 8th edn. (London, 1762), letter 48, 233.
[71] *The Complete Letter-Writer, Containing a Great Variety of Plain, Easy, Entertaining & Familiar Letters* (London, 1808).
[72] *The Complete Letter-Writer: Or, Polite English Secretary*, 5th edn. (London, 1758), pt. IV, letter 33, p. 211.

for they are an Image of private and familiar Conversation.'[73] These letters by real letter-writers generally formed a section of its own at the end of the book, and they were meant to be entertaining as well as instructive.

These letter-writing manuals thus tapped into the vogue for letter collections, many of which appeared and circulated widely in the eighteenth century. Many letters by both British and French authors were compiled and published. These were usually those of well-known authors, but in some cases the literary reputations followed the collections. These letters varied in tone, but many also demonstrated familiarity, and claims to friendship. Like epistolary novels, they offered the same vicarious thrill of entering into a different circle of familiarity, one especially enthralling if the author were celebrated, or the letters especially pleasing. Such letters appealed both to the well-born and to the less well-off. The preface to *Letters of Mr. Alexander Pope, and Several of his Friends* declared: 'Many of these having been written on the most trying occurrences, and all in the openness of friendship, are a proof what were his real Sentiments, as they flow'd warm, from the heart, and fresh from the occasion.'[74] As warm and fresh as these letters might have been, their appearance in two large, expensive volumes meant their reach was limited, a point reinforced by the classical references in them. Other, later collections made familiarity much more accessible, whether in the tear-stained letters of Laurence Sterne or Ignatius Sancho, or in the enormously popular letters of Lord Chesterfield to his son.[75] So popular were the published collections of Sterne and Chesterfield that their letters then came to be incorporated into letter-writing manuals, as in the sixteenth edition of *The Complete Letter-Writer*.[76]

These letter collections and manuals were closely connected with the other form of letters many would have read in this period: epistolary novels, along with epistolary periodical stories, which also demonstrated the virtues of familiarity. All of them make clear that the polite, familiar letter was the genre *par excellence* of the eighteenth century. Part of the pleasure and interest of epistolary novels, as well as these other epistolary forms, lay in their allowing a reader to enter into a different circle of familiarity, to gain access to a privileged world. Reading letters of all kinds was something that most elite, educated people would have done, and they learned the lesson of writing in a familiar style. Most notably, Samuel Richardson developed the idea for *Pamela: or, Virtue Rewarded*. In a

---

[73] 'A Letter from Bishop *Atterbury* to his Son *Obadiah*, at *Christchurch* College, in *Oxford*', *The Complete Letter-Writer: Or, Polite English Secretary*, 6th edn. (London, 1759), pt. 4, letter 1, p. 155.
[74] Alexander Pope, *Letters of Mr. Alexander Pope, and Several of his Friends*, 2 vols. (London, 1737), preface.
[75] Laurence Sterne, *Letters of the Late Rev. Mr. Laurence Sterne, To his most intimate Friends*, 3 vols. (London, 1775); Ignatius Sancho, *Letters of the Late Ignatius Sancho, an African*, 2 vols. (London, 1782); and Philip Dormer Stanhope, Earl of Chesterfield, *Letters written by the late Right Honourable Philip Dormer Stanhope, Earl of Chesterfield, to his son, Philip Stanhope, Esq.*, 2 vols. (London, 1774).
[76] *The Complete Letter-Writers: Or, Polite English Secretary*, 16th edn. (London, 1778), title-page.

Series of Familiar Letters from a Beautiful Young Damsel to her Parents, out of his volume of collected familiar epistles, *Letters to and from Particular Friends, on the Most Important Occasions*.[77] The letters modeled in most epistolary novels were familiar ones, often between family members, and often written in a familiar style. As literary scholars have pointed out, they also dealt frequently, even dizzyingly, with families in crisis.

The fact that so many of these novels were titles of the protagonist's first name, with no family name, indicates in part the way they invited familiarity, but also demonstrated that the protagonist was cut off from the family of birth. There were many kinds of crises (generally stemming from seduction and betrayal), but what all of them tend to privilege was family distance. This situation had occasioned the letters in the first place, so the relationship between crisis, distance, and letter-writing is always at the forefront. Heroines such as Pamela, Evelina, and Julia de Roubigné conveyed their stories in familiar letters, with Evelina, for instance, making that classic statement of conversational familiarity to her guardian, the Revd Mr Villars: 'I shall write to you every evening all that passes in the day, and that in the same manner as, if I could see, I should tell you.'[78] The letters were familiar, but the story-lines, too, often revolved around who was being let into the bounds of the familiar, and whether that individual was trustworthy or not. Familiarity was indeed their major concern, as well as their major style. These fictional tales, like many historical ones, also raised issues about whether letters could be trusted. This is a central preoccupation in *Clarissa*, in which Clarissa's family distrusts her letters because of her 'silver tongue'.[79] This trope appears throughout the novel, as well as in many other fictional epistolary stories, both in magazines and in novels. Clarissa's brother and uncle complain of her 'knack at letter writing'.[80] When her father received her letter, Clarissa later reported in another letter, he declared: 'tell me of *deeds*!—I'll receive no *words* from her: and so he tore the letter.'[81]

If Clarissa's family evinced no interest in reading her letters, the same could not be said for many other families, who relished them. While the circulation of all these forms of printed familiar letters cannot be pinned down with total precision, it would have been difficult for a well-read educated person to avoid reading

---

[77] Richardson, *Pamela*, and Samuel Richardson, *Letters to and from Particular Friends, on the Most Important Occasions* (London, 1741).

[78] 'Evelina to Rev. Mr Villars', 'Queen-Ann-Street, London, Saturday, April 2', letter 10, Fanny Burney, *Evelina, or, A Young Lady's Entrance into the World, in a Series of Letters*, 3 vols. (London, 1779), i. 28.

[79] Bella Harlowe, as quoted in Clarissa Harlowe to Anna Howe, undated, letter XLII, in Samuel Richardson, *Clarissa, or The History of a Young Lady*, 7 vols. (London, 1748), i. 290.

[80] e.g. her uncle does so in Antony Harlowe to Clarissa Harlowe, as included in Clarissa Harlowe to Anna Howe, 'Tuesday, March 14', letter XXXII, ibid. i. 215. Her brother threatens that he will accept no letters from her for this reason: James Harlowe to Clarissa Harlowe, included in Clarissa Harlowe to Anna Howe, 'Thursday March 16', letter XXXIII, ibid. i. 228.

[81] Clarissa Harlowe to Anna Howe, 'Sunday afternoon', letter XIV, ibid. ii. 84.

familiar letters. The most popular novels were epistolary; magazines overflowed with stories involving letters and reprintings of letters; letter-writing manuals appeared frequently, letter collections even more so. The frequent reprintings, in many and varied locales of the anglophone Atlantic, of all of these forms of familiar letters is one indication of their popularity. Library circulation lists also provide evidence for their widespread appeal among literate populations on both sides of the Atlantic.[82] As we shall see, references to epistolary novels in particular pepper personal correspondence of the era, and they also appear in probate and other inventories.

The printed familiar letters circulating throughout the British-Atlantic world dealt with familiarity as a vexed space; so did family letters that were far less publicized. Family letter collections demonstrate that familiarity, while certainly not the only style, was the major chord struck. Some of the impetus stemmed from religion (the plainness nurtured by Protestant forms such as Congregationalism, Quakerism, and Methodism); some of it stemmed from changing forms of education, and a move from classical to more practical learning. Some of it came from the world of business, a world with little patience for literary flourishes and furbelows. One of the obvious sources of learning about letters was both from books and periodicals with letters in them, and from letters written by other family members. Families themselves, then, both reflected and forwarded newer ideas about familiar letter-writing, and thus carved out their own circles of familiarity.

The most explicit mentions of letter-writing models of familiarity occur in the formulaic apologies for badly written letters that fill most family letter collections.

---

[82] e.g. the 1770 printed catalogue for the Library Company of Philadelphia includes letter-writing manuals such as *Epistolary (Polite) Correspondence*, 2nd edn. (London, 1751); Charles Halifax, *Letters (Familiar) on Various Subjects in Business and Amusement, Letters on the Most Common, as well as Important Occasions of Life*, 2nd edn. (London, n.d.); and *Letters written to and for particular Friends, on the Most Important Occasions*, 5th edn. (London, 1752). There were also collections such as the two-volume *Letters: (A Collection of original) Written by the Most Eminent Persons, on Various Entertaining Subjects and on Many Important Occasions* (London, 1755) and *Sevigne's (The Marchioness de) Letters to the Countess de Grignan*, 2nd edn. (London, 1745). And of course there were epistolary novels, from the famous four-volume *Pamela; or Virtue Rewarded*, 8th edn. (London, 1762), to Jean-Jacques Rousseau, *Eloisa: or, a Series of Original Letters*, 4 vols. (London, 1761), to *Delia Stanhope; (The History of Miss) in a Series of Letters*, 4 vols. (London, 1767). All information here is as listed in the catalogue. See Library Company of Philadelphia, *The Charter, Laws, and Catalogue of Books, of the Library Company of Philadelphia* (Philadelphia, 1770). Similarly, a Boston circulating library in 1765 included all of Richardson's novels as well as his *Familiar Letters*. It also held works such as Halifax's *Familiar Letters on Various Subjects of Business and Amusement* (London, 1764), *The Complete Art of Writing Letters* (London, 1764), and *The Ladies Complete Letter-Writer* (London, 1765). See John Mein, *A Catalogue of Mein's Circulating Library* (Boston, 1765), esp. 33. A post-war circulating library in Maryland held Chesterfield's letters in four volumes, as well as several epistolary novels, including Richardson's as well as Burney's *Cecilia* and *Evelina*, among others. It also included letter collections such as 'Letters of the late Ignatius Sancho, an African' and 'Letter writer, or lady's polite secretary'. Stephen Clark, *A Catalogue of the Annapolis Circulating Library* (Annapolis, Md., 1786), 21, 37–3, 30, 41. There is a useful discussion of the circulation of novels such as *Pamela* and *Clarissa* in the Hatboro Circulating Library borrowers' lists in Landsman, 'Presbyterians, Evangelicals, and the Educational Culture', 175.

The innocuous and conventional nature of these apologies belies their profound cultural significance. These references indicate most fundamentally the ways that letter-writers knew about the standard expectations for letters, based on their reading. One scholar has remarked on this aspect, and has argued persuasively that these apologies stemmed in part from the self-consciousness with which these individuals approached the writing of letters.[83] Yet it also demonstrates the recurring emphasis on how a familiar style helped to make a familiar space. In this sense, such remarks on infelicities often functioned to emphasize not incompetence or even simply self-consciousness, but instead to suggest that the freedom of familiarity permitted such kinds of writing.

Statements about the incorrectness of letters functioned to reaffirm what was permitted between familiar friends. Familiarity could create a space separate from politeness or even entertainment in letters. In 1784 one Quaker wife, Rebecca Shoemaker, offered a kind of non-apology to her husband in London:

> I know my incapacity for writing what is called good Letters or entertaining ones, but if they convey to thee proofs of my affection, & give thee a small degree of pleasure, I shall be content, & not make one Single effort or attempt what I know I could not effect... I have some where seen it remarked that letters that pass between such near fr[ie]ds are not the less natural for being unfit to be seen by any other person. Mine I know are only fit for the perusal of one person.[84]

At one level, this statement offered a kind of apology for writing familiar rather than 'good' or 'entertaining' letters, even as it emphasized that she could take the freedom of writing letters that were merely affectionate, as she and her husband were 'near friends'. The letters were better for being written for the perusal of only one person, her husband, rather than as entertainment for a larger audience of individuals in London. This particular letter also demonstrates the ways in which their readership was shifting, from a group, oral reading of letters to a more individual, quieter style of reading and receiving them.

A similar sense comes across from another non-apology, this one from a Virginian, Severn Eyre, writing home from London. Writing in 1785, he advised his friend Littleton not to show his letters to anyone else, although elsewhere he seemed to assume that they would be circulated among a small circle of friends. Admittedly, these letters *were* full of descriptions of women and mentions of visits to prostitutes. However, he was apparently less embarrassed about those—for which he offered no apologies—than about his writing style: 'after a perusal of the last letter I find it will be necessary to caution you against letting any other person read my epistles for they are wrote in a cursory manner just as thoughts present themselves, without any attention to diction or the usual forms

---

[83] Dierks, 'Letter Writing, Gender, and Class in America', ch. 1.
[84] Rebecca Shoemaker to Samuel Shoemaker, 'Nov. 27th 1784', Shoemaker Family Papers, HSP.

of letter writing.'[85] He opened another letter: 'There requires little apology for the introductory lines of my former epistles as they will be perused by friends only... I am sensible you will derive pleasure from a perusal of them even in their incorrect state.'[86] The statements of both Rebecca Shoemaker and Severn Eyre closed off the circle of familiarity narrowly (to 'the perusal of one person', or at least just to a few chosen 'friends'). The fact that they are written in a very familiar style meant that they were not for general entertainment, but were all the more valuable for that. Indeed, elsewhere in Rebecca's letters she hoped that her son would 'give me a little Journal of your tour [of England]; it would put him in the way of familiar writing which I want him to be in'.[87] A master of the style of familiarity herself, she hoped her son would gain similar skills.

The trope of letters as simply a long-distance conversation between friends (a very old trope indeed) also appears in these letter collections. One young man from Pennsylvania, training for the ministry in London, confided to his family: 'Whenever I take my Pen in Hand to write to you, I endeavor to work myself into a Notion that I am sitting by your Side, & relating those Things to you which are the Subjects of my Letters. All my Thoughts are spread before you without the least Disguise, & I think I see you either smile or sadden as I am happy or otherwise.'[88] One man used his letters to replace the conversations he could not have with his cousin: 'I would give the Indies, if I had them, that I could only have an hours conversation with my perfect cousin—but alas! There is a wide space between us.'[89] Another woman informed her correspondent: 'I have laid every care every thought and every incumbrance aside and retired into my Chamber on porpos [sic] to convers [sic] a little with you my dear.'[90] 'What a Blessing is the art of writing,' declared one woman, 'to be able to convey one's thoughts to & converse with our dearest friends when at such an immense distance; it is a happiness which cannot be too highly prized.'[91] Conversations between friends, made impossible by distance, could take place by letters.

Such familiar epistolary conversations could take place in a familiar style, *'sans ceremonie'*. One writer counseled his sister: 'I should be glad you would strive to excel in writing Letters. I can assure you it is a most genteel Accomplishment, & what will greatly recommend you to the thinking Part of your own Sex, as well as ours.—You will find its whole Art to consist in thinking freely, & writing what

---

[85] Severn Eyre to Littleton, 'London 5th Sep. 1785', Severn Eyre Journal, 1785 (typescript copy), VHS.
[86] Severn Eyre to Littleton, 'London 25th Sep. 1785', ibid.
[87] Rebecca Shoemaker to Samuel Shoemaker, '16th June 1784' from Peggy to E.D. by the Washington 1784', Shoemaker Family Papers, HSP.
[88] Thomas Coombe (jr.) to Thomas Coombe (sr.), 'Wednesday Evening Jany 3d, 1770', F18-1, Coombe Family Papers, HSP.
[89] Patrick Brown to Sophia Waterhouse Brown, 'Nassau Feby. 17th. 1807', John Brown Family Papers, NYHS.
[90] Susanna Brown to Sophia Waterhouse Brown, undated draft, ibid.
[91] Rebecca Shoemaker to Samuel Shoemaker, 'Nov. 27th 1784', Shoemaker Family Papers, HSP.

you think.'[92] Pierce Butler noted of his son's most recent letter: 'it is well written tho a little stiff—You must try to write free; that is, to be acquired only by writing a good deal.'[93] Some letter-writers presumed that friendship would allow for the forgiveness of letters written 'just as thoughts present themselves'. This theme can be seen, for instance, in the non-apology that appeared in a 1769 letter from a man in London to his brother in the Bahamas: 'You'll excuse all incorrectness, but such appologies are more becoming the formality of Courtiers, than the sincerity of Brothers so shall say no more.'[94] Wordy apologies for infelicities of style or grammar or handwriting were courtly; a sincere brother could understand and forgive such problems, because of a relationship of familiarity. One father similarly invoked 'friendship' as a space in which casual letters could be forgiven. In a letter to his son's tutor, he noted the hurry in which he wrote his letter, 'Excuse its wants and imperfections—It is wrote in the spirit of friendship without attending to anything else.'[95] Another man offered a similar sort of apology for the distance between his letters and those of the famous Lord Chesterfield: 'Having written thus far I cannot help thinking what would Lord Chesterfield have said to such a scrawl as this.— . . . however I am writing to a Friend who I hope will excuse it, and consign it over to the Flames when he has read it.'[96] A 'Friend' could excuse the messy handwriting and casual tone of a letter, even if the elegant Lord Chesterfield would have been chagrined.

This invocation of Chesterfield, mentioned more often than any other letter-writer in the late eighteenth century, signaled both the concerns about, and the desire for, familiarity. Looking briefly at familiarity in Chesterfield's letters, and their reception, makes clear both the anxieties about, and the importance of, familiarity in this epistolary culture. Chesterfield's letters demonstrate that epistolary tones other than familiarity remained popular; they were elegant, even courtly, even if at times also familiar. Indeed, their production (in the 1740s and 1750s) and their publication (in the 1770s) witness the transitions in epistolary tones creeping in over the century. They remained aristocratic and courtly, but also privilege familiarity and business. Chesterfield still recommended entertaining letters, telling his son: 'For gay and amusing letters . . . there are none that equal Comte Buffy's and Madame Sevigné's. They are so natural, that they seem to be the extempore conversations of two people of wit; rather than letters.' But he also counseled that his son read 'Cicero's Epistles to Atticus, and

---

[92] Thomas Coombe to Sally Coombe, 'Popodicon August ye 8th 1767', Thomas Coombe Papers, HSP.
[93] Pierce Butler to Thomas Butler, 'Philadelphia March Ye 4th. 1792', Pierce Butler Letter Collection, Add. Mss. 16603, BL.
[94] Alexander Brown to John Brown, 'London the 1st Septr 1769', John Brown Family Papers, NYHS.
[95] Pierce Butler to Weeden Butler, 'Mary-Ville May ye 5th. 1788', Pierce Butler Letter Collection, Add Mss 16603, BL.
[96] Isaac Norris to John Leeds Bozman?, 'Philadelphia Septr. 28. 79', John Leeds Bozman Papers, LoC.

to his familiar friends... the best examples that you can imitate, in the friendly and the familiar style.'[97] He also advised that his son write better familiar letters to him: 'Your letters... neither answer my desires, nor the purpose of letters; which should be familiar conversations, between absent friends. As I desire to live with you upon the footing of an intimate friend, and not of a parent, I could wish that your letters gave me more particular accounts of yourself, and of letter transactions. When you write to me, suppose yourself conversing freely with me, by the fire-side.'[98] Here is the classic trope of letters as familiar conversation; the mention of the 'fire-side' adds a further note of domesticity. Chesterfield went on: 'If you have ever looked into the Letters of Madame de Sevigné, to her daughter, Madame de Grignan; you must have observed the ease, freedom, and friendship, of that correspondence; and yet, I hope, and believe, that they did not love one another better than we do.'[99]

A familiar style, when carried off well, showed familiar love. Familiarity allowed families to enjoy 'ease, freedom, and friendship', even when far apart. It bridged distances of both geography and status, even while excluding many. It was thus a useful virtue for families on the move, helping them to forge fictive families, even across oceans. Even if not sharing a fireside or under the same roof, families could hold their members together. Familiarity was the virtue par excellence of letters, letters that enacted the imaginary links that held fictive families together. While a familiar style makes such letters seem natural, even spontaneous, it was a style inculcated by all kinds of texts, one that did significant cultural work. The tone of such letters, as well as their circulation, helped to forge the links of familiarity. They also helped to maintain lines of feeling, the topic of the next chapter.

---

[97] Lord Chesterfield to his son, letter 91, 'London, July the 20th O.S. 1747', *Chesterfield's Letters*, i. 219.
[98] Lord Chesterfield to his son, letter 132, 'London September the 27th. O.S. 1748', ibid. i. 345.
[99] Ibid.

3

Sensibility in Life and Letters

In 1630 a wife, with a notable New England name, faced the prospect of her dear husband's sojourn across the Atlantic, in the midst of political tumult and complicated family movements (including her husband's frequent absences). She was therefore pleased to hear from him, and so opened her letter to him: 'My Deare Husband, I received thy sweet letter, and doe bless God for all his mercyes to us, in the continuance of thy healthe and welfayre.' Fretting over her husband's 'longe partinge', she knew she would miss his 'sweete presence'. Nevertheless, she continued: 'I desyre the Lord to . . . give me fayth and pacience to submite unto his will . . . I hope, he will supply by the comfort of his holy spirit in the assurance of his love in Jesus Christ our Lord and Savior.' She also reveled in her husband's love: 'I see thy love to me and mine, my good Husband, is more then I can deserve.' She therefore prayed: 'I beseech the Lord to send us a comfortable meetinge, and thus with my best love to thy selfe . . . and all the rest of our frends, I desyre the Lord to send thee a good end to all thy troubles . . . as I trust he will not fayle thee.' She signed her letter: 'thy faithful and obedyent wife Margaret Winthrope.'[1]

In 1778 a wife, with a notable New England name, faced the prospect of her dear husband's sojourn across the Atlantic, in the midst of political tumult and complicated family movements (including her husband's frequent absences). She was therefore pleased to hear from him, and so opened her letter to him: 'Dearest of Friends Shall I tell my dearest that tears of joy filld my Eyes this morning at the sight of his well known hand.' Fretting over her husband's absence, she informed him: 'I have lived a life of fear and anxiety ever since you left me . . . we could not get a word from the Boston [his ship], and most people gave her up as taken or lost, thus has my mind been agitated like a troubled sea.' Complaining at the shortness of his letter, she declared: 'I own I was mortified at so Short a Letter, but I quiet my Heart with thinking there are many more upon their passage.' She continued, implying her resentment that she had not been permitted to come with him: 'Now I know you are Safe I wish myself with you. Whenever you entertain such a wish recollect that I would have willingly hazarded all

---

[1] Margaret Winthrop to John Winthrop, 'Groton, ca. February 15, 1629/30', Malcolm Freiberg (ed.), *The Winthrop Papers*, 6 vols. (Boston: Massachusetts Historical Society, 1931), vol. 2 (*1623–1630*), 209–10.

dangers to have been your companion, but as that was not permitted you must console me in your absence by a Recital of all your adventures.' She presumed one such adventure would be meeting the 'polite Scientifick Ladies of France', whom she commended for being more accomplished than most of her countrywomen. She informed her husband that she had developed this opinion: 'ever since I read the Letters of Dr. Sherbear, who professes... that Women have in general more delicate Sensations than Men.' She thus indicated her familiarity with John Shebbeare's 1755 *Letters on the English Nation*, a set of letters on matters of gender dynamics, religion, politeness, luxury, and sensibility, among other things.[2] She concluded by commending an improvement in female education in France, and wished that it had advanced as far in America, noting of men that, 'if they deserve the title of our Friends, tis an inhumane Tyranny to debar them of privileges of ingenious Education.'[3] Although the end of this letter is missing, she would likely have signed it much as she did another from this same month: 'Remember with unabated ardour her whose chief happiness is calling Herself your affectionate Portia.'[4]

Significant changes had occurred between Margaret Winthrop's letter and that of Abigail Adams. These changes are manifold, but one of the most obvious is the shift from a language of religion into a language of sensibility. To be sure, there are certain continuities between the two letters. Both demonstrate literacy and learning, anxiety over the journey, and affection for the missing husband, with warm marital relations in both cases. Both were written in moments of considerable transatlantic dislocation, at the founding of a colony or a nation. Both wives had already experienced separations from their husbands, and were becoming highly skilled letter-writers. There are also, admittedly, certain atypical aspects: the Winthrops were especially inclined to religion, and Abigail Adams an exceptionally well-read and feisty wife. Nevertheless, these letters are in many respects typical of their times. The tone of the first one is affectionate but measured: the hoped-for reunion will not be blissful but simply comfortable. It dwells neither on the wife's feelings nor on her anxieties, but instead makes those clear through invocations of a need to depend on God. It emphasizes obedience and faith much more than feeling. It also presumes, in keeping with general beliefs of the hotter sort of Protestant, that family affections, however strong, will be subordinate to the greater love of God. Abigail's letter, by contrast, invokes nothing of God or Providence, but dwells much more on her own sentiments and those of her husband. It deploys a typical language of marriage as friendship, and also spends a considerable amount of time on the sensations of the writer. It also demonstrates a familiarity with reading, not the Bible (as Margaret might

---

[2] It was a set of letters by an Italian Jesuit to various correspondents about the mores of the English. This passage quotes letter XX, 'To the Marchioness of *** at Rome', in John Shebbeare, *Letters on the English Nation* (London, 1755), 168–9.
[3] Abigail Adams to John Adams, 'June 30 [1778]', *Adams Family Correspondence*, iii. 51–3.
[4] Abigail Adams to John Adams, 'Boston june 18 1778', ibid. iii. 46–7.

have done), but an epistolary set of writings on gender dynamics and sensibility. Its opening, referring to tears coming from simply seeing handwriting, is what we might expect. Its mention of women's 'more delicate Sensations' also places it squarely in the latter half of the eighteenth century.

One of Abigail Adams's foremost biographers has noticed the language of the heart, the sensations, and the affections in these letters. She has claimed: 'Abigail tended to locate her emotions physically, so that her heart became the bearer of her hurt.'[5] She has contended further that Abigail 'discovered that writing allowed her the satisfactions of recreating her world in letters as well as the therapy that came from this method of confession'.[6] There is indeed something beguiling in a tone like Abigail's, especially when viewed in isolation from other letters of the period. A language of the heart seems sincere, fresh, the words dropping from the pen with utter truthfulness, affection, and even a confessional quality. However, what Abigail did when she wrote letters in this style was not simply confessional, therapeutic, or even personal, though it may have been all of those things. It was a highly mediated and specific cultural act. This is not to say that her letters might not have expressed her emotions. But it is to point out that there is something else going on here. This something else is the subject of this chapter. A language of the heart, for all its fresh and personal quality, was a dominant language of the later eighteenth-century anglophone world, and its origins were domestic, in ways too often overlooked by scholars. These sensations, and ideas about them, underpinned much of the culture of sensibility.

When Abigail Adams approvingly quoted Shebbeare's letters about the naturally delicate sensations of women, she entered into cultural debates about sensation, connections, and sensibility. Other letters of hers invoked concerns about connections between individuals. In a courtship letter from 1763, for instance, she declared:

Humanity obliges us to be affected with the distresses and Miserys of our fellow Creatures. Friendship is a band yet stronger, which causes us to [fee]l with greater tenderness the afflictions of our Friends. And there is a tye more binding than Humanity, and stronger than Friendship, which makes us anxious for the happiness and welfare of those to whom it binds us... Unite these, and there is a threefold cord—by this cord I am not ashamed to own myself bound.[7]

Abigail here identified three types of bands tying individuals together: humanity for all; friendship; and, in essence, marital or romantic love. This typology was a way of expressing her affection for John, and her willingness to marry him, but it was also a larger statement about bands and bonds of varying sorts.

---

[5] Edith B. Gelles, *Portia: The World of Abigail Adams* (Bloomington, Ind.: Indiana University Press, 1992), 32–3.
[6] Ibid. 36.
[7] Abigail Smith to John Adams, 'Weymouth August th 11 1763', in *Adams Family Correspondence*, i. 6–7.

Abigail Adams was hardly alone in devoting attention to the nature of sympathetic bands. Such 'connexions' preoccupied many in the eighteenth century. Between nerves, between objects, between individuals: all of these connections were critical, but also fraught. The notion of sympathetic connections had its origins in medical understandings of the nervous system. So, George Cheyne's 1733 treatise on the nerves, which remained influential throughout the eighteenth century, sounded out some of the principles that underlay sensibility as well as sympathy. Cheyne declared: 'That the Intelligent Principle, or *Soul*, resides Somewhere in the Brain, where all the Nerves, or Instruments of Sensation terminate, like a *Musician* in a finely fram'd and well-tun'd Organ-Case; that these Nerves are like *Keys*, which, being struck or touch'd convey the Sound and Harmony to this Sentient Principle, or Musician.' He also compared the 'intelligent principle' to a 'Bell in a Steeple', with nerves extending down like bell-ropes.[8]

Cheyne's postulations, in which the brain was a kind of musician or bell for the fibers which were plucked together, seems to have influenced numerous other authors, including Samuel Richardson, Adam Smith, and David Hume. Hume, considering the 'nature and force of *sympathy*', contended that: 'The minds of all men are similar in their feelings and operations... As in strings equally wound up, the motion of one communicates itself to the rest; so all the affections readily pass from one person to another, and beget correspondent movements in every human creature.'[9] Hume also claimed: 'No quality of human nature is more remarkable, both in itself and its consequences, than that propensity we have to sympathize with others, and to receive by communication their inclinations and sentiments, however different from, or even contrary to, our own.'[10] Words like 'strike', 'sensation', 'feeling', and 'movement' characterize descriptions of sympathy and sensibility in magazines such as *Town and Country*.[11]

Sensibility shared qualities with sympathy. Both expressed an idea of shared sentiment. Both also stemmed from medical understandings of the relationship between physical objects, and came to be informed by scientific views of the nerves. Notions of sensibility could overlap with sympathy, in that both could refer to feelings (for instance, of suffering). Both were also about physical reactions between objects, and bodies in particular. Yet there were also key differences. Sensibility was a quality within the possessor. It showed an awareness of others and of their emotions, but it represented the sentimental capacities within an individual which rested on physical reactions (and which could be directed at

---

[8] George Cheyne, *The English Malady: or, A Treatise of Nervous Diseases of All Kinds* (London, 1733), 3–4.

[9] David Hume, *A Treatise of Human Nature* [1739–40], ed. L. A. Selby-Bigge and P. H. Nidditch, 2nd edn. (Oxford: Clarendon Press, 1978), book III, pp. 575–6.

[10] Ibid. 316.

[11] See 'An Essay on Humanity', *Town and Country Magazine* (Apr. 1779), 188–9, and 'An Essay on Sympathy', ibid. (Oct. 1779), 530–2.

objects as diverse as a distant spouse, a sublime painting, or a gloomy woods). It was fundamentally about the capacity of the physical body to respond to all kinds of sensory input. By contrast, sympathy described the relationship between two individuals. The notion of one object that could influence another lay at its core. At its most fundamental, it was 'fellow-feeling'.[12] The distinction between sensibility and sympathy is made clear in a quotation from Adam Smith's *Theory of Moral Sentiments*, in which he laments that a 'want of sensibility' within ourselves may result in an 'artificial sympathy'.[13] To be able to respond with sympathy required sensibility, so the two ideals worked in tandem, even though they were distinct in their precise meanings.

Sympathy is a necessity for letter-writers, whatever the age. They have to enter into the same fantasy in which time and distance are obliterated, projecting themselves forward and backward in time and place. Sympathy is in this sense ageless. Sensibility, on the other hand, received its greatest impetus in precisely this era. Of course, there had been claims to hearts and connections before, but they took on a peculiar and novel force in the later eighteenth century. Sensibility came to denote the capacity of certain sensitive individuals to understand and respond to the world around them.[14] It meant an innate trait, related to the nerves and their union, but it was also about exhibiting that trait. In short, it is best defined as the ability to possess and to display a feeling heart. A feeling heart, as we shall see, was critical here, though heads and nerves were also implicated.

The feeling heart was one part of a body animated by sensibility; sensibility, as theories of nerves indicate, was a physical attribute, expressed through the body. Discussing Samuel Richardson's novels, one scholar has noted that 'sentiment displays itself in a repertoire of conventionally involuntary signs—tears, sighs, palpitations'.[15] Tears, facial expressions, bodily contortions: these were the easily discernible signs of sensibility. And it was through the body that sympathy was most easily achieved. For Adam Smith, it was obvious that 'this is the source of our fellow-feeling for the misery of others... When we see a stroke aimed, and

---

[12] Definition of 'Sympathy', *Oxford English Dictionary Online*, 2nd edn., (Oxford University Press, 1989). David Marshall terms sympathy 'the capacity to feel the sentiments of someone else... fellow-feeling'. David Marshall, *The Surprising Effects of Sympathy: Marivaux, Diderot, Rousseau, and Mary Shelley* (Chicago: University of Chicago Press, 1988), 3.

[13] Adam Smith, *Theory of Moral Sentiments* (London and Edinburgh, 1759), pt. I, sec. IV, ch. I, p. 102.

[14] On the relationship between the physical body and sensibility, see Robert A. Erickson, *The Language of the Heart, 1600–1750* (Philadelphia: University of Pennsylvania Press, 1997); John Mullan, *Sentiment and Sociability: The Language of Feeling in the Eighteenth Century* (Oxford: Oxford University Press, 1988), ch. 5; Sarah Knott, 'A Cultural History of Sensibility', ch. 1; Andrew Burstein, *Sentimental Democracy: The Evolution of America's Romantic Self-Image* (New York: Hill & Wang, 1999), ch. 1; and Jessica Riskin, *Science in the Age of Sensibility: The Sentimental Empiricists of the French Enlightenment* (Chicago: University of Chicago Press, 2002).

[15] Mullan, *Sentiment and Sociability*, 74. For France, one scholar has even written a history of tears, focused on the eighteenth century. See Anne Vincent-Buffault, *The History of Tears: Sensibility and Sentimentality in France* (Basingstoke: Macmillan, 1991).

just ready to fall upon the leg or arm of another person, we naturally shrink and draw back our own leg or our own arm.'[16] Even 'men of the most robust make, observe that in looking upon sore eyes they often feel a very sensible soreness in their own'.[17] It was through the sensible nervous system that moral sentiments originated, for Smith as for many others. The body was critical both for the generation of sympathy and for the display of sensibility.

The sensible body first expressed attachments in the family. Many theorists of this period considered that sensibility began first at home, in part because of the sympathy that was felt to be 'natural' in familial relationships. So for Francis Hutcheson, for instance, it was in the circle of the family that sensibility, which led ultimately to benevolence, virtue, and love of God, originated:

> The sensible Pleasure alone must... be esteemed at a very low rate: But the Desires of this kind, as they were by Nature intended to found the most constant uninterrupted Friendship, and to introduce the most venerable and lovely Relations, by Marriages and Families, arise in our Hearts, attended with some of the sweetest Affections, with a disinterested Love and Tenderness, with a most gentle and obliging Deportment, with something great and heroick in our Temper.[18]

For Hutcheson, the limited and natural attachments to family (and even nation) were supposed to help to develop more general, benevolent attachments to all humanity and to God. David Hume also believed in the domestic origins of sensibility.[19] For Abigail Adams, as we have seen, the view was reversed: so that general benevolence could deepen into love for friends and family. In either case, family affection was intimately and importantly related to benevolence and morality.

Adam Smith, too, argued for the domestic origins of sympathy and sentiment. While the more neo-Stoical Smith was less laudatory of the sensible impulses of the domestic setting, he nonetheless argued that sympathy was found first in the individual and then in the familial setting, since 'natural inclination' led toward 'the prosperity of our family'.[20] Affections and benevolence radiated outward from this setting, and it was here that sympathetic sway could work most strongly. Indeed, Smith argued that familiar sympathy not only affected those within the family, but even those who saw the family. In a section of *The Theory of Moral Sentiments* on the topic 'Of Mutual Sympathy,' he posited:

> Their mutual regard renders them happy in one another, and sympathy, with this mutual regard, makes them agreeable to every other person. With what pleasure do we look upon a family, through the whole of which reign mutual love and esteem... where freedom

---

[16] Smith, *Theory of Moral Sentiments*, pt. I, sec. I, ch. 1, p. 3. [17] Ibid. 4.
[18] Francis Hutcheson, *An Essay on the Nature and Conduct of the Passions and Affections with Illustrations on the Moral Sense* [1742], ed. Paul McReynolds, 3rd edn. (Gainesville, Fla.: Scholars' Facsimiles & Reprints, 1969), 309–10.
[19] See David Hume, 'Of Moral Prejudices', *Essays*, 538–44.
[20] Smith, *Theory of Moral Sentiments*, pt. VII, sec. II, ch. II, p. 434.

and fondness, mutual raillery, and mutual kindness show that no opposition of interests divides the brothers, nor any rivalship of favour sets the sisters at variance, and where every thing presents us with the idea of peace, chearfulness, harmony, and contentment.[21]

Smith's theory meant that even to witness familiar harmony would produce good feelings and sympathy in the viewer; family peace, then, was important not only for the family itself, but for those with whom it came into contact. But it is the very fragility of this family harmony, the strong possibility that there might be 'opposition' or 'rivalship', which renders this domestic concord so precious. As Smith continues: 'On the contrary, how uneasy are we made when we go into a house in which jarring contention sets one half of those who dwell in it against the other.'[22] Households of 'jarring contention' caused dismay not only within the family, but also to all who witnessed it. This is partly why sensibility, especially within settings of familiarity, took on such force. Peaceful families were supposed to radiate their peace outward, sending waves of sympathy through society. Dislocated ones discomfited all. This emphasis is an acknowledgement of the pain and rivalries that are part of family life, but it also suggests that such pains and rivalries need to be avoided, both for those within the family and for those with whom the family comes into contact.

What family letters from this period indicate is that sensibility often had significant compensatory elements. Sensibility developed as a style for many reasons, as scholars have been at pains to demonstrate.[23] Writing about eighteenth-century Scotland, a literary critic has observed that the 'Man of Feeling' was 'the fantasy of a ruling class about what it has lost', as this class became ever more mired in a system of commerce which increasingly strained society.[24] The appearance of the language of sensibility in family letters, as we shall see, often occurred at the very moments when feeling seemed most imperiled, whether because of distance, war, death, or conflict. As Smith's contentions about the family indicate, the very fragility of familiar sensibility was what made it so valuable, for families themselves and for those around them. After all, when a husband reminded his wife that 'distance ought never to disunite our Hearts', he expressed both his anxiety that it might, and his hope that it would not.[25] In that particular case, the husband had chosen to go from Virginia to Scotland on family business, for commercial reasons. For him, this language of feeling allowed him to sidestep these financial realities and focus instead on love and union. This language also allowed him to reassure himself that this distance of persons meant no distance of hearts. The Man—and Woman—of Feeling served as a

---

[21] Smith, *Theory of Moral Sentiments*, pt. I, sec. III, ch. IV, pp. 82–3. [22] Ibid. 83.
[23] See Barker-Benfield, *Culture of Sensibility*, and Knott, 'A Cultural History of Sensibility'.
[24] John Mullan, 'The Language of Sentiment: Hume, Smith, and Henry Mackenzie', in Andrew Hook (ed.), *The History of Scottish Literature* (Aberdeen: Aberdeen University Press, 1987), ii. 273–90, at 284.
[25] James Stevens to Martha Stevens, 'Greenock 12th September 1786', typescript, Stevens Family Papers, VHS.

fantasy for these men and women, in the face of an Atlantic economy, and a political world, in which indifference and even cruelty could be paramount. In theory, languages of sensibility could be used by all, but in practice, they were used more, and more efficaciously, by some than by others.[26] The association of sensibility and domesticity meant that there were limits to the force of these styles. Not all individuals privileged the language of feeling, but many did so, often self-consciously borrowing the language of love in order to ameliorate the harder realities of the choices that lay underneath. The efficacy of such rhetoric varied enormously depending on individual circumstances, especially since it always butted against other forces within the household.

Sensibility, like familiarity, then, had its origins in the domestic setting. Both moved outward from the smallest circles of domesticity (husbands and wives, parents and children) into other realms in the eighteenth century. The great explosion of the language of feeling as a larger political statement (to end the slave trade, for instance) stemmed in part from the family. This point clarifies, again, the agency of the family in instigating, nurturing, and maintaining political changes in broader realms. Sensibility, like familiarity, could not only support but also work against familial hierarchies (and later other sorts of hierarchies). That is, if sensibility was to some degree in the body, and could thrive in the family, then it did not require special rank, and it could indeed subvert traditional hierarchies (so women, legally subordinate, could be more sensible than men, in some cases). It could thus replace or at least join, other modes of address. Sensible appeals to the self and its sufferings could gain force over traditional appeals to deference, to courtliness and gallantry, or to godliness and charity. So, it had potentially leveling effects, as familiarity did. On the other hand, as we shall see, its force in the body meant that, as with familiarity, it could also exclude. If sensibility was something one either had or did not have, if the fibers were sufficiently delicate or were not, then it could exclude populations declared to be lacking those delicate fibers.

The very physicality that lay behind notions of the sensible connections meant that not only might some people have more of it than others, but that this distinction was ingrained or 'natural'. George Cheyne declared that: 'There are as many and as different Degrees of *Sensibility* or of *Feeling* as there are Degrees of *Intelligence*... none can choose *his* own Degree of *Sensibility*.'[27] Having too much sensibility could cause enervation or weakness; Cheyne's treatise, indeed, was trying to deal with precisely these maladies. Some felt that women might have such an over-delicacy of feeling, or might attach that sensible feeling to 'trifling' notions or events. One letter-writing manual specifically designed for

---

[26] Sarah Knott, in approaching a different set of sources though a related set of concerns, has reached similar conclusions. See her 'Sensibility and the American War of Independence', *American Historical Review*, 109 (2004), 19–39.
[27] Cheyne, *The English Malady*, 48–9, as quoted in Barker-Benfield, *Culture of Sensibility*, 9.

women claimed that: 'though Nature has bestowed on them a Delicacy and Ease of Expression... nothing can appear, in general, more trifling and empty than their Language and Sentiments.'[28] Having too much sensibility, or a sensibility wrongly directed, could be a problem.

But equally, having too little sensibility indicated an association with brute animals, and was thus also a concern. As we shall see in ensuing chapters, there were accusations of insensibility directed at all kinds of individuals: tyrannical fathers in novels and stories; political enemies in times of war and political conflict; masters of slaves, and slaves themselves. The myriad uses of accusations of insensibility served important political ends. Claims about the insensibility of entire peoples, indeed, became significant in the maintenance of slavery, especially in the later eighteenth century, as some contended that Africans had a brute insensibility that enabled them to survive and labor in the torrid zones, and to withstand the pain of whipping and other punishments. In 1799 Benjamin Rush, patriot and doctor, argued that 'Negroes' had an 'insensibility in the nerves' which rendered them better able to bear pain than whites.[29] In this he echoed others. One traveler in North America, sympathetic and awestruck by the arduous labor performed by slaves, posited that: 'It is the poor Negroes who alone work hard... Incredible is the fatigue which the poor wretches undergo, and that nature should be able to support it; there certainly must be something in their constitutions, as well as their color, different from us, that enables them to endure it.'[30] A less sympathetic sojourner in the Caribbean in the early nineteenth century had imbibed such beliefs, when she informed her friend in England that the Africans 'are a sluggish, inert, self-willed race of people, apparently inaccessible to gentle & kindly impulses'.[31] This sense of 'inaccessibility' to sensible impulses was one of the ways in which ideas about the physical body were grafted on to beliefs in cultural inferiority. This sojourner worried that her son might be infected in turn by having to suppress feelings of sympathy for their slaves: 'greatly do I fear the practices of severity, which are really essential in the government of Negroes, may chill & close his heart against those general sympathies which appear to me essential to the excellence

---

[28] Anon., *The Ladies Complete Letter-Writer; Teaching The Art of Inditing Letters on every Subject that can call for their Attention, as Daughters, Wives, Mothers, Relations, Friends, or Acquaintances* (London, 1763), introduction.

[29] Benjamin Rush, 'Observations intended to favor a supposition that the Black Color (as it is called) of the Negroes is derived from LEPROSY', *Transactions of the American Philosophical Society* 4 (1799), 289–97, at 292–4, as quoted in Kirsten Fischer, *Suspect Relations: Sex, Race, and Resistance in Colonial North Carolina* (Ithaca, NY: Cornell University Press, 2002), 191.

[30] Anburey, 'Travels through America During the War', ii. 330–5, as quoted in 'Documents: Travelers' Impressions of Slavery in America from 1750 to 1800', *Journal of Negro History*, 1 (1916), 399–435, at 407.

[31] Eliza Fenwick to Mary Hays, 'Bridge Town, Barbadoes, Dec. 11th, 1814', in A. F. Wedd (ed.), *The Fate of the Fenwicks: Letters to Mary Hays (1798–1828)* (London: Methuen, 1927), 163.

of character.'[32] Sensibility might exist more in some individuals than others, at least according to some commentators, but sympathy might also be limited by practices of 'severity'. When Africans, African-Americans, and Anglo-Africans challenged notions of racial insensibility, they often did so by emphasizing their own sensibility. Olaudah Equiano's narrative was a testament to his sensibility, as were the letters of Ignatius Sancho, as we shall see.

In the culture of sensibility, then, there was a considerable emphasis on the physical, the body, and the thing. Going back to the postulations of Cheyne and other theorists demonstrates the ways in which the languages of fibers striking each other, or being struck together, point to this physicality. At the same time, objects could strike the nerves in the same way, so that a physical object could provoke an emotional reaction. If a fine painting or dark woods could stir a response in a sensible individual, then it is clear that the sentimental token of a letter could do the same. One scholar of eighteenth-century sensibility has devoted considerable attention to the relationship between the 'consumer revolution' of the eighteenth century and the rise of the culture of sensibility.[33] These two developments worked together, in ways that led to the increasingly important sentimental significance of things. Connections and impressions existed that made some things into feelings, and some feelings into things.

WRITING WITH FEELING

It was not enough to have sensible fibers; one had to *show* them. One of the chief ways the body could express its sensibility was through writing about it.[34] Letter-writers sought to render physical objects—a piece of paper, the ink from a quill—into indicators of a feeling heart. The body—with its tears, its expressions, its convulsions—could display authentic affection, approbation, or disapprobation. However, in correspondences, since the body was missing, the letter had to stand in for it. Due to the distance separating writer and recipient, epistolary prose had to take the place of physical feeling. Letter-writers had to believe that their ink-blotted texts of sensibility could inspire sympathy. Writers of letters had to exchange feelings for texts; readers of letters had to exchange texts for feelings. The constant conversion and reconversion between feeling and text was the critical circulation of sensible, familiar letters. One son apologized for sending his letter instead of himself: 'In stead of seeing myself in Person . . . you have little more than a transcript of me, a bare Epistle.'[35] These 'bare epistles' needed, then, to demonstrate sensible affection.

---

[32] Eliza Fenwick to Mary Hays, 'March 21 & April 12th 1815', in ibid. 169–70.
[33] Barker-Benfield, *Culture of Sensibility*, esp. ch. 4.
[34] This feeling was also depicted in family portraits. Retford, *The Art of Domestic Life*, esp. chs. 2–4.
[35] Thomas Ruston to Job Ruston, 'London April 3d: 1766', Thomas Ruston Papers, LoC.

Recipients increasingly assumed that languages of sensibility would infuse the domestic letters they received. Take, for instance, a complaint made by Molly Aitchison Parker, in Richmond, Virginia, in 1797. She was indignant at a 'very cold, formal letter' from her aunt in London, grumbling to her father-in-law: 'when I receive letters from my friends and relations I expect they are to be affectionate and friendly I have no pleasure in receiving Aunt Elmsleys letters—they are so frigid—She dont write as if She felt.'[36] Since the letter no longer survives, it is difficult to know exactly what so roused Molly's ire. But what seems to have been missing in this letter was the display of writing with feeling, a particular requirement for a friendly relation. The letter from Molly's aunt may have been of the more formal, courteous, hierarchical nature, neither entirely familiar nor sensible. In her displeasure, Molly articulated a requirement that was hinted at in hundreds of other family correspondences: to write familiar letters with feeling.

To write letters with feeling required not only the feeling, but also an abiding knowledge of sensible letters. For an even moderately well-read individual, such familiarity was not difficult to come by in the latter half of the eighteenth century. Novels, magazines, books of famous letter-writers, and letter-writing manuals all combined to teach would-be letter-writers how to transform feelings into letters. Such sources provide a good sense of what a letter-writer and reader would have expected of a sensible letter. Epistolary novels necessarily inculcated the heartfelt and yet fictional nature of correspondence in the minds of their readers. Even many novels which were not explicitly epistolary often included letters, or a discussion of them, in some part of the text. In Fanny Burney's *Cecilia*, for instance, one chapter is entitled 'The Letter', and in it Delvile confides to Cecilia in letter form, avowing: 'Thus have I laid open to you my whole heart.'[37]

Many literary protagonists similarly laid their hearts open in letters. Novels such as *Pamela* and *Clarissa* cultivated sensible writers and readers of letters, as it became clear that certain characters, those with whom the reader was expected to sympathize, were sensible themselves. Samuel Richardson's Pamela described the letters she had written elsewhere in the novel: 'I think I have no Reason to be afraid of being found insincere...I know I wrote my Heart; and that is not deceitful.'[38] Such a declaration, which signaled the ability to write from the heart with nothing but sincerity, could have come from any number of epistolary protagonists of the eighteenth century. Anna Howe declared to her friend Clarissa: 'My heart...is a sincere sharer in all your distresses. My sunshine

---

[36] Mary Aitchison Parker to James Parker, 'Richmond 29th April 1797', PA11.144, Parker Family Papers, LRO.

[37] Frances Burney, *Cecilia, or Memoirs of an Heiress*, 5 vols. (London, 1782), vol. iv, ch. 5 ('A Letter'), p. 66.

[38] Pamela to Father and Mother, 'Saturday, Six o'Clock' [no letter number given], Richardson, *Pamela*, ii. 14.

darts but thro' a drizly cloud. My eye... is more than ready to overflow.'[39] The heart's feeling expressed itself in the bodily signs invoked in her letter: tears ready to overflow.

Nowhere does the language of the sensible and feeling heart take on more life than in Fanny Burney's 1778 *Evelina, or the History of a Young Lady's Entrance into the World, in a Series of Letters*, one of the more popular novels of the later eighteenth century. This epistolary novel recounted the tale of another potentially 'loose fish', who remained connected to her family (though not her natural one) by letter. One critic has argued that in *Evelina* 'the heart... becomes the central text'.[40] Hearts do much more than simply feel in *Evelina*; they are practically molten with sensation. In the novel, hearts are 'formed' by love.[41] They 'tremble'.[42] They 'beat with resentment'.[43] They 'throb with joy!'[44] They are 'open' to distress.[45] They 'overflow' with blessings.[46] They 'glow with tenderness and gratitude', even as they are 'oppressed with a sense of [their] own unworthiness'.[47] They often 'bleed'.[48] Hearts are also capable of being impressed with sensations, much as Cheyne and others postulated that the nerves were. Mr Villars, Evelina's guardian and correspondent, describes his ward in the following terms: 'her heart was open to every impression with which love, pity, or art might assail it.'[49] Of her fear of a seemingly unworthy suitor, Evelina declares: 'oh, if this weak heart of mine had been penetrated with too deep an impression of his merit,—my peace and happiness had been lost for ever!'[50]

In *Evelina*, letters and hearts are nearly interchangeable in the text, though sometimes letters apparently cannot quite transmit the liveliness of those active hearts. But this is not for want of trying. Mr Villars proclaims that: 'This letter will be delivered to you by my child... I send you with her the heart of your friend.'[51] Other letters apparently represent the heart less clearly, as when Evelina apologizes for not coming herself: 'My sweet Maria will be much surprised... when, instead of her friend, she receives this letter;—this cold, this inanimate letter, which will but ill express the feelings of the heart which indites

---

[39] Anna Howe to Clarissa Harlowe, 'Thursday Morning', letter XXI, Richardson, *Clarissa*, ii. 134.
[40] Jennifer A. Wagner, 'Privacy and Anonymity in *Evelina*', in Harold Bloom (ed.), *Fanny Burney's 'Evelina'* (New York: Chelsea House, 1988), 99–110, at 106.
[41] 'Evelina to the Rev. Mr. Villars', 'Howard Grove, May 18', letter 5, Burney, *Evelina*, ii. 49.
[42] 'Mr. Villars to Evelina', 'Berry Hill, April 16', letter 15, ibid. i. 86.
[43] 'Evelina in continuation', 'Holborn, June 17th', Letter 15, ibid. ii. 125.
[44] 'Evelina to Miss Mirvan', 'Berry Hill, July 14', letter 26, ibid. i. 235.
[45] 'Evelina to the Rev. Mr. Villars', 'Howard Grove, May 18', letter 5, ibid. ii. 50.
[46] 'Evelina to Miss Mirvan', 'Berry Hill, July 14', letter 26, ibid. i. 236.
[47] 'Evelina in continuation', 'Berry Hill, August 10', letter 29, ibid. ii. 256.
[48] 'Evelina to the Rev. Mr. Villars', 'Howard Grove, May 18', letter 5, ibid. ii. 51.
[49] 'Mr. Villars to Lady Howard', 'Berry Hill, May 2', letter 28, ibid. i. 223.
[50] 'Evelina in continuation', 'Berry Hill, July 21', letter 28, ibid. 242.
[51] 'Mr. Villars to Lady Howard', 'March 18', letter 5, ibid. i. 18.

it.'⁵² Evelina reports of her meeting with her father: ' "Oh, Sir," exclaimed I, "that you could but read my heart!—that you could but see the filial tenderness and concern with which it overflows!" '⁵³ When Mr Villars approves her love-match by letter, Evelina's heart is so full that she cannot even read it: 'Open it, indeed, I did,—but read it I could not . . . the tenderness of your expressions,—the certainty that no obstacle remained to my eternal union with the loved owner of my heart, gave me sensations too various . . . blinded by tears of gratitude and delight which started into my eyes, I have given over the attempt of reading.'⁵⁴ In other scenes the heart itself stands in for the letters, as a text itself. Evelina declines to write more: 'I cannot write the scene that followed, though every word is engraven on my heart.'⁵⁵ At the end of the novel Mr Villars proclaims: 'Yes, my child, thy happiness is engraved in golden characters, upon the tablets of my heart! and their impression is indelible.'⁵⁶ Evelina's own letters maintain a highly conversational style, one filled with many dashes and exclamation-marks, a grammar to indicate the breathless conversational mode they displayed.

This is writing with feeling indeed. While epistolary novels have received the most attention, other, less exalted products of eighteenth-century print culture conveyed similar messages that sustained the idea that the true feelings of the heart could—and should—be captured in familiar letters. Even the relatively scandalous *Town and Country Magazine* included such moralizing letters of sensibility. Letters of feeling serving moral ends provided ballast for the levity of its scandal pages. In 'The Tyrannical Fathers: A Tale', one Madame Niveau informed the hero, Louis, that if he went ahead with his marriage to another, her daughter, who loved him, was likely to die of a broken heart. Madame Niveau had to conclude her letter to Louis because: 'The mother who feels like me, must give vent to her grief.—My tears will not let me proceed.'⁵⁷ Here the physical response to the situation became a reason for discontinuing the letter; feelings had overwhelmed the text, and in so doing had shown themselves to be true and powerful. Naturally, such a letter has a devastating effect on the hero, who is then given the courage to declare his true love.

Magazines thus conveyed the lesson that people should write out their feelings in letters; books of famous letters increasingly did the same. While the language of sensibility was not a major feature of the 1737 *Letters of Mr. Alexander Pope, and Several of His Friends*, it became a far more important feature of later eighteenth-century collections, such as the 1775 *Letters of the Late Rev. Mr. Laurence Sterne, to His Most Intimate Friends*.⁵⁸ While many of Sterne's letters

---

⁵² 'Evelina to Miss Mirvan', 'Berry Hill, July 14', letter 26, ibid. iii. 233.
⁵³ 'Evelina in continuation', 'Oct. 11', letter 19, ibid. iii. 220.
⁵⁴ 'Evelina in continuation', 'Clifton October 13', letter 21, ibid. iii. 259.
⁵⁵ 'Evelina in continuation', 'Oct 6ᵗʰ', letter 15, ibid. iii. 158.
⁵⁶ 'Mr. Villars to Evelina', n.d. letter 22, ibid. iii. 261.
⁵⁷ 'The Tyrannical Fathers: A Tale', *Town and Country Magazine* (Mar. 1775), 137–41.
⁵⁸ Pope, *Letters of Mr. Alexander Pope*, and Sterne, *Letters of the Late Rev. Mr. Laurence Sterne*.

dealt with business matters, in a number of them, as his daughter noted in the preface, 'a good heart breathes in every line'.[59] Here, in a love-letter from a young Sterne to his wife, is what she meant:

> Fanny had prepared me a supper... —but I sat over it with tears; a bitter sauce, my L. but I could eat it with no other—from the moment she began to spread my little table, my heart fainted within me.—One solitary plate, one knife, one fork, one glass!—I gave a thousand pensive, penetrating looks at the chair thou hadst so often graced, in those quiet, and sentimental repasts—then laid down my knife, and fork, and took out my handkerchief, and clapped it across my face, and wept like a child.—I do so this very moment, my L. for as I take up my pen my poor pulse quickens, my pale face glows, and tears are trickling down upon the paper.[60]

This passage could function (and possibly did) as a 'how-to' checklist of every feature for which the sensible letter-writer was to strive: the physical features of sensible suffering (his tears, his paleness, his quickened pulse), the ability of objects (a knife, a plate, a glass, a chair) to impress a sentimental reaction, the privileging of the language of the heart (which 'fainted within' him), the conversational style, made even more 'natural' by the many dashes and exclamation-marks.

This language of the heart also appeared in epistolary manuals. In these guides, as in the novels and magazine stories they paralleled, the bosoms of lovers heave with rapturous love; scorned lovers writhe in agony; and hearts pound and flutter with palpable emotion. One male suitor assured his love: 'I desire you will first look carefully over this Letter, for my whole Heart is in it.'[61] He implored his beloved to take the text as a heart, and expected she would treat his letter (and his heart) with care. Another courting man claimed: 'my Heart [is] purely dictating every Word I say.'[62] Writing to a father who had left for sea only a few days ago, a daughter exclaimed: 'Oh! Sir, though short to some the Interval of Time since I received your Blessing, ere your Departure from us, to me it seems an Age! And when I reflect how many such I am doomed to bear in the Absence of the best of Parents, I am inconsolable!'[63] Similar language occurs in model letters between friends, as in the letters between 'Miss Jones' and 'Lady ____', who had recently parted at the end of the London season. So Miss Jones to Lady ____ declared: 'The first Letter from an absent Friend is surely the most agreeable... Yours from Hatfield revived in me those pleasing Remembrances which not only enliven but expand the Heart; that very Heart, which, but the Moment before, felt itself mightily shrunk and contracted at the Thoughts of your Departure.'[64] Such a description echoed other contemporary texts, such as Smith's *Theory of Moral Sentiments*: 'The sight of a smiling countenance... elevates even the pensive [man] into that gay and airy mood,

---

[59] Sterne, *Letters*, i. 25. [60] Ibid. i. 33–4.
[61] *The Complete Letter-Writer*, 11th edn. (1767), 109.
[62] *The Complete Letter-Writer* 4th edn. (1757), 136.
[63] *The Complete Letter-Writer* 11th edn. (1767), 58. [64] Ibid. 90.

which disposes him to sympathize with, and share, the joy which it expresses; and he feels his heart, which with thought and care was before that shrunk and depressed, instantly expanded and elated.'[65] This imagined letter-writer used such imagery, and, in so doing, embraced the heart as a text, as well as the text as a heart. Miss Jones continued: 'I could tell you many Stories of the sensible Things; but of all the insensible ones upon this Occasion, your Lamp provoked me the most. To see that Creature... burn so prettily... has put me out of all Patience.'[66] Such descriptions not only served to indicate her affection for her absent friend, but also modeled for others how to write with feeling and how to transform things into sentiments (and back again). The interchangeability of things and sentiments both renders the things more meaningful and the sentiments more physical.

The ability to write with feeling was modeled for an ever more extensive range of readers and writers of letters. Adults and children, men and women, rich and poor, masters and servants: all of them wrote sensible letters in these manuals. Pamela, Richardson's sensible servant, had set the tone for the eighteenth century.[67] In so representing this range of writers of sensible letters, these books, consciously or not, made a political statement: all kinds of people could display sensibility, irrespective of class, gender, age, or even race. By the 1770s even Anglo-African authors wrote such model letters. One of the most remarkable—and yet unremarked—additions to successive editions of *The Complete Letter-Writer* was the inclusion, from 1778 on, of an exchange of letters between Ignatius Sancho, a former slave now living in England, and the sensible Laurence Sterne.[68] A few of these letters first appeared in print in 1775, in Sterne's collected letters. In 1782 Sancho would himself publish his own letters. Not only did Sancho model sensible letters (a political statement itself), but he did so specifically on the topic of the slave trade and the treatment of slaves in the West Indies.

Reprinted in a cheap and popular letter collection, Sancho's letters to Sterne evinced a clear anti-slavery ambition. Sancho identified himself as 'one of those People whom the Vulgar and Illiberal call Negroes'.[69] The main point of his letter was not only to thank Sterne for his literary productions, but also to ask Sterne to write more against slavery. In a classic claim of impressionable sensibility, Sancho praised Sterne's sermons as having 'touched me to the Heart'. He goes on to quote from them, particularly approving 'this very affecting Passage—"Consider how great a Part of our Species in all Ages down to this—have been trod under the

---

[65] Smith, *Theory of Moral Sentiments*, pt. I, sec. III, ch. III, p. 75.
[66] *The Complete Letter-Writer*, 11th edn. (1767), 90–1.
[67] As Janet Altman has pointed out, by contrast French manuals virtually never represented the working poor as letter-writers. Altman, 'Political Ideology', 113.
[68] Markman Ellis has adroitly analyzed this correspondence, and the complicated relationship that united the two men. Ellis, *The Politics of Sensibility*, ch 2.
[69] *The Complete Letter-Writer*, 16th edn. (1778), 249–53. Sancho's own letter is on pp. 249–50.

Feet of cruel and capricious Tyrants, who would neither hear their Cries, nor pity their Distresses.—Consider Slavery—what it is—how bitter a Draught—and how many Millions are made to drink of it."' Sterne had presented 'tyrants' as those who were unable to exercise sympathy or sensibility; he also expressed his own sympathy for those forced to endure such cruel treatment. Again in perfect sensible style, one which mirrored Sterne's own, Sancho applauded Sterne for being able to extend sympathy to slaves: 'Of all my favourite Authors, not one has drawn a Tear in favour of my miserable black Brethren—excepting yourself.' Having elegantly made use of the language of tears and sensibility, Sancho then exhorted Sterne to publicize the sufferings of West Indian slaves, since: 'That Subject handled in your striking Manner would ease the Yoke (perhaps) of Many.' Calling now upon Sterne's sympathy, Sancho requested, in a more deferential style, that he perform this 'Act of Charity': 'Grief (you pathetically observe) is eloquent: Figure to yourself their Attitudes; hear their supplicating Addresses! Alas! you cannot refuse.'[70]

It is significant that *The Complete Letter-Writer* included a letter from a 'black' from 1778 onwards, but it is even more significant that this man pleaded against slavery, using the tools of sensibility. He found a willing audience in the ever-sensible Sterne, who noted in his reply that he 'had been writing a tender Tale of the Sorrows of a friendless poor Negro-Girl, and my Eyes had scarce done smarting with it, when your Letter of Recommendation, in behalf of so many of her Brethren and Sisters, came to me.' The eighteenth century had already witnessed many a tale of the sorrows of a friendless girl, but to make that a 'Negro-Girl' rendered the political ambitions even clearer. Sterne went on to declare that her brethren are also his, and, while acknowledging differences in complexion, argued for the ultimate unity of the human family. Thus, making use of a domestic language of sensibility made perfect sense; all human beings should treat each other as sensible family members. Sancho was able to deploy vocabularies of sensibility in part because of an association between the two men, but his appeal was very specifically connected to his feelings and the feelings of slaves themselves. Languages of sensibility helped to try to eradicate differences, even as both men, with their complex languages of race and color, made such distinctions explicit.

Driven by a political ambition to demonstrate the humanity, sensibility, and patriotism of a formerly enslaved African, Sancho sent letters not only to Sterne but to many others, which were, like Sterne's, published posthumously by his family.[71] A 1772 letter from Sancho demonstrates this point: 'I thank you for your kindness to my poor black brethren—I flatter myself you will find them not ungrateful—they act uncommonly from their feelings:—I have observed a dog will love those who use him kindly—and surely, if so, negroes... my soul

---

[70] Ibid. 250.
[71] Ignatius Sancho, *Letters of the Late Ignatius Sancho, an African*, 2 vols. (London, 1782).

melts at kindness.'[72] Sancho responded to the notion that blacks were insensible, and incapable of feeling gratitude, and posited that the reverse was true. He did so very carefully. The reference to 'dogs' was responding to the idea of the alleged brute insensibility of Africans, a restrained way of making his point to an audience of whom he was unsure. In demonstrating his own ability to exhibit sensibility, and to inspire sympathy, Sancho made his points both explicitly and implicitly. As generally in his letters, there is a sense that Sancho represented an entire people, one whom he styles his 'brethren', that his soul melting with kindness stands in for the many slaves who experienced no such kindness.

The feeling heart, written out, thus became the dominant style for all kinds of printed model familiar letters in the later eighteenth century. But it also came to dominate familiar letters that were far more obscure. As Molly's complaint about her aunt's formal letter indicates, family letters often displayed a sensible style. Other types of family letters had dominated in the past; these included religious styles, courtly styles, and deferential styles. It is not that such styles disappeared; it is simply that, more and more often, family letters resonated with the idiom of sensibility and the feeling heart. Before delving into those sensible examples, it is helpful to have some sense of the kinds of languages they were replacing, or at least joining.

In the past, many family letters, such as those from the Winthrops, invoked God and Providence frequently. Family members were supposed to love each other, but such love was to be subordinate to the love of God. This hierarchy of affection was receding in the eighteenth century, as family members invoked their love for each other, with no necessary mention of God. It is not that languages of religion disappeared in the eighteenth century; plenty of letters invoked Providence, and its guidance. One ship's captain, Christopher Ellery, for instance, fretted over the likelihood of rebellion in 1775, in a letter sent from his ship back to Rhode Island: 'I see no prospect of Peace in our Borders, but however it may appear to so short sighted Mortals yet the whole is view'd by the all penetrating Eye of him, who will . . . rule all for the good of his grand Empire & Cause, under whose Protection & Guidance may you and I be ever found trusting.'[73] This type of invocation is typical of many letters, such as the 1767 letter from the Quaker Mary Wanton to her son Edward in Barbados. In an old-fashioned letter full of backward-facing 'e's, spelling that confounds the modern reader, and incessant invocations of God's protection rather than personal feeling, Wanton expressed her love and concern for her son, but with few of the flourishes and furbelows that would have endeared her letter to someone like Molly. Mary prayed that the Lord would keep Edward 'in perfect pees [peace]'. Noting that 'I coul rit [could write] abunden but I

---

[72] Ignatius Sancho, *Letters of the Late Ignatius Sancho, an African*, 45.
[73] Christopher Ellery to Mary Ellery, 'Montegobay Apr. 22d. 1775', Ellery Family Papers, Box 61, Folder 2, NHS.

must Leve the[e] to that devin ascxtence [divine assistance],' Mary desired that 'thes [this] may find the[e] as thay Leve us in helth.' Although she signed it 'thy tender & afectnet [affectionate] mother', the letter does not bloom with effusive emotion.[74] Religious invocations appeared often when the subject was death, a place where individuals met, never to part again. Still, this did not provide the language with the greatest force for requests or for conflict. Languages of God, Providence, and religion remained important, but they were not so paramount in many family letters as they had been earlier.

Courtly languages, too, while they remained in some force in courtship letters, receded in favor of idioms of sensibility. As a result of the eighteenth-century emphasis on women's sensibility, its relative novelty in this era has received comparatively little attention. Traditionally, men's letters in courtship and marriage actually resonated with much more feeling than women's did; this was, after all, a courtly tradition, in which eloquent men pursued silent, beautiful women, as Petrarch did his Laura. Laura was hardly expected to write back with her own love poems. In earlier times even wives were often shy of responding in kind to husbands' declarations of affections. What was new in the eighteenth century was the notion that women could display language of feeling to men, and might even exceed them in such sentiments and expressions. Men's languages in courtship still retained more force than women's, and men were the ones to instigate such epistolary connections (with all due permission of her family, of course). It was a novelty that many eighteenth-century sources emphasized women's naturally delicate sensations and innate ability to excel at writing sensible letters. In part, this reflected not just a shifting gender ideal, but also a shifting domestic one: that the domestic world was thought to be the one in which delicate sensations and attachments would emerge, in part because of its heterosocial and polishing nature. At the same time, women's ability to deploy languages of sensibility helped to reshape the nature of family negotiations.

Traditionally, wives, children, servants, and slaves were subordinate to the male head of the household, and, when they wrote to him, it was expected that they would often, if not exclusively, use letters of deference and petition. In the eighteenth century languages of sensibility and familiarity began to join languages of deference within and eventually outside the household. In the past, the most powerful assertions from subordinates were those, ironically, that relied most heavily on claims of powerlessness and submission. Such styles of negotiation, which tended to highlight the weakness and incapacity of the petitioner, depended on the generosity of the master. This was a strategy used within the household just as it was also used in a variety of other locales (a veteran seeking compensation for his services to the state, a commoner pleading

---

[74] Mary Wanton to Edward Wanton, 'Rhodisland th 4 mo 1767 14 day', Folder 6, Box 43, Wanton Family Papers, NHS.

for the intervention of the monarch). It was a form of negotiation that not only worked within hierarchies, but actually stressed them. While petitions occurred on an informal basis throughout the British-Atlantic world, they were also a legal form with a set tone and style. That some individuals needed to know how to *write* petitions is clear from their inclusion in various how-to manuals of the era, including a swathe of letter-writing manuals. So, *The Universal Letter-Writer* proclaimed in the introduction to a section on petitions: 'the language of Petitions should be at once the most humble and respectful imaginable... we shall here inform such of the most probable means of proving successful, as well as instruct any other persons of inferior station to address their superiors with propriety upon any emergency.'[75] This last line summarizes the imperatives at work here. 'Petitions' are intended for those of 'inferior station', providing them with a means of calling upon a 'superior' person for the fulfilling of a want. In this and in its American counterparts, a range of petitions, all making use of 'humble and respectful' language, then followed.[76]

These petitions were financial and political in nature, addressed not within the household but rather to groups, such as 'churchwardens and overseers of the parish' or the governor of New York (in an American edition).[77] In one example, William Harley, a cabinetmaker forced by incapacitating illness to stop work for six months, begged for help to support his wife and four children. Harley wrote to a 'charitable Gentleman': 'That being still in a languishing condition, and destitute of every manner of subsistence, he has ventured in great humility, to lay his distressed case before you.'[78] These imagined petitioners did not invoke the first-person, referring to themselves formally as 'your petitioner' and making use of a third-person diction. Their focus is on their helplessness as well as on the graciousness of those from whom they seek aid. They seek compassion, but not sympathy.[79] They emphasize neither feeling nor familiarity. Letters of deference continued in all kinds of cases outside of the household. But within the household other forms began to dominate.

By the later eighteenth century—if indeed not before this—it became highly unlikely that a wife would write in such a deferential style to her husband. Once upon a time this had not been the case. One scholar of late medieval women's letters, for instance, notes that: 'Formal and submissive modes of address in letters to husbands easily coexisted with sentiments of affection.'[80] Some of this had to do with conventions of epistolary and secretarial intervention, but some

---

[75] Thomas Cook, *The Universal Letter-Writer; or, New Art of Polite Correspondence* (Norwich, 1808), 130.

[76] Petition sections were much smaller. For example, the 1808 American edition of *The Universal Letter-Writer* had five pages of petitions, and 116 pages of letters. *The Universal Letter-Writer* (Philadelphia, 1808).

[77] *The Universal Letter-Writer* (Norwich), 135, 138.   [78] Ibid. 136.

[79] This distinction is elegantly made in Nicole Elaine Eustace, ' "Passion Is the Gale": Emotion and Power on the Eve of the American Revolution', Ph.D, University of Pennsylvania (2001).

[80] James Daybell, 'Introduction', in Daybell (ed.), *Early Modern Women's Letter Writing*, 10.

had to do with what was considered proper language for any kind of household subordinate, even a wife. This was connected with familiarity, as a mode of interaction, but it was also connected to the relative demise of petitioning and deferential languages in familiar relationships. By the eighteenth century wives and children still echoed claims to submission, but in a more muted way (as we shall see in ensuing chapters). They joined sensibility to deference.

Increasingly, family members invoked their feeling hearts, frequently as a way to call upon another family member to behave differently. Often these ends were affectionate (as when a wife wrote to ask her husband to come home soon). Just as Ignatius Sancho used sensible rhetoric to argue against slavery, so did subordinate family members deploy it to influence the behavior of others in the household, as we shall see in ensuing chapters. Writing with feeling was not about novel feelings, but instead about increasingly acceptable ways for people to express those feelings. Modeled in all kinds of print literature, families also had agency in influencing the adoption of such languages. In particular, family members often invoked their hearts, and images of its physical movement, in their letters. These invocations ensured the emergence of new styles in the family, ones that might ultimately be put in service of requests and negotiations. They also permitted individuals to display their education and cosmopolitanism, as well as their delicate sensations.

Training for the ministry in London in the 1770s, Thomas Coombe used this sensible style to reassure his family in Pennsylvania of his love, while at the same time displaying his learning, high-mindedness, and worldly wisdom. Writing to his sister Sally, Thomas declared: 'I very well know the Pleasure you receive from my Letters, by the Joy which I feel myself at the Arrival of a Ship from Philadelphia. The kind Expressions in your last Letter can only be exceeded by the same Heart which indited them—indeed, my Sally, they were painful to my Soul, in as much as they were expressive of too great Grief for my Absence.' Just as Evelina apologized for 'this cold, this inanimate letter, which will but ill express the feelings of the heart which indites it', so did Thomas mention his sister's heart 'inditing' her kind and affectionate letters.[81] It is hardly surprising that Thomas also recommended Henry Mackenzie's *The Man of Feeling* to his sister.[82] He signed off his own letter: 'My Heart bounds with Transport when I reflect that my Return will be the least Addition to the Happiness of our Family, which is the chief Object of my Prayers & Wishes.'[83] These kinds of claims demonstrated his affectionate sensibility, but they also

---

[81] 'Evelina to Miss Mirvan', 'Berry Hill, July 14', letter 26, ibid. iii. 233.

[82] Thomas Coombe noted: 'Among my books, you will find one entitled the "Man of feeling," in the reading which, you will find a noble entertainment. It possesses all the humanity, & the sentiment of Sterne, without his too notorious indelicacy. Read it, & let me have your opinion of it, when I see you.' Thomas Coombe to Sally Coombe, 'London Sepr 26, 1771', Thomas Coombe Papers, HSP.

[83] Thomas Coombe to Sally Coombe, 'London Feb: 24/[17]69', ibid.

served to reassure his family that his expensive education was not going to waste. They also provided a way for a patronizing older brother to lord it over a younger sister back home.

Thomas Coombe's heart was hardly the only one to leap around in familiar letters of the era. Margaret Cowper, daughter of a Loyalist who moved throughout the British-Atlantic world (from Georgia to Britain to Jamaica), prized sensibility in her many letters. The dislocations of her life seem to have led her to cling ever more tenaciously to sensible styles, using them in an attempt to maintain ties imperiled by revolution and exile. Also, as with Thomas Coombe, they functioned to demonstrate educational attainment, cosmopolitanism, and delicacy. Margaret used the heart metaphor in order to express her longing to be with her cousin and sister, as well as her frustration at being left behind. In one example, Margaret transformed herself from an irritated girl kept at home by a bad cold into a divided presence, separated from her own heart: 'My Heart has played Truant my Dear Girls ever since you left us, it followed you to Town . . . has taken up its abode there, & keep it quietly & peacably at this Cottage I cannot . . . I never felt more disposed to repine at sickness.'[84] In a later letter from Bristol to her cousin, she bewailed her separation from a new friend, Miss Fitzgerald: 'I have half left my heart behind me . . . to think of seeing those who have <u>attracted</u> us for the last time is exceedingly painful.'[85] Repeatedly, over decades, Margaret emphasized a heart so very full of feeling that sometimes it nearly took on a life of its own. Like the fictional 'Miss J' who had so lamented her separation from Lady ____ and Miss L, so too did Margaret lament her absence from Eliza and Miss Fitzgerald, and its deplorable effects on her heart.

Other letter-writers also invoked hearts and kisses, thus displaying their delicacy, education, and desire to reinforce connections. Writing from New Jersey in the 1790s, to her cousin, Sophia Brown declared, in classic style, 'as I am truly sensible that your feeling heart will sympathize with me in my joy I must tell you I have just received letters from my Husband that inform me he is now on his passage home'.[86] She encouraged her mother-in-law, to whom she wrote not to be overcome by her own 'feeling heart': 'my beloved Mama, keep up your spirits that no more sorrow may distress thy feeling heart.'[87] She praised other friends for their 'benevolent hearts', even as she invoked her own feeling one: 'Our good & kind friend Mrs Pinder, how my heart feels for her.'[88] Mary Malbone envisioned seeing her family again: 'Oh my Mamma! . . . My heart's in my mouth at seeing the dear old Lady take off her spectacle & come forward

---

[84] Margaret Cowper to Eliza McQueen and Mary Anne Cowper, 'Friday Night [October 1796]', Mackay–Stiles Papers, SHC.
[85] Margaret Cowper to Eliza McQueen Mackay, 'Gloucester Sept 26 1809', ibid.
[86] Susanna Brown to Cousin, undated, Brown Family Papers, NYHS.
[87] Sophia Brown to Susanna Brown, 'Perth Amboy August 1st 1791', ibid.
[88] Sophia W. Brown to Susanna Brown, 'Perth Amboy April 21st 1796', and Sophia Brown to Susanna Brown, 'Perth Amboy Oct 31st 1795', ibid.

smiling, to meet me, the deuce take the paltry tears, they flow so fast.'[89] Writing to her son, one mother, Mary Butler, felt that knowing that his father, Pierce, was also sending a letter would 'make your little heart rejoice'.[90] One woman hoped her brother had recovered from illness: 'Poor fellow how grieved I was at the account of your illness, absence from a beloved object is much more supportable, when we are assured things go on prosperously.' She continued: 'had I known... you were so ill, how should I have wished to have annihilated space, and to have thrown myself in a moment in your arms, how should I have wished to have been at your bed side, to have kissed your burning cheek, & soothed you into slumbers.'[91] These women thus demonstrated their continued affection, as well as their sensibility and education.

Men could and did exchange letters of sensibility, especially in moments of domestic tragedy, emphasizing friendship but also borrowing shared vocabularies of grief and feeling. When the oldest son of Robert Mackay died, his friend William Mein opened a letter alerting Robert to this terrible news: 'My hand shakes my Pen trembles And I want language to impart to you My feelings.' Although he may have struggled to find 'language' adequate to this tragedy, the one he fell back on was that of sensibility, in words reminiscent of Sterne and others. With these physical manifestations of shared grief made clear, William went on to mourn with Robert: 'Would to God I could take you by the hand & mingle my Tears with yours for the Loss (how shall I name it) of your oldest & Darling Son.'[92] Mein here invoked the language of shared physicality and also of tears in order to convey news that was unspeakably bad. It was a sign of his familiarity with the Mackay family that he was able to do so. When John Brownrigg received news in Dublin of the death of his sister in North Carolina, he declaimed: 'I am almost overcome with grief so that I am hardly able to compose myself to write.'[93] In another letter he similarly exclaimed: 'penn can't Describe the Shock and agonie I was in at the Loss of so sincere and affectionate a Sister and Friend.'[94]

Still, while men performed sensibility for each other, they more frequently did so in the presence of a woman and in domestic settings. One man wrote his cousin: 'How often my dear Sophia, do we wish we could all live in the same Country. It seems hard to be deprived of the dearest friend we have on Earth.

[89] Mary Malbone Chilcott to John Malbone, 'Augusta May 14th 1770', Malbone–Hunter Papers, Folder 8, Box 22, NHS.
[90] Mary Butler to Thomas Butler, 'New York August ye 2d 1787', Pierce Butler Letter Collection, Add. Mss. 16603, BL.
[91] D. Hunter to William Hunter, 'Hammersmith Mall June 4th 1798', Malbone–Hunter Papers, Folder 8, Box 22, NHS.
[92] William Mein to Robert Mackay, '[Savannah, October 1 1804]', in Hartridge (ed.), *The Letters of Robert Mackay*, 37–8.
[93] John Brownrigg to Thomas Brownrigg, 'Dublin Novbr 20th 1791', Brownrigg Family Papers, SHC.
[94] John Brownrigg to Thomas Brownrigg, 'Dublin Sepbr 18th—1789', ibid.

My Eyes fill with tears. God bless you.'[95] Here is how one young man in London described receiving a letter from his mother in Virginia: 'how shall I describe my feelings, when . . . the Postman surprised me with the sight of my Mother's handwriting while preparing a mess of cold beef & potatoes, my appetite, before keen, even in an instant sated, & while perusing it eagerly three times, fits of joy & an involuntary flow of tears, alternately succeeded.'[96] In 1786 James Stevens wrote to his daughter that he was 'a Father whose heart is fill'd with the most tender emotions for the future happyness of his dear Child'.[97] Robert Mackay informed his wife in 1801 that: 'I assure you my dear Eliza I feel your absence most forcibly . . . —the house appears vacant & lost without you—no cheering smile to welcome me home when I return from the labours of the day, nobody to hearken to & soothe ones little cares—hasten to return my dear Girl.'[98] His reference to the house once again suggests that physical objects could conjure up certain sentimental responses. It was also an idealization of domestic bliss and a kind of invocation of burgeoning separate spheres: his 'labour' but her soothing. In this he joined Thomas Jefferson and John Adams, among others, who invoked their domestic happiness, thus constructing separations between tough public worlds and reassuring private ones. This kind of idealization served to reinforce the notion that women's role was to soothe the men who went into the wide world of work and worry.

Another husband, Christopher Ellery, used these kinds of vocabularies to stress his continued affection, and also to reassure his wife Mary, left in Rhode Island, of his continued virtue as he plied the Atlantic and Caribbean as a ship's captain in the 1760s and 1770s. Receiving a letter from his wife created 'so rapturous a sensation', that he hoped his letters did the same for her.[99] Here is his description of receiving such a line from her:

As I was coming to this Port a Brig [carrying your letter] had just come too . . . upon which such an Agitation of Mind, or rather such an entire stagnation of the Blood at the Heart seiz'd me, as can't be expressed, 'till I heard you were all well, and then, O then, what a quick transition what a flash like the Sun breakg. thro the thickest Cloud, after a long Absence from the Earth—so the Blood flowed to different parts, and warm'd and animated the before Cold almost Lifeless parts—And my Joy was heightned when I received your Letter[100]

---

[95] Patrick Brown to Sophia Waterhouse Brown, 'Nassau N.P. 24th Octr 1807', John Brown Family Papers, NYHS.

[96] Severn Eyre to Littleton, 'London 15th Jany. 1785', Severn Eyre Journal, 1785 (typescript copy), VHS.

[97] James Stevens to Anne Oliver Stevens, 'Clover Forest Sunday 22d April 1786', Stevens Family Papers, VHS.

[98] Robert Mackay to Eliza McQueen Mackay, 'Savannah 22nd. June 180[1]', in Hartridge (ed.), *The Letters of Robert Mackay*, 31–2.

[99] Christopher Ellery to Mary Ellery, 'Montegobay 8th April 1765', Ellery Family Papers, Box 62, Folder 2, NHS.

[100] Christopher Ellery to Mary Ellery, 'Montegobay Decr. 15t. 1774', ibid.

Elsewhere, he was pleased that his own letters 'were receiv'd with a Thankfull heart... They came from a true Heart and a tender one, and answered the End proposed to give you the most agreeable Sensation.'[101] Thinking upon his children, he confided at the end of another letter: 'O those little Pledges of our Love, I can say no more, my Bosom swells, and my Eyes are bursting with Tears, at the Thought of their future Welfare, and their present Danger... In daily expectation of a Line of Comfort from you from the overflowing of your Love convey a stream that may rejoice Y[ou]r. Affect[ionate] Husband.'[102]

A brief case study of one man's sensible letters will serve to sketch out the various ends such letters could serve. We have already encountered Pierce Butler, an Irish immigrant turned plantation-owner, who also served as delegate from South Carolina at the Constitutional Convention, and as senator from South Carolina. Despite these patriotic credentials, Pierce sent his only son Thomas to England for his education. While Pierce wrestled with his part in shaping a new United States, attending the Constitutional Convention 'to form a stronger Constitution', he sent his son to another family, and another country, in order to form the boy's constitution and character.[103] His letters to his son, but more particularly to his son's tutor, Weeden Butler (apparently no relation), show how such letters worked to display his continued affections as well as his sensibility, in the face of evidence to the contrary. Pierce Butler was a slave-owner, living on a rural plantation in South Carolina; he notably defended slavery in the Constitutional Convention. He also willingly sent his only son to England—the late enemy of American Patriots—at considerable cost to himself.

Pierce Butler had an investment in demonstrating that he was not a vicious slave-owner, an American rube, or an unfeeling parent. Mastering sensible rhetoric allowed him to perform the parts of a caring, cultivated gentleman and loving family man. On hearing of Weeden's illness, he declared that: 'My heart my Dear Sir, has palpitated for You... I can not express to You my feelings.'[104] When he did not receive a letter from his son, he complained half-jokingly: 'If the Young Rogue knew the feelings of my heart towards Him, He would not be inattentive to anything that could give me pleasure.'[105] When Pierce received good news from his son's English tutor, he thanked him, in terms reminiscent of novels such as *Evelina*: 'Your account of my dear Boy is heart-gratifying. It is to my drooping Spirits, and fatigued mind, as the "cooling brook to the

---

[101] Christopher Ellery to Mary Ellery, undated, ibid.
[102] Christopher Ellery to Mary Ellery, undated, ibid.
[103] Pierce Butler to Weeden Butler, 'Charleston ye 18th of February 1786', Pierce Butler Letter Collection, Add. Mss. 16603, BL. For further biographical and political information on this family, see Bell, *Major Butler's Legacy*, esp. ch. 4.
[104] Pierce Butler to Weeden Butler, 'Philadelphia Decbr. ye 14th 1791', Pierce Butler Letter Collection, Add. Mss. 16603, BL.
[105] Pierce Butler to Weeden Butler, 'Amsterdam August ye 30th. 1785', ibid.

hunted Deer"—It is doubly comforting coming from You who are truth and sincerity—coming from any other quarter I might place it to politeness and a disposition to please; but I put it down as your real opinion, as such I have recorded it on the tablet of my heart.'[106] Just like Evelina's guardian, Villars, Pierce Butler made his heart a tablet upon which a true account of his dear child could be engraved. Such imagery neatly, if slightly oddly, conflates the conversions between heart and text, making the heart a text itself, but also allowing that feeling (and truthful) texts could gratify the heart.

Pierce emphasized his fatherly feelings. When he had not received a letter for some time, he invoked sympathy and sensibility to complain: 'Knowing as I do the fineness of Your feelings, I am sure You are not indifferent to mine—to the anxious throbbings of the heart of a fond Father... My mind forebodes some unpleasant tidings from You! I am distressd!'[107] When he finally received news, he apologized for his anxiety and for his 'feminine feelings'.[108] Still, such did not prevent further expressions of 'feminine' sensibility, as when, that same year, he proclaimed: 'my pen will not do justice to the emotions of my breast; and, with all my endeavours, but faintly make known my sense of Your kindness—Your friendship to me, in your Paternal Attention to my Son—I thank You!—The silent tear of gratitude expresses much.'[109] Later, he exclaimed that 'while I express my thanks the tear of gratitude wets my papers... and the Blood thrill[s] in my veins'.[110] That Pierce's sensibility appealed to Weeden is demonstrated in the tutor's few surviving letters. When Weeden received a letter from Thomas, who had by 1796 returned to the United States, he informed Pierce: 'His grateful Letter was the best Poultice to my Heart[,] was received with Sensations better to be imagined than capable of my Expression.'[111] That the son, Thomas, also learned this language is clear from one of his letters, in which he regretted his inability to 'imitate Sterne' (even as he claimed that Sterne used too many dashes in his writing).[112]

The death of Pierce's wife, Mary, in 1790 caused something of a predicament, one that allowed Pierce ultimately to decide that he was truly sensible. When Mary lay on her deathbed in 1790, his letters to London conveyed his horror: 'It is impossible my Dear Sir, to convey to You the feelings of my mind... My Dearest Wife, the friend of my bosom, the partner of my sufferings and losses in a long Civil War, is in that painful state... When I call to mind Her many Virtues I cling to Her! I fondly wish to hold Her back!... Great God! how shall I bear the separation! I need the hand of friendship to pour balm in to

---

[106] Pierce Butler to Weeden Butler, 'Charleston ye 30th of Novr [1786]', ibid.
[107] Pierce Butler to Weeden Butler, 'Charleston February ye 8th. 1789', ibid.
[108] Pierce Butler to Weeden Butler, 'MaryVille Sunday ye 15th. of March 1789', ibid.
[109] Pierce Butler to Weeden Butler, 'New York June ye. 21st. 1789', ibid.
[110] Pierce Butler to Weeden Butler, 'Philadelphia September ye 2d 1792', ibid.
[111] Weeden Butler to Pierce Butler, 'Chelsea 19th January 1796', ibid.
[112] Thomas Butler to Weeden Butler, 'Philadelphia, Sepr. 9th 1796', ibid.

my afflicted breast.'[113] Here again is the language of physical suffering, and the shared language of grief, expressed between men. When she died, Pierce later related, he fell into 'a stupor', at which:

> I wondered at myself. I almost began to think I had no sensibility—that I was a monster of ingratitude. I detested my own breast, I was unable to assign to myself a cause, knowing that from my Youth Upwards I had not been insensible to the distress even of a Stranger. Was I then to be indifferent to such a loss! In a little time I awakened to a full sense of my situation. I felt the weight of the stroke. I feel it still severely.

This crisis provoked him to worry that he was an insensible brute. Pierce echoed one of his own earlier letters, in which he had derided slaves as 'strangers to the feelings of gratitude'.[114] Was he perhaps concerned that his life on the plantation was having deleterious effects on his character? Emphasizing the restoration of his full sense, he could thus maintain his status as a sensible family man. Using the language of sensibility transported him from the questionable choices of slavery, in which he was immersed, into an arena of shared sensibility and refinement. Returned to the rightful state of sensibility, Pierce went on to lament the loss of his wife, ending finally by noting: 'My breast is too full for utterance.' He also thanked the tutor for his sympathetic letters to the Butler family: 'the feeling sentiments, prove in lively colours the goodness of the heart that dictated them. Even my daughters, tho' at a distance, benefit from your cultivated Mind, Your feeling breast.'[115] Cultivation and feeling could traverse distance.

Claims of sensibility allowed Pierce Butler to deny that being part of a world of slavery had affected his character as a man of feeling; they also allowed him to make statements about current politics. In 1794 he argued for the lenient treatment of the Whiskey rebels. He proclaimed: 'there are among Us a few bad Men who wished to proceed to extremities at Once and to draw the Sword of Civil discord for a small aggression; against a handful of Men not sensible of doing wrong—may such unfeeling blood thirsty Scoundrells be banishd [from] Society!'[116] 'Unfeelingness', again, was condemned as a personal and a political state. Pierce, by contrast, demonstrated his sensibility in personal as well as political realms. Expressing his horror at events in France in 1793, he noted: 'From French affairs I turn my mind as a benevolent Man turns his Eyes, from a distress he Can neither prevent nor relieve.'[117] Later, he lamented: 'the situation of France is to a feeling mind painfull to an extreme.'[118] A sensible man felt horror at the distresses of the French, just as he did at the distresses of other families or his own.

---

113 Pierce Butler to Weeden Butler, 'N Y October Ye 6th. 1790', ibid.
114 Pierce Butler to Weeden Butler, 'So Carolina July ye 18th. 1788', ibid.
115 Pierce Butler to Weeden Butler, 'Philadelphia March the 5th. 1791', ibid.
116 Pierce Butler to Weeden Butler, 'Philadelphia September ye 1st. 1794', ibid.
117 Pierce Butler to Weeden Butler, 'Philadelphia November ye 1st. 1793', ibid.
118 Pierce Butler to Weeden Butler, 'Philadelphia December ye. 7th. 1793', ibid.

These examples indicate the ways in which sensibility became a dominant tone of family letters. They demonstrate that these letters did considerable work, connecting individuals but also allowing them to display delicacy, education, cosmopolitanism, and virtue. They also indicate the agency of women, as both writers and recipients of letters. Sensible rhetoric could be equally powerful outside the family. It began to appear, albeit hesitantly, in letters even from the enslaved. Many servants and slaves continued to have recourse to deferential and petitioning languages in the household. Some domestic letters read much as petitions, as in a letter from Jamaica in the 1770s, written on behalf of some slave children. Nathaniel Pierce, who seems to have been a slave or perhaps a freedman, wrote to his absentee master, Roger Hope Elletson, hoping to buy his children out of slavery. Before departing Jamaica, Roger had told Nathaniel that he could not sell the children, but he would allow them to remain in school. Despite these assurances, once his master had left, the plantation manager had decided to hire the children out for wages. Nathaniel thus used the letter form to implore his master to let him buy the children, as Roger Elletson had promised. Nathaniel noted that it would be good deed to himself and to Diana, a trusted house slave and mother of these children, to allow them this liberty. He sought to win pity by invoking his and Diana's infirmity, asserting: 'As I am grown weak & Criple it will be doing a deed of Charity for me allso. Diana is Grown Sick & Weak.' In the deferential language typical of a petitioner, Nathaniel went on to 'beg your Honour will Excuse the Liberty of Troubleing you . . . I shall be grately, Oblidged to your Honour for an Answer.'[119] Conspicuously absent in this letter is any mention of his tender affections for his children, his fidelity and attachment to Roger, or of his own feelings. Instead, he invokes his need for 'charity', not sympathy.[120] It is not clear where Nathaniel had learned this form, nor is it clear whether his letter was successful. Nonetheless, he had learned to make use of petitioning language, and this style remained one way in which subordinates could seek to alter the behavior of those in a superior position of authority.

His wife, Diana Pierce, also used this kind of petitioning rhetoric in her letter from Jamaica to her mistress in England in 1777. It is highly unusual that Diana, almost certainly an Afro-Caribbean slave, wrote such a letter at all; indeed, it is one of the earliest such letters that exists. She had spent time with the Elletson family in England, and so presumably learned how to write letters there. Her

[119] Nathaniel Pierce to Roger Hope Elletson, 'Liguanea August 13th 1774', STB 25/18, Brydges Correspondence, Stowe Collection, HL.

[120] Nathaniel Pierce to Roger Hope Elletson, 'Liguanea August 13th 1774', ibid. The fact that Nathaniel had a surname implies he might have been a freed man. Still, his status was considerably below that of Roger Elletson, and he was petitioning on behalf of his children who were in slavery on the Elletson estate. In a letter from a manager of the Elletson estates in 1769 there is a mention of the 'house Negroes' and the statement 'Diana's Children & Peirce are well'. Joseph Stewart to Roger Hope Elletson, undated [Oct./Nov. 1769], Elletson Letterbooks, Volume 1, Brydges Correspondence, Stowe Collection, HL.

script is polished, and her address formulaic. It is also highly deferential. While she 'condoles' with her mistress for the loss of her husband, she does so 'in ye most submissive Manner'. The letter asked for rum and sugar from the estate, as well as clothes and shoes from England, as 'I want to goe to Church to serve my God Every Sunday'.[121] Such languages of deference hardly disappeared in the late eighteenth century, and they continued to be a useful resource for numerous individuals.

Nevertheless, in domestic and other contexts they were increasingly joined by a different form of supplication, one that exploited newer ideals of sensibility and sympathy. This was a different style from that of the simple petitioner, although it too could depend on claims of weakness. It was no third-person style. Instead, it was all about the first-person, and that person's feelings. Some in this period managed to graft sensible languages onto deferential ones, in ways that still begged assistance from a powerful master, but that also gestured towards distress, sympathy, and feeling. This is the case in the letter of one Bahamian slave, Caesar Brown, who, like Nathaniel Pierce, sought to persuade his master to honor a promise of freedom earlier made. John and Susannah Brown had apparently pledged that on their deaths they would free Caesar Brown, but they failed to honor this vow. Caesar thus took up his pen to ask their heir and daughter-in-law, Sophia, to lower his valuation price that he might buy his freedom. Caesar opened the letter first by offering condolence for the death of his late mistress, 'which I regret most sincerely'. Like Nathaniel Pierce, Caesar Brown invoked the strength of the promise made, but, unlike Nathaniel, he also invoked his sentiments. He noted: 'you... know with what Zeal & fidelity I have served him and his wife, and you must be convinced of my attachment.' He invoked the deference expected, acknowledging that he was 'intruding' and 'begging' Sophia to honor the family promise, in part because of his long and faithful service. However, he also reminded her of his 'regret' and 'attachment' to the family, a newer, more sentimental language.[122] This is not a letter written in as sensible style as Ignatius Sancho's, but it did invoke languages of sensibility, albeit in a highly deferential way.

Enslaved men seeking freedom deployed sensible languages in personal letters and also in wider arenas. Invocations of 'family feeling' appeared in petitions to the Massachusetts Assembly to end slavery in the 1770s. These petitions show the enduring power of deferential appeals to charity and humanity. They also begin to demonstrate the creeping influence of 'rights talk' and appeals to liberty, perhaps attributable in part to the American Revolution. But in general this emphasis on liberty and rights has obscured an equally powerful trend

---

[121] Diana Pierce (or Dianna Pierse) to Anna Eliza Elletson, 'April ye 1.—1777—Hope Estate', Brydges Correspondence, Stowe Collection, HL.

[122] Caesar Brown to Sophia Waterhouse Brown, 'Nassau N[ew] P[rovidence] May 30th 1800', Brown Family Papers, NYHS.

in these petitions: the emphasis on sensibility and domesticity. The first such petition, from 1773, made use of traditional petitioning language, with appeals to charity and Christianity rather than to feelings and sympathy. The petitioners did remind the Assembly: 'We have no Wives! No Children!... But we have a Father in Heaven.' These petitioners mentioned the family, as well as their unhappiness, but they did not dwell on their sufferings in having their families taken from them.[123]

By contrast, later petitions overflow with claims to sensible suffering and fractured families. A 1774 petition began with a mention of 'naturel right to our freedoms', which had not been willingly forfeited 'by aney compact or agreement whatsoever'. But, it went on:

We were unjustly dragged by the cruel hand of power from our dearest friends and sum of us stolen from the bosoms of our tender Parents.... Thus we are deprived of every thing that hath a tendency to make life even tolerable, the endearing ties of husband and wife we are strangers to... Our children are also taken from us by force and sent maney miles from us wear we seldom or ever see them there being made slaves of for Life which sumtimes is vere short by Reson of Being dragged from their mothers Breest[124]

Such a set of claims emphasized domestic sentiment in order to highlight the familial and sensible heartache endured by slaves. This is a language different from an appeal to rights, but an equally important one. Emphasizing their own sensibility, they also implied the insensibility in the willingness of masters and mistresses to separate husbands and wives, parents and children. To rip the child from the mother's breast, in a transatlantic culture in which breastfeeding had taken on considerable cultural capital as a key symbol of the sentimental mother in the family, was the height of cruelty.[125] Petitioners in 1777 used similar expressions: 'wher Unjustly Dragged by the hand of cruel Power and their Derest friends and sum of them Even torn from the Embraces of their tender Parents... in Defiance of all the tender feelings of humanity.'[126] These were public political petitions made to the Massachusetts Assembly. Yet the invocations of 'Derest friends', 'tender Parents', and 'all the tender feelings of humanity' was a language more consonant with emerging idioms of sensibility, as well as familiarity. By invoking the sufferings of slaves torn from family and country, it emphasized that they, too, shared the 'natural sensibility'.

---

[123] Felix's Petition (1773), in Herbert Aptheker (ed.), *A Documentary History of the Negro People in the United States* (New York: Citadel Press, 1951), 6–7.

[124] Petition, 'May 25 1774', in ibid. 8–9.

[125] On the cultural import of breast-feeding in the eighteenth century, see Londa Schiebinger, 'Why Mammals Are Called Mammals: Gender Politics in Eighteenth-Century Natural History', *American Historical Review*, 98 (1993), 382–411, and Ruth Perry, 'Colonizing the Breast: Sexuality and Maternity in Eighteenth-Century England', *Journal of the History of Sexuality*, 2 (1991), 204–23.

[126] Petition, 'January 13, 1777', in Aptheker, *A Documentary History*, 9–10.

Other political writings of the period did much the same, sometimes in explicitly epistolary form. Such was the case with John Dickinson's *Letters from a Farmer in Pennsylvania, To the Inhabitants of the British Colonies*. In language we have now come to recognize, here is how he opened his third letter, challenging British authority in the colonies, in the wake of the Stamp Act:

My dear COUNTRYMEN,
I rejoice to find that my two former letters to you, have been generally received with so much favor by such of you, whose sentiments I have had an opportunity of knowing. Could you look into my heart, you would instantly perceive a zealous attachment to your interests and a lively resentment of every insult and injury offered to you, to be the motives that have engaged me to address you.[127]

Here, then, is language of sensible attachments, in letter form. Elsewhere, Dickinson noted his desire to affect the sensations of the colonists: 'So should not any honest man suppress his sentiments, concerning freedom, however small their influence is likely to be. Perhaps he "may touch some wheel" that will have an effect greater than he could reasonably expect.'[128] Hopeful that he might alter the sentiments of others, here was the belief that his letters might resonate powerfully across a whole people.

This language indeed 'touched the wheel', because so many men and women, on both sides of the Atlantic, were already primed for such feeling sensations. Looking at family letters of this era makes clear that it is not simply that families borrowed political language (as Abigail Adams did, when she exhorted her husband to 'remember the Ladies'), but that political writers, in all kinds of realms, used domestic, familiar, and sensible languages in their own texts. There is no precise cause and effect, and of course political languages also influenced domestic situations. But at least some of the impetus for the use of this language of familiar sensibility, of invocations of tender feelings and the attachments of the heart, came from the family itself.

This concatenation demonstrates again the intermingling of what have been termed private and public worlds. Individuals in circumstances domestic, economic, and political pressed claims increasingly in terms of affection and attachment, invoking family feeling. This language could have efficacy in certain situations, but it often met with little reward, in families, communities, or nations. It did become a political language in both families and nations, and it could influence behavior sometimes. It is hard to know whether letters from Nathaniel Pierce or Caesar Brown resulted in freedom for slaves; likewise, it took several years and considerable legal agitation to bring freedom to slaves in Massachusetts. However, this kind of language provided another arrow in a

---

[127] John Dickinson, *Letters from a Farmer in Pennsylvania, To the Inhabitants of the British Colonies* (Philadelphia, 1768), letter 3, p. 14.
[128] Ibid., letter 1, p. 4.

quiver of means of persuasion. Its flight was halted, though, in situations where it conflicted with economic and long-term prospects. If politics and assemblies could be filled with feeling hearts and tender attachments, then families could equally be filled with cold calculation and long-term group strategies in which individuals suffered. It is this area to which we now turn.

4
Credit in Life and Letters

Seeing his father's familiar handwriting on a letter, young Warner Lewis Wormeley, in London in 1801, would probably not have felt his heart leap, nor would it have provoked tears of joy. It would instead have been likely to cause squirming discomfiture. Here is what he would have opened it to find: 'I very much fear your usual idleness and indisposition to your literary pursuits still attend you . . . you ought to have known better than to employ your time so unprofitably, especially as you have lost so much of it, & are for a boy of your age remarkably ignorant—nothing but assiduity and labour can make amends for this ignorance and loss of time.' So began the first surviving letter from Ralph Wormeley, in Virginia, to his son. Fretful about whether his son was succeeding in obtaining the education for which his father was paying dearly, Ralph instigated a course of letter-writing designed to impress upon the boy that he had better work hard and learn how to prosper.

The opening of this letter makes Ralph Wormeley seem a classic patriarch, anxious over his son's behavior, castigating him for idleness, and ordering him to behave differently. But Ralph then announced that he preferred to have Warner 'led by silken cords, not driven, induced, not compelled'. Crafting his own letters into such affectionate 'silken cords', Ralph explicitly pointed to the horrors of parental tyranny, much as those who had revolted against patriarchal authority were expected to do. This is the language we might expect of a post-Revolutionary paternalistic father, especially a reader of novels such as *The Infidel Father*.[1] Yet then he continued the letter: 'However, if gentle methods and mild parental exhortation will not avail, contrary to my nature, other means must be adopted, and if these fail, you will repent of your conduct all days of your life—I will leave my estate to my daughters.'[2] Ralph thus used threats of disinheritance to bolster his authority, thereby seeming more like an old-style patriarch than a new-style paternalist. Terms such as patriarch or paternalist ultimately do little to further the analysis of Ralph's letter. One historian has pointed out, rightly, that the

---

[1] Ralph wrote his son: 'I would recommend to your perusal? the "Infidel Father", (called a novel).' Ralph Wormeley to Warner Wormely, 'Rosegill 16th Novr. 1803', Mss1/W8945/a-10, Wormeley Family Papers, 1791–1952, VHS.

[2] Ralph Wormeley to Warner Lewis Wormely, 'Rosegill 29 June 1801', Mss1/W8945/a-1, ibid.

same man could act like a patriarch in some settings but a paternalist in others.[3] But here is a man acting as both patriarch and paternalist in the same letter to the same person in the same situation. These terms simply do not help to make sense of this letter.

It is more helpful to attend carefully to the concerns raised here. While Ralph saw his letters as highly personal to their situation, in fact the kind of language used here appears repeatedly in letters from fathers from all kinds of areas in the British-Atlantic world. Its points—about idleness, the failure to obtain literary skills, the unprofitability of how his son spent his time, the need to balance ledgers by paying for loss of time with assiduity—were all themes resonating through many letters from fathers. One historian has identified similar exhortations in Virginia letters, arguing that child-rearing in Virginia created habits of indolence that did not square with desires for independence.[4] Yet such letters hardly came only from Virginia—they were also written from New England, the mid-Atlantic, other parts of the South, the British Caribbean, Scotland, and England. Numerous fathers worried incessantly over the possible idleness and extravagance of sons.

Sensibility became a dominant tone in family letters, but other tones, related to credit and industry, also prevailed. Looking at this second style can reveal much about the family and the Atlantic world. The family had agency in shaping not only cultures of sensibility, but also economic cultures of credit, ones upon which the very creation and maintenance of the Atlantic world depended. After all, while numerous sensible familiar letters crossed the Atlantic, so did even more business ones (though these categories were hardly mutually exclusive). Although it has long been recognized that families were a central financial entity in this period, few have paid attention to the ways that families in their letters shaped Atlantic cultures of credit, the topic of this chapter.[5] In order to understand the family's role in teaching credit in letters, it is necessary first to understand the general significance of the culture of credit, especially for men, in the eighteenth century. It is also vital to comprehend the ways that Atlantic movements and trade served not only to increase the importance of that culture of credit, but

---

[3] Kathleen Brown has concluded that 'paternalism—in the guise of the ideal of domestic tranquility—[was] . . . one face of patriarchy, not a softer replacement of it'. Kathleen M. Brown, *Good Wives, Nasty Wenches, and Anxious Patriarchs: Gender, Race, and Power in Colonial Virginia* (Chapel Hill, NC: University of North Carolina for the Institute of Early American History and Culture for the University of North Carolina Press, 1996), 366.

[4] Lewis, *Pursuit of Happiness*, ch. 4.

[5] One important exception is Peter Mathias, who argues persuasively that 'the family matrix was . . . central to the operation of business'. Mathias points out that families were critical in ameliorating the risks of the early modern economy. He also maintains that: 'The word "friend" widely in use in the eighteenth century when referring to a trusted personal acquaintance or collaborator in business . . . is resonant with implications of personal trust and the obligations which friendship entailed . . . Personal and business considerations would not be separated.' Peter Mathias, 'Risk, Credit and Kinship in Early Modern Enterprise', in McCusker and Morgan (eds.), *The Early Modern Atlantic Economy*, 15–35, at 16, 30.

also to imperil it. This chapter also assesses how families taught epistolary values of credit across the Atlantic, and the ways that fathers in particular nurtured them in sons, for whom credit was all-important to success in uncertain Atlantic economies.

Recovering the ways in which families inculcated credit alters unsatisfying and ultimately untenable divisions between market values and family values, demands a restructuring of distinctions between public and private, and explodes once and for all any thought that modern families functioned as a haven in a heartless world.[6] As several historians have pointed out, credit was an issue that transcended the realm of economics.[7] Still, credit's importance as a domestic source of authority, one instilled by a particular style of monitoring in the family, has yet to be understood fully. Credit was as much a domestic issue as it was a political and national one. A nation's credit depended on the accumulated credit of its households and its members, and ruin terrified politicians as much as it did fathers. Ruin in the family needed to be averted not only to preserve the welfare of the individual and the family, but also to preserve the welfare of the nation. Personal choices resonated powerfully in much larger realms. As one English tract put it, 'the want of oeconomy, so little attended to in the education of our youth, saps the integrity, and undermines the honour of individuals, carries... the most insupportable distresses into private families'. But it did not stop there: 'it moves on, canker-like, to the whole body, and introduces venality and corruption into a whole nation.'[8]

---

[6] It thus amplifies arguments made in Margaret R. Hunt, *The Middling Sort: Commerce, Gender, and the Family in England, 1680–1780* (Berkeley: University of California Press, 1996).

[7] For England, see Julian Hoppit, *Risk and Failure in English Business, 1700–1800* (Cambridge: Cambridge University Press, 1987); Craig Muldrew, *The Economy of Obligation: The Culture of Credit and Social Relations in Early Modern England*, ed. Rab Houston, Edward Muir, and Bob Scribner, Early Modern History: Society and Culture (Basingstoke: Macmillan, 1998); Margot C. Finn, *The Character of Credit: Personal Debt in English Culture, 1740–1914* (Cambridge: Cambridge University Press, 2003); and John Smail, 'Credit, Risk, and Honor in Eighteenth-Century Commerce', *Journal of British Studies*, 44 (2005), 439–56. For early America there are useful discussions in Bruce H. Mann, *Republic of Debtors: Bankruptcy in the Age of American Independence* (Cambridge, Mass.: Harvard University Press, 2002); T. H. Breen, *Tobacco Culture: The Mentality of the Great Tidewater Planters on the Eve of Revolution* (Princeton: Princeton University Press, 1985); Allan Kulikoff, *Tobacco and Slaves: The Development of Southern Cultures in the Chesapeake, 1680–1800* (Chapel Hill, NC: University of North Carolina Press for the Institute of Early American History and Culture, 1986); and Thomas A. M. Doerflinger, *A Vigorous Spirit of Enterprise: Merchants and Economic Development in Revolutionary Philadelphia* (Chapel Hill, NC: University of North Carolina Press for the Institute of Early American History and Culture, 1986), among others. For the Atlantic world, see Jacob Price, *Capital and Credit in British Overseas Trade* (Cambridge, Mass.: Harvard University Press, 1980), as well as various collections such as Olaf Uwe Janzen (ed.), *Merchant Organization and Maritime Trade in the North Atlantic, 1660–1815*, (St, John's, Newfoundland: International Maritime Economic History Association, 1998); McCusker and Morgan (eds.), *The Early Modern Atlantic Economy*; and Coclanis (ed.), *The Atlantic Economy During the Seventeenth and Eighteenth Centuries*. Merchant letters receive helpful attention in Toby L. Ditz: 'Shipwrecked', 'Formative Ventures', and 'Secret Selves, Credible Personas'.

[8] THE REMEMBRANCER: *Addressed to Young Men in Business. Shewing How they may attain the Way to be* RICH *and* RESPECTABLE (London, 1793), 25.

When fathers attempted to shape their sons, then, this act was both a private and a public one, because ruin and credit were personal, economic, and political issues. Much was at stake. Fathers wanted their sons to develop a strong basis of credit. As Daniel Defoe noted, credit was 'the foundation, the life and soul of business in a private tradesman; it is his prosperity, 'tis the support in the substance of his whole trade; even in publick matters 'tis the strength and fund of a nation'.[9] The individual tradesman depended on it, the family depended on it, and the nation depended on it. So, to have this foundation was critical, which is why fathers in particular were so intent upon inculcating credit and industry in their sons. They were willing to use brutal, punitive methods, ones looking suspiciously harsh and patriarchal in a period of alleged paternalism, in order to achieve this objective. Understanding this point recasts what we think we know about both the rise of the Atlantic economy and the rise of the affectionate family. The line of interpretation that argues that there was something remarkable about 'the vigorous spirit of enterprise' of these 'citizens of the world', with their willingness to take on and manage risk in an uncertain world, is correct and also insufficient.[10] These entrepreneurs, merchants, traders, planters, and others undeniably built a prosperous Atlantic world. But its costs were enormously high, even for those who found success in it. There are many ways to witness those costs, but one is to consider the domestic implications of creating 'men of credit' in the family. Such men (and they were mostly men), with their risk-taking and their capital, did not spring fully grown, blazing forth in this Atlantic world like Athena erupting from the head of Zeus. Families created these men, and it is worth considering these domestic sources, and the agency that families had in inculcating a set of values that might initially seem more closely aligned to the market than to the family.

For the families under discussion here, market values were inseparable from family values. As Max Weber posited in *The Protestant Ethic and the Spirit of Capitalism*: 'In order that a manner of life so well adapted to the peculiarities of capitalism could be selected at all . . . it had to originate somewhere, and not in isolated individuals alone, but as a way of life common to whole groups of men.'[11] Weber's insight, that such attitudes did not originate in 'isolated individuals alone', is relevant here. The ideal of the man of credit was partly formed within the family, and was inculcated by 'strict scrutiny', a style of monitoring deployed by fathers. It was not isolated individuals but family members in domestic settings who learned to select aspects of a capitalist economy. These individuals felt the need to instill in boys an underpinning of

---

[9] Defoe, *Complete English Tradesman*, 408.
[10] See Doerflinger, *A Vigorous Spirit of Enterprise*, and David Hancock, *Citizens of the World: London Merchants and the Integration of the British Atlantic Community, 1735–1785* (Cambridge: Cambridge University Press, 1995).
[11] Max Weber, *The Protestant Ethic and the Spirit of Capitalism*, trans. Talcott Parsons (London: George Allen & Unwin, 1930), 55.

credit, because of its immense fragility and yet critical importance. In the family context, this imperative translated into domestic debate, wrangling, dunning (or as one boy called it, 'quizzing'), scrutiny, scoldings, harangues, and a brutality that coexisted effortlessly, ominously, with a culture of politeness, refinement, and self-mastery. These men held on to power with great effort, but what made them anxious was not colonial status, as some historians of early America have argued, but instead this constant threat of ruin, ruin to 'unman' them, ruin to undermine even a commonwealth.[12] The kind of scrutiny they would later exhibit to their own business associates they first experienced as sons.[13]

Concerns about ruin and credit animated a great deal of behavior in the anglophone Atlantic world, both in families and outside of them. 'Creditors are a kind of People, that have the sharpest Eyes and Ears, as well as the best Memories of any in the World', cautioned Benjamin Franklin, in his guise as an old tradesman writing a letter to a young one.[14] To offset the dread surveillance of creditors, it was important to become 'a Man of Credit', as Franklin phrased it, or at least to *appear* 'a careful as well as an honest Man'.[15] One important commodity that a man carried with him as he made his way was his credit. But it took time, time and constant effort, to earn credit. Franklin, as many others, also emphasized both the vital importance and the terrifying fragility of credit: 'The most trifling Actions that affect a Man's Credit, are to be regarded.' To spot a debtor at a 'Billiard Table', to hear his voice 'in a Tavern', to see that debtor's wife wearing 'Finer Cloaths' than his own wife wore: any or all of these actions might prompt a creditor to demand immediate payment—or to dun—the misguided debtor.[16] In other words, a debtor had better watch everything he and his family did, said, or wore, as even the smallest slip could prompt a possible loss of credit.

Credit had long held several meanings in English, since it allied belief and trust with what might be called economic probity. It had for some time had connotations of both economics and personal standing, due to the nature of the early modern economy.[17] Goods could be offered without immediate payment due because the creditor believed in the trustworthiness of the debtor. Into the eighteenth century, a person with a 'character of credit' was someone who could be believed. Samuel Johnson declared 'reputation', in fact, to be the second

---

[12] As colonials, such men would always be marginal to London, Kathleen Brown has argued, so they needed to prevent any 'small usurpations of power'. Kenneth Lockridge has posited: 'Byrd and Jefferson epitomize the eternal vulnerability of a new-world, would-be gentry.' Brown, *Good Wives*, 319, and Kenneth A. Lockridge, *On the Sources of Patriarchal Rage: The Commonplace Books of William Byrd and Thomas Jefferson and the Gendering of Power in the Eighteenth Century* (New York: New York University Press, 1992), 101.

[13] On these adult disputes, see Ditz, 'Shipwrecked', *passim*.

[14] Benjamin Franklin, *Advice to a Young Tradesman. Written by an Old One* (Boston, 1762), 3.

[15] Ibid. 2–3. As Max Weber pointed out: 'The peculiarity of this philosophy of avarice appears to be the ideal of the honest man of recognized credit.' Weber, *The Protestant Ethic*, 51.

[16] Franklin, *Advice to a Young Tradesman*, 2–3.

[17] Julian Hoppit has posited: 'Creditors had to enquire into a man's financial worth and his character; financial and personal issues were impossible to separate.' Hoppit, *Risk and Failure*, 163.

definition of this word. From this reputation for reliability flowed a positive standing within the community. Johnson considered that 'honour' was one definition of credit; he also defined it as 'good opinion'.[18] To be a man of credit, then, was to be a man who had a good name and who had honor in the community. This good name was itself a valuable commodity, since another meaning of credit was 'Influence; power not compulsive', as Johnson phrased it, or 'right to be believed', as the *Oxford English Dictionary* notes.[19]

Credit, then, was about more than even reputation or honor; it was about authority, power, and the 'right to be believed'. Unpicking the threads that tied 'credit' to 'authority' in part clarifies why it was so often a masculine possession. Credit as a form of reputation was more important for men than for women. Women could and did have credit, especially when they entered into trade, but it did not define their character in the same way it did for men. Women's credit tended to rely on men's: their father's, their husband's, or their son's.[20] A woman could damage household credit, for example, by charging debts to her husband's name. Widows often maintained household credit begun by husbands. But men and women did not share the same credit, thanks in part to the unequal distribution of wealth that followed marriages. The phrase 'woman of credit' was not used with anything like the same frequency as the phrase 'man of credit'. Indeed, many considered masculine credit to be paralleled not by feminine credit, but by feminine sexual virtue. Daniel Defoe claimed that 'the credit of a tradesman . . . is the same thing in its nature as the virtue of a Lady'.[21]

As a form of social capital, then, credit was primarily a masculine prerogative. Indeed, the possession of good credit was one of the ways in which elite men set themselves apart from dependants, who did not possess the same credit, and thus the same authority. Independence was in part tied to credit, since it implied that a man was out of debt. In reality, even the wealthiest men of the British-Atlantic world were generally in debt, but this did not mean that they lacked credit, in social and cultural terms. They could repay their debts, or so it was believed, and this state of affairs added to their credit. To be a man of credit did not mean one had to be a creditor, nor did it depend strictly on capital. Credit accrued more easily to men who already had capital, but it was not strictly about money. A man with fewer resources, possessing the character of working hard and being trustworthy, could outstrip in credit men with greater financial reserves. To be a man of credit thus had both economic and social implications.

A man of credit's words about anything could be trusted: such was its essence. Newspapers regularly made reference to reports coming from a 'man

---

[18] Johnson, *Dictionary*, 'credit', defs. 2–3.
[19] Ibid., def. 7, and *Oxford English Dictionary*, 'credit', defs. 2b, and 6. The *OED* here uses examples from the sixteenth century on.
[20] As Craig Muldrew has pointed out, households had credit, but his analysis leaves out the way that household credit relied on men's credit. Muldrew, *Economy of Obligation, passim*.
[21] Defoe, *Complete English Tradesman*, 228–9.

of credit'. When newspapers referred to men in such terms, they were implying not an economic status, but rather a reputation for honesty and accuracy. The *Pennsylvania Gazette* reported that: 'We have the following Account from a Gentleman of Credit...that may be depended on.'[22] The weight of credit was meant to counteract even implausible assertions. Discussing a storm, the author noted that 'Capt. Strachan is a man of credit, and from him I have the account'.[23] To name the source, and to identify him as a man of credit, was to lend credibility even to a story about how a warehouse had been borne off of its foundation, carried down the river, finally landing upright, with no damage to its contents.[24]

It is thus no wonder that men were so jealous of their credit. Young men did not yet possess it, and it was an act of will, a constant and strict guard over one's self, to earn it. To build up such a reputation took time and great effort. It could also be lost in a New World minute. Franklin emphasized the many ways in which credit might be imperiled, but in this he was merely echoing other writers. One early seventeenth-century writer declared that 'the Credit of Merchants is so delicate and tender, that it must bee cared for as the apple of a man's eye'.[25] Defoe's *Complete English Tradesman* asserted unequivocally that 'CREDIT is the tradesman's life'. He warned that if credit was weakened, then 'the tradesman is sick, hangs his head, is dejected and discouraged; and if he does go on, it is...with difficulty'.[26] Nothing could be more important—or more fragile—than credit, and Defoe's metaphors sought to emphasize both its delicacy and its importance: 'A tradesman's reputation is of the nicest nature imaginable, like a blite upon a fine flower, if it is but toucht, the beauty of it...is lost.'[27] If people did not give a good 'character' of a tradesman to others, then the tradesman might well be sunk. He concluded that credit was 'the life and soul of his trade, and it requires his utmost vigilance to preserve it'.[28]

Unremitting vigilance was the way to maintain credit, upon which the entire economy of the Atlantic depended. To be in debt was no longer a sin or a crime, although it could become both if the debts were not paid off in a timely fashion. Rather, debt was an essential aspect of how this economy worked. One historian has noted: 'Choice of creditor and choice of debtor...were central to the success of a business...without credit there would have been far less chance for growth in eighteenth-century England.'[29] For the system to run properly,

---

[22] 'Headline: From the Virginia *Gazette*, Williamsburg, May 22,' *Pennsylvania Gazette*, 11 June 1741, in *Early American Newspapers, Series I, 1690–1876* (Readex).
[23] 'Headline: Philadelphia, October 26', *Pennsylvania Gazette*, 26 Oct. 1749, in ibid.
[24] Ibid.
[25] Gerard Malynes, *Consuetudo, vel lex mercatoria, or the Ancient Law-merchant* (London, 1622), 104.
[26] Defoe, *Complete English Tradesman*, 235–6. [27] Ibid. 232. [28] Ibid. 193–4.
[29] Hoppit, *Risk and Failure*, 160.

people needed to believe that debtors would repay debts. As another historian contends: 'Trust had to be extended, even when the risk of non-payment was very high. It was simply impossible to trade in any other way.'[30] Trust was necessary within England, and also across the Atlantic.

For decades, even centuries, face-to-face transactions that depended solely on the immediate reputation and behavior of the debtor or creditor had been receding in the face of long-distance trade exchanges and burgeoning economic growth that relied as much on the circulation of capital and credit as on the circulation of goods. Franklin imagined a creditor who could personally observe his debtor, thus witnessing games at the billiard tables or extravagant clothes. However, as in Johnson's definition of family in Chapter 2, Franklin's vision of debtor–creditor relations obscured the fact that increasingly large numbers of creditors could not personally monitor their debtors. As the economy developed in the eighteenth century, it became increasingly likely that a creditor might well be separated from his debtor by an ocean. As one historian has noted in a case study from eighteenth-century England, 'the largest debts lay overseas'.[31] Overseas debts produced the largest outlays of capital, and also incurred the highest levels of risk. But face-to-face surveillance could not work, so reports and letters about credit became essential to economic functioning and, quite simply, the growth of this Atlantic world.

To give a man goods and money across the ocean meant that his credit needed to be strong indeed. Certain individuals had to be trusted (a Jamaican planter had to send sugar to *someone* for sale in London; a Glasgow merchant had to send goods to Virginia without going there himself). Factors, intermediaries, and others filled in many of these fissures in this Atlantic, and ultimately global, system. But all of the links in these chains of credit and goods had to be reliable. At the same time, the sheer facelessness of many of these transactions caused credit as an issue to be highly charged, and constantly evolving. Here is how one historian phrases it: 'trust was still more fragile in proportion to the distance over which it was extended, and this meant that the credit of a merchant and his household was of even greater concern than for anyone else'.[32] The longer the distances, the slower the communications networks, and increasingly the more problematic, and yet equally critical, became the already all-too-perishable system of credit.

This Atlantic world was perilous, even for those who commanded it. Goods, as well as bills of exchange, could be lost in so many different ways. Anyone involved with planting, or dependent on people who were, was plagued by choking droughts, sudden blights, ravaging insects, chilling frosts, and poor harvests, not to mention disasters like hurricanes or earthquakes (common events especially in areas of major staple crop production in the Lower South and the

---

[30] Muldrew, *Economy of Obligation*, 194.   [31] Hoppit, *Risk and Failure*, 157.
[32] Muldrew, *Economy of Obligation*, 188.

Caribbean).³³ Crops did not harvest themselves, so there were also potential problems of labor. Wars might also impact on trade adversely. Epidemics like smallpox might decimate communities; they might also detain ships in port, waiting to clear quarantine measures. These problems might ruin a man who had planted crops, or who had overseen their planting. But they could equally ruin the man who had sold goods to those planters on the credit of harvests and sales to come.³⁴ Even once the goods made their way onto ships, a series of hazards awaited them on the seas. Fearsome pirates or privateers might seize booty. Captures of all sorts were ubiquitous in times of war, which meant most of the long eighteenth century. When the 'cargo' of a ship consisted of living, breathing individuals capable of resistance, and increasingly prone to disease due to the revolting conditions in which they were held, then these problems were intensified.

These human dangers were amplified by the hazards already present in any voyage over a vast, merciless ocean: blasting salty winds; massive pounding waves; sharp, deadly rocks lying silently in wait. Books like *Lex Mercatoria Rediviva*, a treatise on merchant law, devoted literally hundreds of pages to enumerating these oceanic dangers, and the legal problems that might ensue from them. Many in this world needed to be clear about the legal distinctions between 'flotsam' (goods that floated up from a perished ship) and 'jetsam' (goods cast into the sea to preserve a ship from sinking, 'notwithstanding which she afterwards perishes').³⁵ That such distinctions were considered critical knowledge for merchants of all sorts demonstrates the relative ubiquity of such disasters. There were also problems of transport and communication. A ship might reach port late, after rival vessels, so lowering the price its cargo could command, or losing its market altogether. A trader might sell for too low a price, and so not make all the money expected. Or the goods might provoke only complaints from the purchasers, thus losing future sales. There might not have been monsters there, but there was nevertheless plenty to terrify and destroy people and goods making their slow way across the Atlantic.

Then there were the smaller but no less needling problems of personal trust and credit. Laws governing credit related especially to moveable and mercantile property.³⁶ While loss of goods might be covered by insurance to an extent,

---

³³ This point receives extended treatment in Matthew Mulcahy, *Hurricanes and Society in the British Greater Caribbean, 1624–1783* (Baltimore, Md.: Johns Hopkins University Press, 2006).

³⁴ While there were many distinctions to be drawn between planters and merchants, and while they often held competing and even conflicting views, they also shared a world-view in which hazards beyond their control might imperil their prospects, and even destroy them, all too easily. There is a useful discussion of the definition of the particular 'overseas merchant' (as opposed to general traders) in Perry Gauci, *The Overseas Merchant in State and Society, 1660–1720* (Oxford: Oxford University Press, 2001), 8–9, 20–1.

³⁵ Beawes, *Lex Mercatoria Rediviva*, 130.

³⁶ See Claire Priest, 'Creating an American Property Law: Alienability and its Limits in American History', *Harvard Law Review*, 120 (2006), 385–459.

insurance offered no protection against bad business choices. A man might be dunned before ships had come into port with his goods ready for sale, thus terminating his credit. A man might sell items to a buyer who offered him bills of exchange that turned out to be worthless. A man might dun a debtor, but obtain no payment. Even a lawsuit might prove costly and pointless, if the debtor could not pay, or if other creditors were able to settle their claims first. One of the most common instruments for circulating capital, and an increasingly dominant one in the eighteenth century, was a bill of exchange; such a bill depended on at least three, and sometimes four, distinct individuals and institutions on different sides of the ocean, in order to work properly.[37] If even one link in that chain defaulted, or protested payment, the whole chain could be lost. A man needed to be able to discern as precisely between good credit and bad credit, as he did between 'flotsam' and 'jetsam'. There were all too many potential problems for traders and others who sought to become men of credit.

Indeed, for centuries these kinds of worries had plagued those who traded in lands abroad. An early seventeenth-century tract summarized what a merchant faced: 'he must indure a number of daungerous adventures, both outward and inward, shipwracks at Sea, peril of Pirats, and other robbers; at his place of sale, there he must give credit to those hee never saw... he must abide to answer all defects found.' This author noted that such fears penetrated deeply into the consciousness of these merchants: 'These and many other casualties causeth cares to abridge his rest, and keepes him waking when others sleepe, everie stormie wind breedes his feare, and everie flying report makes him doubtfull, and not without great cause, seeing so many fall sodainly to the utter overthrow, not onely of themselves, but divers others depending on them.'[38] There was cause for the incessant fretful monitoring of 'everie flying report'. The merchant's ruin was an unceasing fear plaguing the men who did business in these worlds. Too many letters, papers, and associates could and did tell shocking stories of sudden, eviscerating ruin, which destroyed not only the merchant but also his business associates, as well as his household. One historian claims: 'commerce in eighteenth-century Philadelphia was a brutally demanding and financially dangerous occupation.'[39] Such a description might serve the entire world of British overseas trade; it certainly resonated tellingly for those involved in the rich and risky Atlantic and Caribbean basins.

---

[37] The clearest articulation of how a bill of exchange functioned can be found in John J. McCusker, *Money and Exchange in Europe and America, 1600–1775: A Handbook* (Chapel Hill, NC: University of North Carolina Press for the Institute of Early American History and Culture, 1978), 21–2. Smail argues that it took on particular importance, and thus exacerbated concerns about risk, in the eighteenth century. See Smail, 'Credit, Risk, and Honor', 442–4.

[38] John May, *A Declaration of the Estate of Clothing Now Used Within this Realme of England (London, 1613)*, The English Experience: Its Record in Early Printed Books Published in Facsimile (Amsterdam: Da Capo Press, 1971), 38–9.

[39] Doerflinger, *Vigorous Spirit of Enterprise*, 44.

These anxieties go some way to explaining the power of oceanic metaphors of destruction circulating in all kinds of materials in this period. An island, Britain had long depended on trading overseas. Literate individuals were also familiar with ancient seafarers (such as Odysseus). Oceanic metaphors signaled risk and uncertainty. So, in *Lex Mercatoria Rediviva* the author reminded his readers: 'permit me... to shew you the Causes which naturally drive Men to split on that Rock, where so many thousands have been wrecked... I shall direct my Advice... and endeavour to guide them from running on the aforementioned Shoals, by persuading them to aim at the Dissipation of the Fogs of *Ignorance* by the Sunshine of Learning.'[40] Daniel Defoe similarly deployed such metaphors:

Hitherto I have written to you of tradesmen ruin'd by lawful and innocent diversions... a ship may as well be lost in a calm smooth sea, and an easy fair gale of wind, as in a storm, if they have no pilot, or the pilot be ignorant and unwary... when rocks are apparent, and the pilot bold and wilful runs directly upon them... we know the fate of the ship, it must perish... but in a smooth sea, a bold shoar, an easy gale, the unseen rocks or shoals are the only dangers, and nothing can hazard them, but the skilfulness of the pilot; and thus it is in trade.[41]

These metaphors conflated real dangers for traders, and metaphors for these dangers. They also emphasized the need for a person to learn how to steer a good course through a sea of menaces to avoid ruin.

Ruin terrified men of credit because it could push them into a state of dependence. In that case, they might be not much better off than their wives, their children, or their servants. And what would their dependants do? As with credit, ruin functioned differently for men than for women. For men, it meant grave financial loss bringing poverty and disgrace. For women, ruin implied sexual violation. The gender connotations of ruin are important for what they demonstrate about the ideal of female sexual virtue, and its enduring social, cultural, and political significance in Anglo-American culture in the early modern period.[42] Yet they are also important for what they reveal about men, and their worst fears. Connecticut farmers protested colonial policies in the 1760s by claiming that 'they should be absolutely ruined, and rendered incapable to pay their Debts, or support their Families'.[43] One writer in favor of bankruptcy reform in the early United States wondered if 'the malignant creditor' could comprehend 'the ruin and wretchedness' he caused when he 'tear[s] a man from his family... and the tears of his wife and children are falling at your feet', and asked: 'After depriving the wife of a husband, and the children of a father,

---

[40] Beawes, *Lex Mercatoria Rediviva*, 486. [41] Defoe, *Complete English Tradesman*, 133.
[42] See Ruth H. Bloch, 'The Gendered Meaning of Virtue in Revolutionary America', *Signs*, 13 (1987), 37–58.
[43] 'Headline: NEW YORK, July 10', *Pennsylvania Gazette*, 17 July 1766, in *Early American Newspapers, Series I, 1690–1876* (Readex).

what is their chance in a cold and hostile world?'[44] To suffer such a shame was, as historians have pointed out, to be 'unmann'd', to lose masculine credit, to lose, as one author put it, 'every Thing that is dear and valuable in Life'.[45] Much as it encapsulated immense changes, this eighteenth-century world also maintained deep continuities with older periods. Slander cases in both Britain and the mainland colonies had long made it clear that men were most concerned with their economic status, women with their sexual status.[46] This situation continued in the eighteenth century.

Claims about potential and actual 'ruin' were rhetorical devices, used by agitators, propagandists, and others.[47] Such rhetorical claims, both personal and general, had power precisely because ruin was so fearsome, threatening destruction far beyond its original source. Devastation might cause a domino-like collapse that could affect all kinds of people, and personal catastrophe might ultimately result in general ruin. One typical example, which conflates meanings of physical destruction, financial loss, and general colonial hardship, comes from the report of a fire that had raged across Bridgetown, Barbados: 'Near half the Houses of our late flourishing Town is now a Heap of Rubbish; many of our Merchants ruined... Unless proper salutary Measures are pursued... Trade and Commerce will decay, and the whole Island be ruined.'[48] For merchants to be ruined, and for trade to decay, might spell the wreck of 'the whole Island'.

Ruin affected families, as well as individuals, and if enough families were devastated, the entire country might be too. A 1760s article in the *Pennsylvania Gazette* deplored the rise in lawsuits for debt, which had 'ruined Hundred of Families... and yet threatens Destruction and Desolation to many more'.[49] Another piece from the 1780s condemned taverns, 'whereby numberless families suffer, many are ruined, morals corrupted, industry lessened, and the

---

[44] William Keteltas, 'Hotchpotch (No. 2)', *Forlorn Hope*, 7 Apr. 1800, as quoted in Mann, *Republic of Debtors*, 142.

[45] See Ditz, 'Shipwreck'd', *passim* and Mann, *Republic of Debtors*, 120–1. Quotations from *The Ill Policy and Inhumanity of Imprisoning Insolvent Debtors Fairly Stated and Discussed* (Rhode Island, 1754), as quoted in Mann, *Republic of Debtors*, 83.

[46] For England, see Laura Gowing, *Domestic Dangers: Women, Words, and Sex in Early Modern London* (Oxford: Clarendon Press, 1996), and Martin Ingram, *Church Courts, Sex and Marriage in England, 1570–1640* (Cambridge: Cambridge University Press, 1987). For American colonies, see Mary Beth Norton, 'Gender and Defamation in Seventeenth-Century Maryland', *William and Mary Quarterly*, 44 (1987), 3–39; C. Dallett Hemphill, 'Women in Court: Sex-Role Differentiation in Salem, Massachusetts, 1636 to 1683', *William and Mary Quarterly*, 39 (1982), 164–75; and Cornelia Hughes Dayton, *Women Before the Bar: Gender, Law, and Society in Connecticut, 1639–1789*, (Chapel Hill, NC: University of North Carolina for the Institute of Early American History and Culture, 1995) Ch. 6.

[47] e.g. a typical claim made by those who opposed the Stamp Act was that 'we shall all be ruined'. 'Headline: PHILADELPHIA, October 24', *Pennsylvania Gazette*, 24 Oct. 1765, in *Early American Newspapers, Series I, 1690–1876* (Readex).

[48] 'Headline: PHILADELPHIA, February 12', *Pennsylvania Gazette*, 12 Feb. 1767, in ibid.

[49] 'Headline: To his Excellency WILLIAM FRANKLIN, Esq.', *Pennsylvania Gazette*, 26 Oct. 1769, in ibid.

commonwealth greatly injured'.⁵⁰ This concern took on particular force when national debt, to cover wars, was increasing over the eighteenth century. One 1793 English tract, in the years of the French Revolution, argued that young men in particular had better turn away from habits of dissipation and extravagance, warning ominously: 'we must resolve upon an immediate and entire reform, or the kingdom is undone: destroy those bonds of society, integrity, industry, confidence, and shame, and our enemies shall triumph; they will come upon us like a thief in the night, whilst we are dancing and revelling upon the ruins of our credit.'⁵¹ The good order of the colony and the nation depended on these individual households, and their disintegration might well carry with them the destruction of the entire commonwealth.

The desire to avert ruin, and the sense that young men in particular needed to develop mechanisms by which to do so, influenced all kinds of men. Credit was especially critical for the merchants, traders, and agents in these Atlantic worlds, and these concerns about producing men of credit took on an intensified importance in these families. Still, to be a man of credit, or at least a man of honor in a more general sense, was important for all kinds of men, even aristocrats whose fortunes seemed assured. Even men of the greatest wealth worried that their property might be dissipated by young men who spent too much time and money in taverns, in brothels, and at gaming tables, or that sudden reversals of fortune might require them to come to depend on credit and good habits. This was an individual concern, a family concern, and a national concern, and it was sufficiently important that all kinds of people attempted to produce a sense of credit in sons especially.

Fathers knew the vulnerability of their sons, and they sought to minimize it by teaching them to be masters of themselves and of the worlds around them. Men learned to gain credit in the market, but they also learned it in the family. Men shaped themselves in accordance with what other men, including their fathers and sons, might think of them. Points of conflict between fathers and sons can demonstrate the ways in which family members sought to mold each other. They also indicate that credit was a commodity and bone of contention within the family.⁵² After all, 'everie flying report' could rob a man of sleep, and in no place was this more obvious than in his own house, or in the larger household held within the bounds of familiarity and letter-writing. For parents, and parental figures, separated from children by dint of economic or political circumstances, or by the decision to send a son across the ocean, these reports were critical.

---

⁵⁰ 'Headline: To the PRINTERS of the PENNSYLVANIA GAZETTE', *Pennsylvania Gazette*, 25 Feb. 1784, in ibid.

⁵¹ REMEMBRANCER, 3.

⁵² While Craig Muldrew's work on credit has reshaped our understandings of early modern society and economy, he tends to treat households as though all members shared the same interests. This is an assumption of which, as numerous historians of gender and the family have reminded us, we need to be wary.

Their own letters in return were equally important, as they sought to shape a child, even when an ocean lay between them. Many fathers deployed strategies of monitoring and advice-giving, in both verbal and written form, to their sons, and in some cases to nephews, cousins, and other young men who sought some form of patronage from them.

Although an established English aristocrat, Lord Chesterfield paralleled many other fathers in this British-Atlantic world in his insistence on a form of monitoring which he termed 'strict scrutiny'.[53] Here is how he introduced the concept, in one of his many letters to his son:

> You know I have often told you, that my affection for you was not a weak womanish one; and, far from blinding me, it makes me but more quick-sighted, as to your faults: those it is not only my right, but my duty, to tell you of; and it is your duty and your interest to correct them. In the strict scrutiny which I have made into you, I have (thank God) hitherto not discovered any vice of the heart... but I have discovered laziness, inattention, and indifference; faults which are only pardonable in old men... But a young man should be ambitious to shine, and excel; alert, active, and indefatigable in the means of doing it.[54]

Despite his aristocratic status and wealth, Lord Chesterfield was still eager that his son be ambitious and successful. These desires were equally, if not more, compelling for the Atlantic traders, merchants, and planters who also populated this world. Like Chesterfield, such men had recourse to showing affection by sternness. They avoided feminine, forgiving methods that a mother might use (a 'weak womanish one'), but instead made their sons aware of manifold faults. Chesterfield, with his desire to be friend, not simply father, has been used as a classic example of 'rational equalitarian friendship' with his son, and thus part of the 'revolution against patriarchal authority'.[55] This description does not capture the incessantly domineering tone of most of his letters to his son.[56] To shape each facet of a son, whether his dress, his handwriting, or his love of virtue, was to be a good father. In fact, to point out his son's manifold faults was 'not only my *right*, but my *duty*'. Such a claim summarized the imperatives at work here. Fathers had the right, the privilege, to offer strict scrutiny to their sons; his son had only *duty* and *interest* in return.

Like other fathers, Chesterfield wanted to create a man who could withstand the pressures of a busy, scheming world. Chesterfield had high hopes for these

---

[53] 'Strict scrutiny' now applies to judicial monitoring to ensure compliance with US federal law; in the eighteenth century it had different connotations.

[54] Lord Chesterfield to his son, letter 81, 'Bath, October the 9th, O.S. 1746', Chesterfield, *Letters*, i. 197–8.

[55] Fliegelman, *Prodigals and Pilgrims*, 41.

[56] Fliegelman contends: 'Recognizing that the purest bond between father and son is affection rather than consanguinity, Chesterfield humbly relinquishes the aristocratic name of "father" for the sentimental name of "friend".' There are many words to describe Chesterfield, but 'humble' is not one I would use. Ibid. 40.

methods, declaring in that same letter: 'I am very sure that any man of common understanding may, by proper culture, care, attention, and labour, make himself whatever he pleases.'[57] It was part of a father's responsibility to provide that care and attention, and to ensure that the son used his own 'labour' to succeed. Simon Taylor, who spent decades offering strict scrutiny to his nephew and heir, wrote to his sister-in-law about the young man that: 'I have nothing in the World so much at Heart as that he shall turn out a worthy good Man and be a Creditt to his Family and Connexions, and a usefull Man in Society, not an Empty vain... Gambler or Lounger.'[58] To be a useful man was to be a credit to the family, as one man noted when he wrote about his desire to become a merchant, 'not that I may riot in luxury but that I may have it in my power of being an useful and honorable member of society, and a credit to my name and family'.[59] John Adams implored his son: 'Make it a Rule, my dear Son, to loose no Time.... Make it the grand Maxim of your Life, and it [you] cannot fail to be happy, and usefull to the World.'[60] To become a credit to the family required methods of strict scrutiny. A 1793 tract painted a dark picture of the effects of extravagance in youth, noting that for such a debtor: 'His conduct will not bear a strict scrutiny; and the deeper he enters into it, the more formidable is the scene that opens!'[61]

In part, what many commentators—from fathers in their personal letters to Benjamin Franklin and Daniel Defoe in their advice to tradesmen, and even to letter-writing manuals—were attempting to do was to inculcate habits of credit and industry in young men, who could then face the world on their own, bolstered by connections. Even the seemingly innocent letters reprinted in juvenile sections in letter-writing manuals echoed this message: 'that you will always remember, however distant you are, or however secret you may think yourself from your Friends and Relations, you will never be able to conceal your Faults; for some of our prying tattling Tribe, will be continually carrying them home, to... the Ears of your Papa, much to your Shame and Discredit.'[62] One of the ways to show industry and credit was by letter; for sons away from home, letters were a way of monitoring, a way of offering 'strict scrutiny', a way both of nurturing and demonstrating credit. It was something of a fiction, since in fact the father was not able to survey personally, but instead relied on reports, as well as uneasy readings of the son's letters.

---

[57] Lord Chesterfield to his son, letter 81, 'Bath, October the 9th, O.S. 1746', Chesterfield, *Letters*, i. 198.
[58] Simon Taylor to Lady Taylor, 'Kingston Jamaica October 6. 1780 [sic—1800]', I/D/34, Simon Taylor Papers, ICS.
[59] John Pintard to Elisha Boudinot, from Bayard–Boudinot–Pintard Papers, NYHS, as quoted in Mann, *Republic of Debtors*, 111.
[60] John Adams to John Quincy Adams, 'Amsterdam Decr. 14. 1781', Butterfield and Friedlaender (eds.), *Adams Family Correspondence*, iv. 263.
[61] REMEMBRANCER, 31.
[62] Letter XII, 'From ROBIN REDBREAST in the *Garden*, to Master BILLY CARELESS, abroad at School', in *The Complete Letter-Writer*, 6th edn. (1759), 74–5.

Letters were a critical means of circulating information and especially credit. All kinds of letters, from the most domestic to the most public, carried with them evaluations of credit and probity, and a man's prospects could rise or fall due to them. Bills of exchange, the chief means of sending capital between separate locales, depended on pieces of paper that included assumptions about credit on both sides of the Atlantic. Here is how one merchants' manual described such bills: 'a Bartering or Exchanging the Money of one Kingdom with those of another, which is always effected by the Intervention of two or three Lines of Writing on a Slip of Paper'.[63] In this Atlantic world, much depended on 'the Intervention of two or three Lines of Writing on a Slip of Paper'.

WRITING 'IN THE MERCANTILE STILE'[64]

The men and women in the families under discussion here attempted, even in sensible familiar letter exchanges, to create men of credit. The entire nexus of familiar letter-writing in these families was informed by the need to balance epistolary accounts, and to be 'in credit' in terms of letters. Such families created systems of exchange that paralleled and in some cases reinforced those of the world of merchandise and trade. Market values coexisted entirely comfortably with ideas about sentiment and sensibility. There was a belief in the evenness of letter exchange, just as in the fairness of a bill of exchange. When a recipient failed to reply, it put his or her credit into dispute. There was a careful calculus of barter and sentiment in letter exchanges, as no one wanted to find themselves sending more letters than were received, or vice versa. Letter-writers surveyed themselves and their epistolary partners, to ensure that debts were paid, remittances made. Although this concern had appeared in letters for centuries, it took on a new force in this period.[65]

This rhetoric of epistolary exchange revises the strict dichotomy that many early American historians have been eager to draw between the market and the family, especially for the later eighteenth century. Certainly, many if not most of these letter-writers belonged to merchant families, and so their familiarity with this language of trade comes as little surprise. Nonetheless, its ubiquity bears some

---

[63] Beawes, *Lex Mercatoria Rediviva*, 416.
[64] Ann Hulton to Mrs Lightbody, 'Boston Jany, 25 1774', Ann Hulton, *Letters of a Loyalist Lady* (Cambridge, Mass.: Harvard University Press, 1927), 66.
[65] This kind of language had appeared in letters since at least the sixteenth century, an indication of the increasing integration of the market and the family even at that early stage. But it seems to have become far more common in the eighteenth century. James Daybell notes that: 'Other letter-writers textualized the reciprocal ideal of communicating by letter by expressing unease or embarrassment at being in somebody's "debt" or by "owing" them a letter.' The one example he gives of such language comes from a merchant to his wife. James Daybell, *Women Letter-Writers in Tudor England* (Oxford: Oxford University Press, 2006), 161–2.

explaining. Both men and women deployed this language of the counting-house in the realm of the affective family. Epistolary exchanges were supposed to be even ones: affectionate remembrances exchanged for one another. Even though there were often disparities between the status of letter-writers, these were to be obviated by the fair exchange of sentiment. This is not a language of patronage, but of exchange. People could become angry when these expectations were not met. In a larger debate about the origins of anti-slavery humanitarianism, historians have set the values of the family against those of the market.[66] One scholar has argued that: 'the whole pre-Romantic and Romantic cults of sensibility and domesticity... were pitted against the brutality and insensitivity of the marketplace.'[67] The letters at hand indicate that, in this period at least, market values and family values of sensibility were not in opposition to each other. This world was one that privileged fair exchange, whether for cargo or for feeling. The 'cognitive style', to use Thomas Haskell's phrase, taught by this world of epistolary exchanges was that each action deserved a reply, that fair exchanges governed relations between people of a certain environment and type. It was a problem for someone to be 'out of credit', however this was understood. This mercantile language of affection, along with the notions underpinning it, indicates that the family had agency in teaching people about fair exchange. It also conveys that individuals sought to mold family and friends into the sorts of people, the good characters, who paid their debts, whether monetary or sentimental. Keeping in credit was a critical value, one especially important for men whose livelihoods depended on the reputation of credit, but instilled by both men and women in the family.[68]

Many references can seem casual—letters are 'owed', and letter-writers are 'in debt'. This language offers a clue to the lessons they are teaching. So Anna Eliza Clark harangued Dorothy Forbes in 1798: 'I sit down to beg you to write me some time when you find a moments leisure—... really dear Madam you

---

[66] This debate is to be found in: David Brion Davis, *The Problem of Slavery in the Age of Revolution* (Ithaca, NY: Cornell University Press, 1975); Thomas L. Haskell, 'Capitalism and the Origins of Humanitarian Sensibility, Part 1', *American Historical Review*, 90 (1985), 339–61 and 'Part 2', ibid. 547–66; David Brion Davis, 'AHR Forum: Reflections on Abolitionism and Ideological Hegemony', *American Historical Review*, 92 (1987), 797–812; John Ashworth, 'AHR Forum: The Relationship between Capitalism and Humanitarianism', ibid. 813–28; and Thomas L. Haskell, 'AHR Forum: Convention and the Hegemonic Interest in the Debate over Antislavery: A Reply to Davis and Ashworth', ibid. 829–878.

[67] Davis, 'AHR Forum: Reflections', 179. Davis was partly responding to Haskell's assertion that capitalism taught people the kind of long-distance sense of consequences, the 'cognitive style', that would lead to humanitarian anti-slavery campaigns. Haskell thereby in a way acknowledges the debt language, but does not place it within the family either. Instead, he claims it was a virtue of the market. But the market was not the only place where people learned to balance accounts, as this discussion shows.

[68] This 'domestic economy of debt' broadens the argument made most forcefully by Margaret Hunt about 'the ways "the market" *transcended* the so-called "public sphere" and went to the heart of family life'. Hunt, *The Middling Sort*, 9.

owe me a letter.'[69] Similar themes inform another letter to Dorothy Forbes, this one from her aunt in Scotland, Jean Bennet. Jean apologized for her own sister's silence, but: 'she (Annie I mean) is not wanting in affection but is a bad scribe & Averse to her pen.' Jean also reminded Dorothy that 'My Sister & I will be glad of Remittance too, as soon as is Convenient.' 'Remittance' in this era generally referred to the payment of bills, but here Jean adopted the language of merchants to refer to these familiar epistles.[70]

Many letter-writers complained when they felt their correspondent was in epistolary debt to them, and sometimes refused to send more letters for that reason. Thomas Coombe excused himself for not writing to his sister Sally, 'but she is still in my Debt'.[71] Rebecca Shoemaker apologized to her son for not writing sooner, while upbraiding him for not writing more frequently: 'So long an Interval should not have elapsed without my writing to my D[ea]r Edward, if thee had not been 2 or 3 letters in my Debt.'[72] Elizabeth Hadwen chided: 'I would just remind my Cousin that he is indebted to me a Letter.'[73] Isaac Low, writing to his brother, reported of his son: 'Isaac comes on very well at his new School, expects soon to write you a French letter, though he says you are already several in his Debt.'[74] At other points, he noted of his son: 'Isaac... thanks you kindly for the promised Reply... and says he will not remain long in your Debt.'[75] Other correspondents complained of 'arrears'. Thomas Ruston justified not writing more to his father: 'You seem to complain of my not writing more frequently, but... I cannot help thinking I have wrote fully as often as I have been honour'd with a letter from you... Have I not in this letter nearly balanced accounts, by paying up arrears in Answering the several queries that have from time to time been proposed to me.'[76] Mercy Otis Warren similarly accused her son of being 'rather in arrears', and demanding that he send answers to her letters.[77] Elsewhere, Isaac Norris launched a letter with no salutation but the following: 'I fear I am out of credit with you—appearances I own are against me, but be assured it has not been thro neglect that your last Letters have remained

---

[69] Anna Eliza Clark to Dorothy Forbes, 'September 10 1798', Forbes Family Papers, MHS.

[70] Jean Bennet to Dorothy Forbes, 'Kelso, September 12th 1788', typed transcription, ibid.

[71] Thomas Coombe to Thomas Coombe, 'London Novr 1st. 1769', Thomas Coombe Papers, HSP.

[72] Rebecca Shoemaker to Edward Shoemaker, '19 Sept. [17]84', Shoemaker Family Papers, HSP.

[73] Elizabeth Hadwen to John Bragg, 'Portsmouth 12th Mo 2d 1775', Hadwen–Bragg Family Papers, microfilm, LoC (originals at Whitehaven Public Library, Cumberland, England).

[74] Isaac Low to Nicholas Low, 'London March 2d. 1785', Nicholas Low Papers, Box 1, File: 'Low, Isaac 1785', LoC.

[75] Isaac Low to Nicholas Low, 'Mortlake Septr. 3d. and 8th: 1785', ibid.

[76] Thomas Ruston to Job Ruston?, 'Camberwell Feb: 5 1772', Thomas Ruston Papers, LoC.

[77] Mercy Otis Warren to Winslow Warren, 'Dec 24, 1779', as quoted in Edmund M. Hayes, 'Notes and Documents: Mercy Otis Warren versus Lord Chesterfield 1779', *William and Mary Quarterly*, 40 (1983), 616–621, at 621.

'till now unanswered.'[78] One of Thomas Butler's sisters complained that her brother was 'one or two letters in my Debt', while another worried that she was 'indebted' to him for his.[79]

This metaphor becomes far more elaborate in some letters. Charles Parker, himself a trader, deployed such language with his sister, Susan, who had sent her brother letters in proud schoolgirl French. When Charles had not received a letter from her in some time, he humorously tallied up her French epistles against his English ones, carping to his father: 'as for Susan I suppose she thinks the Exchange is so much in favor of the French at present that one French letter is worth 2 English ones tell [her] for gods sake to write me & not to be afraid that I'll run in debt to her.'[80] Thomas Pinckney similarly argued that his sister as well as his mother should reply to his letter: 'I expect double return all idle Excuses laid aside.'[81] Idleness should be avoided in letter-writing as in all other aspects of life. Other correspondents read silence not as idleness but as political division, so that the wife of a Loyalist in London complained to her brother in New York: 'not a line for Either of us it is a hard task but I am Endeavouring to reconcile My Connexions Conduct to Me... I write at least 6 letters for one I receive tis hard that Cursed politics should divest people of all regard for those that ought to be dearest to them.'[82] Whatever its cause, failure to remit and to balance accounts could be considered bad behavior.

By contrast, fair exchange of letters demonstrated not simply good mercantile behavior, but also good sentiments. Pierce Butler repeatedly made use of these metaphors in his letters to his son and his son's tutor. He worried over being 'in arrears' and 'in Debt' in the exchange.[83] Elsewhere, Pierce self-consciously toyed with usual dictates of mercantile letters, opening one such missive: 'Without regularity there is no getting properly on: Now tho' it may appear more like the begining of a Mercantile Correspondence than a less shakled, but more sincere exchange of friendly Sentiments, I will, for the sake of Order, note my Epistolary

---

[78] Isaac Norris to John Leeds Bozman?, 'Philadelphia Sept. 28. 79', Box 5, John Leeds Bozman Papers, LoC.

[79] Harriett Butler to Thomas Butler, 'Philadelphia, March ye 3d. 1792', and Sarah Butler to Thomas Butler, 'GermanTown August ye 25th 1794', Pierce Butler Letter Collection, Add. Mss. 16603, BL.

[80] Charles Parker to James Parker, 'Grenada 12t. March 1790', 1/43, Parker Family Papers, LRO.

[81] Thomas Pinckney to Harriott, 'Camp at Redlap...June 18th. 1778', Charles Cotesworth Pinckney Papers, Series 1, Box 6, Folder 1, LoC.

[82] Ann Watts Kennedy to Robert Watts, 'decr 3d 1788 Perez? St Bedford Sq London', Robert Watts Papers, Box IV, Folder 1, NYHS.

[83] Pierce Butler to Thomas Butler, 'MaryVille Sunday morn November ye 23d. 1788', Pierce Butler to Weeden Butler, 'New York July 15th, 1789', Pierce Butler to Weeden Butler, 'NY May ye 22d 1790', Pierce Butler to Weeden Butler, 'Philadelphia March ye 3d. 1792', Pierce Butler to Weeden Butler, 'Philadelphia August ye 7th 1793', Pierce Butler Letter Collection, Add. Mss. 16603, BL.

Debt to You.'[84] Pierce Butler thanked his son's tutor for letters, as well as the care of his son, in an extended metaphor of debt and credit:

> I stand indebted to You for three letters—If this was my only debt to you I could soon pay it, but I have a debt to You that the short period of my days will not admit of my paying—a debt which You are hourly adding—it is the debt of gratitude, for your Parental attention to and tenderness of my dear Boy—what return my Dear Sir, is adequate to the obligation! . . . I must still remain your Debtor . . . I am sure I can't have a more feeling Creditor.[85]

This intermingling of feeling and tenderness, with the language of credit and debt, demonstrates the ways in which metaphors of debt and credit were deeply embedded even in the sensible family.

Occasionally correspondents claimed that their willingness to send a letter demonstrated their exceptional 'disinterestedness' because they did not expect a return. So, Thomas Pinckney informed his sister: 'I hope my Dear Sister is now satisfied with the length of my Epistle; indeed it is a most disinterested one as I do not expect a return for it, not being able to tell you where to direct for me.'[86] Other writers noted that they could never be impartial in such a matter. In one lengthy usage of this trope, Ann Hulton, writing from Boston, informed her friend in England: 'I must own, I am not disinterested in my correspondence, but expect a return of pleasure & satisfaction, for what I send out, however trifling be the value of the Adventure. You will allow me to treat with you in the Mercantile Stile, who have been conversant in these matters lately. Yet be assured a kind regard to you & the hopes of hearing of y[ou]r health and welfare is the first Motive.'[87] While her motives were affectionate and familiar, her rhetoric, as she herself noted, was that of the counting-house. Fair exchange was the expectation in epistolary relations for both men and women. Nevertheless, for reasons already elaborated, it was far more often men who needed to write 'in the Mercantile Stile', as families, businesses, and nations depended on such letters.

To become a man of credit, as well as a man of business, meant first becoming a man of letters. This was no small task, nor was it an insignificant one. Many merchants' manuals read as a series of letters from an experienced man of business to an inexperienced one in need of advice. In adopting this format, such books attempted not only to inculcate particular messages in the letters, but also to display conspicuously the way to write letters. That idleness had long been considered a problem that letters could solve is illustrated by the fact that the first letter-writing manual in English, appearing in 1568, was itself entitled *The Enimie*

---

[84] Pierce Butler to Weeden Butler, 'Mary-Ville May Ye 5th. 1788', ibid.
[85] Pierce Butler to Weeden Butler, 'Mary Ville March Ye 2d. 1788', ibid.
[86] Thomas Pinckney to Harriott Pinckney, 'Camden Novr. 2d. 1775', Charles Cotesworth Pinckney Papers, Series 1, Box 6, Folder 1, LoC.
[87] Ann Hulton to Mrs. Lightbody, 'Boston Jany, 25 1774', Hulton, *Letters of a Loyalist Lady*, 66.

*of Idlenesse.*⁸⁸ One of the most well-known epistolary merchants' manuals was *The Marchant's Avizo* (1589), which offered advice to young men on the importance of trade and credit. Trade with other nations depended on international travel, transport, and communication, and many of these books emphasized that they could help a man as he crossed the oceans. The subtitle of *The Marchant's Avizo* was: 'very necessarie for their sons and servants, when they first send them beyond the seas.'⁸⁹ Letters became important for ever wider realms of individuals, as both literacy and trade abroad accelerated. This connection of letters and trade abroad would continue to be a critical one. Letters circulated a great deal of information about credit, not only in their contents but also in their style.

To write well was the first thing a man needed to do to become a man of credit. This imperative outranked even knowing how to calculate sums or to balance ledgers. The first instruction to would-be merchants given by *Lex Mercatoria Rediviva* was: 'To write properly and correctly.'⁹⁰ Daniel Defoe opened his *Complete Tradesman* with advice on how to write letters, since, as he noted, 'I have mentioned this [letter style] in the beginning of this work, because indeed it is the beginning of a tradesman's business'.⁹¹ Defoe sought to teach styles of letter-writing associated with business, not literature: 'an easie free concise way of writing is the best stile . . . He that affects a rumbling and bombast stile, and fills his letters with long harangues, compliments, and flourishes, should turn poet instead of tradesman.'⁹² Defoe proceeded to give an example of one ludicrously literary letter, in which a young trader wrote: 'Sɪʀ, The destinies having so appointed it, and my dark stars concurring, that I, who by nature was fram'd for better things, should be put out to trade . . . [I] hereby let you know that I shall have occasion for the goods hereafter mention'd.' Such a letter, Defoe mocked, 'put his correspondent in *London* into a fit of laughter, and instead of sending him the goods he wrote for, put him . . . to enquire after his character . . . or else . . . to be fil'd up among such letters as deserv'd no answer.'⁹³ Defoe then offered the contrast of a succinct, well-written letter: 'Bᴇɪɴɢ obliged, Sir, by my late master's decease to enter immediately upon his business . . . I here send you a small order . . . I have enclosed a bill of exchange . . . that you will send me the goods well stored, and well chosen, and as cheap as possible, that I may be encourag'd to a farther correspondence.' This letter, Defoe proclaimed, caused 'his correspondent in *London* [to] presently say, this young man writes like a man of business; pray let us take care to use him well.'⁹⁴ To be a man of business and of credit demanded first that a man *write* like one, and this style, both easy and concise, was one that many fathers also modeled.

---

⁸⁸ This book was a translation from a French manual. See Hornbeak, *The Complete Letter-Writer in English*, 1–13.
⁸⁹ John Browne, *The Marchants Avizo* [1589], ed. Patrick McGrath (Boston: Baker Library, Harvard Graduate School of Business Administration, 1957), title-page.
⁹⁰ Beawes, *Lex Mercatoria Rediviva*, 30.   ⁹¹ Defoe, *Complete English Tradesman*, 27.
⁹² Ibid. 23.   ⁹³ Ibid. 23–4.   ⁹⁴ Ibid. 24.

Like Defoe, even the aristocratic Lord Chesterfield repeated to his son such injunctions about the need for a plain and clear style in business letters: 'The first thing necessary, in writing letters of business, is extreme clearness and perspicuity; every paragraph should be so clear, and unambiguous, that the dullest fellow in the world may not be able to mistake it.' He continued: 'Business must be well, not affectedly dressed; but by no means negligently. Let your first attention be to clearness.'[95] Elegance was still requisite, but of far greater import was clarity. Chesterfield reiterated his point: 'No flourishes, no declamation. But (I repeat it again) there is an elegant simplicity and dignity of style absolutely necessary for good letters of business; attend to that carefully.' He used this advice to point out particular epistolary failings of his son's: 'I should not mention correct orthography, but that you very often fail in that particular, which will bring ridicule upon you; for no man is allowed to spell ill. I wish too that your hand-writing were much better . . . Neatness in folding up, sealing, and directing your packets, is by no means to be neglected . . . But there is something in the exterior, even of a packet, that may please or displease.'[96] Even the appearance of the letter mattered in business, and carefulness needed to attend even the way the letter was sealed.

Numerous fathers and father-figures repeated these kinds of injunctions to their sons, nephews, and others. Twinned exhortations—to industry and good behavior, and to learning and letters—occur frequently in these epistles. Signs of sloppiness in letter-writing signaled to fathers far graver crimes. Let us return to Ralph Wormeley, the father with whom this chapter began. Ralph was eager to impress habits of industry and honesty on his son. So, in the same letter with which we began, Ralph proclaimed: 'if you keep bad company, if you indulge in idleness, temptation will assail you, and no way sooner would you be conducted to ruin.'[97] Elsewhere, Ralph painted a dark picture of the ways of vice and idleness that had already proved 'the ruin of thousands of easy-minded Youths'.[98] He reminded his son that such idleness 'will never do for you, who must be devoted to business, must be a man of business, or, must be a vagabond through life'.[99] The lesson was clear: 'never be idle . . . lose no time.'[100] Success depended on the right use of time, as well as on the right use of resources. As Charles Carroll wrote to his son, he hoped that the boy would 'avoid the many temptations wch by being Idle you will be exposed to, for nothing is more certain

---

[95] Lord Chesterfield to his son, letter 45, 'London, December the 19th, O.S., 1751', Chesterfield, *Letters*, ii. 189.
[96] Ibid. ii. 191.
[97] Ralph Wormeley to Warner Wormely, 'Rosegill 29 June 1801', Mss1/W8945/a-1, Wormeley Family Papers, 1791–1952, VHS.
[98] Ralph Wormeley to Warner Wormely, 'Rosegill 24 April 1802', Mss1/W8945/a-3, ibid.
[99] Ibid.   [100] Ibid.

than that Idleness is the Root of all Evil'.[101] Several of Ralph's letters castigated his son for spending too much, since 'I sent you to London to try to make you a man of mercantile business'.[102] To become a man of business meant living within his allowance, as well as being honest. Ralph cautioned his son: 'never on any occasion to prevaricate; never resort to duplicity . . . —if you once say the thing that is not, your character for veracity will be blasted for ever—and, if your actions be double, if, you are false, indeed, you had better fly to the solitude of the desert, than the busy haunts of men.' It would not do to have his character as a man of credit 'blasted'. Ralph exhorted his son to demonstrate virtue and learning in his letters: 'I hope to hear of your progress in learning, and of your distinguished rectitude of conduct.'[103]

Far too often, however, young Warner's letters did not demonstrate much progress. Such epistolary problems signaled to Ralph failings of a deeper sort. Ralph admonished his son: 'I am sorry to say, that you do not improve (by your letters) up to my expectation—if you be vain and frivolous, instead of solid and steady, given to laziness, instead of to thought and reflection, you will come to nothing, nay, come to ruin.'[104] He fretted over his son's spelling: 'I am concerned . . . that you do not write either as to language or orthography, as I expected you would from the opportunities you have enjoyed.' He continued: 'your wrong spelling of the local adverb here, which you confounded with the verb to hear, is such a gross error, that a youth of your age, who has been at a grammar school, ought not to have committed. Lord Chesterfield tells his son that he knew a nobleman (more shame for him!) who was ridiculed all his life for writing, upon the hole, instead of whole.' Ralph ended this section by exhorting his son: 'study English grammar . . . read Epistolary compositions.' He ended the letter: 'I intreat you, as well, for your future advantages in your future vocation, as for your own happiness through life, to apply to your scholastic pursuits.'[105] Nearly two years later, Ralph continued to be disappointed in his son's letters: 'I have written to you most frequently & am sorry to find you so little improved—in your mother's letter which, by no means, pleased me, I find you do not know the difference between accepted & Excepted, and use the latter word, instead of, the former. In your's to me you have this word, unequalable

---

[101] Charles Carroll to Charley Carroll, 'Octr 7th 1759', Ronald Hoffman, Sally D. Mason, and Eleanor S. Darcy (eds.), *Dear Papa, Dear Charley: The Peregrinations of a Revolutionary Aristocrat, as told by Charles Carroll of Carrollton and his father, Charles Carroll of Annapolis*, 3 vols. (Chapel Hill, NC: University of North Carolina Press for the Omohundro Institute of Early American History and Culture, 2001), i. 129.
[102] Ralph Wormeley to Warner Wormely, 'Rosegill 16 May 1803', Mss1/W8945/a-5, Wormeley Family Papers, 1791–1952, VHS
[103] Ralph Wormeley to Warner Wormely, 'Rosegill 29 June 1801', Mss1/W8945/a-1, ibid.
[104] Ralph Wormeley to Warner Wormely, 'Rosegill 29th June 1803', Mss1/W8945/a-6, ibid.
[105] Ralph Wormeley to Warner Wormely, 'Rosegill 16 Decr 1801', Mss1/W8945/a-2, ibid.

advice, there is no such word.'[106] Elsewhere, Ralph saw in colloquial diction signs of lack of trustworthiness: 'Where did you collect this elegant expression, "any how"... my own opinion is, that you are not fit to be trusted.'[107]

That sons chafed and buckled under such censures is clear, even in the absence of their own letters. Sons learned to defend themselves, their letters, and their characters in their replies to fathers. The echoes of Warner's frustrated replies come through even in Ralph's letters. So, Warner must have provided proof to his father that the word 'unequalable' did exist, since Ralph replied: 'I find, I was hypocritical in saying there was no such word as "unequalable," the truth is, it is become obsolete.'[108] Warner must further have complained that by making this claim, his father assumed he was 'an idiot', since Ralph continued his own letter by noting that it did not follow that 'I thought or took you for an idiot'.[109] Warner must also have accused his father of being too 'acute' in his attacks. Ralph responded by pointing out, much as Lord Chesterfield did, that it was his duty to correct his son's mistakes: 'you are so little delicate, as to say to your Father, "you are certainly very acute in taking me up in my letters;" whereas you ought to be obliged to me for taking this trouble of criticizing your mistakes when you commit any, and not like a self-sufficient & ignorant youth express your indignation at it'.[110] Self-sufficiency was not acceptable behavior from a son dependent on a father, at least in matters of personal criticism. Elsewhere, Ralph refused to admit he had been scolding his son: 'neither have I upbraided your conduct, tho' it do [sic!] not meet my full approbation: it is the duty of a parent to advise his child for his sake; it is the duty of a parent for the sake of all his children to restrain any form [of] licentiousness and extravagance.'[111] Like Chesterfield, Ralph considered it his duty to offer 'strict scrutiny' to correct a son.

Like Ralph Wormeley, Michael Keane, originally from Ireland but relocated to St Vincent in the West Indies, also offered 'strict scrutiny' when his son attended Harrow, Cambridge, and the Inns of Court in England. In a letter-book, Michael copied letters to his son in which he hoped that Hugh's tutor would 'not encourage Idleness & Extravagance nor suffer himself to be prevailed upon under any Pretence to advance a Shilling for Hugh'.[112] Frequently Michael recorded not the full letter but simply its main point, so that he noted: 'wrote to Hugh... expressing much Surprize at the largness of his Extra Expences', or

---

[106] Ralph Wormeley to Warner Wormely, 'Rosegill 16 May 1803', Mss1/W8945/a-5, ibid.
[107] Ralph Wormeley to Warner Wormely, 'Rosegill 8th: Septr: 1803', Mss1/W8945/a-8, ibid.
[108] Ralph Wormeley to Warner Lewis Wormely, 'Rosegill 8th: Novr: 1803', Mss1/W8945/a-9, ibid.
[109] Ibid.   [110] Ibid.
[111] Ralph Wormeley to Warner Lewis Wormely, 'Rosegill 8th: Septr: 1803', Mss1/W8945/a-8, ibid.
[112] Michael Keane to Mrs Greg, 'St. Vincent 3d May 1789', Letterbook of Michael Keane, Box 1, Keane Family Papers, VHS, p. 221.

'Wrote to Hugh P. Keane expressive of my Dissatisfaction with him upon many Grounds'.[113] That Michael had little belief in the efficacy of these letters is clear in the opening of one:

Having experienced... how little you regard my advice... I shall forbear to obtrude either Advice or Observation upon you in future under a persuasion that when you find yourself obliged to provide Payment for what you want by your own Industry and professional Application without any other Resource or Friend to resort to you will find it necessary to be much more careful & œconomical... than all I have been saying or wishing to you for 10 years could have inculcated.[114]

Independence and the need to support himself would, Michael claimed, help his son become an orderly man of business, even if his own letters did not succeed in doing so. Elsewhere, he harangued his son: 'Believe me young Man: you have been playing a foolish Game & I shall not be much surprized if I soon hear of your being in Difficulties Your Want of Candour & Confidence in me leaves me not the smallest Room to expect that I shall distress or embarrass myself for you... I remain Dear Hugh, Your much dissatisfied father.'[115]

Like Warner Lewis, who complained of 'acuteness', Hugh Keane apparently grumbled about his father's 'quizzing'. In two of his own letters, Michael noted: 'it was the Extremity of Folly & Dissipation in you to attempt to keep an Horse, for besides the Expence it must have drawn your Attention from more useful matters. This you will call "quizzing you."'[116] In another, Michael smarted at Hugh's own smarting: 'I hope to hear you have disposed Of your dashing Molly [the horse] & that you will mend your Reading & not mak[in]g Excursions to Bedfordshire You See I cannot help "Quizzing You—."'[117] To quiz a son in such a manner was his duty, since, as he himself noted, 'it is now your Time to exert yourself in those Pursuits, the attainment of which to a certain Degree must make you either respectable or contemptible in your professional Line'.[118] To make a son respectable required a marshalling of effort on the part of both the father far away (who then offered scrutiny) and the son himself.

Even the highly sensible Pierce Butler used such methods in his letters to his son. Pierce was the classic paternalist, calling himself his son's friend, but the focus of his letters, as with these other fathers, was on 'strict scrutiny'. In a typical example, written as Thomas was close to turning 11, Pierce noted: 'I have therefore a right to look for some fruits—I expect some budings at least, of a Cultivated Mind—If I am mistaken in You I shall be a miserable disappointed Father.' He continued by exhorting Thomas always to keep these hopes in

---

[113] '13th May 1788', and 'Sepr. 20 1789', ibid. pp. 67, 258.
[114] Michael Keane to Hugh Keane, 'St. Vincent 5th April 1789', ibid. p. 187.
[115] Michael Keane to Hugh Keane, 'St. Vincent 16th April 1789', ibid. p. 208.
[116] Michael Keane to Hugh Keane, 'St. Vincent 3d May 1789', ibid. p. 211.
[117] Michael Keane to Hugh Keane, 'St. Vincent 10 May 1789', ibid. p. 225.
[118] Michael Keane to Mrs. Greg, 'St. Vincent 3d May 1789', ibid. p. 211.

mind: 'You must therefore think of nothing but improving your mind... When your School fellows ask You out to play remember this; and say, I must go read or write, otherwise I can not accomplish what my Father, my best friend, expects of me.' He concluded the letter by shaming Thomas by comparing him, unfavorably, to his older sisters: 'If You do not apply... Your Sisters will have more acquired Knowledge than You; which, however tenderly I love them, would hurt me much. I am never under a necessity of Exhorting them to apply; they do it without my requiring.'[119] Such themes—of worries over possible disappointment, of exhortations to work hard and improve, of embarrassing comparisons with more learned sisters—sounded repeatedly in Pierce Butler's letters to his son. In one, he invoked Jonathan Swift's willingness to study for thirteen hours a day for eight years: 'Why may not my Son do the same! If He loves me—if He regards my peace, and the satisfaction of His Sisters; But above all, if He reveres the Memory of his Mother He will do it.'[120] In another letter, he pointed out: 'If You wish then for my love and Esteem You must read a great deal... You must write a fine fair hand.'[121]

For Pierce Butler, as for many fathers, his son could prove himself not only through reports of the tutor but also in the 'fine fair hand' he showed in the very letters he sent home. These were really the only means by which a father some 3,000 miles away could divine whether his son was learning good lessons. In one letter to the tutor, Pierce noted: 'I am very desirous of His writing a good hand—My anxiety in every particular increases as He advances towards Manhood.'[122] Pierce, like other fathers, fretfully scrutinized his son's letters, even the very shape of the words on the page, for evidence of industry or idleness, of talents or failings. After declaring: 'If You realy love me You will forego play, and improve your mind,' he also launched into a detailed critique of his son's writing: 'The writing of Your two letters is not quite so well as I expected. On the last strokes of Your m's n's and w's, there are Corners—Your Sisters all write well—When will You write as well as the inclosed letter from your Sister Sally?'[123] Later, he praised the hand of some letters, but not unreservedly, informing his son that his last letter 'is written in the best hand of any that I have received from You, except the Capital J in Your Name, which is in a Vulgar Shape'.[124] There were gender and status pressures exerted in these comments: would his son want to be 'vulgar' or worse than a girl in his writing? This point receives further clarification in a later letter in which Pierce complained to the tutor: 'His last letter to me is illy executed—the Letters are vulgarly shaped, liker

---

[119] Pierce Butler to Thomas Butler, 'MaryVille Sunday morn Ye 22d. February 1789', Pierce Butler Letter Collection, Add. Mss. 16603, BL.
[120] Pierce Butler to Weeden Butler, 'Philadelphia November ye 19th 1792', ibid.
[121] Pierce Butler to Thomas Butler, 'Philadelphia October ye 5th 1789', ibid.
[122] Pierce Butler to Weeden Butler, 'Philadelphia March Ye 4th. 1793', ibid.
[123] Pierce Butler to Thomas Butler, 'New York September ye 28th. 1789', ibid.
[124] Pierce Butler to Thomas Butler, 'Sunday November Ye 13th. 1791', ibid.

to the writing of a Stable boy than a Gentleman—how mortifying! How is it possible that with such penmanship He can ever get through much business!'[125] Pierce claimed he was forced to drop the subject: 'I find it agitates my mind too much.'[126] Handwriting would show his son to be a 'gentleman' or not, might help or hinder his chances at business success.

Such letters became an exaggerated version of what might have happened had the sons been closer to home. Reading the words came to stand in for actually being able to view, monitor, or chastize a son. This distance begins to explain the insistent and fretful tone found in so many of them. The financial investment in the son's education was another reason for the nervousness. Even though Pierce Butler's daughter Sarah showed great academic ability, and was as 'good a Mathematician . . . as any Mathematician in Carolina', it was her brother who received the more expensive education.[127] At one point, Pierce fussed: 'His Sisters are fortunate enough to distinguish themselves Shall I have one Son only, and He alone the Blockhead of my Family.'[128] Paying handsomely for the education of the male heir, blockhead or not, represented a considerable family investment for its future prosperity. Investment of capital had again as much place in the family as on the plantation or in the port. It was a way to achieve and maintain prosperity.

Similar themes resonate in the relationship between Simon Taylor (whom I will call Simon), a Jamaican planter, and his nephew and heir, Sir Simon Taylor (whom I will call Sir Simon). Pierce Butler and Simon Taylor were very different men, but their methods were remarkably similar. Although he made occasional visits to England, Simon, an exceptionally rich planter and agent, spent most of his life in Jamaica. In keeping with Jamaican traditions, he never legally married. So, although he maintained a decades-long relationship with his free black housekeeper, Grace Donne, and although he sired at least two illegitimate children, he had no recognized legal offspring.[129] Therefore his attention was focused on his nephew, whose father had died when Sir Simon was an infant. Sir Simon was raised in Britain, while Simon resided in Jamaica, so

---

125 Pierce Butler to Weeden Butler, 'Philadelphia February Ye 3rd. 1793', ibid.
126 Ibid.
127 Pierce Butler to Thomas Butler, 'Mary Ville Sunday ye. 5th of April 1789', ibid. Even Pierce Butler eventually conceded: 'I find, with some degree of Mortification, yet with resignation . . . that Tom's parts are not bright.' Pierce Butler to Weeden Butler, 'Charleston May ye 6th 1792', ibid. See Bell, *Major Butler's Legacy*, 45. Ultimately, Pierce was to grow so disappointed with Thomas that he directed the bulk of his estate in inheritance to Thomas's older sister Sarah, and two of her sons: ibid. 486.
128 Pierce Butler to Weeden Butler, 'Philadelphia November ye 19th 1792', Pierce Butler Letter Collection, Add. Mss. 16603, BL.
129 Details of the relationship with Grace Donne and her children can be found in Simon Taylor Papers, ICS. Lady Maria Nugent, who recorded her friendship with Simon Taylor, confided on 10 March 1802 that she was told he had illegitimate children on all of his plantations. Frank Cundal (ed.), *Lady Nugent's Journal: Jamaica One Hundred Years Ago* (London: Adam & Charles Black for the Institute of Jamaica, 1907), 93.

the two only saw each other twice, for brief visits. Despite the paucity of physical contact, the two Simon Taylors developed a complex, if troubled, relationship in hundreds of letters exchanged between 1792 and 1811.[130] Simon was both rich and irascible; he was also deeply concerned to mold his heir into the sort of man who would superintend and develop properties worth hundreds of thousands of pounds. He wanted his nephew to avoid what he saw as the dissipations of metropolitan life, as well as the new revolutionary philosophies that swirled throughout this Atlantic world. Simon used his letters in order to create the sort of man he wanted Sir Simon to be, and Simon was not a man with whom to trifle.

Like Pierce Butler, Simon sought to make his heir an industrious man of business, one who wrote well and was ready to take over plantations. Also like Pierce Butler, Simon was unable to monitor him personally, and therefore resorted to letters as the way both to read Sir Simon's abilities and to impart his own lessons. Also like Pierce Butler, Simon used gender and status pressures in order to achieve his ends. So, in the first of his surviving letters, Simon chided: 'You do write better than you did, but not half so well as your Sister . . . and will you lett a Lady write better than you, it is my particular desire that you learn to write exceeding well.'[131] Elsewhere, Simon complained: 'I am really ashamed to see how ill you spell, such a thing might be pardonable in a Footman . . . but is not so in any one who has been supposed to have had a liberall Education.'[132] He summarized: 'I must try and insist . . . that you apply in good earnest to write a good legible hand, Spell well, and Ground yourself thoroughly in Arithmetick . . . for it would be a Shame and a Scandall to you to be pointed at as a Blockhead.'[133]

Sir Simon's handwriting, spelling, and diction all were signals of whether he was heeding his uncle's advice, and so avoiding idleness, extravagance, drunkenness, and other vices. For Simon, such failings were the 'rocks on which many a Man splits'.[134] In telling a morality tale of another man who ended up in debt, Simon prayed: 'God grant you may avoid the Shoals and Rocks that he has shipwrecked himself on.'[135] In one letter, Simon noted that: 'Drinking and

---

[130] There are some gaps for when letters or letter-books were lost, but this still leaves hundreds of letters.

[131] Simon Taylor to Sir Simon Richard Brissett Taylor, 'Kingston Jamaica March 27. 1798', I/B/15, Simon Taylor Papers, ICS.

[132] Simon Taylor to Sir Simon Richard Brissett Taylor, 'Kingston Jamaica Octr. 22. 1801', I/E/7, ibid.

[133] Simon Taylor to Sir Simon Richard Brissett Taylor, 'Kingston Jamaica Aprill 11. 1799', I/C/1, ibid.

[134] Simon Taylor to Sir Simon Richard Brissett Taylor, 'Kingston Jamaica Feby. 6 [1799]', I/B/43, ibid.

[135] Simon Taylor to Sir Simon Richard Brissett Taylor, 'Kingston Jamaica May 14. 1800', I/D/15, ibid.

Gaming are the two most pernicious Vices that a Man can learn.'[136] But idleness and extravagance were equally bad. He cautioned his nephew not to harbor any aspirations to be a man of fashion, or, as Simon phrased it, 'a Coxcomb & Puppy'.[137] In Simon's representation, Sir Simon sought merely to be a man of fashion, while Simon himself sought to be (and indeed succeeded in being) a man of hard work and moderation:

You consider an Indolent lounging life to dress Gayly fine Cloaths Horses Equipages Dissipation and to have nothing to do I on the Contrary think far otherwise I think that every person should dedicate the Whole of the Morning from the Hour he rises Untill He goes to dress for Dinner to the Study of some thing usefull looking over his own Affairs inspecting his Accounts writing & conserving letters and seeing all his Accounts entered in to proper Books avoiding all debts whatsoever never giving way to Idleness nor Dissipation nor leaving that to be done to tomorrow that can be done today.[138]

In 1799 Simon exhorted his nephew: 'I myself who am an old Man think nothing of sitting down twelve Hours in the 24 ... and if I can do it at my Age what should hinder you from doing the Same ... you must make a Fortune before you dissipate one and I wish to putt you in a Way both to make the one and preserve the other.'[139] Five years later Simon made his desires for Sir Simon explicit: 'Your situation in life will require you should be active and Stirring and continually overlooking your own Matters with your own eyes.'[140] Simon was thus concerned to inculcate the 'vigorous spirit of enterprise', even advising his nephew to avoid 'hovering by the fire' and instead to learn 'Manual Exercises'.[141] Simon reminded his nephew that his father had died in debt, and that it was only Simon's own generosity and labor that ensured the future of the family's fortunes. As Simon summarized: 'Indolence is ruin to the Man that possesses a West India Property, and therefore I mention it to you so often.'[142] Unremitting threats of disinheritance also accompanied Simon's advice.

More than other employment, Sir Simon's whole livelihood depended on the letters he sent across the Atlantic. Sir Simon recognized that his future lay in pleasing his uncle, and so in his letters he constantly represented himself as

---

[136] Ibid.
[137] Simon Taylor to Sir Simon Richard Brissett Taylor, 'Kingston Jamaica Aprill 11. 1799', I/C/1, ibid.
[138] Simon Taylor to Sir Simon Richard Brissett Taylor, 'Kingston Jamaica Janry. 15. 1801', I/D/47, ibid.
[139] Simon Taylor to Sir Simon Richard Brissett Taylor, 'Kingston Jamaica October 27. 1799', I/C/30 and 'Kingston Jamaica May 14. 1800', I/D/15, ibid.
[140] Simon Taylor to Sir Simon Richard Brissett Taylor, 'Kingston Jamaica Novr. 30. 1799', I/C/38, ibid.
[141] Simon Taylor to Sir Simon Richard Brissett Taylor, 'Kingston Jamaica feby. 6 [1799]', I/B/43, ibid.
[142] Simon Taylor to Sir Simon Richard Brissett Taylor, 'Kingston Jamaica May 14. 1800', I/D/15, ibid.

hard-working, upright, patriotic, and studious. His handwriting and spelling also steadily improved. He also explicitly claimed to be following his uncle's advice. So, for instance, as Simon had suggested, he carefully procured Blackstone's *Commentaries*.[143] Indeed, such a good boy was Simon that he even quoted from it in later letters to his uncle.[144] Still, as careful as Sir Simon was in his self-representations, sometimes he was not careful enough. In two episodes, in 1805–6 and again in 1810, Sir Simon blundered in his replies to proposals from his uncle, thereby unleashing the terror of disinheritance. In one infuriated reply in 1806, Simon informed his nephew: 'the expressions you have thought proper to make use of in your letter have made those impressions on my mind that I have resolved firmly to close you for ever from my Affection and Fortune and therefore do not busy yourself in the expectations or hopes that you will be my Heir.'[145] In his reply, Sir Simon attempted to distance himself from his epistolary missteps: 'I solemnly declare they [my expressions] proceeded from a bad choice of words and not from any intention to give you offence.'[146] Although Sir Simon won grudging forgiveness in 1806, another similar problem occurred in 1810, in an episode over his choice of marriage partner, in which his uncle declared: 'the letter which you have thought proper to write and send me has made [me] alter every thing in my Will which was in your Favor.'[147] In horror, Sir Simon replied with profuse apologies for 'those unguarded expressions which have given you so much offence'.[148] He sent several letters sounding this same theme. When these seemed to have no effect, Sir Simon made a surprise voyage to Jamaica to beg forgiveness in person. When the visit failed in its purpose, Sir Simon again resorted to letters, the mainstay of his relationship with his uncle. In a letter from Simon's own property of Jamaica in 1812, Sir Simon opened: 'Having no opportunity of conversing with you since my residence in your house in the friendly manner which I flattered myself you would have allowed of, and which was the cause of my coming to this country, I feel myself reluctantly compeled to

---

[143] Ibid.

[144] Writing in 1803, acknowledging that the war recently declared between France and England would prevent his uncle from visiting England, Sir Simon grumbled: 'If I were not too loyal subject to find fault with any measure of the Government and were I not perfectly disposed to believe in a moral sense what Blackstone has taught me is Constitutionally true "that the King can do no wrong" I confess I should be very much inclined to murmur at an event which may perhaps deprive me of a pleasure.' Sir Simon Richard Brissett Taylor to Simon Taylor, 'Lausanne July 14th. 1803', VI/A/40, ibid.

[145] Simon Taylor to Sir Simon Richard Brissett Taylor, 'Kingston Jamaica Jany. 15. 1806', I/G/41, ibid.

[146] Sir Simon Richard Brissett Taylor to Simon Taylor, 'Cumberland Place April 1st 1806', VI/A/54, ibid.

[147] Simon Taylor to Sir Simon Richard Brissett, 'Kingston Jamaica Aug. 1. 1811', I/J/45, ibid.

[148] Sir Simon Richard Brissett Taylor to Simon Taylor, 'Great Cumberland Place October. 11th. 1811', VI/A/104, ibid.

address you in writing, trusting that you will not refuse to receive my letter.'[149] With that, Sir Simon gave up and returned to England, though he continued to send letters pleading for forgiveness. Whether because of these letters or for some other reason, it appears that Simon did not in fact disinherit his nephew, despite his threats.[150] Still, Sir Simon had learned the hard way how to write letters to his uncle, a fierce critic eager to make his heir into the kind of man he wanted him to be.

Simon Taylor seems in many respects a classic patriarch, exercising his powers in the most terrifying ways possible, in his letters and on his Jamaican estates. A harsh tone, and threats of disinheritance, formed the backbone of his letters to his nephew. By contrast, Pierce Butler seems a classic paternalist, concerned to be a friend to his son, and much more given to the language of sensibility. Simon Taylor detested anything that smacked of reform or revolution, while Pierce Butler was an ardent Revolutionary leader. Yet both men adopted similar methods in their letters, in order to shape boys into deserving heirs and men of credit. Both pressured these boys to learn to write well and to become men of business, twinned desires for both. The surviving letters of both men testify to their hopes of monitoring these boys and turning them into hard-working men who could write well and prosper. These kinds of desires demonstrate the unity of the Atlantic world they inhabited, as well as the worries that swirled around the prosperity that both men, and many others, had achieved.

Such prosperity seemed ever elusive, even to those men who had achieved it. In the financially difficult years after the American Revolution, on both sides of the Atlantic, the ability to succeed needed, these fathers felt, to be drummed into their sons especially. If this meant 'dunning', 'quizzing', or 'strict scrutiny', then it was a father's duty and right to inculcate habits and proofs of industry and credit in his son, above all. It showed both his paternalist affection and his patriarchal power, to try to ensure the future prosperity of his male heir. In one letter Pierce Butler enquired about Thomas's talents: 'Is there, or is there not, a good foundation to build on?'[151] At the same time that Butler was writing these letters, he was also involved in the Constitutional Convention, seeking to build a 'good foundation' for this new nation. In one letter, explaining the system of government in the United States, he quoted General Washington: 'much

---

[149] Sir Simon Richard Brissett Taylor to Simon Taylor, 'Prospect Penn March 28th. 1812', VI/A/107, ibid.

[150] The bulk of Simon Taylor's estate, worth a mind-boggling £ 881,966 5s. 7 1/4d., was left to Sir Simon. See 'Will of Simon Taylor', made 2 December 1808 and proved 27 April 1813, LRO Wills, vol. 87, fos. 1–34, Jamaica Record Office. Many thanks to Betty Wood for providing me with this reference.

[151] Pierce Butler to Weeden Butler, 'New York October ye 8th 1787', Pierce Butler Letter Collection, Add. Mss. 16603, BL.

must depend on the Morals and manners of the People at large.'[152] All kinds of economies, those of nations as well as those of families, depended on these good foundations, and so fathers and politicians worried about them incessantly. Such foundations were laid in the loving bosom of the family. In addition, by displaying forms of scrutinizing letters, father modeled both behavior and prose. Both were equally important in order for a son to make his way in the world, a world in which credit was so crucial to individuals, families, households, and nations. In the next chapter we shall see how these desires and methods played out in one family in particular.

[152] Pierce Butler to Weeden Butler, 'undated', ibid.

PART II

'WHAT MAY BE OUR LOT': STORIES OF CONNECTION AND DISCONNECTION

Introduction

Our Youth, however well inclined, are too apt to be disgusted by the Formality of Precepts; and to slight the most important Truths, when inculcated by the dry Maxims of Philosophy, or enforced in a magisterial Manner: But the Case is quite otherwise, when the World is thus set before them; when the Consequences of Virtue and Vice are exhibited in Characters and Events drawn from Nature and real Life, and the Human Heart is laid open, and all the Springs that gave it Motion exposed to View.

(The Complete Letter-Writer, 1757)[1]

All history, that descends to a sufficient detail of human actions and characters, is useful to bring us acquainted with our species, nay with ourselves.

(Bolingbroke, 1752)[2]

The next part focuses on three Atlantic families in crisis. It is possible in these stories to see both the disruptions and the benefits of Atlantic distance for individual families. Letters allowed these families to remain in contact despite distance, and they also provided an arena in which complex family dynamics played out. Letter-writers deployed certain cultural tropes in order to attempt to persuade other family members in particular directions. Themes of familiarity, sensibility, and credit resonate in these letters and these narratives. The individuals under focus here relied on connections, both familial and otherwise, as they made their ways on different sides of the Atlantic. Sensibility formed a key style, as well as a critical means of justification for a variety of decisions and claims. These stories also highlight the importance of credit in the decision-making that went on in these families, for whom the entire North Atlantic represented a locale in which to pursue personal and dynastic ambitions. These people moved with some ease across the ocean, helped along by family connections, feelings, and credit.

The families under focus in these last three chapters were chosen for several reasons. First, they all experienced significant Atlantic sojourns, and distances

---

[1] *The Complete Letter-Writer*, 4th edn. (London, 1757), n.p.
[2] Viscount Henry St John Bolingbroke, Letter V, in *Letters on the Study and Use of History*, 2nd edn. (London, 1752), 138.

between members, remedied in part by letters. They also experienced crisis, for a variety of reasons, and a need to find equilibrium in their domestic lives. Families functioned as both sources of anxiety and as sources of the alleviation of that anxiety, in all of these cases. Perhaps most importantly, all left rich epistolary and other accounts, which provide access into the complicated dialogues and disputes that characterized them. Most centrally, there are surviving letters for the chief protagonists; this is essential. They also represent different regions and colonies, and so provide at least some sense of unifying themes, as well as more particular trajectories.

One such trajectory concerns the story of an unhappy series of disputes between a father and a son, the subject of Chapter 5, 'The Repentant Son and the Unforgiving Father: Making a Man of Feeling, a Man of Credit'. This chapter, which focuses on the Chesapeake and Scotland, looks at a rupture between a father and son, over issues of sentiment, but mainly over issues of credit. It seeks to understand why a father remained so furious at a son who died young that it was difficult for the son to obtain forgiveness, even in death. The importance of credit, in economic, political, and domestic terms, is central to this story. It also traces the ways that the social and political merged, so that a political background could deeply affect the way a father–son relationship played out. It corrects notions of rigid Loyalists or anxious patriarchs, and instead concentrates on the pressures of an Atlantic economic and credit system.

Chapter 6, 'The Farewell Between Husband and Wife: The Politics of Family Feeling', looks at the separation of a husband and a wife during and immediately after the American Revolution, considering those moments when the 'silken cords' of 'matrimonial bondage' were stretched by distance and disorder. Concentrating on New England and England, it seeks to answer the question of why a husband did not return to his wife at the war's end, and what this meant. Women in such circumstances could obtain a kind of limited leverage from eloquent sensibility. Charges of unfeelingness, an important domestic claim, could also take on additional political meaning in wartime situations. At the same time, claims of 'family feeling' could also be put in service of some rather dubious political and domestic choices.

Some couples suffered because of geographical separations; others endured different kinds of division. Chapter 7, 'The Old Husband and the Young Wife: Scandal, Feeling, and Distance', looks at a moment of outrageous adultery in a family, tracking why a cuckolded 'old husband' was willing to offer forgiveness to the wife who betrayed him. It raises issues about the lives of Anglo-Jamaican families, and the complicated ways in which distance between family members created both crises and the solutions to them. This chapter also attends to women's ability to deploy eloquent sensibility, and the limits of this language. It also tracks how Atlantic distance could both undermine and make possible 'family feeling'.

Why should we care about these three families? After all, as one 1769 letter-writer declared: 'It matters little to the World what may happen to me or any Individual, & few care what may be our Lot except a small Circle of Friends & Acquaintance, who may perhaps give us a passing Sigh, cry "Poor Fellow" & so wind up the Story.'[3] There are three major reasons. First, these tales allow us to witness the exigencies of everyday life in tandem with cultural imperatives, of the sort we have seen in the last three chapters. Cultural and social ideals created the scripts that gave meaning to individual actions, that provided justification for personal decisions, and that ameliorated the anxieties provoked by dramatic events. Individuals made decisions (to forgive an erring son, to choose a side in war, to leave a wife behind) within the parameters of certain possibilities available to them. To comprehend those parameters, it is necessary to understand the larger culture, as well as the ways in which such choices were communicated and articulated. But to answer the far more difficult question—why did a particular individual do what he or she did?—requires a grasp of a complex amalgamation of social, political, economic, military, and cultural circumstances. This complicated mix brings us to the second reason why it is worth caring about these families. To examine these narratives carefully is to face head-on the ways that a variety of imperatives affected behavior. Political loyalties as well as economic imperatives influenced the ways that domestic decisions proceeded, while at the same time, domestic concerns informed political and economic determinations. Rather than focusing narrowly on patriarchy or paternalism, or on political motivations, it is possible to see the potency of domestic imperatives, which affected men as much as women.

Finally, this investigation of particular families provides a much-needed corrective to stereotypes, both from the time and from subsequent historians. These case studies juxtapose stock images from the time, subsequent historical categories, and a detailed examination of motivations. Thus, each chapter begins with an archetypal image from the time, such as the penitent son, the husband heading to war, or the cuckolded old husband. Starting in this way allows access into the kinds of images that influenced these letter-writers, and the kinds of anxieties and comforts that animated both imagined and historical families. Just as readers of magazines and novels relied on certain stock types, so too have historians. Slotting individuals into categories such as conservative Loyalist or anxious patriarch or West Indian tyrant has allowed historians to make sense of the chaos of particular lives. This tendency is understandable, but it is not always terribly productive.[4] Such labels make it all too easy to dismiss an individual as

---

[3] Thomas Coombe to Sally Coombe, 'London Feb: 24/69', Thomas Coombe Papers, HSP.

[4] As Ira Berlin has observed in other contexts, 'as always, close examination of the particulars of the human condition subverts general ideas, for it exposes contradictions and unearths exceptions to the most powerful generalizations'. Ira Berlin, *Many Thousands Gone: The First Two Centuries of Slavery in North America* (Cambridge, Mass.: Harvard University Press, 1998), 4. Along similar

simply a typical member of a group, thus encouraging a certain unwillingness to pursue particular motivations and circumstances. However, these particularities can often reveal more general points about the times than we might have realized. In so investigating these tales, it is possible, then, to move beyond the historical and historiographical stereotypes that surround such families, and to reveal something new about their worlds.

One final point: to tell these tales is not to exonerate or condone. We needn't like the protagonists at the end of all this. Many of these people made bad decisions, with dismal consequences for other human beings. Still, to explore those choices, the ways in which they were articulated, and the context in which they were made, is indeed, as Lord Bolingbroke suggested, to know something more about our species in the past. To enter into family life, to watch loving hearts laid open, is messy but fascinating work.

lines, John Demos has contended: 'The closer one gets to the details of power relations within the family, the more complicated—and the less amenable to summary formulas—they come to seem.' John Demos, 'Digging Up Family History', in Anya Jabour (ed.), *Major Problems in the History of American Families and Children: Documents and Essays* (Boston: Houghton Mifflin, 2005), 1–18, at 6.

5

The Repentant Son and the Unforgiving Father: Making a Man of Feeling, a Man of Credit

> Alas! My heart was full—and we parted without conviction on either side.—How rarely do men understand one another!
>
> (Goethe, 1779)[1]

Would the father forgive his erring son (Fig. 5.1)? The answer would come only on the sickbed. The son, Charles, waited in a corner of the bedroom, where his father was recovering. Like the prodigal son in Jesus's parable, Charles knew that he had been a bad son: he had ignored his father's wishes; he had married without his family's permission; his wife proved to be profligate and pregnant by a servant; and so he had run himself badly into debt. He had thrown away the Scottish education lavished upon him by his father. Yet on the advice of his tutor, Charles was nonetheless hopeful. He watched his father read the letter that the tutor had sent explaining Charles's contrition. He sought the signs of forgiveness that he hoped would be etched upon his father's worn physiognomy. They came soon enough: expressions of commiseration, tears coursing down the cheeks, and a cracking voice that proclaimed: 'My poor boy—I pity—I forgive him—would he were here!' With that, Charles crept up to his father's bed and found absolution. An 'elegant plate' illustrated the heart-rending scene.[2]

The story of this prodigal son and his reconciliation with his father appeared in the *Town and Country Magazine* in March 1776, a year in which unhappy divisions and faltering, painful steps to independence engrossed audiences in Britain and North America. Like many similar prodigal-son tales, it raised issues often covered in such periodicals: family relations, patrimony, debt and credit, clandestine marriages, confused and disobedient young men, frustrated

---

[1] Werter, 'August 12', letter XXIX, Johann Wolfgang von Goethe, *The Sorrows of Werter: A German Story*, 2 vols. (London, 1779), i. 136.

[2] 'The Repentant Son: A Moral Tale', *Town and Country Magazine* (Mar. 1776), 137–41. Although the picture was labeled 'The Penitent Son', the story itself was called 'The Repentant Son'. I have followed the story title here.

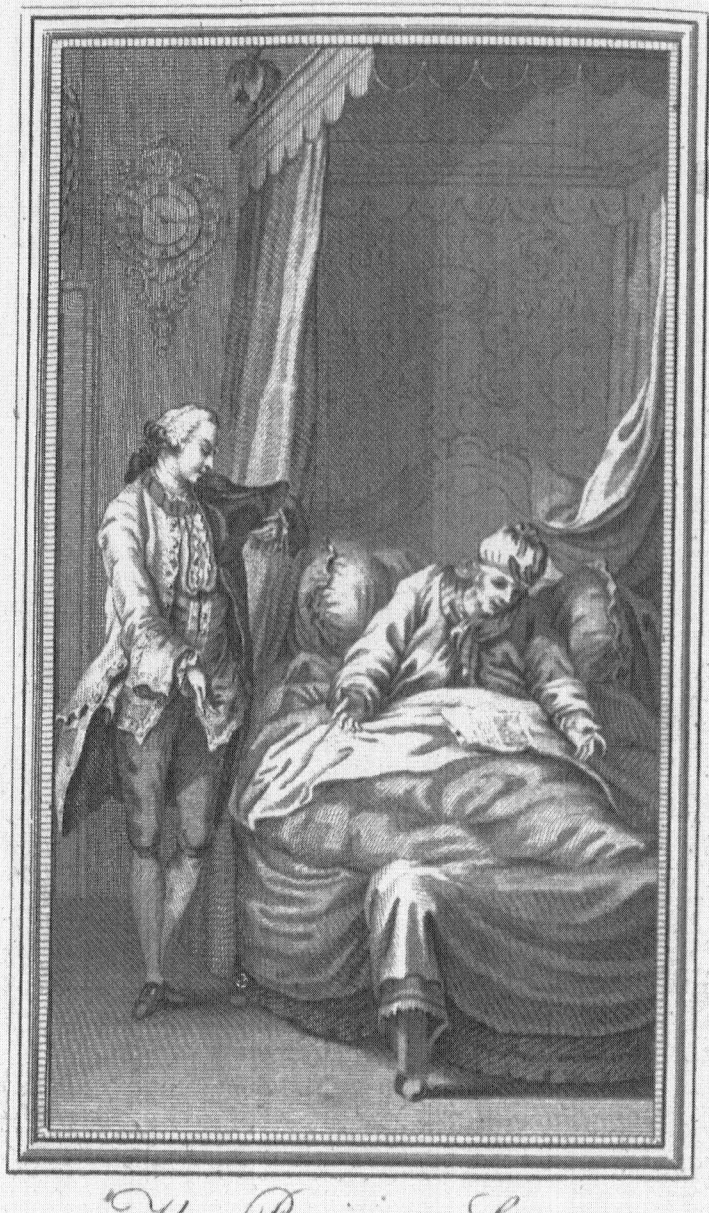

Fig. 5.1. 'The Penitent Son', to accompany 'The Repentant Son: A Moral Tale', *Town and Country Magazine*, 8 (Mar. 1776), 137–41. Cambridge University Library, T900.c.38.8.

fathers, interventions by others, letter-writing and its effects, and sensibility. Such themes are echoed, too, in the story of another prodigal son, Patrick Parker—this one historical rather than fictional. Both the fictional and the historical actors used familiar letters in order to represent their ideals and to attempt to coerce others into behaving in a certain way. Letter-writing was central to the stories of both sons, as anxieties about representation, familiarity, and communication informed both. Both the fictional and historical actors connected their relationships with newer literary models associated with domestic feeling and a reshaping of patriarchal authority.[3] At the same time, in both cases, the languages of sensibility obscured the issues of debt, extravagance, and property that figured strongly in both. Still, while Patrick's story could equally be called the tale of 'The Repentant Son', it ended quite differently for him than for the fictional Charles.

His fragile frame racked with blood-flecked coughs, Patrick Parker struggled to sit up in bed in New York and pen a letter to his father, James, in London. It was July 1795. Patrick, having left his native Virginia, was awaiting passage to Britain, where he planned to meet his father. Patrick also hoped a sea voyage would relieve his lung disorder. However, 'the fatigue of the Jaunt from Virginia here brot on a fever here I Expected w[oul]d have Carried me allmost off My Cough is still unrelenting.'[4] Patrick was determined to reach his father one last time, writing in shaky hand: 'I Am now propped up in a bed with pillows while I am writing this letter to you I could say a Vollume but neither Strength nor recollection will admit—I could wish . . . for many reasons to go home & see you.' Like a romantic hero in a novel, Patrick highlighted the contrast between the weakness of his body and the strength of his emotions.

Patrick's sickbed missive was only the final, and most poignant, in a series of letters from this prodigal son to his embittered father. Ever since Patrick had enraged his exiled Loyalist father by returning to Virginia and, despite his poverty, marrying his cousin in 1787, the relationship between the father, in Britain, and the son, in Virginia, had gone from bad to worse. Patrick expressed contrition: 'W[oul]d to God I had Gone home when you asked . . . if you knew my Situation your mind is not not [*sic*] so unrelenting but all w[oul]d be forgiven.' It is impossible to state whether Patrick genuinely regretted his past behavior, or whether he merely hoped to obtain forgiveness and money from a father who had cut him off financially, leaving him to flounder in an ever deeper sea of debt. What is clear, however, is that Patrick, unlike the fortunate Charles Hanbury, never found the forgiveness he desired: he drew his last ragged breaths on the ship that was to have carried him to London. All his father had left of his son were his letters and his debts.[5]

---

[3] See Fliegelman, *Prodigals and Pilgrims*.
[4] Patrick Parker to James Parker, 'New York the 16 of July 95', PA 10.19, Parker Family Papers, LRO. All Parker letters are from this collection unless otherwise noted. I have used the older system of notation where possible (to match the more readily available microfilmed version).
[5] In the will he completed on board, Patrick noted: 'for the Remainder of my [estate] both real and personal which I hereby direct to be sold by my Executor hereafter for the purpose of paying

Was 'all . . . forgiven' in the wake of Patrick's untimely end? It does not seem so. We might expect that James would have labeled this letter as something like 'the last letter from my poor son', rather than 'P Parker. Self Refflections when too late'.[6] In letters to his old friend, Charles Steuart, James recounted his distress at the untimely death of his son, and next-to-last surviving child (he had already lost four children). James noted that 'I Shall ever lament his loss, he had once as good a heart as ever animated a humane breast, & could I have drawn him from amongst the Wretches where he Was, things would have been very different'.[7] However, he also admitted that 'he & I have unfortunately have [*sic*] not been upon good terms for some time'.[8] James continued to claim that 'he regreats much not having followed my frequent advices to him'.[9] Even after Patrick's death, then, James continued to cling to his fatherly righteousness. Why do the two sickbed scenes involving penitent sons end so differently, and what is the relationship between them? What other imperatives influenced the relationship between the father and the son?

It might seem unsurprising that James would not forgive his son for disobedience. James was a slave-owner in Virginia. It might be tempting to conclude that James was an anxious, enraged patriarch, furious at the rebellion of his son. Add to this the fact that James was also a Loyalist, and it is only surprising that he tolerated his Patriot son for as long as he did. But here, as elsewhere, further inspection reveals that these usual lines of explanation have only limited force. If we simply slot James Parker into what we think we know about the broad lines of patriarchy in Virginia, we will see only what we have always seen: a conservative man who fought off challenges to authority in brutal ways. This historiographical framework no better captures the lines of the Parker story than do magazine stories like 'The Repentant Son', or indeed the parable of the prodigal son that informed it.

Before it is possible to pursue more persuasive lines of analysis, it is necessary to have some sense of the key players. In 1776, when 'The Repentant Son' appeared, Patrick, a native Virginian, was in Edinburgh, living with a tutor, enjoying the Scottish education lavished upon him by his father. A Glasgow native, James had immigrated to Virginia in 1747.[10] There he built up business as a merchant

---

all my just and Lawfull debts.' Patrick Parker Will, 29 August 1795, Reel 19, Norfolk City Wills & Administration 1795/1796, LV.

[6] James labeled most of his incoming letters from Patrick.

[7] James Parker to Charles Steuart, 'London the 26th of Novr 1795', MS. 5038, fos. 281–2, Charles Steuart Papers, NLS.

[8] James Parker to Charles Steuart, 'London the 7th of Sepr 1795', MS. 5038, fos. 252–3, ibid.

[9] James Parker to Charles Steuart, 'London the 26th of Novr 1795', MS. 5038, fos. 281–2, ibid.

[10] I have not found the records to corroborate this officially. It is from Margaret Rainy Parker, 'Extract from Memorandum by Mrs Parker of Fairlie daughter-in-law of Capt. James Parker Dec. 1835', PA18.6, Parker Papers, LRO.

(most notably, in a business as Aitchison & Parker).¹¹ By 1776 James was in North America, married to Margaret Ellegood Parker, whose sister, Rebecca, was married to James's business partner, William Aitchison.¹² The Ellegoods were a prosperous family of long standing in Lynnhaven Parish, Princess Anne County.¹³ In the 1750s and 1760s James's business flourished, and so did the family. Although at least three children died early, three more—Patrick, Charles, and Susan—arrived and generally thrived.¹⁴ The family lived in an impressive two-story house; they also held lands and several slaves in Virginia and North Carolina. As a Royal Navy commander later informed the commission on Loyalist losses, James's 'manner of living had all the appearance of great opulence; his dealings were very extensive, and his character for probity and commercial knowledge in the highest and most universal esteem'.¹⁵ Near the end of 1776, while on a military campaign, James himself noted wistfully that he looked back on his life in Virginia 'as our first Parents did when they left Eden'.¹⁶ James lost his Eden not for disobedience, but for his enduring obedience to crown and country. Even if James had become a prosperous local merchant, he never went native, becoming a Loyalist officer.¹⁷ It was not to be an easy service, a situation to which we shall return.

But what of the other Parkers? The Parkers sent their oldest son, Patrick, to school in Edinburgh before the war broke out, in order to equip him with

---

¹¹ James makes his first appearance in the tithables lists in 1759. See Elizabeth B. Wingo, *Norfolk County, Virginia, Tithables, 1751–1765* (Norfolk, Va.: Wingo, 1981), 147, 211. He is listed for subsequent years in Elizabeth B. Wingo and W. Bruce Wingo, *Norfolk County, Virginia, Tithables, 1766–1780* (Norfolk, Va.: Wingo, 1985), 34, 82, 118, 119, 163, 168, 206, 228, 242.

¹² Record of their marriage has been lost, but it must have been between 1753 (when Margaret, unmarried, is mentioned in her father's will) and 1760, when letters between this couple exist. All possible records at the Library of Virginia have been searched [including both Elizabeth B. Wingo, *Marriages of Princess Anne County, Virginia, 1749–1821* (Norfolk, Va.: Wingo, 1961) and id., *Marriages of Norfolk County, Virginia, 1706–1792* (Norfolk, Va.: Wingo, 1961)]. It also makes no appearance in microfilmed original marriage bonds at LV.

¹³ Margaret's father, Jacob Ellegood, was church warden from 1736 to his death in 1753. Her brother, Jacob Ellegood (jr.), was appointed a vestryman from 1773 until his Loyalist service ended this position in 1776. See George Carrington Mason (ed.), *The Colonial Vestry Book of Lynnhaven Parish, Princess Anne County, Virginia, 1723–1786* (Newport News, Va.: State Archives/George Mason, 1949), and Anne E. Maling, *Princess Anne County, Virginia: Land and Probate Records Abstracted from Deed Books Eight to Eighteen, 1755–1783* (Bowie, Md.: Heritage Books, 1993).

¹⁴ The children who died early are mentioned in Margaret Parker to Charles Steuart, 'Norfolk 10th November 1769', MS. 5040, fos. 76–8, James Parker to Charles Steuart, 'Norfolk 20th. Octr 1769', MS. 5025, fos. 215–21, and Patrick Parker to Charles Steuart, 'Norfolk VA May 8th 1789', MS. 5041, fos. 134–5, Charles Steuart Papers, NLS.

¹⁵ Charles Lyell, 'COPIES of CERTIFICATES and LETTERS respecting Mr. PARKER's Services, Sufferings and Losses', 17 April 1783, p. 415, AO 13/134, NA.

¹⁶ James Parker to Margaret Parker, 'New London. Bedford County. Decr. 10ᵗʰ 1776', PA 7.9, Parker Family Papers, LRO.

¹⁷ See Adele Hast, *Loyalism in Revolutionary Virginia: The Norfolk Area and the Eastern Shore* (Ann Arbor, Mich.: UMI Research Press, 1982), esp. 10–14 and 73–8, and Keith Mason, 'A Loyalist's Journey: James Parker's Response to the Revolutionary Crisis', *Virginia Magazine of History and Biography*, 102 (1994), 139–66.

the skills and background to become a merchant too.[18] In the meantime, the rest of his family was already suffering. Patriots apparently burned down the Parker house in Norfolk in January 1776. When James was officially declared a traitor in 1776, Margaret and the two younger children, Charles and Susan, were attacked, and their land as well as many of their goods were taken or destroyed. So, Margaret, Charles, and Susan ended up at Eastwood, the house of her sister Rebecca, the widow of William Aitchison, who had also been an accused Loyalist traitor. Margaret brought little to housekeeping, beyond the eight enslaved people[19]—Juba, Doctor, Dinah, Sarah, Roger, Nanny, Charles, and Chloe—who accompanied her and were apparently persuaded to stay.[20] In 1779, during the family's stay at Eastwood, James was able to visit. The Parkers then sent Charles to join his brother Patrick in Edinburgh.[21] Meanwhile, Margaret and Susan endured the rest of the war in Virginia.[22] These women seem largely to have been left alone by the locals, probably partly because, with one husband dead and the other gone, women from a prominent local family headed the household. Their own political sentiments are difficult to determine. The women of this family later made claims for goods and cattle given to Patriot troops, although they may have done so under duress.[23] It is hard to know if they supported the Loyalism so explicitly defended by the men in their family (including Margaret's husband, brother, and brother-in-law).

At any rate, the end of the war might have meant the end of separations, once Margaret and Susan went to London, where James and Patrick (now a clerk) were living. But it was not to be. Although financially dispossessed, the Parkers still retained assets, including some land, thanks in part to a Virginia law that allowed Loyalist wives to retain property.[24] James, Margaret, and Susan attempted to forge new lives for themselves in post-war London, as James worked for government compensation. But the presence of his wife was a consolation

---

[18] Like many elite children in this era, Patrick Parker boarded with his private tutor, Thomas MacKnight. See Alexander Law, *Education in Edinburgh in the Eighteenth Century* (London: University of London Press, 1965), esp. ch. 5.

[19] See 'Estimate of Losses sustained by James Parker in Virga and North Carolina in conseqce. Of his taking Arms agreeably to the Calls of Government in 1775', p. 126, AO 12/54, NA.

[20] The names of the slaves, along with a scanty amount of information about them, can be found in Margaret Parker to James Parker, 'Eastwood 27th July 1783', PA 8.26, Parker Family Papers, LRO.

[21] The Petition of James Parker late of Virginia Merchant', London 16th. December 1783, p. 425, AO13/134, NA.

[22] Margaret Parker to Charles Steuart, 'Princess Anne 3d January 1779', MS. 5040, fos. 152–4, CSP, NLS.

[23] See the claims of Rebecca Aitchison and Anne Newton (Margaret's mother) in *Virginia Publick Claims*, microfilm, LV [also in Janice L. Abercrombie (ed.), *Virginia Publick Claims: Princess Anne County* (Athens, Ga.: Iberian Publishing Co., n.d.), 1, 3, 6].

[24] The law stated that the forfeiture of property would be waived in cases where there was 'a wife and child, or child and no wife'. William Waller Hening (ed.), *The Statutes at Large: Being a Collection of All the Laws of Virginia, From the First Session of the Legislature in the Year 1619*, 13 vols. (Richmond, Va., 1819–23), vol. x, ch. 14, May 1779, p. 71.

soon snatched from the hapless James, when Margaret died suddenly in 1785. According to his daughter-in-law: 'Thus was her poor husband left again desolate with his little girl and almost brokenhearted.'[25] James refused to stay in the house that witnessed their reunion, sending Susan to her Aunt Elmsley, Margaret's sister, now residing in London. In the meantime, Patrick returned to Virginia, ostensibly to take care of family property and debt-collection in Virginia. Patrick stayed on in Virginia, well beyond the initial plan. He became a trader there, selling goods that James sent him. Over the ensuing decade Patrick and James exchanged increasingly frustrated letters, with a great crisis in 1787 relating to Patrick's decision to marry his cousin, Molly, and settle permanently in Virginia.[26] Still, after a trip back to Britain, Patrick obtained his father's grudging forgiveness, as well as another loan of £1,000.

After 1787 events were to unfold in a way that increasingly confirmed James's suspicions about his son's credit, the cause, ultimately, of the breakdown of their relationship. In part, Patrick apparently expected that their family ties would cause his father to treat him *better* than other debtors; James did not apparently share this view. Indeed, James seems to have felt that the familial relation required him to be even more rigorous, in offering 'strict scrutiny' to a wayward son. Patrick also continued to be a debtor to his father, and he ceased to repay loans. By 1794 James had so given up on Patrick that he simply stopped writing altogether. If James hoped to use his fearsome silence to obtain repayment, he was to be sorely disappointed. By the summer of 1795 Patrick's respiratory illness prompted him to borrow further money against his father's credit, in order to travel from Virginia to London.[27] As we know, he did not make it.

How do we explain James's unwillingness to offer any kind of tear-stained forgiveness to his repentant son? Real life does not have the happy endings of magazine stories. Still, Patrick, internalizing the fictions of his era, expected forgiveness of the sort Charles Hanbury had received. It may seem a simple matter to explain this refusal. Some historians might pinpoint James's Loyalism, others his patriarchal anxiety and an old-fashioned view of marriage. These points would not be wrong, but they would be incomplete. Those explanations that offer much greater analytical purchase include James's experiences in Virginia, both before and after the marriage; the early death of Margaret Parker; and a general but critical concern to make a son into an independent trader who could be a man of credit.

---

[25] Margaret Rainy Parker, 'Extract from Memorandum by Mrs Parker of Fairlie daughter-in-law of Capt. James Parker Dated Dec. 1835', PA18.6, Parker Family Papers, LRO. This memorandum was written 50 years later, after the death of James himself. Still, it is the best surviving account.

[26] Nearly all of James's letters to Patrick have been lost (with the exception of one draft copy), but it is possible to hear his words, at least faintly, both in Patrick's replies and in the brief annotations he made on Patrick's letters.

[27] Patrick Parker to James Parker, 'Norfo. Virga. June the 20th 1795', PA 10.18, Parker Family Papers, LRO.

James's avid Loyalism affected his handling of the situation with his son, but not in precisely the ways that historians have assumed. After all, given traditional understandings of Loyalism, it seems unsurprising that James would be unwilling to forgive disobedience.[28] With a few exceptions, the picture that emerges from existing work on Loyalism is one of conservatives virtually incapable of envisioning a new order. One historian's phrase, echoed by another, best exemplifies this characterization: ' "I Believe," "I obey," these were part of the Loyalist code.'[29] From this perspective, it makes sense that such a man would treat a wayward son with great severity, since disobedience was not something that could be countenanced, in political or personal life. Another historian has asserted that: 'With his deep-seated desire for order, intolerance of ambiguity, faith in deference, and respect for authority and due process, [James] Parker displayed many of the traits of the Loyalist personality.'[30]

This line of argument does something of a disservice to James Parker and others like him. Admittedly, there were ways in which he was conservative and obedience-oriented, but in other respects he was forward-looking and progressive, in some ways more so than his allegedly modern-minded son Patrick. His wife, his other son Charles, and his daughter Susan all had fairly easy and affectionate relationships with him. It is true that James did believe in compliance at home. In a letter to Margaret when Charles was a little boy, James used language associated with an older view of child-raising as a will-breaking endeavor: 'do you sufficiently correct his little . . . faults, keep him in due subjection?'[31] Still, in that same letter James also used language that implied different views of child-rearing, as he referred to the children as 'dear little things' and hoped that his wife was 'permitt[ing] Charlie to run half naked as he should do'.[32] James may have shown some aspects of an older, more 'rigid' way of social thinking, but in other respects he was much more consonant with cultures of sensible child-rearing. At

---

[28] Tracing James Parker's decision to become a Loyalist, Keith Mason argues that the dispute between father and son was primarily a political one. Mason, 'A Loyalist's Journey', 165.

[29] Edward Countryman, *A People in Revolution: The American Revolution and Political Society in New York, 1760–1790* (New York: W. W. Norton & Co., 1989), 285. Countryman is quoting from Esmond Wright, 'The New York Loyalists: A Cross-Section of Colonial Society', in Robert A. East and Jacob Judd (eds.), *The Loyalist Americans: A Focus on Greater New York* (Tarrytown, NY: Sleepy Hollow Restorations, 1975), 89.

[30] Mason, 'A Loyalist's Journey', 163.

[31] James Parker to Margaret Parker, '8 Mar 1776', PA 8.18, Parker Family Papers, LRO. On views of child-rearing as a will-breaking endeavor, see Philip J. Greven, *The Protestant Temperament: Patterns of Child-Rearing, Religious Experience, and the Self in Early America* (New York: Knopf, 1977).

[32] James Parker to Margaret Parker, '8 Mar 1776', PA 8.18. In a letter later that year he desired to know how his little girl, who had been laid low with a fever, was doing: 'God grant that I may Soon hear of our Poor little Susies recovery, as it would be hard on me just to have a sight of the dear little blooming innocent & then have it snatched away.' James Parker to Margaret Parker, '8 Novmr. 1776', PA 7.8, Parker Family Papers, LRO. Indeed, Smith has used this as evidence of the development of the sentimental family in later eighteenth-century Virginia. Smith, *Inside the Great House*, 25–6.

any rate, such ways of thinking and writing—a balance of what might called older patriarchal notions and newer sentimental ones—would hardly have been considered unusual by most of his Virginia neighbors, even those who became ardent Patriots.[33]

It is more accurate, for James as well as for other Loyalists, to characterize him as someone who was attuned to transatlantic developments, not simply obedience-minded. For example, James was a man who flouted local convention—and unwittingly provoked a riot against himself and his family—by choosing smallpox inoculations for his family and himself in 1768–9, a controversial decision.[34] Even after the Revolution, James maintained a lively interest in new developments in science and philosophy. In 1789 he recommended Voltaire, Rousseau, and other writers to Patrick, who furiously rejected them.[35] James did follow British, and especially Scottish, developments, but this does not mean he was conservative.[36] In fact, in certain respects it made him more radical than a lot of Americans, many of whom recognized the advances of eighteenth-century Scottish medicine.[37] Even if it were true, it does not actually help very much. After all, James forgave his son for marrying too soon and for settling in Virginia, and continued to send letters, credit, and money to him after this breach. Simply dismissing James as a typical regressive Loyalist, or even just as a cantankerous grouch, does not get us very far in explicating his refusal to forgive his son.

Also, Loyalism does not capture the long-standing tense relations that James had had in Virginia, which had much more to do with his status as a Scot. Even before the Revolution intervened, James, as part of a well-off Scottish minority, apparently never overcame the suspicions of his neighbors, whom James termed a 'Weak prejudiced people'.[38] Many Virginians resented successful Scottish creditors such as James.[39] Historians have demonstrated that, in part due

---

[33] See e.g. Lewis, *Pursuit of Happiness*, and Smith, *Inside the Great House*.
[34] See Hast, *Loyalism in Revolutionary Virginia*, 11–13, and Mason, 'A Loyalist's Journey', *passim*.
[35] Patrick Parker to James Parker, 'Norfolk Virginia Sep: 29th. 1789', PA10.15, Parker Family Papers, LRO.
[36] This point supports Countryman's contentions that many Loyalists 'looked eastward toward Britain'. Countryman, *A People in Revolution*, 285. It also supports Woody Holton's characterization of Parker and others like him as 'transatlantic traders'. Woody Holton, *Forced Founders: Indians, Debtors, Slaves, and the Making of the American Revolution in Virginia* (Chapel Hill, NC: University of North Carolina Press for the Omohundro Institute of Early American History and Culture, 1999), ch. 2.
[37] See e.g. Kariann Yokota, 'A Culture of Insecurity: The United States as a Post-Colonial Nation', Ph.D, University of California, Los Angeles (2002).
[38] James Parker to Charles Steuart, 'Norfolk 27 Jany. 1775', MS 5029, fos. 14–15, Charles Steuart Papers, NLS.
[39] Woody Holton has argued that, by the 1760s, merchants like James Parker inspired such resentment in Virginia that the term 'Scottish' demarcated not simply an ethnic or national identity but in fact an economic stratum of fortune-seeking, temporary sojourners trading British-manufactured goods for tobacco. According to Holton, such men inspired hatred among locals, who feared their positions might be usurped by these powerful creditors. Holton, *Forced Founders*, 41.

to the lengthy period from planting to shipping for tobacco (fifteen months), the Chesapeake depended more heavily than many other places on credit, especially British credit.[40] Virginia nurtured a significant culture of debt, but this fact did not make debt any more bearable for those who were burdened with it (or their creditors). Of course, antipathy towards successful Scots was nothing new in the Anglo-American world. English political culture had long satirized Scots as penurious upstarts who could become all-too wealthy, especially in colonial contexts.[41] As a flourishing merchant, and therefore creditor, in the area, James apparently provoked local frustrations for having brought lawsuits against defaulting debtors.

These tensions came to a head in inoculation riots in 1769.[42] Many locals were furious that the Parkers and other Scots inoculated themselves against smallpox, thus risking bringing infection into the community. It seems likely, however, that this riot was one aspect of a long-standing set of conflicts. According to James, one of the demands of a set of rioters was that James 'drop all lawSuits I had against them'. James also pointed out that the chief speaker of the mob at his house 'was one Singleton a Carpenter whom he had Sued a year ago for Debit'.[43] After these riots, during which a pregnant Margaret had to flee with a toddler to escape an attack on the family home, James and his fellow Scots sought justice from the governor of Virginia, to whom James complained: 'Such is the spirit of rioting & licentiousness here, that . . . we are at present actually obliged to disperse our families', invoking the separation of his family as a reason for the need of protection.[44] He also informed him 'that I hop'd in time the people of Norfolk would be Convinced . . . that the people they were pleased to Call forreigners had as good a Claim to protection & justice'.[45]

As a Scot, a successful trader and creditor, and a believer in inoculation, James had more than enough to make him feel a 'forreigner' in pre-Revolutionary Virginia, even as he established himself enough to win a local wife, strong connections, and the friendship of many. The war exacerbated James's sense of himself as an outsider in a place where, to his mind, too many individuals were given to debt, disorder, and demagoguery. As early as 1774, William Aitchison, his brother-in-law and partner, reported on the tarrings-and-featherings going

---

[40] See Breen, *Tobacco Culture*, and Bruce Mann, *Republic of Debtors*, 136–7.

[41] As Linda Colley has noted, 'many [of the English] regarded the Scots as poor and pushy relations'. Linda Colley, *Britons: Forging the Nation 1707–1837* (New Haven: Yale University Press, 1987), 13. See also Karras, *Sojourners in the Sun*, Ned. C. Landsman, *Scotland and Its First American Colony, 1683–1765* (Princeton: Princeton University Press, 1985), and Hamilton, *Scotland, the Caribbean and the Atlantic World*.

[42] See Hast, *Loyalism in Revolutionary Virginia*, and Mason, 'A Loyalist's Journey'.

[43] James Parker to Charles Steuart, 'May 1769,' MSS 5025, fos. 123–4, Charles Steuart Papers, NLS.

[44] Undated letter to 'My Lord', in James Parker to Charles Steuart, 'May 1769', MSS 5025, fos. 125–6, ibid.

[45] James Parker to Charles Steuart, 'Norfolk 6 May 1769', MSS 5025, fos. 128–9, ibid.

on at Norfolk, and noted that it was fortunate that James was no longer there, as 'had you been upon the spot there is little doubt but you would have been as roughly handled as any of 'em'.[46] In 1775, when the Earl of Dunmore first began recruiting Loyalist troops in Virginia, James joined him. James disagreed with the tactics of the Patriots, who deployed the 'mobility' (as he sardonically termed it) to such fearsome effect. Equally, too, James felt that Patriots were far more concerned to throw off their own debts than to reform the empire. In 1774 he informed his friend Charles Steuart: 'the more a Man is in debit here the Stronger he is possessed with the Spirit of Patriotism.'[47] For James, 'Patriot' meant the kind of man who would deploy tactics of the mob in order to avoid making good his debts.

James's lengthy wartime adventures embittered him still further, as he watched the world he had worked so hard to create crumble around him. In 1775 he was wounded.[48] In 1776 he was shipwrecked off the coast of Virginia. When the local minister came out in a canoe to learn the situation, he 'informed me the people were highly exasperated against me'. James was already marked as a traitor. Nonetheless, he pulled himself up in the wreck of a sloop, and proclaimed to the minister that: 'I had the honour to bear a Commission under his Excellency Lord Dunmore his Majestys representatives, & that I expected to be treated as a Gentleman.'[49] While the minister had some sympathy for another 'Gentleman', rebel leaders in Virginia were not so accommodating; James 'was made Prisoner by the Rebels'.[50] Having been shipwrecked near his old home had advantages and disadvantages. Even as soldiers guarded James and his party, preventing anybody from coming near them, one former neighbor 'sent us Supply of fresh provision'.[51] James was later permitted sufficient parole to visit his family and to write letters.

However, like many in the war, James also experienced a new perspective on his old home. As he found to his consternation: 'In this county I formerly liv[ed] . . . in the greatest harmony with all rank, male & femal Young & old, They were greatly altered, very few would speak with me.'[52] Given James's inoculation problems, as well as the constant strains of running a business

---

[46] William Aitchison to James Parker, 'Norfo. 14th Novr 1774', PA 6.2, Parker Family Papers, LRO.

[47] James Parker to Charles Steuart, 'Norfolk 17th May 1774', MS 5028, fos. 200–1, Charles Steuart Papers, NLS.

[48] James Parker, 'The MEMORIAL of JAMES PARKER, late of *Norfolk*, in *Virginia*', 9 March 1783, pp. 247–51, AO 12/54, and again (a printed version) in p. 414, AO 13/134, NA. As the commander of the vessel later told the Commission, 'during the action Mr. Parker received a contusion upon his head by a swivel shot'. Tyrone Howe, 'COPIES of CERTIFICATES and LETTERS respecting Mr. PARKER's Services, Sufferings and Losses', 3 April 1783, p. 415, AO 13/134, NA.

[49] Transcription of James's wartime 'diary', Gwins Island Monday 8 [June] 1776', PA 9.83, Parker Family Papers, LRO.

[50] A. P?. Hammond, certification of James Parker's service, 'on board His Majesty's Ship Roebuck in Delaware River 10th June 1778', PA 7.14, ibid.

[51] Transcription of James' wartime 'diary', Gwins Island Monday 8 [June] 1776', PA 9.83, ibid.

[52] Transcription of James' wartime 'diary', 18/26 June [*sic* - July] 1776, PA 9.83, ibid.

that involved carrying debt and sometimes suing debtors, this rosy vision of the pre-war years was not strictly believable. Nonetheless, it must have been a profound shock for this 'gentleman', who had generally received deference, now to be treated as a pariah. He also witnessed the severe treatment of several old friends, including William Aitchison, who 'tho' very infirm was greatly harrassed' (treatment thought to have hastened his death).[53] James was himself soon tried as a traitor and condemned to imprisonment, with his Virginia property confiscated.[54]

After nine months of 'tedious and cruel imprisonment' and the dispiriting news that North Carolina, too, had taken possession of his land there, James and other prisoners were unwilling to continue pawns to Providence and Patriots.[55] Instead they escaped, with James traveling over 500 miles to join the British forces anchored in the Delaware river.[56] A sympathetic friend reported the escape to Margaret Parker in May 1777, asking her: 'Have you seen Mr. Parker lately? Or did you expect to see him advertised as a Runaway?'[57] Such a status, befitting a slave or servant, did not well befit a 'Gentleman' who himself employed slaves and servants. Indeed, in 1760 James had been mentioned in a runaway advertisement, when a slave named Ned, husband of one of James's slaves and apparently 'a bold obstinate Fellow', ran away in Norfolk.[58] The man who placed the advertisement entreated readers to return Ned to James Parker. Both Ned and James, then, apparently were 'bold obstinate Fellows', willing to take considerable risks to find liberty. Throughout the eighteenth century, but especially in the years of the Revolutionary War, the American landscape was full of fugitives seeking to re-establish connections, some more tolerated than others.

To be marked as a runaway surely did not please James. Still, he eventually resurfaced and managed to rejoin British units. In waters off the coast of what must have begun to seem the cursed land of Virginia, he was taken prisoner again, this time by the French fleet. Once more at the mercy of his enemies, James was sent first to Rhode Island, then to Boston, then to San Domingo, where he was held for another five months. Carried from San Domingo, his ship was once again shipwrecked, this time off the coast of France. He was

---

[53] Transcription of James' wartime 'diary', 18/26 June [sic - July] 1776, PA 9.83, Parker Family Papers, LRO.

[54] In November 1776 the Council at Williamsburg affirmed the 'forfeiture of the Appellants Estate', and ordered that he be detained as prisoner of war. 'Order of the Council of Virginia against Mr Parker', 'Williamsburg Novr 16 1776', PA 7.10, and POW order by Patrick Henry Jr., 'Williamsburg 18th November 1776', PA 7.10a, ibid.

[55] A. P?. Hammond, certification of James Parker's service, 'on board His Majesty's Ship Roebuck in Delaware River 10th June 1778', PA 7.14, ibid.

[56] Ibid.

[57] Andrew Ronald to Margaret Parker, 'Williamsburg 1st May 1777', PA7.12, ibid.

[58] See runaway-slave advertisement for 'Ned' by Christopher Wright, *Virginia Gazette (Hunter)*, Williamsburg, 16 Jan. 1761, 'The Geography of Slavery in Virginia' (Virginia Center for Digital History, 2005).

then imprisoned in various dank French castles.[59] Even peace did not free him immediately. Whether by accident or design, James was left imprisoned and waiting in France long after informal peace negotiations had taken place. In April 1782, thanks to 'the friendship of... M. St. John de Creve Coeur', James was able to win parole in Normandy.[60] James recorded his French sojourn in the following terms: 'I was very unjustly detained prisoner at the request of the Americans.'[61] Once freed, he began the tiresome process of trying to gain compensation from the British government. However, the final settlement for Loyalists proved particularly ungenerous for merchants, thanks to the fact that no claims were accepted for unpaid debts. Since most of James's business depended on credit and unpaid debts, his losses were considerable.[62]

James's experience in Virginia prior to the Revolution had been fairly typical of many other enterprising, imperial-minded Scots. His decision to become a Loyalist was also what we might expect of a well-heeled Scottish creditor. His wartime experience, joined with the outsider status he had long endured, left him with an overwhelming grudge against Virginians in particular. How it must have galled him to be brought before a court of jeering Patriots, among them perhaps his former debtors (as we have seen, the conflation of these two terms was obvious for him), condemned as a traitor, treated as a common criminal, forced to run away like a slave, and given the news that his family had been left destitute and dependent. When James was attainted as a traitor, he lost what apparently amounted to nearly £30,000. Such a loss meant that his wife and children were 'obliged to resort to the benevolence of their relations for the common necessaries of life'.[63] This standard Commission claim suggested the enforced abdication of family responsibility that James had suffered. Such dependence was precisely the fate that James had worked so assiduously to avoid. This blow to his position in both his household and his community must have been harrowing, and one from which it was difficult to recover. And so it is that a man's experiences with Virginia both before and during the war affected considerably his ensuing personal relations with his son. For his son to embrace a Virginian identity was

---

[59] See James Parker, 'The MEMORIAL...', 9 March 1783, pp. 247–51, AO 12/54, and again (a printed version) in p. 414, AO 13/134 and 'COPIES OF CERTIFICATES...', AO 13/134, and other documents in AO13/134, NA, and also James's wartime diary and letters in PAR I, Parker Family Papers, LRO.

[60] James noted that: 'My gratitude to Mr St. John will last for life.' James Parker to Mr LeCamus de Limare, Paris, 'St Malo 26 April 1782', PA7.18, ibid. See Hector St John de Crèvecoeur, *Letters from an American Farmer*, ed. Susan Manning (Oxford: Oxford University Press, 1997), among others.

[61] Jon Williams to James Parker, 'St Germain Nov. 14 1782', PA7.22, Parker Family Papers, LRO.

[62] Indeed, Mary Beth Norton has pointed out that: 'The group of claimants that suffered the most in relative terms was the merchants.' Mary Beth Norton, *The British-Americans: The Loyalist Exiles in England, 1774–1789*, (Boston: Little, Brown & Co., 1972), 220–1.

[63] See James Parker, 'The MEMORIAL...', 9 March 1783, pp. 247–51, AO 12/54 and (a printed version) in p. 414, AO 13/134, NA.

treachery to everything for which James had fought, and it must have cut him to the quick.

As should be clear from much of his story, James could fit classic understandings of patriarchy, and he did expect 'to be treated as a Gentleman'. It may seem unsurprising that he refused in the end to listen to his son, since the portrait we have of a number of elite Virginian men is that they were anxious patriarchs, fretting about the ways in which subordinates of all kinds were challenging them.[64] James could conform to these notions, but at the same time he also deployed sentimental language and ideals with many in his family. Moreover, he advised, rather than ordered, his son most of the time. James did not punish his son simply to show that he could, or because he was infuriated by his son's lack of deference. He punished him because his son had ceased to be a man of credit, and this was so troubling, for so many reasons, that he could not countenance it. He was fearful for the credit of his son, himself, and future generations.

James was a man much more attuned with newer ideals of sensibility and sympathy than the usual portrait of such patriarchs.[65] He engaged in negotiated relations with his wife, his son Charles, and his daughter Susan, and even sought to avoid hard mastery with his slaves. None of this makes him a believer in egalitarianism, which he emphatically was not, but it does suggest that simply to label him as a patriarch provides little analytical purchase.[66] Let us first look at his relations with his slaves. Although he was hardly a great planter, James's businesses and his life depended on the labor of slaves, and he owned several.[67] Based on the limited available evidence, his attitude was much more paternal than patriarchal. In the post-war correspondence, both James and Margaret seemingly worried over the future of these slaves, even if they ultimately privileged their own futures. When James enquired about them, Margaret noted that their Virginia slaves continued to stay with her: 'poor creatures the thoughts of leaving them & the chance of their geting cruel Masters distresses me greatly, they are all so much attached to me, & have so long promisd themselves the happiness of being settled with us again.' Much of this rhetoric is self-serving. Still, she also canvassed an emancipation plan: 'I wish we were able to set them free if they cannot live with us.'[68]

---

[64] See: Lockridge, *On the Sources of Patriarchal Rage*; Brown, *Good Wives, Nasty Wenches, and Anxious Patriarchs*; and Rhys Isaac, *The Transformation of Virginia, 1740–1790* (New York: Norton, 1982) and *Landon Carter's Uneasy Kingdom*. Woody Holton also emphasizes the ways in which such men were challenged before and during the Revolution. Holton, *Forced Founders*.

[65] Isaac elegantly explores similar tensions in the world of Landon Carter, in his *Landon Carter's Uneasy Kingdom*.

[66] See e.g. his extraordinary critique of Tom Paine's *Rights of Man*, in James Parker to Charles Steuart, 'London the 10th. of May 1791', MS 5036, fos. 282–3, Charles Steuart Papers, NLS.

[67] See entries in Elizabeth B. Wingo and W. Bruce Wingo, *Norfolk County, Virginia, Tithables, 1730–1750* (Norfolk, Va.: Wingo, 1979); Wingo, *Norfolk County, Virginia, Tithables, 1751–1765*; and Wingo and Wingo, *Norfolk County, Virginia, Tithables, 1766–1780*.

[68] Margaret Parker to James Parker, 'Eastwood 27th July 1783', PA 8.26, Parker Family Papers, LRO.

James was already concerned about how the family would live on the £200 *per annum* settled on him by the government, and he seems not to have paid any attention to Margaret's hopes here. Still, this did not mean that he was unwilling to listen either to her, or indeed, in a minor way, to the desires of the slaves themselves. He instructed Margaret that they should be hired out, as 'I cannot bring myself to think of selling the poor creatures who have served us so well'; 'poor creatures' echoes Margaret's own phrasing. He continued: 'God knows what we may be forced to do, but at Present I would rather suffer a little myself as sell them for any consideration to a Tyrant who would use them cruily.'[69] He did not rule out the possibility that the slaves would have to be sold off and separated, and freeing them was not among the options he entertained. But here James joined Margaret in the typical language of paternalism: concerns for the 'poor creatures' who might end up with tyrants who lacked the kindness of the Parkers. None of this adds up to an enlightened view of emancipation, or a genuine consideration of their feelings. On the other hand, it does not demonstrate a typically patriarchal view.[70]

That James wanted to appear in a certain way to his wife, and adopted her language in his letters, indicates too that his marital relations were also not captured by the notion of patriarchy. Like many men of his era, James relied on the notion of marriage as friendship and affection. In 1776 he proclaimed: 'Nothing so much distresses me as being Seperated from my famillie,' and he concluded his letter to Margaret: 'I shall with affectionate heart forever Remain Your[s].'[71] Margaret repeatedly termed James 'my Dearest friend'.[72] James also referred to himself as 'your affectionate friend'.[73] Both wife and husband were eager to display their sympathy for each other. After the war Margaret was loath to leave Virginia, and did so only reluctantly. This point underscores the limited legal and financial leverage she had, but James's letters offered sympathy for the 'distress' his wife was suffering: 'I really sympathize with you on this trying scene of leaving your Country and all our friends... with whom I always wished and hoped to finish my life. Providence has ordered it otherwise & we must

---

[69] James Parker to Margaret Parker, 'London 5th feby. 1784', PA 8.30, ibid.

[70] Indeed, Philip Morgan has used these letters as evidence of the shifting views from 'austere patriarchalism' to 'mellow paternalism', and so it would be difficult to categorize James Parker in this respect as simply an unforgiving patriarch. Morgan, *Slave Counterpoint*, 259, 270.

[71] James Parker to Margaret Parker, '8 Mar 1776', PA 8.18, Parker Family Papers, LRO.

[72] See Margaret Parker to James Parker, 'Eastwood October 21 1783', and Margaret Parker to James Parker, undated but labeled 'recd 22nd July 1784 from Mrs Parker', ibid. Margaret Parker was herself conversant with languages of affectionate sensibility. Indeed, in a 1772 letter, Margaret had written approvingly of Henry Mackenzie's *The Man of Feeling*: 'I got the man of feeling... and am much pleased with it there are Several Scenes in it... that I could not get over with dry eyes.' Margaret Parker to Charles Steuart, 'Feby 1772', MS 5027, fos. 130–2, Charles Steuart Papers, NLS. See also Henry Mackenzie, *The Man of Feeling* (London, 1771).

[73] James Parker to Margaret Parker, 'London 5th feby 1784', PA 8.30, and James Parker to Margaret Parker, 'London 23d August 1783', PA 8.27, Parker Family Papers, LRO.

submit.'74 Such a claim was a touch disingenuous. While James had had to submit to Providence and to the new political regimes, Margaret had to submit to James and join him in what was to her a foreign land. Still, this is the language of a man of feeling.

Indeed, had Margaret lived she might well have intervened and influenced James to treat Patrick differently. Like her son, she was also a Virginia native, with strong allegiances there. When she was reluctant to depart for Britain, she reminded James of her pain at leaving her 'native Country & friends'.75 Due to his mother's connections, when Patrick returned to Virginia in 1785 he received a warm welcome: 'contrary to my Expectation I was shook by the hand & Wellcomed to Virginia.'76 In 1786 he assured his father that 'I have hitherto had all the Princess Anne [County] Men, they have All of them Told me that . . . I shall have all their Custom, for my mothers Sake.'77 Although his father was viewed as a Loyalist villain, many locals respected Margaret, and Patrick was apparently able to take advantage of this situation. Patrick's and Margaret's shared allegiance to their 'native land', as well as their mutual affection, can be discerned from their few surviving letters. In 1785 Patrick emphasized to his mother how kind everyone in Virginia had been: 'Every Body I see enquires after you with the sincerest friendship . . . the poor negroes even say that times are quite altered since you Left us.'78 Patrick also echoed his parents in his paternalistic reference to the 'poor negroes': his mother's son indeed.

But the most telling piece of evidence for Margaret's influence comes from a line in James's draft letter to Patrick about the 1787 conflict. James reminded his son that 'you very well know that it was only in obedience to your amiable mothers request that I consented to your going there at all'.79 Margaret had died in 1785, after having persuaded her husband to allow Patrick to return to Virginia. Women often retained leverage in the family, particularly based, as we have seen, on their ability to make use of languages of sensibility. In intervening for errant children, mothers such as Margaret were able to persuade masters of households to alter their behavior.80 Margaret, an influential member of the family, might have understood her son's longing to remain in Virginia in ways her husband did not. Also, Margaret had spent the war with the Aitchisons at

---

74 James Parker to Margaret Parker, 'London 5th March 1784', PA 8.31, Parker Family Papers, LRO.
75 Margaret Parker to James Parker, 'Eastwood 27th July 1783', PA 8.26, ibid.
76 Patrick Parker to James Parker, 'Eastwood May 12th 1785', PA 11.11, ibid.
77 Patrick Parker to James Parker, 'July 10th 1786 Norfk', PA 11.24, ibid.
78 Patrick Parker to Margaret Parker, 'Eastwd May 9th 1785', PA 10.6, ibid.
79 Letter (copy) from James Parker to Patrick Parker 'Portglasgow 20 Octr. 1787', PA 11.162, ibid.
80 Ron Hoffman and Sally Mason argue that, for the Carrolls: 'Unlike Mama's letters, filled with the warmth, encouragement, and news of home that provided Charley with an emotional bridge between the world he had once lived in and the one he now inhabited, Papa's sterner correspondence reflected his didactic commitment to shaping his son.' This situation thus parallels the Parker family dynamic. Hoffman with Mason, *Princes of Ireland*, 147.

Eastwood, and was close to Molly; she had helped to raise this little girl. She very likely would have calmed James's fury at the marriage, and would probably have continued to lobby on behalf of her beloved older son (who named his only daughter Margaret, a tribute to personal and familial loyalties).[81] In this case, the absence of the mother skewed these disagreements into an out-of-control conflict between the two men. Women's domestic influence is clear even in their absence.

James's relations with Margaret, as well as his two other children, seem to have been much warmer than those with Patrick. With his younger son Charles, James also had a long-term epistolary relationship, since Charles did what his father meant him to do: become a merchant in the West Indies (chiefly Grenada), returning to Britain after these imperial economic successes. Throughout the 1790s and 1800s James and Charles corresponded in far more pleasant terms than James had with Patrick. Unlike his brother, Charles consistently thanked his father for his advice: 'Your good advices my Dear Father have a great Influence over me which . . . you may depend upon being followed as far as a young man new launched into the World can have command enough over himself to comply with . . . I observe the Justice of your remarks on giving Credit to foreigners.'[82] Charles repeatedly mentioned that he was working hard to support his father and his younger sister.[83] While his actions may not have been as upstanding as his words, his father does not seem to have suspected the disjunction between them that he did with Patrick. Susan's letters to her father were equally even and affectionate in tone. They report on her progress in her lessons, her need for shoes (as she hoped 'you have too much regard for me to let me go to the ball in ugly shoes'), and reports of her health, which seems always to have been delicate.[84] After learning of her early death in 1792, James wrote: 'there has not been a more unhappy man on Earth . . . In her I have lost all worth living for, I thought I Saw the Mother reanimated in her Daughter . . . & the sooner I follow the better.'[85] To summarize, there is little to indicate anything other than the rather typical elite man of family and feeling in his correspondence with his wife and two other children. Sympathy, not tyranny, was the dominant strain of James Parker's family relations.

---

[81] Charles S. Parker wrote to his father that Patrick had informed him in late 1792 that he 'had a fine daughter, which he had Christened Margaret, after my dear departed Mother'. See Charles S. Parker to James Parker, 'Grenada 13t. January 1793', PAR III 1/70, Parker Family Papers, LRO.

[82] Charles S. Parker to James Parker, 'Grenada 6th. June 1790', PAR III 1/47, ibid. The lengthy correspondence between the two men fills PAR III of the Parker Family Papers.

[83] See e.g. Charles S. Parker to James Parker, 'Grenada 14th. November 1790', PAR III 1/51, ibid.

[84] Susan Parker to James Parker, '[Ramsgate] Augt 11 1789', PAR II 1/2; Susan Parker to James Parker, 'Strangeways-Hall August 2d 1786', PAR III 2/2; and Susan Parker to James Parker, 'from Ramsgate, September 1785', PAR III 2/1, ibid.

[85] James Parker to Charles Steuart, 'London the 3d of November 1792', MS 5037, fos. 199–200, Charles Steuart Papers, NLS.

Now, none of this adds up to a man who might not respond adversely to the perceived misbehavior of a son. That he did not always need to enforce his patriarchal prerogative does not mean that he did not still possess it, or that he was incapable of imposing obedience when he chose to do so. Yet he did not do so. In understanding why, there are first certain features about Patrick's decision to marry Molly that require further attention: namely, their relative poverty and Molly's age. Also, even though Patrick entirely cast off his father's patriarchal authority, James still forgave him, lent him money, and remained in touch. What needs explanation is why the relations broke down later, and it is here where a focus on the exigencies of an Atlantic economy, and James's concern for making his son a 'man of credit,' can help a great deal.

In fact it was these very issues, of debt and credit, which informed much of the marriage conflict, in ways that have not always been appreciated. Many of James's objections to the marriage were based on his sense that Patrick's status as a man of credit was in peril. Such explanations are ultimately far more persuasive than issues of affection or patriarchy. Surveying the 1787 rift, other historians have used the Parker case to argue for a change over time in terms of views of marriages. In these readings, Patrick's decision was related to his privileging affection (for Molly) over duty (to his father), or in seeing marriage as more about feeling than economics.[86] There are some ways in which this is correct: Patrick did willfully ignore economics when he chose to marry Molly. But this was not all there was to it.

As early as 1786 Patrick's credit in his family was already under suspicion, because he had bungled a bill of exchange for Jennie Steuart, the daughter of James's friend Charles, and an informal sister to Patrick.[87] His relations in London concluded that he had deliberately miscalculated. Patrick was shocked. He wrote to his father: 'what were my immotions at reading the Contents of Mrs Elmslys letter wherein she openly accuses me of enviging money from an Orphan.' He went on: 'I declare this affair has allmost made me Raving

---

[86] Jan Lewis has posited that 'The father could not provide the settlement to which the younger man felt himself entitled, and the son could not yield the obedience that the older man demanded. Thus, neither man was able to give what tradition said he should, but neither man was willing to forgo what tradition said he should receive.' Such a view is based on her portrait of James Parker as a Loyalist conservative: 'Whereas the older man [James] was rigid when faced with the new situation, the younger one was beginning to think and act in ways that were to become more common in the nineteenth century.' She has concluded that Patrick was 'torn between an older ideal of family relationships, duty (to his father) and a newer one, affection (for a fiancée)'. Lewis, *Pursuit of Happiness*, 175–9, 189 (quotations at pp. 177–8). Like Lewis, Daniel Blake Smith also focuses on the marriage, using it as evidence that older generations had married for property but newer ones married for love and personal happiness. In point of fact, James's own marriage had been both strategic *and* affectionate. These are not mutually exclusive categories, and there is no simple dichotomy to be drawn between older views of marriage as economic strategy and newer ones of marriage as love. Smith, *Inside the Great House*, 149–50.

[87] Patrick drew the bill with a short period of sight, so it was disadvantageous to Jennie. See McCusker, *Money and Exchange in Europe and America, 1600–1775*, 21. See also Beawes, *Lex Mercatoria Rediviva*, 416–51, esp. 448–51.

mad... [at] the idea of my Character being forever Blasted.' He even avowed: 'O my Dear father the Tears are now upon my Cheeck,' a claim of sensible suffering, it might be noted, he never made during the marriage dispute.[88] This fear of a 'blasted character' was profound, and the strength of Patrick's replies shows that his credit in the family was already at risk.

These problems were exacerbated by his decision to marry Molly in 1787. James was not against Patrick's marriage to Molly per se, but he did not want his son to marry until he was financially independent.[89] Responding to James's fears, Patrick aimed to win sympathy as both a man of feeling and a man of credit. He adopted four central methods in trying to persuade his father to approve this marriage and his decision to settle with his new wife in Virginia. First, he emphasized his affection for Molly, playing the sentimental hero: 'I am an unfortunate young man—I loved a girl, pay'd my addresses to her—& won her affections.'[90] Second, he also made a claim on the basis of his affection for his father, and so, like Charles Hanbury, relied on him to be forgiving in return, stressing his father's indulgence as well as his own affectionate duty. Acting the role of a son torn between duty and love, Patrick asked his father for advice on this dilemma: 'it is the reall Sentiments of my heart—my engagements to her I never can breack but if it is your wish I shall endeavour to forget her—But I seem to Look up to an indulgent parent—Every thing rests with You.'[91] Patrick also toyed with the image of himself as a prodigal son, who depended on the affections of a merciful father: 'I shall forever let you take what means you will with me [,] look upon you as an Affec:[tionate] Parent, who perhaps has been treated too ill by an ungratefull Son.'[92] Third, he asked that his father empathize with his decisions: 'my Dear Father put yr self in my Situation I think you can feel for others especially a Son.'[93] Finally, even as he stressed his own sentiments, he also focused on his own credit, and the importance of keeping his vows to Molly: 'I am in hopes my former behaviour will have some weight in your opinion... if instantaneous ruin ensue I never w[oul]d breack such a Sacred promise.'[94] This talk of ruin and promises is the language of business.

Patrick evidently hoped this combination of languages of feeling and credit would help him to win his father's approbation. He had reason for thinking such a strategy might work; after all, it had done so for countless fictional characters.

---

[88] Patrick Parker to James Parker, 'Norfolk Nov: 13th. 1786', PA 11.28a. See also Patrick Parker to James Parker, undated, PA 11.27, Parker Family Papers, LRO.
[89] Cousin marriage was relatively common among Southern gentry families, and few would have voiced an objection based on the family ties. See Kulikoff, *Tobacco and Slaves*, esp. 252–5.
[90] Patrick Parker to James Parker, 'Norfolk Virginia August 1st. 1787', PA 11.41, Parker Family Papers, LRO.
[91] Patrick Parker to James Parker, 'Charleston South Carolina March 22d 1787', PA11.37a, ibid.
[92] Patrick Parker to James Parker, 'Norfolk Virginia August 20th. 1787', ibid.
[93] Patrick Parker to James Parker, 'Charleston So Carolina Mar 31st 1787', PA 11.38, ibid.
[94] Patrick Parker to James Parker, 'Norfolk Virginia August 20th. 1787', PA 11.42, ibid.

Patrick's letters testify to his familiarity with novels by Fanny Burney, in which her eponymous heroines exhibited sensibility as they made their way in the rough world, and thus engaged the sympathy of the reader.[95] During this period he sent Molly a copy of Goethe's *The Sorrows of Young Werther*.[96] Patrick's letters expressed a muted form of the kind of language that informs Werther's correspondence. Here is a typical Wertherian claim:

Let us suppose a man attached to a young woman, dedicating to her every hour of the day . . . Then comes a man of cold and correct understanding . . . and this very respectable person says to him, 'My young friend, love is a natural passion, but it should be kept within due bounds . . . reserve the rest [of your time] for business' . . . If the young man takes this advice, he may be a very useful member of society . . . but as to his love it is annihilated.[97]

At points, Patrick aligned himself with the Wertherian ideal of the romantic hero. Yet his problem was different from Werther's. He needed to convince his father that he was a man of feeling who loved, but he needed as well to persuade his father, who was also his financial backer, that he was trustworthy, a 'useful member of society'. So, even as Patrick emphasized the sentimental, he also privileged his word of honor and his good character. Thus, he joined the language of sentimental attachments to that of commitments and ruin.

Initially at least, these entreaties did not meet with anything like the forgiveness that had greeted Charles Hanbury. Invoking the language of sensible suffering, a livid James portrayed his son's set of decisions as an abandonment of his family, country, and everything right: 'If heaven had granted my warmest wish it was that my sons might be independent . . . & to have them settled in a land of real liberty, but you have abandoned me become an Alien & made choice of a society whose principles every honest man abhors.' Playing Cassandra, James croaked out dire warnings: 'I am extremely concerned . . . to find you still in Virginia persevering in a plan which all your freinds here think will be productive of ruin & to the poor girl.' James also lamented that he had funded Patrick's return journey to Virginia, since 'I soon saw ruin Coming upon you'.[98] He added an infuriated postscript: 'why consult me, after announcing your will?' James was especially upset that Patrick claimed to be seeking parental advice, when he apparently had no intention of following it. James concluded, finally ending

---

[95] Molly complained in a letter to Patrick that: 'Old Delville is as crabbed as ever.' ' Delville' was a coded reference to a character in Burney's *Cecilia*, her erstwhile guardian who is austere and all too conscious of his importance. See Burney, *Cecilia*, as well as Mary Aitchison (Parker) to Patrick Parker, 'Eastwood April 13th 1787', PA 11.138, Parker Family Papers, LRO.

[96] Molly thanked Patrick: 'I am much oblig'd to you my Dear Couzin for the Sorrows of Werter.' Mary Aitchison (Parker) to Patrick Parker, 'Eastwood April 13th 1787', PA 11.138, ibid.

[97] Werther, 'May 26', letter VIII, Goethe, *The Sorrows of Werter*, i. 30–1.

[98] Letter (copy), James Parker to Patrick Parker, 'Portglasgow 20 Octr. 1787', PA 11.162, Parker Family Papers, LRO.

the letter: 'I hope you will have the justice to consider, that you with a seeming compliance to my designs, have only been anouncing your fixed resolution & will.'[99] Patrick's 'seeming compliance', unsupported by the *reality* of compliance, undermined his credit within the family. It seems that it was less the disobedience than the false self-representation that most upset James.

Economic and other concerns also shaped James's reaction to the marriage of Patrick and Molly. He felt that they were both too young and too poor to be able to support a family. Molly was under the legal age of consent for marriage in Virginia in the 1780s.[100] This legal age of consent for girls was *12*.[101] Moreover, in a 1787 letter from Patrick, James wrote the following: 'his Cousin Molly Aitchison was the very Girl Id have Chosen for him, but at that time both their Ages together was not 32, without a farthing between them.'[102] While putting their combined ages at 32 may have been an exaggeration (Patrick was 23, and Molly has to have been at least 10), it was undeniable that they were young, Molly especially, and that neither could contribute much to keeping up a home.

James's objections to the timing of the marriage point also to a more general cultural concern about young men marrying too soon, while still in debt. James wanted them to wait until Patrick was financially independent and able to support fully his wife and children; in this desire he was not alone. Daniel Defoe, in his *Complete Tradesman*, devoted several pages to 'the ordinary Occasions of a Tradesman's Ruin; such as . . . Too early Marrying'.[103] He declared 'that a young beginner should never marry too soon',[104] and went on to tell stories of young tradesmen who had married too early, generally without a father's permission, and had thereby ruined themselves. Defoe concluded by advising his reader 'not to marry too soon; not to marry, 'till by a frugal industrious management of his trade in the beginning, he has laid a foundation for maintaining a wife, and bringing up a family . . . that he may not cripple his fortune at first, and be ruin'd before he has begun to thrive'.[105] His was not the only voice so to caution young men. Even Patrick's brother Charles wrote condescendingly to his father from

---

[99] Ibid.

[100] In Virginia, parents signed a bond demonstrating their agreement with the marriage of a child under the legal age. Such a bond, signed by Rebecca Aitchison, exists for Molly's marriage to Patrick. See Marriage Bond for Mary Aitchison and Patrick Parker, 11 Dec. 1787, LV.

[101] In the British-Atlantic world, in general, the age of consent for marriage was 14 for boys and 12 for girls. See William Blackstone, *Commentaries on the Laws of England*, ed. John Frederick Archbold, 4 vols. (London, 1811), vol. i. ch. 15 ('Of Husband and Wife'), p. 436. For a discussion of Virginia's age-of-consent laws in particular, see Holly Brewer, *By Birth or Consent: Children, Law, and the Anglo-American Revolution in Authority* (Chapel Hill, NC: University of North Carolina Press for the Omohundro Institute of Early American History and Culture, 2005), chs. 5, 8.

[102] Patrick Parker to James Parker, 'Norfolk feb: 9th. 1787', PA 11.32, Parker Family Papers, LRO.

[103] Defoe, *The Complete English Tradesman*, title-page.

[104] Ibid. 154.   [105] Ibid. 176.

Grenada: 'I do not know the ideas of the virginia gentlemen, but our ideas here, are that when a dependent man takes a wife here <u>he is done for</u>.'[106]

James Parker knew that marrying too soon was one sure way to increase financial worries. He wrote his friend Charles Steuart in 1787, of Patrick: 'he wants to Marrie his Cuzen Molly Aitchison which in their Present Situation would be ruinous to both, & I therefore Cannot agree to it.'[107] James felt that marriage choices deserved to be made in a nexus of other considerations, not least of which was the achievement of financial independence. Even a wife's thrift could not counteract the decision to take on dependants while still a dependant oneself; it could devastate all concerned. Patrick probably knew all of this, which is why he and Molly were eager in their letters to demonstrate their frugality.[108] In September 1789 he assured his father that Molly's 'Œconomy of her family matters... has improven'.[109] At the same time, borrowing a reference from Fanny Burney's *Cecilia*, Patrick stressed that he himself was so thrifty as to be practically a miser.[110] In that same letter, as in others, Patrick also assured his father that he was not making a related mistake of giving too much credit, a point against which Defoe, and apparently also James, had warned. Patrick wrote: 'I shall therefore take your advice give no Creditt.'[111] Here was a frugal, careful man of business who knew that his personal household management was related to his ability to prosper. This claim is somewhat belied by later ads in Virginia newspapers, in which Patrick advertised the sale of dry goods: 'On which, a reasonable credit will be allowed.'[112]

Patrick's desire to appear as a prudent man of business demonstrates that he shared James's concern about his credit, as well as the deleterious consequences for himself and his family should it perish. Both men were eager to avoid ruin. As we have seen in Chapter 4, ruin was the fierce specter that haunted correspondences

---

[106] Charles S. Parker to James Parker, 'Grenada 1st. September 1791', PAR III 1/54, Parker Family Papers, LRO.

[107] James Parker to Charles Steuart, 'Portglasgow 5th. Octr 1787', MS 5035, fos. 72–3, Charles Steuart Papers, NLS.

[108] Patrick Parker to James Parker, 'Norfolk Virginia Sep: 29th. 1789', PA 10.15, and Mary (Molly) Aitchison Parker to James Parker, 'Eastwood September 4th 1788', PA 10.13, Parker Family Papers, LRO.

[109] Patrick Parker to James Parker, 'Norfolk Virginia Sep 20th 1789', PA 11.63, ibid.

[110] He declared that Molly's 'Relations have Christened me Briggs for whose Character I shall refer you to a Novell... Called Cicilia'. Patrick Parker to James Parker, 'Norfolk Virginia Sep 20th 1789', PA 11.63, ibid. This was a rather overblown way of making his point, as Briggs is a consummate miser: see Burney, *Cecilia*, iii. 97.

[111] Patrick Parker to James Parker, 'Norfolk Virginia Sep 20th 1789', PA 11.63, Parker Family Papers, LRO.

[112] This may have been partly because by 1794, having been cut off from James's money, he was sufficiently desperate so to do (or because this was his standard practice). See advertisement, 'For Sale, an assortment of Dry Goods', by Patrick Parker, 'Norfolk, Sept. 17th. 1794', *Virginia Chronicle, & General Advertiser*, 9 Oct. 1794; *Virginia Chronicle*, 13 Nov. 1794; 20 Nov. 1794; 24 Nov. 1794, in *Early American Newspapers, Series I, 1690–1876* (Readex).

of this type. It seems, though, that James decided that, in addition to being an untrustworthy son, Patrick was also an untrustworthy debtor. As early as August 1789, Patrick grumbled: 'your... Constant distrust in me makes me feel That if I am Ever to be in arrears to you a Little you w[oul]d immediately conclude That I was going to Take advantage of You.'[113] James had more than one reason to be worried about his son's lack of credit. He was personally worried by it, but it was also professionally important. First, it damaged his reputation as a father who could shape his son correctly. Second, James had been financially devastated by the Revolution and its war. Third, his own credit was at stake, partly because of the nature of the eighteenth-century Atlantic economy. The credit of the parties in bills of exchange actually affected the exchange rate, and hence the price, of bills so drawn.[114] If James Parker, as the drawee, had to protest bills, it was a loss of that reputation and hence of his ability to do business at an advantageous exchange rate. So, if his son owed him money and did not pay it back, and if James was therefore unable to pay bills of exchange, he might lose not just the money his son owed, but also his own financial and personal standing in a community of transatlantic traders.

Patrick added to his father's suspicions about his lack of credit by his business dealings, as his letters from the 1790s protest constantly about his honesty, and business acumen.[115] He argued that James was too harsh a creditor, because his credit came with 'strict scrutiny'. The gentle treatment of his debtors was one indicator of a gentleman's character, as it showed both his economic standing (he could afford to be gentle) and also his feelingness. One pre-Revolutionary Virginian, Robert Beverley, noted: 'I am Sensible... that we ought to be as tender with Respect to each others Credit as possible.'[116] Such was the case even when the ties between men were not those of father and son. Patrick felt that James ought to be more 'tender', as both creditor and father: 'Were I a person you [never] knew... you Could not be more severe.'[117] He griped that his father's constant discouragement would end any chance of success in trade: 'it is impossible for me to Succeed... when every Letter from you is fill'd with the most disheartening encouragem[en]t—In every letter I receive There is Allways

---

[113] Patrick Parker to James Parker, 'Norfolk 26th August 1789', PA 11.60, Parker Family Papers, LRO.
[114] McCusker, *Money and Exchange in Europe and America*, 22.
[115] Indeed, a 1789 letter from Patrick to his father admitted as much: 'I observe what you say abt my Giving Creditt... you may rest Satisfy[d] That The Little The very Little Creditt I have given... I have got mostly paid for.' Patrick Parker to James Parker, 'Norfolk Virginia Sep 20th 1789', PA 11.63. See also Patrick Parker to James Parker, 'Norfo 13th May 1790', PA 11.78, Parker Family Papers, LRO.
[116] Robert Beverley to Dixon, 26 March 1765, Beverley Letter Book, 1761–1793, Library of Congress, Washington, DC, as quoted in Breen, *Tobacco Culture*, 166.
[117] Patrick Parker to James Parker, 'Norfo 13th May 1790', PA 11.78, Parker Family Papers, LRO.

Something wrong.'[118] Patrick's business was not going especially well, in the lackluster economy of post-war Virginia.[119] It seems from his letters that he began to blame his father's discouragement for his lack of success.[120] Patrick was frustrated that his father wrote to him 'as if I was a rascall', and stated that he did 'not deserve it, particularly from a Father'.[121] He rejected his father's plans for him to resettle in South Carolina, Nova Scotia, or New York, where James thought trade prospects were brighter. Patrick also went ahead with building a house he could ill afford.[122]

As his debts to his father caused ever more friction, Patrick exploited an emotionally charged language of debt, merging idioms of sensibility with those of credit. Although Patrick had been repaying at least the interest on the loan from his father, whether from want or anger Patrick stopped being 'punctuall' in paying it in 1792, resulting in the nadir of the epistolary relationship. By 1793 James was so suspicious of his son's credit that he dunned Patrick, charging him with dishonesty. Patrick rebutted such allegations in the heated disputes of 1793 on, agreeing only that 'if to be in Debt to you is a Crime . . . Then I agree I stand Convicted'. Still, he could not help smarting at his father's accusations: 'Before I draw my Letter To a Conclusion my D[ea]r Father I think you are cruell in saying That I have forsaken my Father & Brother it is rather I am Sure the Other way.'[123] When Patrick used the word 'cruell' here, he implied the heartlessness of his father's accusation as well as the distress it caused him.[124] One fictional prodigal son in a similar situation complained to his sister that 'my father is cruel, and tyrannises over my distress'.[125] A month later Patrick was again begging for credit and time: 'For Godsake my Dear f[athe]r dont Distress me. I will pay as I have said . . . if you push me harder . . . you will only have the Satisfaction of ruining me and my family.'[126] Here is emotionally loaded language of financial insolvency, in which one man's ruin, like a stone tossed in a pond, rippled outward ominously to all those about him, starting with his own family. Ruin had economic implications, but it also implied considerable loss of prestige in

---

[118] Patrick Parker to James Parker, 'Norfolk 6th Septr. 1790—', PA11.83c, Parker Family Papers, LRO.

[119] Allan Kulikoff discusses at some length the 'decline of opportunity' in the Tidewater area in the 1790s. See Kulikoff, *Tobacco and Slaves*, ch. 4. See, too, Lewis, *Pursuit of Happiness*, ch. 4.

[120] Petitioners from other debtors in this period indicate that rare was the debtor who did not blame circumstances beyond his own control (rather than his own choices) for his failure to honor debts. There is a helpful discussion of these petitions in Mann, *Republic of Debtors*, 72–8.

[121] Patrick Parker to James Parker, 'Norfo Virginia 4th Novr 1791', PA 11.104, Parker Family Papers, LRO.

[122] Patrick Parker to James Parker, 'Norfolk Virga August 16th 1791', PA 11.99, ibid.

[123] Patrick Parker to James Parker, 'Norfolk Virginia April 29th 1793', PA 11.119, ibid.

[124] *Oxford English Dictionary* online, second edn., (1989), definition of 'cruel,' definition 1a.

[125] Daniel Defoe, *The Family Instructor*, in *The Novels and Miscellaneous Works of Daniel Defoe*, 15 vols. (Oxford, 1841), i. 379.

[126] Patrick Parker to James Parker, 'Nor? Virga October 22nd 1793', PA 11.124, Parker Family Papers, LRO.

family and community.¹²⁷ Surely, Patrick insinuated, a good father would not want to cause such ruin; only a 'cruel tyrant' would delight in 'ruining' a son and thus causing 'distress' for the son and his innocent wife and child.

'Distress' implied emotional suffering sufficient to provoke pity in another, but it also implied financial hardship. Both meanings occurred together here, as in many other texts of the era. So in the King James Bible: 'And every one that was in distress, and every one that was in debt, and every one that was discontented, gathered themselves unto him.'¹²⁸ A British advice manual to young men in business lamented that too many men embraced 'difficulties, distress, shame, bankruptcy, and imprisonment'.¹²⁹ One woman whose husband had lost much by his Loyalism expressed her hope that 'our Distresses may be considered' by the new British ministry.¹³⁰ A fictional petitioner, writing from debtors' prison, pleaded with a wealthy benefactor to help him, since 'your petitioner has often heard of your great goodness to your fellow creatures in distress'.¹³¹ When Patrick pleaded with his father not to 'distress' him (and noted that it would only serve to 'ruin' him), he was begging his father not to exert unbearable financial pressure on him *and* not to cause emotional suffering.

James surely hardly relished seeing a son, even one whose misrepresentations had long caused suspicions, 'distressed.' But apparently he argued that in fact it was Patrick who allowed his old father to live in 'distress', thus ignoring the duty an affectionate son owed his father. Patrick turned his father's allegations upside-down: 'you mention that by my unjust barbarous and unnatural behaviour that I have reduced you to ye. most dreadfull necessity—being so much conscious of the reverse the accusation hangs ye heavyer on me.'¹³² He also decried his father's accusations of 'Villainy Dishonesty [and] ingratitude', again resorting to the language of merchants' disputes.¹³³ But he also deployed the language of sympathy and anti-tyranny, claiming that James preferred to 'harass and Distress' him rather than 'making Something Comfortable for His family'.¹³⁴ According to the Declaration of Independence, 'harassing' was what George III did to the people of America when he 'sent hither swarms of officers to harass our people'. Only a man 'whose character is thus marked' as a tyrant would do such a

---

127 The obsessive concern with ruin and dependence, and its political implications, are insightfully treated in Breen, *Tobacco Culture*. The economic, social, and cultural implications of ruin, and the concomitant importance of credit, are ably discussed in Muldrew, *The Economy of Obligation*, Finn, *The Character of Credit*, and esp. Mann, *Republic of Debtors*.
128 *The Bible* (King James Version), 1 Sam. 22: 2.   129 REMEMBRANCER, 3.
130 Rebecca Shoemaker to Samuel Shoemaker, '1 July 1784 by the Skinner', Shoemaker Family Papers, HSP.
131 'A Prisoner for Debt to a Gentleman celebrated for his Humanity To G.E. Esq. The humble Petition of A.B.', *The Universal Letter-Writer* (Philadelphia, 1808), 139.
132 Patrick Parker to James Parker, 'Norf. Virga Octr. 5th. 1793', PA 11.122, Parker Family Papers, LRO.
133 Cf. Ditz, 'Shipwrecked'.
134 Patrick Parker to James Parker, 'Norfolk Virginia Novr 13t 93', PA 11.125a, Parker Family Papers, LRO.

thing to his own people. Both 'distressing' and 'harassing' implied the deliberate inflicting of pain on another party, and a father and man of sympathy would surely do all in his power not to inflict but to alleviate suffering. Had Patrick been capable of financial and emotional independence, this would have been his declaration of it.

But if some achieve independence, others have independence thrust upon 'em, as Patrick found in 1794. James stopped writing altogether; Patrick then came to rely even more strongly on the language of sensibility and familiar affection. By contrast, James focused ever more resolutely on debt. Even in 1793, James commented sardonically on the back of one letter: 'P. Parker... Proposals but no payment.'[135] By May 1794, when still no letters had arrived, Patrick was beginning to panic. Rather than starting a long letter with his usual 'My Dear Father', Patrick began with the obsequious: 'My Dearly Beloved & much Esteemed Father.' Uncharacteristically brief, the letter invoked the suffering of himself and his family: 'Look over what is heretofore past the most vigorous exertions... shall Shortly be used, to pay you... Write... as formerly... you know not in what Confusion and melancholy y[ou]r long silence throws us all.' This pathetic bare epistle elicited no response from James, beyond a further label: 'P. Parker promises as made years ago, without a farther payment.'[136] Promises not backed up by performance and payment meant only a total loss of credit in both personal and professional terms. In July 1794 Patrick was again appealing for a letter in terms of sentiment: 'Your long and y[ou]r Cruell silence really distresses me in the Extreme.' Although Patrick reported on his wife and daughter, he continued bitterly: 'but why should I... Trouble you ab[ou]t a family you Seem entirely to have thrown off—and a Son... who has no other Crime but that of being in debt.' Patrick ended the letter plaintively: 'never was there a poorer outcast from his family.'[137] James greeted these lamentations with silent scorn, annotating the letter: 'P. Parker promises 500£ payment this Year, but as usual without any intention of Performing.'[138] James here echoed an earlier tobacco trader who, in 1760, termed the Chesapeake area 'the Land of Promis without any intension of Performing'.[139] Similarly, James now saw Patrick's self-representations and promises as empty shells. Patrick had lost all credit with his father.

In the end, if marriage and settlement issues were the winds and waves that mightily shook and damaged James's and Patrick's fragile transatlantic

---

[135] Patrick Parker to James Parker, 'Norfo Virginia Septr 20th 1793', PA 11.121, Parker Family Papers, LRO.
[136] Patrick Parker to James Parker, 'Norfolk Virga 30th May 1794', PA 11.127, ibid.
[137] Patrick Parker to James Parker, 'Norfolk Virginia July 18 94', PA 11.128, ibid.
[138] ibid.
[139] Edmund Wilcox to James Russell, 6 May 1760, Hubard Family Papers, Southern Historical Collection, University of North Carolina, Chapel Hill, quoted in Mann, *Republic of Debtors*, 133. This was a classic charge leveled against defaulting debtors. See also Ditz, 'Shipwrecked', *passim*.

relationship, debt and a failure to honor it—with concomitant implications for character and credit—were the sharp rocks on which their relationship finally split for good. James did not stop communicating with his son or sending him money when his son had taken a child-bride whom he could not independently support, or when he had decided to settle in Virginia, or when he chose to set up business there, handing over James's money to business associates denounced by James as a 'crew of perdition'. James stopped communicating and sending money only when he decided that his son was not a man of credit. His decision here was partly financial; after all, to cut off debtors and even to sue them were standard practices of the era.[140]

At the heart of the conflict lay the fact that James was horrified that his son had become what he most feared: a true Virginian, a debtor who would make promises without payment or even any 'intention of performing'. James loathed what he saw as the sham liberty of Virginia. He viewed Virginia, like his son, as capable of claims of independence and authenticity, but incapable of delivering anything like a true 'performance'. As he phrased it to Charles Steuart: 'P & I have not been upon good terms for some time, owing to his failing to pay me according to promise, & Putting himself into that Situation, After promise, which disqualified him to fullfill, Virginia like.'[141] As we have seen, for James, 'Virginia Patriot' meant 'debtor' as well as 'enemy.' While it is not simply Loyalism that caused James to hate Virginia, his wartime experiences, as well as the defaulting debtors and rioters well before the war, caused him to feel an intense resentment against Virginians in particular. In James's view, Patrick had chosen familiarity with the wrong people, had cast off the connections in South Carolina, the West Indies, and Britain that James had arranged, in order to choose his own 'friends' in Virginia. But James knew these 'friends' to be nothing of the sort. Equally, he felt that Virginia would only bring loss and ruin to his son, just as it had done to himself (and in this, it transpires, he was not far wrong).

In his personal dealings no less than his professional ones, Patrick was all pretense and promise, where he should have been performance, at least according to James. Although he had consulted his father about whether or not to marry Molly, he did not actually wait for his father's approbation, going ahead despite the explicit objections penned by James. Against his will, Patrick did agree to follow his father's wishes and go to Charleston in 1787. However, he had stayed such a short time as to render the trip a 'farce', productive only of unnecessary expense and aggravation for himself and his father.[142] Again, Patrick had not bothered to wait for his father's replies when he asked whether he ought to

---

[140] Mann, *Republic of Debtors*.
[141] James Parker to Charles Steuart, 'Monday morning the 28th Ocr. 1793', MS 5038, fos. 63, Charles Steuart Papers, NLS.
[142] His father termed this journey 'The Farce of going to Charleston'. James Parker to Patrick Parker (copy), 'Portglasgow 20 Octr. 1787', PA 11.162, Parker Family Papers, LRO.

leave Charleston, although his letters appeared to ask his father for advice. So his claim of consulting his father was not backed by his actions. Against his father's objections, Patrick also chose to settle permanently in Virginia and refused to consider moving anywhere else, even when his father promised contacts, connection, and credit. Equally, he had gone ahead in building a house for himself against James's desires, while still considerably in his father's debt. Patrick's cessation of remittances was only final confirmation of what James had long feared: that his son could or would not truly be a man of credit, one who kept his word and repaid his debts. In becoming a debtor, a committed Virginian, and, in the end, a man without credit, Patrick came to embody everything that James most despised. So, James could not entirely forgive him.

James had tried to ensure his children's prosperity. In 1776, after the death of his brother-in-law and while he himself was being detained as a prisoner, James had informed Margaret of his melancholy sentiments: 'God help us, our friends drop off very fast, were it not the Hopes of better times, & that Ardent desire of doing all we can for the little folks who are to Succeed us... there are but very few [enticements?] at present w[ould] prompt us to desire Staying behind our friends.'[143] For James, working for the future success of children could preserve the spirits of a man in prison with little prospect of liberty and happiness any time soon. To be a good man was to be a good father who worked for the future of his 'little folks'. When those children chose not to listen, and not to tell the truth, then it was a difficult, embittering, and ultimately futile process to make them understand. James knew he had not succeeded with his son Patrick, who died before he could put things to right. Patrick and Molly produced no surviving children themselves, since their little girl, Margaret, died even before her father did. The death of Patrick's child might have brought him closer to his own father, who had also lost a precious daughter and a beloved Margaret. But by this point his relationship with his father brought Patrick no solace.

This tragic ending would not have surprised many. In his cautions about marrying too early, Daniel Defoe provided a narrative about a young man whose father set him up in business, who married without his father's knowledge and permission, and who ended up ruined as a result. Defoe summarized this imagined story in a way which might have described Patrick's own trajectory: 'he sunk gradually, and then broke, and died poor: in a word, he broke the heart of his father, wasted what he had, and could never recover it, and at last it broke his own heart too.'[144] To lose credit was also to court emotional disaster. How gloomy the world must have seemed to the heartbroken Patrick when his own child perished and his father cut him off, the future and the past felled and the grim specter of ruin haunting him and his prospects. If his father felt that he had

---

[143] James Parker to Margaret Parker, 'New London. Bedford County. Decmr. 10th 1776', PA 7.9, Parker Family Papers, LRO.
[144] Defoe, *Complete English Tradesman*, 157.

chosen to become an alien, Patrick saw himself as a 'poor Outcast', cast adrift in a cruel Atlantic world and economy by a stern, unforgiving father and creditor.

To remedy these problems Patrick had tried to use languages of sensibility, as Charles Hanbury successfully did. Fictions like those of the Hanburys, as well as many novels, provided vocabularies and a storyline which a young man, struggling to make his way in the world, could believe. Sensible languages seemed powerful. A son, like his mother, could use them, and indeed they could smooth conflict up to a point. Even if a son married a young girl with no money, and chose to settle in a place that had destroyed much of his father's patrimony, this behavior could be forgiven, especially at the behest of that son, as long as that son succeeded in becoming a man of credit and a man of honor, as well as a man of feeling. If many wanted to believe in the power of sympathy, it was nonetheless clear that its power extended only so far, especially when it came into conflict with credit and the prospects of a family in the long term. In the end, the aspects of life such languages of sensibility either deliberately or inadvertently attempted to submerge—issues of credit, debt, and promise-keeping—came bobbing back to the surface.

Relations of credit were so important that they could also provoke feeling responses, even when the creditor was not a father. Benjamin Franklin pointed this out when he reminded young tradesmen that 'Good-natur'd Creditors... feel Pain when they are oblig'd to ask you for Money. Spare 'em that Pain, and they will love you.'[145] Even creditors, sharp of eye and ear, could love a man of credit, as James knew. Still, if a man ceased to have credit, then he risked losing that love. Credit and sensibility could work together, but they could also cut against each other, as Patrick found to his horror. Family members, like others in this Atlantic world, depended on each other's credit, and it could gain overwhelming importance in certain situations. Dependence was a state of life, though many, like Patrick, found it galling. The ideal of independence motivated Patriots and Loyalists alike. But in the eighteenth century choices made by an individual on one side of the ocean could have severe ramifications for an individual on the other. To focus on the family is to be reminded of the enduring nature of dependence in this Atlantic world, even for men who embraced ideals of independence and liberty. It is also to be reminded that Patriotism and Loyalism, or patriarchy and paternalism, may be less useful in explaining certain kinds of behavior than an emphasis on dependence, credit, and sentiment.

Financial and emotional dependence on fathers inspired both historical and fictional sons to pursue penitence and to seek forgiveness, but with very different results. The story of the Parkers forces these issues of independence, credit, and ruin to the forefront in a way that the happy sentimentality of the Hanburys did not. In fact, the final scene in the correspondence between James and Patrick reverses that of the fictional story, as the unforgiven son died on a sickbed

[145] Franklin, *Advice to a Young Tradesman*, 3.

far from an embittered father. Two men, on different sides of the Atlantic, connected by the closest of blood, emotional, and economic ties, saw only terrible alienation and betrayal stemming from the other. There are no powerful patriarchs here, enforcing their prerogative vigorously, but neither are there forgiving paternalists. There is also no merciful father, no returned son, no open arms, no fatted calves. There are no heroes here. There are instead two flawed, frustrated men trying their best to avoid ruin, distress, and dependence, in a world and an economy that made those fears all too pressing. When Patrick avowed in his last letters that he was on the verge of death, his father might have wondered whether his son's declarations were genuine. When Patrick's death provided dreadful proof of the truth of his claims, it made him, at last, a man of credit. By then, however, it was 'too late'.

6

The Farewell Between Husband and Wife: The Politics of Family Feeling

> There is nothing so bad as a separation.
> (Jane Austen, 1818)[1]

Would the husband return to his wife after the war was over? (Fig. 6.1) Prospects did not seem hopeful, when Horatius left his tearful Flavilla. Horatius, in red coat and riding boots, gestured to the townscape awaiting him, one pulling him away from his loving wife and her supportive sister. Flavilla herself cut a figure of nature, as her form blended into the tree behind her, her ruffles like leaves. She could hardly overcome the natural sentiments of sorrow, sure to follow when her husband unclasped his hand and moved out into the world beyond. As in many portraits, darkening clouds split the sky, intimating the couple's impending separation.[2] While a classic vision of war, it also would have resonated powerfully in July 1781, when it appeared in the *Town and Country Magazine*, as the American Revolutionary War was drawing to its bloody close.[3] There had been many such farewells since 1775, as something like one out of eight adult military-age males in Britain and America fought in the war.[4]

In the picture's accompanying story, Flavilla and Horatius had wed with happiness, but then the husband's unit was 'ordered abroad'. It was difficult to surmount the pain they felt at 'the Farewell!—the cruel, the afflicting, the agonizing Farewell!', a farewell, the story did not need to state, which might all

---

[1] Mrs Musgrove in Jane Austen, *Persuasion* [1818], ed. Gillian Beer (London: Penguin Books, 1998), 66.
[2] This portrait echoes themes raised by marital 'double portraits' in Retford, *The Art of Domestic Life*, ch. 2.
[3] 'The Farewel: or, the History of Horatius and Flavilla', *Town and Country Magazine* (July 1781), 376–8.
[4] Numbers in Britain were one out of seven or eight: Stephen Conway, *The British Isles and the War of American Independence* (Oxford: Oxford University Press, 2000), 29. John Shy reckons that, tallying the Patriot side and excluding slaves, 'military service approached one in ten of the available population'. Presumably if including Loyalists and slaves, the numbers would be higher. John Shy, *A People Numerous and Armed: Reflections on the Military Struggle for American Independence*, rev. edn. (Ann Arbor, Mich.: University of Michigan Press, 1990), 248–9.

Fig. 6.1. 'The Farewell', to accompany 'The Farewel: or, the History of Horatius and Flavilla', *Town and Country Magazine* (July 1781), 376–8. Bodleian Library, University of Oxford, Per. 2705 e.674, pp. 376–7, vol. 13.

too easily prove permanent. Horatius could comfort Flavilla only with sensible assurances of his love: 'My dear angel, said he, I must go—my country calls—my honour, nay every thing that is dear to a gentleman is at stake; but... with you I leave my heart—place it next your own, where it has long entwined in sympathy—there let it unite, and cherish it till my return.' Yet even as this story foreground the hell of those farewells, it also offered hope. By the end, Horatius, accompanying Admiral Rodney, had not only survived but triumphed, returning to Flavilla with the spoils from St Eustatius in the Caribbean.[5] The story ended on a cheering note: 'as the reader will necessarily anticipate all the blissful circumstances that must succeed an interview with his delectable Flavilla.' Moving beyond this domestic scene, the author concluded 'with a hearty wish that every pair so deserving of the most refined enjoyments... may meet with them'.

Unlike this happy couple, many others endured only sorrowful separation due to the Revolutionary War, never finding 'blissful' reunions. This magazine story raises issues refracted in the real-life stories of individuals caught in a war that altered forever many homes. After all, as we have seen in the Parker family story, the war divided not only countries but also married couples. Even peace did not necessarily bring reunion, as other factors, including political views, economic situations, and complicated webs of loyalties, sometimes kept loving couples apart. Letters, although not used in this story, were a critical means of keeping together and reordering the world, as uncertain futures greeted those caught up in war and revolution. As with other sentimental tales of the period, including domestic letters, this magazine story deliberately excluded the possibility of loss and permanent derangement of prospects, even as it made a pathetic scene of separation its center. Taking pain as its main theme, it also promised the amelioration of that agony, soothing suffering audiences who themselves longed for those reunions, that bliss.

Among many such possible readers might have been Charles and Catherine Dudley, who also experienced first-hand the American Revolution. The story of Charles and Catherine, like that of Horatius and Flavilla, raises a number of salient issues about family feeling in a state of considerable political, economic, and military flux. Their story also offers a useful case study of how marriage functioned for a loving couple who nevertheless found themselves divided both by the Atlantic and also by their distinct senses of what their future should be. Historians who have addressed marital separations have tended either to focus on

---

[5] The prosperous St Eustatius was taken from the Dutch (thought to be smuggling to American allies), on 3 February 1781, a few months earlier. According to a naval historian, while not of military importance, 'the booty was enormous'. Kenneth Breen, 'Sir George Rodney and St Eustatius in the American War: A Commercial and Naval Distraction, 1775–81', *The Mariner's Mirror*, 84 (1998), 193–203, at 197. See also Andrew Jackson O'Shaughnessy, *An Empire Divided: The American Revolution and the British Caribbean* (Philadelphia: University of Pennsylvania Press, 2000), ch. 9.

marital breakdown or on the effects of such separations on women left alone.[6] Few have observed that such partings put pressure on marriage itself, for individuals and for societies. Children were expected eventually to separate from parents; but husband and wives were supposed to stay together. Nevertheless, the reality of empire and war in the lives of particular couples subverted this social ideal. Narratives like 'The Farewell', generated by the worries of an empire at war with itself, reassured audiences that reunion, and the return of the social order, was the rightful state of society. So did familiar letters between husbands and wives. In such situations, women and men had recourse to expressions of sensibility and family feeling, although these were cut against by the grim exigencies of war, economics, and separation. In addition, such rhetoric transcended individual couples and offered a politicized language for all kinds of individuals caught in trying circumstances.

To tell tales about the disordering of couples and families by war and empire was not only to highlight the anguish of such individuals, for domestic and political purposes, but also to emphasize that such anguish was, or should be, temporary and aberrant. Many different kinds of people—from wives and husbands to generals and politicians—recounted narratives of distress for such purposes. Sensibility as a means of expression might initially seem to be at odds with war. Soldiers like Horatius (a name invoking Roman martial prowess) were to be stoical even under duress.[7] Nevertheless, eloquent sensibility, especially within a familiar setting, was an ideal held dear by many individuals before

---

[6] On marital conflict, see, among others, Lawrence Stone, *Broken Lives: Separation and Divorce in England, 1660–1857* (Oxford: Oxford University Press, 1993), and his *Road to Divorce*; Merril D. Smith, *Breaking the Bonds: Marital Discord in Pennsylvania, 1730–1830* (New York: New York University Press, 1991); Norma Basch, *Framing American Divorce: From the Revolutionary Generation to the Victorians* (Berkeley: University of California Press, 1999); Joanne Bailey, *Unquiet Lives: Marriage and Marriage Breakdown in England, 1660–1800* (Cambridge: Cambridge University Press, 2003); and Mary Beth Sievens, *Stray Wives: Marital Conflict in Early National New England* (New York: New York University Press, 2005). On the effects of marital separations on women, see the discussion of 'deputy husbands' in Laurel Thatcher Ulrich, *Good Wives: Image and Reality in the Lives of Women in Northern New England, 1650–1750* (New York: Knopf, 1980). Mary Beth Norton argues for women finding independence from such situations in her *Liberty's Daughters: The Revolutionary Experience of American Women, 1750–1800* (Boston: Little, Brown & Co., 1980). Other have considered the difficulties of poorer women, especially sailors' wives, left alone. See Lisa Norling, *Captain Ahab Had a Wife: New England Women and the Whalefishery, 1720–1870*, ed. Thadious M. Davis and Linda K. Kerber, Gender and American Culture (Chapel Hill, NC: University of North Carolina Press, 2000); Elaine Forman Crane, *Ebb Tide in New England: Women, Seaports, and Social Change, 1630–1800* (Boston: Northeastern University Press, 1998); Ruth Wallis Herndon, 'The Domestic Cost of Seafaring: Town Leaders and Seamen's Families in Eighteenth-Century Rhode Island', in Margaret S. Creighton and Lisa Norling (eds.), *Iron Men, Wooden Women: Gender and Seafaring in the Atlantic World, 1700–1920*, Gender Relations in the American Experience (Baltimore, Md.: Johns Hopkins University Press, 1996), 55–69; and Paul A. Gilje, *Liberty on the Waterfront: American Maritime Culture in the Age of Revolution* (Philadelphia: University of Pennsylvania Press, 2004), ch. 2.

[7] For instance, Livy and Polybius lauded Horatius Cocles, who 'held the Sublician bridge against the invading army'. See 'Horatius Cocles', in Simon Hornblower and Antony Spawforth (eds.), *The Oxford Classical Dictionary*, 3rd edn. (Oxford: Oxford University Press, 1996), 727.

the American Revolution ever began, and one that retained importance after that war had ended. Such languages provided points of reassurance in a world turned upside-down, and they were also a means by which to measure behavior and to press for other kinds of it, for all types of people. The Revolutionary emphasis on liberty, equality, and independence was for many less important than more long-standing transatlantic commitments to sensibility and sympathy.

The story of Charles and Catherine Dudley, then, reveals how sensibility and family feeling functioned as ideologies, as well as a means of invoking authority. But it also demonstrates the economic and political imperatives that constantly cut against them. Although Horatius returned to Flavilla at war's end, not every couple was so fortunate, though Charles, unlike Horatius, was no soldier. Still, even for civilians like the Dudleys, the end of the war did not necessarily spell the end of divisions. Separated for a second time in 1784, Charles stayed on in exile in England, while Catherine returned to Rhode Island with the children. Apparently, both desired reunion in Rhode Island, but Charles remained in London for six long years. How can we explain this long absence? Slotting Charles into standard ideas about Loyalists or patriarchs might lead us to assume that this separation was inflicted by him on his wife, against her wishes, because he was her master. In fact, explanations relying on these historical and historiographical characterizations do little to help explain their long time apart. Instead, it is more helpful to attend to concerns about credit and independence, as well as considering the ways in which Charles's identity as a man of feeling helped to justify this difficult decision. Altogether, their trajectory illuminates the ways that narratives of sensible suffering had social, cultural, and political leverage, both within and outside the family.

Before it is possible to understand why the Dudleys made the choices they did, it is necessary to understand first how they ended up with limited choices. Let us start, then, in happier times. A 31-year-old Englishman, Charles arrived as His Majesty's Collector of Customs in Newport, Rhode Island, in May, 1768, after having unsuccessfully tried his hand at making his fortune in South Carolina.[8] In a town full of merchants, traders, and smugglers (terms which could describe the same individual), the customs officer, a tax collector for the crown, was

---

[8] Charles was probably born in Staffordshire, May 1737. Baptism record, 'Charles Son of Thomas and Mary Dudley bapt 15 May 1737', entry in 'A True Copy of St. Mary's Register in Stafford in the County of Stafford from September ye 4th 1735 to August ye 29th 1738 given into the Bishops Court of the Triennial Visitation held in the Said Parish Church of St. Marys in Staffordshire', in *Bishop's Transcripts: Baptisms, Marriages, Burials for Staffordshire, 1673–1809* (IGI Film No. 0421592). His attempt at living in South Carolina is mentioned in his claim before the Loyalist Commission. 'Office or Employment lost by the Enemy's getting Possession of the Province', AO 12/104, pp. 94–5, NA. On 21 May 1768, *the Providence Gazette* reported that Charles had arrived there the week before. 'Providence, May 21 [1768]', *The Providence Gazette; and Country Journal*, 21 May 1768, Issue 228, in *Early American Newspapers, Series I, 1690–1876* (Readex).

never a popular figure in the British-Atlantic world.⁹ Just as Charles was arriving to Newport, for instance, reports were circulated about the brutal murder of a customs official in Penzance, England.¹⁰ Resistance to customs collectors became enormously politicized after the Stamp Act made non-compliance a patriotic act.¹¹ Customs duties were even the focus of one 1765 Newport pamphlet justifying the Stamp Act. Its author, Martin Howard, defended tough treatment of miscreants: 'When every mild expedient, to stop the atrocious and infamous practice of smuggling, has been try'd in vain, the government is justifiable in making laws against it, even like those of *Draco*, which were written in blood.'¹² On the bustling wharves of Newport, few applauded schemes for Draconian punishments for smugglers. During the 1765 Stamp Act riots, Howard was hanged in effigy.¹³

Charles must have arrived with a sense that Newport had its share of those eager to make trouble for a new customs collector, and may have attempted to thwart them. In 1772 Ezra Stiles, a local diarist, recorded that 'there is such a swarm of [Customs] Officers, that like the plague of Locusts they devour all before them. They very particularly torment the Sons of Liberty.' Nevertheless, even Stiles admitted that 'Dudley behaves in Office as well as any of them'.¹⁴ Still, Stiles went on darkly, 'bad is the best', calling Dudley an 'accessory to the daily Perjuries which he midwifes into the World of Error & Sin'.¹⁵ It is difficult to discern how much of Stiles's assessment was accurate. What is clear is that Charles Dudley was looked upon as an enemy of the Patriot cause, well before shots were fired at Lexington and Concord.¹⁶ In fact, others in Newport had already shown

---

⁹ Marcus Rediker posits that even by the early eighteenth century Newport was a 'town notorious for its slave trade, privateering, and smuggling'. Rediker, *Between the Devil and the Deep Blue Sea*, 66.

¹⁰ Smugglers apparently stoned and beat to death William Odgers, a Customs officer, there. See Edward Stanley to Thomas Bradshaw, 'Customhouse London 21st April 1768', in Gertrude Selwyn Kimball (ed.), *The Correspondence of the Colonial Governors of Rhode Island, 1723–1775*, 2 vols. (Boston: Houghton, Mifflin & Co., 1903), ii. 402–7.

¹¹ Even before 1750, as Marcus Rediker has pointed out, this was not an easy town for Customs officers: 'Newport's customs officials...dared not "exercise their office for fear of the fury and unruliness" of a threatening mob.' Rediker, *Between the Devil and the Deep Blue Sea*, 66.

¹² Martin Howard, *A Letter from a Gentleman at Halifax, to his Friend in Rhode-Island, Containing Remarks upon a Pamphlet, Entitled, The Rights of Colonies Examined* (Newport, RI, 1765), 18.

¹³ A discussion of this hanging occurs in Robert Blair St George, *Conversing by Signs: Poetics of Implication in Colonial New England Culture* (Chapel Hill, NC: University of North Carolina Press, 1998), 260–1. During those riots, Customs officers fled to a British ship in harbor for shelter, and refused to allow trade to continue. They eventually returned, but smoldering resentments remained. See Kimball (ed.), *The Correspondence of the Colonial Governors*, ii. 372–3, as well as John Russell Bartlett (ed.), *Records of the Colony of Rhode Island and Providence Plantations in New England*, 10 vols. (Providence, RI, 1861), vol. 6: (*1757 to 1769*), 453–60.

¹⁴ Customs collectors generally did function by taking bribes; this is what made the position lucrative.

¹⁵ Ezra Stiles, *The Literary Diary of Ezra Stiles*, ed. Franklin Bowditch Dexter, 3 vols. (New York: Charles Scribner's Sons, 1901), vol. 1: (*January 1, 1769–March 13, 1776*), 270–1.

¹⁶ See also Larry R. Gerlach, 'Charles Dudley and the Customs Quandary in Pre-Revolutionary Rhode Island', *Rhode Island History*, 30 (1971), 52–9.

their agreement with Stiles's assessments with their fists. In 1771, while Charles on a ship collecting customs, unknown assailants seriously injured him. One sympathetic supporter reported to the governor of Rhode Island that Charles 'was... grossly ill-treated, even to the danger of his life, by a number of the inhabitants, without any protection being given him'. Admittedly, this witness was eager to prove to the governor that 'the laws of this kingdom are suffered to be trampled upon'.[17] Nevertheless, even the governor of Rhode Island, Joseph Wanton, did not dispute the event, although he fiercely denied that Rhode Islanders were responsible, conveniently blaming instead a drunken 'company of lawless seamen'.[18] No one was ever prosecuted. Far from offering support, Wanton claimed the problem lay with Charles and others, 'for their abusing and misrepresenting the colony of Rhode Island', proclaiming 'how unkind and ungentlemanly-like, is it for officers, sent abroad by the crown... to traduce and even falsely accuse His Majesty's faithful subjects'.[19] In the end, not only was Charles assaulted by men who went unpunished, but he was also attacked for his 'ungentlemanly-like' behavior in reporting it. In a colony ever more frustrated by what was perceived as unfair British surveillance, he was a marked man.

Whether Dudley was a midwife to daily perjuries or innocent victim of men who trampled upon laws and bodies with impunity (or most likely somewhere in between), his position had brought him into dangerous proximity with Newport's merchant families. But in late 1768 it also brought him into romantic proximity with one such family. Although Stiles claimed that Charles took the trouble to 'torment the Sons of Liberty', he also managed to woo and win the daughter of a Son of Liberty. Born in 1750, Catherine Crooke was the child of a prosperous merchant, Robert Crooke, and his wife Ann Wickham Crooke.[20] Like many of Newport's fortunes, part of the Crooke wealth came from the slave trade, which Robert had joined in 1754.[21] In 1767 Ezra Stiles described Robert Crooke as 'a Merchant of figure and of good Connexions', as well as a Son of Liberty.[22] Robert's most notable political act, his involvement in the Newport Stamp Act riot, had occurred before Charles had even arrived there. In this episode, allegedly, Robert, along with two other merchants, instigated

---

[17] 'The Earl of Hillsborough to the Governor and Company of Rhode Island, 'Whitehall, July 19th, 1771,' in Bartlett (ed.), *Records of the Colony...*, vol. 7: (*1770–1776*), 35.

[18] 'Joseph Wanton, Governor of Rhode Island, to the Earl of Hillsborough, Rhode Island, November 2, 1771', in ibid. vii. 42–3. Sailors were a convenient scapegoat.

[19] Ibid.

[20] Ann Wickham and Robert Crooke married on 12 March 1747, in Trinity Church, Newport's Anglican church. Catherine was their first surviving child (of seven), christened on 18 November 1750. See *Trinity Parish Registers, 1709–1799* (Microfilm, Historical Society of Rhode Island).

[21] In the 1760 Newport Tax List, Robert Crooke was listed as the forty-third wealthiest taxpayer in Newport, out of a list of 962 names. Crane, *A Dependent People*, 32.

[22] Ezra Stiles, Stamp Act Notebook, Stiles Papers, Yale University Library, as quoted in Edmund S. Morgan and Helen M. Morgan, *The Stamp Act Crisis: Prologue to Revolution* (Chapel Hill, NC: University of North Carolina Press for the Institute of Early American History and Culture, 1953), 185–6.

a Stamp Tax protest and effigy-burning that flared into a riot.[23] Admittedly, Robert's protests against the Stamp Act do not necessarily mean he became an equally forceful Patriot when the Revolutionary War broke out. Many Loyalists had actively protested the Stamp Act (one such Loyalist was Joseph Wanton, the governor, who so hotly defended his colony in 1771).[24]

At any rate, a Providence newspaper announced the marriage of Charles and Catherine in April 1769.[25] Catherine's background is hard to gauge with any precision, but she would have received an education typical for an elite girl of the period. More difficult to know are Catherine's political sentiments. Most would probably simply call her a 'Loyalist wife'. Yet such a description would both over- and under-describe her. It would over-describe her, because we do not know whether she believed in the Loyalist cause as her husband did. It would also under-describe her, because she, like many in this era, maintained a complicated set of allegiances, ones that transcended such simplified categories. At any rate, the Dudleys lived together through the early 1770s.

By 1775 Charles himself was watching in presumably ever greater horror as revolution rolled like a great wave into his world. It would ultimately sweep him out on a British ship, the *Rose*, which had been preventing the import of goods into Newport for the better part of 1775. By November 1775 the Rhode Island Assembly had determined that 'all the Silver and Gold and Paper Bills of Credit, and Bills of Exchange' of the Customs House should be handed over.[26] Charles flatly refused. Responding to the threat that General Esek Hopkins would take any crown money 'at the Peril of my Person and private Property', Charles noted warily that 'My Person I trust will soon be out of his reach'. He asserted his readiness to forfeit his private property if necessary: 'confiding in the power and Justice of that Government which I have the honor to serve; I shall submit my private Property to his Disposal.'[27] With that, he fled to the *Rose*,

---

[23] A contemporaneous, if negative, account implicates Robert Crook for the effigy-burning. Dr Thomas Moffat to Joseph Harrison, 16 Oct. 1765, Chalmers Papers, New York Public Library, repr. in Edmund S. Morgan, *Prologue to Revolution: Sources and Documents on the Stamp Act Crisis, 1764–1766* (Chapel Hill, NC: University of North Carolina Press for the Institute of Early American History and Culture, 1959), 109–13, at 112. See also Crane, *A Dependent People*, 113, and Florence Parker Simister, *The Fire's Center: Rhode Island in the Revolutionary Era, 1763–1790* (Providence, RI: Rhode Island Bicentennial Foundation, 1979), 17–21.

[24] David S. Lovejoy, *Rhode Island Politics and the American Revolution, 1760–1776* (Providence, RI: Brown University Press, 1958), 179–86.

[25] Charles, like the Crookes, was a member of Trinity Church. *Annals of Trinity Church, Newport, Rhode Island, 1698–1821* (Newport, RI, 1890), 146–7. The marriage was announced in the *Providence Gazette; and Country Journal*, 29 Apr. 1769, Issue 277, in *Early American Newspapers, Series I, 1690–1876* (Readex).

[26] 'Proceedings of the General Assembly, held for the Colony of Rhode Island and Providence Plantations, at Providence, on Tuesday, the 31st day of October, 1775', in Bartlett (ed.), *Records of the Colony*, vii. 375–408.

[27] Charles Dudley to Nicholas Cooke, Governor of Rhode Island, 'Custom House Newport 14 Novr. 1775', in Nicholas Cooke, 'Revolutionary Correspondence of Governor Nicholas Cooke', ed. Matt B. Jones, *Proceedings of the American Antiquarian Society*, 36 (1926), 231–353, at 288–9.

in the harbor, on 15 November 1775.[28] But Catherine, like many such wives, stayed behind.[29] She sent letters to Charles, and also visited him; we will explore those letters later. The two managed to flee to England by 1778, when they settled in Staffordshire, where Charles's brother lived. Familiar ties eased their temporary settlement, and Catherine gave birth to a son, Charles, and then to Mary-Ann.[30] They also made numerous friends.[31] In 1784 the Dudleys made the monumental decision for Catherine to return to Newport.[32] For Catherine, then pregnant, to take two children across the Atlantic, was no small matter.[33] Other elite women whose husbands exhorted them to make them such a transatlantic voyage, even those with neither pregnancy to endure nor children to shepherd, balked at such a request.[34] For Catherine to make such a trip means that Charles surely intended to follow soon. Shortly after her departure Charles wrote for the first time, reassuring Catherine that 'I shall certainly soon be at R[hode] I[sland]'.[35] This prediction was pronounced confidently, but was not fulfilled. In fact, for six long years their only contact was through their correspondence. In one of his letters Charles quoted her plaintive question: 'You say why do I not come to You.'[36] This is the question we must consider here: why did he not come?

---

[28] It was reported on 18 November (a Saturday) that 'Wednesday Evening last Charles Dudley, Esq. Collector of the Customs for the Port of Rhode-Island, fled for Refuge on board the Rose Ship of War, at Newport', 'Providence, Nov. 18 [1775]', *Connecticut Journal*, 29 Nov. 1775, Issue 424, in *Early American Newspapers, Series I, 1690–1876* (Readex).

[29] See Norton, *Liberty's Daughters*, and her 'Eighteenth-Century American Women in Peace and War: The Case of the Loyalists', *William and Mary Quarterly*, 33 (1976), 386–409.

[30] There is no baptism registered for Mary-Anne, but Charles's baptism is listed for 6 October 1781: 'Charles Edward son of Charles & Catherine Dudley Born May the 23rd. 1780 Johnson Hall.' *A Copy of the Register of the Parish of Eccleshall Bap. Bur 1703 to Octr 1783*', from Church of England, Parish Church of Eccleshall (Staffordshire), *Parish Registers, 1573–1848* (Microfilm, IGI). A book recording graves in Albany cemetery includes gravestones for: 'Charles Edward Dudley born May 23d, 1780 at Johnson's Hall Stafford Shire England, Baptised in the parish church of Eccles hall by the Rev. Dr. Catlow. Departed this Life Jan 23 1841 at his residence in Albany' and 'Mary Ann only sister of Charles E. Dudley died Dec 12, 1806 at New York Aged 23 years'. Henry P. Phelps, *The Albany Rural Cemetery: Its Beauties, Its Memories* (Albany, NY, 1893), 186.

[31] Her friend Mary Meeke maintained correspondence with Catherine for the rest of her life. See Dudley Papers, NHS.

[32] For the period of 1775 only Catherine's letters to Charles survive. After that period only his letters to her survive.

[33] Catherine had help from a servant named Lydia. Charles Dudley to Catherine Dudley, 'London 6th February 1785. No. 27 Suffolk Street', Dudley Papers, NHS.

[34] Margaret Parker, along with other elite women such as Betsey Brown Maunsell of the Bahamas, prevaricated when their husbands asked them to cross the ocean by themselves. Margaret Parker to James Parker, undated but labeled 'recd 22nd July 1784 from Mrs Parker', PA 8.36, Parker Family Papers, LRO, and Betsey Brown Maunsell to Sewell Maunsell, 'Nassau New Providence June 28th 1781', Brown Family Papers, NYHS. Even a woman who willingly crossed the Atlantic alone complained of 'very Ill and disrespectful... treatment' from her ship's captain. Edward and Ann Chandler to Samuel Thorne, 'Portsmouth February 11th. 1783', Edward and Ann Chandler Letters, NYPL.

[35] Charles Dudley to Catherine Dudley, 'London Sept. 21st 1784', Dudley Papers, NHS.

[36] Charles Dudley to Catherine Dudley, 'London No 27 Suffolk Street 6 December 1785', ibid.

Charles's letters give every indication that he wished to return to America soon. Repeatedly, he declared: 'Oh! how happy woud it make me coud I say I shall soon clasp You all in these longing Arms.'[37] After hearing the news that Catherine's pregnancy had resulted in a stillborn child, Charles prayed: 'May God preserve You and the Dear Sweet Innocents for these longing Arms which I hope will embrace You all before You see another Winter!'[38] In the meantime, he continued to press his compensation case, with a government reluctant to make up for lost income rather than property.[39] This situation changed in 1788, however, when the government passed a more generous compensation package for Loyalists.[40] By November 1788 Charles learned that he had received an annuity of £320, one not tied to residence within British dominions.[41] It was not the pre-war £800 *per annum*, but it was still 'a decent support'.[42] Charles seemed on the verge of returning, but then he remained in England through 1789, informing Catherine that he was trying to sort out one last property issue, that around 'Potters Affair'.[43] Catherine was apparently growing suspicious as to why, months after her husband had been given a solid, portable annuity, he remained in England. In a 1789 letter Charles thanked her for her most recent missive, but added: 'when We meet, & I can unbosom myself, You will be sorry if You Have ever for one [moment] thought unfavorably of my Conduct in this long long interval of our Separation.'[44]

Charles never did get the chance to 'unbosom' himself to Catherine. By 1789 the ill health that had plagued him for years caught up with him. Even as he emphasized 'the fast approach of our being united, and . . . the happy time when You and our Dear Boy & Girl will have the Care and attention of a fond Father & affectionate Husband', he complained of illness, and died shortly thereafter.[45] Charles's death, far from his family, renders all the more poignant their lengthy separation; why had he allowed it to continue for so long?[46] In seeking to ascertain

---

[37] Charles Dudley to Catherine Dudley, 'London 27 May 1785', ibid.
[38] Charles Dudley to Catherine Dudley, 'London 6 July 1785 No. 27 Suffolk Street', ibid.
[39] Such losses of income were not included for compensation in 1785 or 1786. See Norton, *The British-Americans*, ch. 7.
[40] Ibid.
[41] See Charles Dudley to Catherine Dudley, 'London 5 November 1788', Dudley Papers, NHS. According to Mary Beth Norton: 'These annuities provided some loyalists with the financial security that all of them had been seeking for years.' Norton, *The British-Americans*, 229. She cites Charles Dudley as an example of this pattern: ibid. 212–13, 228–9.
[42] Charles Dudley to Catherine Dudley, 'August 6th, 1788', Dudley Papers, NHS. See also AO 12/84, 104, 109, NA and Charles Dudley to Catherine Dudley, 'London 5 November 1788', Dudley Papers, NHS.
[43] Charles Dudley to Catherine Dudley, '7 May 1789', Dudley Papers, NHS. In addition to his annuity of £320, he also gained compensation for the £928 he had claimed. See AO 12/84, 104, 109 and 13/68, 83, NA.
[44] Charles Dudley to Catherine Dudley, 'London 1 July 1789', Dudley Papers, NHS.
[45] Charles Dudley to Catherine Dudley, 'Bath 1st. December 1789', ibid. Charles was buried in Bath in 1790. Mr Irving to Mr Dudley [Charles's brother], 'Feby. 3rd. 1790', ibid.
[46] It is possible, if highly unlikely, that Charles Dudley was a master dissimulator, sending letters about his longing to see his wife and children, while visiting prostitutes and gambling and drinking

the reasons for his non-return, it is possible to understand both those imperatives of sensibility, familiarity, and affection, as well as those of war, loss, and desire for independence that cut against them. As in the Parker case, explanations that rely on political motivations or on structural considerations (such as patriarchy) are less helpful than ones based upon domestic concerns. Three explanations for Charles's continued decisions to stay in England might seem plausible, but are not satisfactory. Let us investigate them in turn.

The first of these is his political resentment against, or fear of, the United States, strong factors for many. For instance, Edward Chandler, a Loyalist exile in England, believed in 1783 that: 'The poor Refugee's & Loyalists are to expect no mercy.'[47] Many shared such sentiments, and relatively few Loyalists returned to the United States.[48] In 1785 some, like Rebecca Shoemaker, whose husband was a Loyalist exile, were still reporting the rough handling of Loyalists who had tried to return.[49] One historian has noted specifically that 'some of the most dedicated—and affluent—loyalists could not or would not return to Newport'.[50] Nevertheless, as another historian has observed, those Loyalists who returned after 1784 were much less likely to encounter problems. Newport may have been especially welcoming to former Loyalists, given its considerable population loss (especially of men) in the war.[51] One former resident considered returning there in 1790: 'I have had Serious thoughts of going to your parts, provided I was Sure of being Treated Civilly By the Inhabitants.'[52] Charles does not seem to have worried unduly about this issue, or to have expressed particular rancor about the United States in his letters to Catherine.

A second reason for his reluctance to return might be his conservative disposition as a Loyalist patriarch, or indeed a sense that he was not a man eager to go along with his wife's wishes. But there is little in Charles's letters, or indeed his story more generally, to support this notion. Charles did retain the services of a black man, Polydore, who may have been one of his slaves before the Revolution, but he was a paid servant.[53] Charles's frequent use of languages of sensibility also imply a man of feeling much more than an old-style patriarch,

---

away whatever he had left. However, there is no evidence whatsoever to support this view, and indeed much to suggest the opposite.

[47] Edward and Ann Chandler to Samuel Thorne, 'Lindsey Row, Chelsea, September 2d. 1783', Edward and Ann Chandler Letters to Samuel Thorne, NYPL.

[48] As Mary Beth Norton has pointed out, 'the vast majority of the loyalists remained outside of the independent United States'. Norton, *The British-Americans*, 249.

[49] Rebecca Shoemaker recounted the attack on the whole family of a returned Loyalist in Rebecca Shoemaker to Samuel Shoemaker, 'April 23, 1785', Shoemaker Family Papers, HSP.

[50] Crane, *A Dependent People*, 160.   [51] Ibid. and Norton, *The British-Americans*.

[52] John Murray to Francis Brinley, 'Saint John 13th. Septemr 1790', Malbone–Brinley Papers, Box 174, Series IV, Folder 1, NHS.

[53] See Charles Dudley to Catherine Dudley, 'London 6th February 1785', and 'London 4 April 1787', and Mr Irving to Mr Dudley [Charles's brother], 'Feby. 3rd. 1790', Dudley Papers, NHS.

a point corroborated by his reading matter. Within his personal collection in London were several works by Rousseau (including the epistolary novel '*Eloisa*', that is, *Julie, ou la Nouvelle Héloïse*) as well as that classic novel of epistolary sensibility, the '*Sorrows of Werter*'.[54] Owning books is not the same as reading them (alas). Still, there is little here to suggest a man who preferred tyranny to tender and endearing friendship.

A third possible reason for his decision to stay might be England's attractiveness. London especially was famous in this era (as in many) as an alluring place.[55] An Englishman, Charles might have wished to stay on there.[56] If so, though, there is little sense of this affection for his native land in his letters. Indeed, he repeatedly emphasized how little interest he had in the happenings of his native land. In 1784 he wrote to Catherine: 'As to public or private News I am not in a State of Mind to trouble myself about them, all my thoughts bend towards You and our Dear Babes.'[57] Although he reported news from mutual friends in Staffordshire, he expressed little in the way of nostalgia concerning his and Catherine's time there. In 1786 he averred: 'I have not . . . for the last nine months been a single evening out of my own room. I have determined to bear my misfortunes in secrecy.'[58] He even declared unequivocally: 'here I have no chance of getting any thing at all suited either to my turn of mind or my situation in Life.'[59] He also informed Catherine that he did not intend to visit Staffordshire before departing England, and at no point did he raise the possibility that he would be sorry to leave.[60]

What, then, kept Charles Dudley in London? Of the greatest importance was, not his Loyalist tendencies or temperament, but his desire for compensation for his Loyalist losses. From this situation flows all else, including his desire for independence and his hopes of avoiding debt and setting up a patrimony for his children. Charles's need for compensation stemmed partly from his sense of his rightful entitlement to what he had lost in service to the government. Recall that in 1775 he had refused to turn over the Newport customs revenue, because he trusted 'in the power and Justice of that Government', even to make up for

---

[54] Inventory of Goods, in T. Dudley [Charles's brother] to Catherine Dudley, undated [1790?], ibid. On the effects of reading Rousseau, see Darnton, *The Great Cat Massacre*, ch. 6.

[55] The daughter of one Loyalist refugee, like many colonial and provincial visitors to London, declared on arrival from Pennsylvania: 'london is the most agreable place I can have an Idea of.' Elizabeth Galloway to Grace Galloway, undated, File: Betsey Galloway (correspondence to mother and others), Joseph Galloway Papers, LoC.

[56] On favorable colonial impressions of London, see Susan Lindsey Lively, 'Going Home: Americans in Britain, 1740–1776', Ph.D, Harvard University (1996), and Julie M. Flavell, 'The 'School for Modesty and Humility': Colonial American Youth in London and Their Parents, 1755–1775', *Historical Journal*, 42 (1999), 377–403.

[57] Charles Dudley to Catherine Dudley, 'London Septr. 21 1784', Dudley Papers, NHS.

[58] Charles Dudley to Catherine Dudley, 'London 2d, August 1786', ibid.

[59] Charles Dudley to Catherine Dudley, 'London 6th. Septr. 1785 No. 27 Suffolk St Charing Cross', ibid.

[60] Charles Dudley to Catherine Dudley, 'London 7 May 1789', ibid.

any personal property he forfeited.⁶¹ His letters make clear that he was eager for restitution, partly because, like many other Loyalists, he felt entitled to it, given his exile and losses. In 1785 Charles replied to Catherine's apparent wish for him to return by demanding: 'woud You have me... relinquish the fair and just title I have upon this Government for my Sufferings?'⁶² In a 1786 letter he argued that the compensation would also 'make You some reparation for the sorrows You have suffered'.⁶³ Even after news of a likely annuity, he again claimed: 'I cannot bring myself instantly to relinquish my very just pretentions to something more.'⁶⁴ He referred to an initial small annuity as 'a sum so shamefully disproportion'd to my loss of Office, and... so scandalously unjust', as to be unacceptable.⁶⁵ This sense of *justice* was one he shared with many other Loyalist claimants.⁶⁶ There was a general sense of outrage that, as one Member of the House of Lords put it: 'To desert men who had constantly adhered to loyalty and attachment, was a circumstance of such CRUELTY as had never been heard of.'⁶⁷

In addition, compensation from the government became a way for Charles to restore his capacity as an independent man of credit to support a household, a second major reason for his refusal to return. To understand the force of this situation, it is important to consider the financial situation in which the Dudleys were living. Charles Dudley had lost a lucrative position worth a minimum of £800 a year. They had spent the war living on the generosity of his family. Catherine's parents provided for her and the children on their return to Rhode Island. For wives, it was not uncommon, in cases of marital difficulty, for the woman to be supported by her family of birth.⁶⁸ While Charles may have been sending money, he seems more often to have been apologizing for not sending any, an embarrassment. He invoked the languages of the heart to communicate his pain at being unable to provide for her and their children: 'My heart bleeds for my inability to send You any assistance.' He continued by assuring her that this situation would not last forever: 'I cannot write upon it... was it not that I am

---

⁶¹ Charles Dudley to Nicholas Cooke, Governor of Rhode Island, 'Custom House Newport 14 Novr. 1775', in Cooke, 'Revolutionary Correspondence of Governor Nicholas Cooke', 288–9.
⁶² Charles Dudley to Catherine Dudley, 'London No 27 Suffolk Street 6 December 1785', Dudley Papers, NHS.
⁶³ Charles Dudley to Catherine Dudley, 'London 3d May 1786', ibid.
⁶⁴ Charles Dudley to Catherine Dudley, 'August 6th. 1788', ibid.
⁶⁵ Charles Dudley to Catherine Dudley, 'London 5 November 1788', ibid.
⁶⁶ [Joseph Galloway], *The Claim of the American Loyalists Reviewed and Maintained upon the Incontrovertible Principles of Law and Justice* (London, 1788), pp. vi, vii.
⁶⁷ Lord Viscount Townshend, as quoted in Galloway, *The Claim of the American Loyalists*, 93.
⁶⁸ When John McQueen fled Georgia for Florida because of financial difficulties in the 1780s, for instance, his wife refused to join him and was supported financially by her family. See Walter Charlton Hartridge (ed.), *The Letters of Don Juan McQueen to His Family Written from Spanish East Florida, 1791–1807* (Columbia, SC: Bostick & Thornley for the Georgia Society of the Colonial Dames of America, 1943). Similar episodes are discussed in Sievens, *Stray Wives*, esp. ch. 5.

sure of retrieving my affairs, and of making You and Your friends some amends for the anxiety and distress.'[69] In 1788 he 'lament[ed] the utter impossibility of my sending You any present assistance—relying on the goodness of Your Parents to bear a little longer the burthen.'[70]

Charles was himself also in debt. At one point he hoped for compensation for lost property, not simply income, as this payment would 'go a good way towards the discharge of my old debts, of which indeed I shou'd be greatly ashamed, if they have been owing to any Cause than a Public Calamity'.[71] His debts are corroborated by other sources.[72] Indeed, one of the chief reasons Charles lingered in London after 1788 was because of what he described to Catherine as 'Potters Affair'.[73] Before the Revolution Charles had owed Simon Potter £300. After the war Charles learned that his property had been lost, and that, as he phrased it to the Loyalist Commission, 'his Effects were Seized[,] his Wife and Family turned out of doors, and his House converted into a Barrack'.[74] He had assumed that Potter had been paid back during the war, from the auction of Dudley goods. However, Potter claimed otherwise, and sued for debt in 1788, which had serious repercussions, since unpaid debts of this nature could put a man in debtor's prison.[75] They could also ruin his credit.

Charles's claim to Catherine, that unpaid debts would be a cause of great shame had there not been a war to explain them, indicates the importance he attached to his own credit as well as to his independence. Charles's political losses had badly affected his financial position, so that he could not support his family, a severe blow in a world in which masculine independence was measured by an ability to maintain a household.[76] His domestic position, and his standing in a larger community, depended on his political fortunes, which was partly why he was determined to stay on in London until he was able to return an independent man, his fondest hope. When Catherine demanded why he did not come, he replied: 'would You have me my Dear Mrs Dudley come to You in distress to live upon the bounty of Your Friends... [?] You know I cannot;—nor woud You I am Sure wish me to accept a pitiful Station in

---

[69] Charles Dudley to Catherine Dudley, 'London 25th Sepr 1786', Dudley Papers, NHS.
[70] Charles Dudley to Catherine Dudley, 'August 6th. 1788', ibid.
[71] Charles Dudley to Catherine Dudley, 'London 5 November 1788', ibid.
[72] Mr Irving to Mr Dudley [Charles's brother], 'Feby. 3rd. 1790', and George Rome to Charles Dudley, 'Monday 25th July 1785', ibid. Also see AO 12/84, 104, 109 and AO 13/68, 83, NA.
[73] Charles Dudley to Catherine Dudley, '7 May 1789', Dudley Papers, NHS. In addition to his annuity of £320, he also received compensation of £800 for the £928 he had claimed. See AO 12/84, 104, 109 and 13/68, 83, NA.
[74] 'Memorial of Charles Dudley' before the Loyalist Claims Commission, AO 13/68 A, 72–73, NA.
[75] Josiah Finney, Justice of the Peace, Bristol, Rhode Island, informed the Claims Commission that Simon Potter had appeared before him to testify to the debt. See Josiah Finney to Loyalist Claims Commission, 'Oct 20 1788', AO 13/68A, 273–277, NA.
[76] See e.g. Anne S. Lombard, *Making Manhood: Growing up Male in Colonial New England* (Cambridge, Mass.: Harvard University Press, 2003), 98.

Life.'⁷⁷ Charles Dudley had been a prosperous official; it was a horror for such a man to accept 'a pitiful Station'. The use of the word 'distress' here, as in other contexts, conflated financial and emotional issues. In drawing Catherine into his imagined anguish at this situation, he used the language of sympathy to argue that he needed to privilege financial imperatives over sentimental ones: 'You know one of my wishes has been to place You in a respectable Situation . . . better . . . for us and our Dear Children that we waited even this long, long time, rather than sink into a <u>condition</u> of Life, which was the only alternative.'⁷⁸ Charles was facing the terrifying prospect of a severely downwardly mobile spiral.

Moreover, like many fathers, Charles worried gravely about the possibility of such a downward trajectory because of what it would mean for his children. Disavowing his agency in remaining in England, Charles asserted that it was impossible for him to return to Rhode Island: 'my long Continuance here is *indispensible*, by no means depending on my own will; and its <u>purpose</u> to make You and my Dear Children Some amends for Separation.'⁷⁹ Elsewhere, Charles exhorted Catherine: 'tell them, Dear Babes! . . . how sorrowful their father is for their unfortunate beginning in life, and how much he is striving to give them better prospects, and their Mother happier days.'⁸⁰ In another letter, he again directed his words to their children: 'Dear Dear Children! . . . tell them I am doing all I can for their future comfort in Life.'⁸¹ A good father placed the prospects of his offspring over his own immediate desires. His early death cut short his ability to provide such protection for his dependants.⁸²

At the same time, letters of sensibility and family feeling helped to alleviate the pain of these decisions, this privileging of long-term prospects and masculine independence over the happiness of reunited family life. Charles *could* stay in London in part because his letters justified his behavior in terms calculated to soothe Catherine and himself. To understand how stories of sensibility functioned in the aftermath of war, it is critical to understand how they functioned before and during the war, for Charles and Catherine as well as for others. It is also possible

---

⁷⁷ Charles Dudley to Catherine Dudley, 'London No 27 Suffolk Street 6 December 1785', Dudley Papers, NHS.
⁷⁸ Charles Dudley to Catherine Dudley, 'London 5 December 1787', ibid.
⁷⁹ Charles Dudley to Catherine Dudley, 'London October 3 1787', ibid. Italics mine.
⁸⁰ Charles Dudley to Catherine Dudley, 'London No 27 Suffolk Street 6 December 1785', ibid.
⁸¹ Charles Dudley to Catherine Dudley, 'Fludyer Street Westminster London 2d. August 1786', ibid.
⁸² Catherine never remarried, dying in 1800. Their son, Charles, did enjoy better prospects, becoming a merchant who early exploited American trade connections in India. He also became a politician, serving, eventually, as US Senator. This was quite a trajectory for the son of an exiled Loyalist, one that complicates simple distinctions between Loyalist and Patriot families. 'Death notice of Mrs. Catherine Dudley', *Newport Mercury*, 14 Jan. 1800, p. 3, in *Early American Newspapers, Series I, 1690–1876* (Readex). Charles himself died in 1841: Phelps, *The Albany Rural Cemetery*, 186. See also 'Dudley, Charles Edward', in Allen Johnson and Dumas Malone (eds.), *Dictionary of American Biography*, 20 vols. (New York: Charles Scribner's Sons, 1930), v. 480.

to witness how such domestic languages could be taken up by others, in order to make much more explicit political points. Epistolary claims of sensibility had long provided domestic leverage for Charles and Catherine. The few remaining courtship letters from Charles to his 'Katey' indicate his command of languages of sensibility. In one such letter, after announcing, 'but my head's so full of Wine; that You shall take a Stanza from my Heart', Charles proceeded:

> Harsh and untunefull are the Notes of Love,
> Unless dear Katey strikes the Key,
> Her hand alone can touch the Part,
> Whose dulest movement charms the Heart,
> And governs all the Man with sympathetic Sway.[83]

Both Charles and his Katey apparently rejoiced in classic languages of sensibility. Elsewhere, Charles referred to a heart that 'is made up of Such excellent Materials, such as Friendship, [and] Sensibility'. Even in a more sober frame of mind, Charles pondered on the heart, pronouncing: 'It is Yet a dispute among the Learned, what part of the Body is the Seat of Sense, some say in the head, others in the Heart.' Charles decided in favor of the heart, for 'now if its in the heart, I have no pretentions; for my Heart is not at home— . . . wou'd not it be doing a charitable Act to a Neighbour, if You find a Stray'd Heart at Your house to take it into Your Care'.[84] Like Horatius, who left his heart behind, Charles announced, in this metaphor, both his love for Catherine and his sensible style.

Catherine's letters too, most of which come from Newport in 1775 when her husband was on board the *Rose*, show a firm grasp of languages of sensibility. These letters register little concern about the politics of the matters, but instead assessed the behavior of the men in her world, including her husband, in terms of sensibility and civility. Is this any surprise? We do not know what drew Catherine to Charles in the first place, but it could have been, at least in part, the exuberant command of sensibility demonstrated by his courtship letters. Where historians see Patriots and Loyalists, participants in that war often measured men and women differently, in ways more attuned to general transatlantic ideals. Taking these assessments seriously, rather than expecting all individuals to tally up, like sheep and goats, as Patriots and Loyalists, enriches our perspective on this war and its politics. It also enhances our understanding of other ideals valued by people, especially women like Catherine. The library in their home in Newport held the kinds of books to be expected of an elite couple attuned to sensibility and letter-writing: *The Man of Feeling* and *The History of Miss Betsy Thoughtless*, as well as *Letters* by Lord Chesterfield and Madame de Maintenon.[85] Catherine's letters resonate with themes of feeling. Her interest in masculine display of

---

[83] Charles Dudley to Catherine Crooke [Dudley], undated, Dudley Papers, NHS.
[84] Charles Dudley to Catherine Dudley, '9 o Clock' (pre-1775), ibid.
[85] 'Inventory of Effects', Dudley losses before Loyalist Claims Commission, AO 13/68A, NA, p. 241.

sensibility is significant for several reasons. One is that it indicates that sensibility, more than obvious political differences, was the ideal by which Catherine divided the sheep from the goats. It also demonstrates her concern that, even in dire circumstances, Charles should act as a man of feeling. In fact, her letters often attempted to push Charles into sympathizing more for her situation, because she wanted him to let her come to him.

Catherine's letters also fit into a larger pattern of female assessments of male sensibility, and the ways in which such assessments might even become politicized. This pattern is clear in her letter to Charles describing the taking of their home by Patriot general Esek Hopkins, following Charles's refusal to hand over the customs bills.[86] Catherine's letter highlighted the subversion of her domestic authority by the unfeeling authority of General Hopkins. Even while admitting that throwing her out of her house was 'contrary to my Nature', Hopkins nevertheless backed up his authority with martial powers, as 'at that Instant Gaurd of 100 Men, came and surrounded the house, in triumph'.[87] War had crossed the threshold indeed. Meanwhile, Catherine reported: 'the Savage Genl. went about . . . Ordering the furniture to be carry'd . . . and Inventory's taken.' Watching aghast, Catherine nevertheless 'recover'd my Spirits a little . . . apply'd to him for a Bed—my Harpsichord—horse & Chaise'. Realizing that she was to be shown out of the house, she at least tried to hang on to some critical possessions, one of which, 'my Harpsichord', she specifically identified as her own.[88] However, General Hopkins replied: 'No No nothing shoud be movd, his Cruelty in this is condemn'd by every body.'[89]

Catherine's denunciation of Hopkins's cruelty is part of her assessments of feeling and unfeelingness. Catherine used some version of the word 'cruel' four times in this brief letter; she also used the word 'inhuman[e]' twice, and 'savage' once. As one scholar has argued, to attack a house in this time and place was to commit a defilement analogous to a bodily assault.[90] However, Catherine's outrage was tempered by her approval of the sensibility of Hopkins's underling, Colonel Richmond. When the soldiers surrounded her home, Catherine reported that she burst into tears: 'I coul'd not retain any command of my Reason at such a

---

[86] Catherine Dudley to Charles Dudley, 'Thursday Even: Novr. 16th 1775', Dudley Papers, NHS. Esek Hopkins was the first commander of the Continental Navy, 'energetic . . . and aggressive'. See 'Hopkins, Esek', in Dumas Malone (ed.), *Dictionary of American Biography*, 20 vols. (New York: Charles Scribner's Sons, 1932), ix. 209–10.

[87] Robert St George argues that such 'surroundings' of houses were especially potent forms of attack on the symmetry and order of elite houses: St George, *Conversing by Signs*, 286–7.

[88] Whatever sentimental and personal significance the harpsichord may have had, it also had considerable monetary value. In the list of their property losses, the only single item more expensive than the harpsichord (valued at £42) was the 'Phaeton with harness complete' (worth £46). See 'Inventory of Effects', Dudley losses before Loyalist Claims Commission, AO 13/68A, NA, pp. 234, 233.

[89] Catherine Dudley to Charles Dudley, 'Thursday Even: Novr. 16th 1775', Dudley Papers, NHS.

[90] St George, *Conversing by Signs*, chs. 2–3, esp. p. 284.

Sight, but gave way to my feelings.' But Catherine did not cry alone: 'Richmond shew'd some compassion, he even drop'd a Tear, said it was the most cruel Duty he had ever been upon, he endeavord to comfort me.' Even in the midst of this appalling event, Catherine weighed up which Patriot soldier turning her out of her home was a man of feeling, and which was a cruel tyrant; these categories were the most pressing ones to her. She concluded her tale sadly: 'so you see, they have driven me out without any of the Comforts, or Necessarys of Life—and the comfort they give me, is that others have suffer'd the same before.'

Other Loyalist families did suffer such hardships, though in similar situations some women were more fortunate than Catherine.[91] It was reported, for instance, of Grace Galloway, wife of one well-known British supporter, that: 'A Party of Rebel Troops went to the [Philadelphia] house of Joseph Galloway... with an intent to Plunder and demolish it, but his Lady made immediate Application to Mr Arnold, who orderd them immeadiately to desist.'[92] In a situation similar to Catherine's, Grace was able to stop rebel troops from taking over her household. In that instance the sensible entreaties of a woman worked to stay the hand of war, at least temporarily.[93] Some generals were less willing than Hopkins to perform deeds which even he acknowledged were 'contrary to [his] Nature'. Grace's ability to persuade the general not to throw her out of her home, at least for a while, demonstrates the power that feminine eloquence could possess, especially with other elite and possibly sympathetic individuals, but it also shows how strongly war militated against this power.[94]

However, Catherine continued to rely on her husband being sympathetic to her appeals. In late 1775, when Charles had fled to the *Rose*, Catherine wanted to stay with him there; Charles apparently felt that the ship was an inappropriate place for her.[95] So she used her letters to him to persuade him to attend to her suffering and allow her to spend more time with him. Catherine had visited Charles on the *Rose* on 18 November, and described the way she was harassed on her way home. While walking up the wharf, 'there was two men... they walkd down to me

---

[91] In contrast to later American wars such as the Civil War, it was considered entirely acceptable in the Revolutionary War to confiscate enemy property. See Daniel W. Hamilton, *The Limits of Sovereignty: Property Confiscation in the Union and the Confederacy During the Civil War* (Chicago: University of Chicago Press, 2007), ch. 1.

[92] Anonymous scrap, labeled 'Mr. Galloway... of the American rebels 1780', Joseph Galloway Papers, HL.

[93] Grace may have been helped both by her connections in the city, and by the fact that the general in question was Benedict Arnold.

[94] Indeed, even Grace Galloway was eventually forced out of her home. See Joseph Galloway Papers, Library of Congress and Galloway Papers, HSP, as well as Grace Growden Galloway, 'Diary of Grace Growden Galloway, 1778–1779', *Pennsylvania Magazine of History and Biography*, 55 (1931), 35–94 and 58 (1934), 152–89.

[95] Catherine Dudley to Charles Dudley, 'Wednesday Evening [29. Nov 1775]', Dudley Papers, NHS. The conflict between Charles and Catherine was echoed in a later discussion of the place of women aboard British ships, in Jane Austen's *Persuasion*. In this, Captain Wentworth noted that he 'would never willingly admit any ladies on board a ship of his'; his sister, by contrast, argued that 'Women may be as comfortable on board, as in the best house in England'. Austen, *Persuasion*, 64.

watch'd me try'd to look under my Bonnet... I expected every moment, they woud have seiz'd me I hurry'd thro' the Street.' She stopped in the doorway of the house of Simon Pease, one of Newport's 'most stalwart Royalists'.[96] But they were not done with her yet: 'the fellow I first saw on the Wharf was after me the whole way, when I stop'd at Mr Pease's Door he said, Damn you, you Bitch, you shall be mark'd as a Black Sheep.' Using language to shock a woman of Catherine's standing, this unknown assailant so terrified her that the members of the Pease household 'were oblig'd to drag me in the Door, for I was unable to move Fear, Grief, Resentment, had got the better'.[97] Catherine's language here echoes that in an October 1765 *Newport Mercury* article. The anonymous author reported the reaction to the Stamp Act: 'Rage, resentment and grief appeared painted in every countenance... but I cannot proceed—tears of vexation and sorrow stop my pen.'[98] Such language echoes that found in novels and other texts of the period; many other authors, from Laurence Sterne to the imagined Pamela, had to stop writing because of tears. But this appeal to feeling was also a means of calling upon authority, of making claims about the ways in which proper authority was being subverted by abuse or unfeelingness. This vocabulary was at once both highly sentimental and highly political. Catherine was attuned to the ways in which appeals to sentiment acted as a means of calling upon others to use their authority for good. Her resentment at this assault might have been exacerbated by the sense of grievance she already nursed for the violent taking of her home. In the face of this attack, and against the unfeelingness of her would-be assailants, Catherine's own extreme sensibility caused her body to freeze.

What were Catherine's motives in drawing her husband into her terrifying tale? She was not especially eager to prove the cruelty of Patriots; she was more intent on insinuating the indifference of her own husband in forcing her to return to shore: 'it is too cruel a fate for me to be left behind, if you have the affection for me you profess, and I will not doubt it for that woud be the greatest of all Miserys to me—let me come to you... wherever you are.'[99] Now, 'cruelty' was the word she used to imply her sense of desertion by her husband. This was the theme to which she returned constantly for the rest of her letters. In one, she demanded: 'why woud you not let me go[?]'[100] In another, she announced that she was 'more at a loss than ever to account for your objections to my coming... remember you woud not consent to my coming the last day I spent with you, and yet no terrible consequences happen'd from it'. So, Catherine had previously gone ahead with a visit despite Charles's refusal to sanction it. She continued: 'good god how can you refuse me such a thing[?]' In fact, she flatly refused to accept her husband's

---

[96] Crane, *A Dependent People*, 132.
[97] Catherine Dudley to Charles Dudley, 'Sunday Morng. 19 Nov- 1775', Dudley Papers, NHS.
[98] 'American Intelligence, Philadelphia, October 3 [1765]', *The Newport Mercury*, 14 Oct. 1765, Issue 371, in *Early American Newspapers, Series I, 1690–1876* (Readex).
[99] Catherine Dudley to Charles Dudley, 'Sunday Morng. 19 Nov- 1775', Dudley Papers, NHS.
[100] Ibid.

wishes, going on to state firmly: 'I am determined I will [come] you must not say to the contrary—for if possible I woud not do a thing you woud dispprove.'[101] In fact, apparently she would, as she had already shown in her decision to come to Charles earlier. Elsewhere, even while emphasizing her desire to be with him, she noted that 'you are determin'd—and I must submit'.[102] Submission was the proper posture for a wife, as Catherine indubitably knew, even as the remainder of her letters made clear that she sought to change her husband's mind. She made a similar claim in her last latter: 'you must consent to what I propose—surely I am not unreasonable—make me as happy as you can.'[103] She couched her decisions as requests requiring Charles's consent, even while noting that, whatever Charles wrote to her, she was determined to be with him.

Other wives similarly invoked their submission while circumventing husbandly authority. When conflict arose, as it did here, wives tended to forward their own desires while at the same time explicitly mentioning the ideal of submission. They also invoked their sensible affection for their spouses, as did husbands in their replies. Margaret Parker playfully informed her husband at one point: 'well now you see I am all submission as good Wives ought to be.'[104] Submission was the way 'good Wives ought to be', even as Margaret balked at returning to James. However, she constantly stressed her willingness to follow her beloved husband anywhere: 'tho I would not hesitate one moment to go with you my Dearest friend to any place on earth.'[105] Such a dynamic also characterizes the marital correspondence of Betsey and Sewell Maunsell of the Bahamas. In 1773 Sewell, a British military officer, went to England to deal with family matters, while Betsey remained in New Providence. Business detained him in England long enough for him to be placed in a regiment fighting in the Revolutionary War.[106] Before the war Sewell had implored Betsey to join him in England; after the war he begged her to come to him in Jamaica or, later, England. She consistently refused, and demanded instead that he come home to her, even while avowing her submission: 'I hope you will not impute my not complying with your request to any want of affection to you, & that no circumstance on Earth can make me happy without you.'[107] Like Catherine, Betsey also highlighted the anguish resulting from their

---

[101] Catherine Dudley to Charles Dudley, 'Wednesday Evening [29. Nov 1775]', Dudley Papers, NHS.
[102] Catherine Dudley to Charles Dudley, 'Tuesday Morning ['December 26th 1775]', ibid.
[103] Catherine Dudley to Charles Dudley, 'Thursday evening [28th of December 1775]', ibid.
[104] Margaret Parker to James Parker, 'Norfolk 5th Sepbr 1760', PA 8.3, Parker Family Papers, LRO.
[105] Margaret Parker to James Parker, 'Eastwood 27th July 1783', PA 8.26, ibid. For further on Margaret's tactics with James, see Sarah M. S. Pearsall, 'Hume—and Others—on Marriage', in Marina Frasca-Spada and P. J. E. Kail (eds.), *Impressions of Hume* (Oxford: Clarendon Press, 2005), 269–91.
[106] Betsey Brown Maunsell to Sewell Maunsell, 'New Providence August the 25th 1779', Brown Family Papers, NYHS.
[107] Betsey Brown Maunsell to Sewell Maunsell, 'Nassau New Providence June 28th 1781', ibid.

separation. Like Charles, Sewell responded with sympathy and declarations of his undying affection.[108] This uneasy balance between submission and friendship remained a feature of many marital correspondences in this era. Languages of sensibility provided a way of avoiding the implications of the imbalance, of stressing friendship rather than a disparity in terms of authority and resources.

Sensible suffering was also a posture adopted by many a woman, fictional and historical, in this period. It was used both to describe situations (which in many cases were wretched) and to influence the recipient of a letter. Catherine's leitmotifs were distress, bodily pain, lost happiness, and distraction. Catherine opened one letter: 'had you, my dearest Friend but consented to my going with you, it would not have been a greater Indulgence, than my tenderness deserv'd, my distress is such, I cannot help wishing to be with you.'[109] As we have seen, distress was about emotional suffering, but it was also about provoking a reaction of compassion.[110] Feeling individuals were expected to respond favorably to distress, especially when it was confirmed by physical symptoms. In Catherine's telling, her bodily suffering should similarly have provoked sympathy from her husband. In his (lost) replies, Charles was apparently attempting to point out that she was well cared for by her family. Catherine could not heed this advice: 'tis true I've Friends . . . but . . . you are the World to me and without you there is no Comfort—my thought is constantly fix'd on my Dearest Friend . . . I can't think on you without Tears . . . my heart must be lost to all sence of Feeling, was'nt I uneasy now.'[111] The implication was that Charles, too, could not have lost his own 'sence of Feeling', and would accommodate her desires to come and stay with him. The mention of tears reinforced the words. Catherine also repeatedly drew a strong contrast between their present misery and their past (and imagined future) happiness: 'happy shoud I be if I was with you this moment. I cannot forget our happy, peaceful House, how lost to us.'[112] All of these appeals combined to demonstrate her sensible suffering, to provoke Charles to show sympathy and to behave differently. He was supposed to respond in such a way because he was her 'Dearest Friend', her 'Dearest & best Friend', her 'belov'd friend'.[113] These terms worked to cement their connections, while also reminding him of his obligations to her.

---

[108] Sewell Maunsell to Betsey Brown Maunsell, 'London Decr. 15th 1773', ibid.
[109] Catherine Dudley to Charles Dudley, 'Tuesday Morning ['December 26th 1775]', Dudley Papers, NHS.
[110] This was how Adam Smith used it: 'Our joy for the deliverance of those heroes . . . is as sincere as our grief for their distress.' Adam Smith, *Theory of Moral Sentiments*, pt. I, sec. I, ch. 1, p. 3. One Virginia merchant described a widow as 'in great Distress, & real object of Compassion'. W. Nelson to John Norton, 'Virginia Nover. 14th 1768', in Frances Norton Mason (ed.), *John Norton and Sons, Merchants of London and Virginia, Being the Papers from their Counting House for the Years 1750 to 1795* (New York: Augustus M. Kelley, 1968), 75.
[111] Catherine Dudley to Charles Dudley, 'Tuesday Morning ['December 26th 1775]', Dudley Papers, NHS.
[112] Catherine Dudley to Charles Dudley, 'Wednesday Evening ['29. Nov. 1775]', ibid.
[113] Catherine Dudley to Charles Dudley, 'Tuesday Morning ['December 26th 1775]', ibid.

The language of marriage as friendship provided a nexus for negotiation for many in this era, and indicates the ways that appeals to friendship and sympathy might allow a sidestepping of the actual imbalances, in resources and authority, available to husbands as opposed to wives. Many others in the eighteenth century termed marriage a friendship, or called spouses their 'dearest friends'. For example, Francis Hutcheson proclaimed in his 1755 *System of Moral Philosophy* that: 'Nature has designed the conjugal state to be a constant reciprocal friendship of two... The tender sentiments and affections which engage the parties into this relation of marriage, plainly declare it to be a state of equal partnership or friendship.'[114] Samuel Richardson, in *Pamela*, counseled that '*Wives and Husbands are, or should be, Friends.*'[115] Thomas Turner, an eighteenth-century English diarist, frequently referred to his wife as his friend, and one historian has argued convincingly that: 'Turner used the language of friendship not only to reflect on his marriage, but also to negotiate some very difficult experiences.'[116] For Catherine, these invocations of marital friendship provided a framework in which she could both express her own sympathy and affection for her husband and her sense that he should acquiesce to her own desires.

This sense of marriage as friendship, even with an unstated imbalance between husband and wife, continued to inflect the Dudley letters, even after the War. In 1788 Charles asked Catherine what her opinion was on where they should settle: 'it becomes a matter of great concern, not only to our own happiness, but to the welfare of our Dear Children, what Country we sit down in.'[117] He gave the impression of seeking her advice on this crucial question. Charles went on to sketch the differences in prospects in England and Rhode Island: 'Look to a future day... Consider my time of life... and weighing all these things with that judgment and discretion of which You are capable; & with that local knowledge of affairs in America to whch I am a Stranger, give me Your opinion what I had best do.—Fearfull, and unwilling at the same time, to embarrass You by this question: I shall candidly offer You my own opinion.'[118] This statement by Charles exactly fits in with notions of masculine authority, tempered by new languages, but hardly diminished. Even as he explicitly sought Catherine's ideas on where to settle, he felt that such a question would 'embarrass' her. Also, even as he asked her opinion, he went on to declare that Rhode Island seemed the better place, since their income would go further there. Even as he explicitly solicited her views, he intended to follow the course he thought best.

Catherine had written to Charles on these subjects, and although her letters are missing for this period, it is possible to discern that she had advised his return to Rhode Island (which had been the plan all along!) Still, he did not couch the

---

[114] Francis Hutcheson, *A System of Moral Philosophy (1755)*, ed. Bernhard Fabian, 3rd edn., facsimile (Hildesheim: Georg Olms Verlag, 1990), II, III, I, v, 159, 163.
[115] Richardson, *Pamela*, ii. 323.   [116] Tadmor, *Family and Friends*, 192–8, at 192.
[117] Charles Dudley to Catherine Dudley, 'August 6th. 1788', Dudley Papers, NHS.
[118] Ibid.

decision to return there in terms of their joint resolution. Rather, he continued to develop a fiction that she would be reticent to offer her own ideas on this issue (which seems unlikely): 'I know how very much You wou'd wish to leave every thing relating to our future residence entirely to me, and with what reluctance You wou'd even advise to any measure whatever.' He continued: 'I pray to God therefore that I may have determined right for Your future happiness.'[119] This formulation, that *he* would determine *her* future, neatly summarizes the way that both spouses accommodated visions of Catherine's submission even as they privileged marriage as friendship. Yet, in fact, he was going ahead with the plan of which she apparently approved, which implies the strength of her requests for him to return. Whatever he asked Catherine, his determination was that he would come to Rhode Island, safe in the knowledge of a sizable annuity.[120] Charles repeatedly stressed his tenderness and affection in his letters: 'I feel every anxiety and concern for You that a tender husband can have for a virtuous wife.'[121] Elsewhere, he assured Catherine that he could not even write the names of their children 'without a suffusion of tears', adding: 'I leave You to Judge what a tender Parent and most affectionate Husband must feel.'[122] In 1787 he reassured her: 'how ardently I wish to press them and their Dear Mother to the fond bosom of a tender Parent and Affectionate Husband.'[123] Both Catherine and Charles, as we have seen, often emphasized their own ties of affection and tenderness, and Charles's language was no less warm and sensible than Catherine's own had been.

Languages of sensibility allowed Charles and Catherine to express their own desires, within a context of larger family feeling. They also allowed them to navigate the difficult situations of separation in which they found themselves. Such rhetoric could also have considerable political import. Notable failures of sensibility might serve as a form of political capital, in a war, which like other wars, was also a war of words. The ways in which Americans painted British and Hessian soldiers as cruel has received coverage, but less attention has been paid to the way in which this kind of propaganda might function for British supporters.[124] Yet it is clear that such narratives circulated in private and public letters at the time, drumming up support, in both America and Britain, for the

---

[119] Charles Dudley to Catherine Dudley, 'London 1st. April 1789', ibid.
[120] Charles Dudley to Catherine Dudley, 'August 6th. 1788', ibid.
[121] Charles Dudley to Catherine Dudley, 'London 6th February 1785. No. 27 Suffolk Street', ibid.
[122] Charles Dudley to Catherine Dudley, 'London 3d May 1785', ibid.
[123] Charles Dudley to Catherine Dudley, 'London October 3 1787', ibid.
[124] Sharon Block argues that narratives of rape in the Revolution formed uniquely American critiques of British power: 'The rhetorical power of stories of British rapes of American women lay in their stark portrayal of villains and victims, a portrayal that paralleled American belief in the British empire's betrayal of its American subjects.' I am not sure the traffic is one way here, since British and Loyalist accounts similarly emphasized cruelty directed specifically against the bodies of women by men with too much power (though not, in these cases, rape). Sharon Block, *Rape and Sexual Power in Early America* (Chapel Hill, NC: University of North Carolina Press for the Omohundro Institute of Early American History and Culture, 2006), 230–8, at 237.

British cause. Prime examples of these tales are the letters of Ann Hulton, sister of the Boston Commissioner of Customs, and a more enthusiastic commentator on political events than Catherine herself was. Her letters were written to a female friend in England, but they repeatedly mentioned the ways in which Patriots relished causing pain among supporters of the British cause. Ann reported with horror on the 'destruction of the tea' in Boston in 1773, the Non-importation Act of 1774, and the outbreak of fighting at Lexington and Concord in 1775.[125] She also told many less well-known tales of the miseries of British supporters. She reported on the case of Governor Hutchinson and his wife, who were turned out into a blizzard by angry locals.[126] Ann went into considerable detail about gruesome treatment of those singled out for their support of the British, such as the violent tarring-and-feathering of John Malcolm in Boston: 'This Spectacle of horror & sportive cruelty was exhibited for about five hours.' Ann made a point of highlighting that not only did Malcolm suffer this 'cruel torture' from 'inhuman' Patriots, but in addition, 'he has a Wife & family & an Aged Father & Mother who they say saw the Spectacle w[hi]ch no indifer[en]t person can mention without horror'. The display of this 'torture' to Malcolm's wife and parents exacerbated the pain Malcolm had already endured.[127]

Ann Hulton even used the case of Catherine and Charles Dudley, though unnamed, in her reports of the 'barbarism' that she implied was taking over America. In February 1776, Ann recounted several narratives of the distresses of British sympathizers throughout New England. She began with the Dudleys: 'The Rebels made a demand on the Collector at Rhode Island of the Kings Money upon which he had fled on board the Rose Man of War, they then Seized on his house & effects & turnd his Wife out of doors.' Again, to have turned the wife out was the height of insensibility, precisely the terms in which Catherine Dudley herself saw her situation. Emphasizing again the 'sportive cruelty' of the Americans, especially against women, Ann also described the way that 'Mr Ed: Brinleys wife whilst laying in, had a guard of Rebels always in her room, who treated her wth great rudeness & indecency, exposing her to the view of their banditti, as a sight "See a tory woman" stripd her & her Children of all their Linnen & Cloths.' Again, it is both the punishment (Malcolm's tarring-and-feathering, Mrs Brinley's being kept under guard while giving birth) and the display of the punishment (to Malcolm's family, to the chilling gaze of 'banditti') that were so troubling, as well, again, as the 'stripping' of a woman of her possessions. Ann concluded from all these reports that 'the

---

[125] Ann Hulton to Mrs Lightbody, 'Boston Novr 25. 1773', 'Boston Jany 25. 1774', 'July 8th 1774', and 'April 1775?', in Hulton, *Letters*, 62–80.
[126] Ann Hulton to Mrs. Lightbody, 'Jany 31st 1774', ibid.
[127] This episode is discussed in Alfred F. Young, *The Shoemaker and the Tea Party: Memory and the American Revolution* (Boston: Beacon Press, 1999), 46–51, and in Benjamin H. Irvin, 'Tar, Feathers, and the Enemies of American Liberties, 1768–1776', *New England Quarterly*, 76 (2003), 197–238, esp. 210–13. Ann Hulton to Mrs. Lightbody, 'Jany 31st 1774', in Hulton, *Letters*, 71–2.

cruelties w[hi]ch are exercised on all those who are in their power is shocking'.[128] Another woman, the daughter of a Pennsylvania Loyalist, condemned those Americans who under the guise of 'disinterested patriotism' in fact had little sympathy for the trials of Loyalists: 'There is a meaness and depravity of mind in extracting pleasure from the grievous afflictions of others which nothing can excuse.'[129] For some, unfeelingness could not be forgiven, even in war.

The unfeelingness of American rebels was a theme also taken up in British periodicals as early as 1775. While some of these accounts were in actual newspaper reports, others were couched in subtler terms, as in fictional stories in magazines. An October 1775 story, 'The Fair American', appearing in the *Town and Country Magazine,* was a Romeo-and-Juliet tale updated for the times, about the aptly named Miss Betty Washington, daughter of a Patriot, who fell in love with the aptly named Mr Lovemore, a man who sided with the British. Betty Washington's father forbade his daughter from having further contact with Lovemore. Like many a fictional and historical daughter, Betty tried to use the leverage of sensible pleas to persuade her father otherwise: 'In vain did she urge every alleviating and every soothing argument—the warmth of the dispute; the merit of the youth; her father's [earlier] approbation; and the hardship of being separated at once from all that we love. He was deaf to every remonstrance.' Forbidden to see each other publicly, naturally, 'Miss Washington still continued to see Mr. Lovemore in secret, and poured out her soul to him in many a tender epistle.' One night, when trying to sneak in to visit her, Lovemore was shot and killed, and so 'she fell on his bosom in a transport of grief and despair, and seemed for some time as dead as he.' Mr. Washington was insensible to his daughter's despair: 'instead of compassionating his daughter's distress, he appeared only to rejoice at the fate of her lover.' His ability not only to ignore but to 'rejoice' in pain echoed reports, such as those from Ann Hulton to her English friends, about the unfeelingness of Patriots. The story editorialized: 'Such a tendency has party-rage to banish the feelings of nature and humanity!—Nay, when she began to recover, he . . . ordered her to be excluded [from] his house for ever.' As with Ann Hulton, the turning out of a woman from her home indicated a repudiation of humanity and sensibility and was also a way of contrasting vengeful American rebels with loyal British supporters. Miss Washington, 'almost frantic with grief, and all bathed in tears . . . wandered to the town of Boston; where her story was known to general Gage, who treated her with great tenderness.' The British General Gage acted as her father should have, showing 'compassion' to 'this helpless beauty' by helping her get to England.[130] A romantic tale with a clear

---

[128] Ann Hulton to Mrs. Lightbody, 'Chester Feby 22 1776', in ibid. 85–6.
[129] Anna (Shoemaker) Rawle to Rebecca Shoemaker, '[Phila] March 27, 1781', Shoemaker Family Papers, HSP.
[130] 'The Fair American. A True Story', *Town and Country Magazine* (Oct. 1775), 518–19.

political message, this narrative also emphasized the horrors likely to ensue when 'party-rage' overcame the ties of nature and humanity.

Sensibility and family feeling could also inform more explicitly political debates, even after the war.[131] For example, many of those who argued in parliament for Loyalist compensation used similar terms. One supporter deployed the languages of seduction novels to paint a grim picture of betrayed Loyalists, arguing that the loss of the American territories 'was nothing when put in competition with another of the crimes of the present peace: *the . . . delivering over to confiscation, tyranny, resentment, and oppression, the unhappy men who* TRUSTED to our fair PROMISES *and* DECEITFUL WORDS.'[132] Another could apparently scarcely bring himself to speak of this horror, 'as an assembly of human beings could scarcely trust their judgements when so powerful an attack was made upon their feelings. If they had hearts and nerves they must necessarily overwhelm their understandings. He turned his eyes therefore from that subject, by a kind of natural impulse, as from a *corpse* or a *grave*.'[133] One Loyalist hoped his letter to the Commission would 'affect their Feelings, and may ultimately produce a good Effect'.[134] Another MP claimed that when he spoke for the Loyalists, he '*expressed the* EMOTIONS *of his* HEART', while another averred that 'his heart *bled* . . . Being a man himself, he could not but feel for men so cruelly abandoned to the malice of their ENEMIES'.[135] One member of the House of Lords also invoked his '*own bleeding heart*', demanding: '*is England so lost to gratitude, and all the feelings of humanity*, as not to afford them asylum?' Lord North noted that the clause about the Loyalists in the peace treaty 'awakens human sensibility in a very irresistible and lamentable degree', going on: 'I cannot but lament the fate of those unhappy men . . . the Loyalists, from their attachments, surely had some claim on our affection.' This is not the language of honor, obligation, and justice (though these terms were used elsewhere), but rather the languages of sensible suffering and the invocation of ties of humanity and even affection. North concluded: 'I cannot but feel for men *thus sacrificed* for their bravery and principles; men who have sacrificed all the dearest possessions of the human heart . . . Had we not espoused their cause from a *principle of affection* and *gratitude*, we should, at least, have *protected* them . . . If not tender of their FEELINGS, we should have been

---

[131] This political use of sensibility suggests that a re-evaluation may be in order of Sarah Knott's and others' claims that sensibility in Britain was discredited even during the Revolutionary War, and certainly after it ended. These debates, among many others (such as those agitating for the end of the slave trade in the 1790s) indicate the extent to which sensibility remained a critical aspect of British political discourse. See Knott, 'Sensibility and the American War for Independence'.

[132] Mr Lee, as quoted in Galloway, *The Claim of the American Loyalists*, 90. The italics in all of the quotations given from this volume are original.

[133] Mr MacDonald, as quoted in ibid. 91.

[134] Isaac Low to Nicholas Low, 'London April 4th: 1787', Nicholas Low Papers, Box 1, File: 'Low, Isaac 1787–88', LoC.

[135] Sir Peter Burrell and Sir Wilbraham Bootle, as quoted in Galloway, *The Claim of the American Loyalists*, 90–1.

tender of our CHARACTER.'¹³⁶ The character of Britain depended on its ability to protect, and by implication, to honor its affectionate attachments.

The connection between honoring affectionate ties (a domestic imperative now translated into political discourse) and political protection also highlights the strong connection made between concerns about domestic disorder and political disorder. It is not simply that individuals used political languages in their domestic negotiations; it is rather that some used domestic languages in their political ones. For instance, a few of these defenders of the Loyalists specifically invoked domestic disturbance as a reason to press their case. Lord North fretted that: 'They have *exposed* their lives... *lost* their connections, and *ruined their families*.'¹³⁷ The ruin of families was one of the most terrible aspects of their anguish. A member of the House of Lords similarly argued that these men 'have given up *their all*, and (a pang more grievous to minds of feeling) *the all of their little families*'.¹³⁸ Charles and Catherine could have corroborated this rather patronizing supposition of family suffering. Indeed, Charles himself justified his Memorial to the Loyalist Claims Commission in just such terms: 'Your Memorialist therefore humbly hopes it will be considered by this Honorable Board as no more than a duty he owes to his distressed Family.'¹³⁹ Other Loyalists also complained they had 'lost their all in Support of Government by which means they have begga[are]d themselves and [their] family's'.¹⁴⁰

This invocation of family demonstrates, again, the political capital of such claims, but it also demonstrates that these politicians, among others, were aiming to appear as 'men of feeling' who cared about the domestic anguish of the Loyalists and their families. This disposition showed their tenderness, both to the feelings of the Loyalists and to their own character as men of feeling. Generals and politicians needed to exhibit tenderness to troubled families as much as husbands and wives did, at least in theory. As the stories of Charles Dudley and James Parker make clear, arguments that the British government should act with tenderness and sympathy to the distressed Loyalists did not always mean that it did. As in domestic situations, these languages could sometimes simply justify unfortunate, painful decisions. Husbands and wives might have been friends, but they did not enjoy the true equality necessary for friendship. Similarly, Loyalist petitioners relied on a government with far more resources. In both cases, claims to sensible suffering could help to provide a limited leverage for those lacking power. However, such languages also worked to obscure the imbalance of resources.

---

¹³⁶ Lord North, as quoted in ibid. 86–7.   ¹³⁷ Ibid.
¹³⁸ Lord Sackville, as quoted in ibid. 96.
¹³⁹ 'The Memorial of Charles Dudley', Dudley File (nos. 229–30), AO 13/68 A, NA.
¹⁴⁰ Edward and Ann Chandler to Samuel Thorne, 'Lindsey Row Chelsea Feby. 10ᵗʰ 1785', Edward and Ann Chandler Letters to Samuel Thorne, NYPL.

Invocations of family could justify some difficult, painful, and even sometimes downright questionable decisions, whether for husbands, politicians, or generals. Let us return to the story with which this chapter began, that of Flavilla and Horatius, which hid within it another story of family invoked to justify dubious choices. Horatius shared the prizes from the plunder of St Eustatius under Admiral George Rodney's command. But, though the sentimental tale made no mention of it, this was an event that had generated enormous controversy. Rodney attacked and plundered St Eustatius, a Dutch island that had been involved in smuggling contraband to Americans. The lack of resistance by residents did not prevent the confiscation of all private property, including food. Like the 'savage General' Hopkins, the equally (if not more) savage Rodney ransacked houses, gardens, and even graves. Ironically, and tragically, some of those whose property was confiscated were actually Loyalist refugees from the mainland, including a number of Jews, whom Rodney gratuitously imprisoned. Despite the violation of international law, Rodney quickly auctioned off the goods, selling even to the French, active enemies of the British in 1781. Rodney justified this behavior by claiming that 'a perfidious people, wearing the mask of friendship, traitors to their country, and rebelling against their king deserve no favor or consideration'.[141] He apparently believed they deserved neither tenderness nor justice. Even another British admiral declared that Rodney and the other commanders at St Eustatius 'will find it very difficult to convince the world that they have not proved themselves wickedly rapacious'.[142]

It was Rodney's domestic and financial situation that inspired his 'rapaciousness'. At the start of the Revolutionary War he had actually been imprisoned for debt, and had fled to Paris to avoid his creditors. As one scholar has pointed out, 'St. Eustatius represented the best chance for this sixty-two-year-old naval commander to make a fortune from prize money and to leave his family in comfortable circumstances'.[143] Some months prior to the sacking of St Eustatius, in fact, Rodney wrote to his wife: 'All I want is, to pay off my debts as soon as possible: I shall not be easy till this is done... I cannot bear waiting [to pay them] till a peace.' He continued: 'Many prizes have been taken since my command here, but none very valuable. I hope Fortune may soon smile upon me, for all your sakes.'[144] A man determined to force Fortune to smile upon him, he acted

---

[141] 'Copy of a Letter from Admiral Rodney to the Marquis de Bouillé', *New Jersey Gazette*, 23 May 1781, in *Early American Newspapers, Series I, 1690–1876* (Readex).

[142] In this same letter, Hood noted that: 'The Admiral and the General have a great deal to answer for... as many of their actions will [not] well bear the daylight.' Sir Samuel Hood to Jackson, 'Barbadoes, 24th of June, 1781', in David Hannay (ed.), *Letters Written by Sir Samuel Hood (Viscount Hood) in 1781–2–3*, Publications of the Navy Records Society, 3 vols. (London, 1895), iii. 22–3.

[143] O'Shaughnessy, *An Empire Divided*, 221.

[144] Admiral George Rodney to Lady Rodney, 'Sandwich, St. Christopher's, July 30th, 1780', in Godfrey Basil Mundy (ed.), *The Life and Correspondence of the Late Admiral Lord Rodney*, 2 vols. (London, 1830), i. 360–1.

with ferocity to the inhabitants of St Eustatius. Rodney felt justified, and he also exalted at the prospect offered for clearing his debts. In fact, he informed his wife after the sale of plunder: 'I shall be happy as, exclusive of satisfying all debts, something will be left for my dear children... My chief anxiety is, that neither yourself nor my girls shall ever again be necessitous, nor be under obligations to others.'[145] Taking the island and its wealth, he planned exultantly to buy a new house and to pay for marriage settlements for his children. Seeking independence (and not obligations) for his family, Rodney's newly restored circumstances rested on the violation and plunder of other families.

Charles Dudley was no Rodney, but nevertheless there were certain parallels: a desire for personal prosperity, even if it required going far from his native land to achieve it; a wish to set their children up in independence and good circumstances, even if it meant suffering considerable unpleasantness overseas far from their wives and children; a loyalty to the British crown in the face of all kinds of circumstances; a desperate hope of avoiding debt, even as they endured it; a glossing over of grim realities with invocation of family and sentiment. They were not the only men to share such desires and such willingness, as the history of the British Atlantic (and indeed the British empire) makes clear. Many men were willing to suffer separation from their families, and horrors far from home, in order to make their children independent.

Between his desire for justice, independence, and a long-term future for his family, Charles argued that his presence in London was 'indispensible' and beyond the power of personal choice. This may not have been strictly true. Judging from remarks in Charles's letters, Catherine was unhappy about what she perceived to be his decision. In this, she faced an age-old dilemma: of wanting her husband and the father of her children back, even when he argued strenuously for the financial imperatives of their separation. Indeed, a similar situation appeared in the very first letter-writing manual in England, the 1568 *Enimie of Idlenesse*. In it, a wife demanded to know why her husband had been gone for so long, and argued that his presence to her and their children was more important than 'riches'. She closed her letter: 'Therefore I beseech and require you that you will come unto us, for we have great neede of you, & not of money.' The husband replied: 'I am not covetous, as peradventure you suppose: true it is, that I am come unto the Court to advantage us and our children as much as I can, which may hereafter be cause of joyfull quietnesse.'[146] Couples had been longing for 'joyfull quietnesse' for centuries, even as husbands ended up privileging long-term prospects for children over more short-term desires.

That such epistolary marital negotiations had been going on for centuries in fact and fiction indicates both what was old and what was new about the dilemmas of Catherine and Charles. Separations, whether caused by business,

---

[145] Admiral George Rodney to Lady Rodney, 'St. Eustatius, April 23d, 1781', in ibid. ii. 98–100.
[146] William Fulwood, *The Enimie of Idlenesse* (London, 1568), 110–11.

war, or other reasons, had long put pressures on marriages and cast spouses into liminal settings, even as they also in some cases generated the letters through which it is possible to witness these marriages. Even when husbands privileged domestic imperatives, they sometimes defined them differently from their wives. Husbands tended to place long-term concerns about inheritance and patrimony at the forefront of their arguments, while wives tended to argue for more immediate concerns. Letters had long provided one way of negotiating these issues between husband and wife, at least within certain circles. Those letters also demonstrate what had changed by the late eighteenth century. More and more, men went into larger imperial worlds. At the same time, blissful, emotional reunions were to replace a desire simply for 'joyfull quietnesse'. Languages of sensible suffering became much more important, on both sides of the Atlantic. Both women and men made use of these vocabularies, in contexts as much political as domestic. Whether in order to rally a population to fight a war or to rally a husband to join his wife, such rhetoric provided an important means of address for many. Wives, among others, gained some leverage from these vocabularies, even if this leverage was greatly constrained by other concerns, especially financial ones tied to a husband's ability to provide for his household.

When Horatius had left his Flavilla, he averred that he had to do so because 'everything that is dear to a gentleman' was at stake. The same might be said for Charles Dudley. While he wanted to privilege his character as a man of feeling, different imperatives pulled him other directions. What he held dear, like many other men in this era, were not only affectionate attachments but also political loyalty, independence, credit, and an ability to provide for future generations. Even while admitting the force of these pressures, both Horatius and Charles underplayed these financial and martial imperatives by invoking languages of sensibility and marital affection. This rhetoric gave men a way to pursue masculine prerogative while still remaining men of feeling. Both Charles and the author of 'The Farewell' recounted imagined happy reunions, even as they skirted over realities of plunder, inhumanity, and horror. In fact, Charles's claims turned out to be as fictional as those put forward by the author of 'The Farewell'. Both promised happy kisses amid scenes of destruction and loss. They could thus avoid the implications of what it meant for a nation to have lost a war against its colonies, for men to have done terrible things because of that war, and for some men never to have come home at all. Stories of sensibility, whether for fictional or historical families, were both a means of expressing sympathy and of ameliorating the horrors of war and separation. No wonder they flourished amid the Revolutionary War.

Family feeling could justify a lot of unfortunate decisions. It could be deployed to justify decisions not always popular or even right, whether the reward of money to Loyalists, the indiscriminant sacking of the houses of St Eustatius, or choosing to stay in London away from a loving wife and children. Charles Dudley could cite the future of his children as a reason not to come home to them; George Rodney could do the same when he sold off goods plundered from Loyalist refugees. Sensibility was a central concern, but so was the family. Sentimental stories made sense of those disconnections by imagining the reconnections that might occur. Whether in domestic letters or in magazines, such stories placed families at their center, and exploited their power for both personal and political ends.

Both Catherine and Charles had placed their faith in those who were supposed to protect and defend them against disorder and painful, financially unsupported independence. Yet such loyalties, whether in a husband or a government, ultimately did not provide the protection they both had desired, leaving them to spend years apart, living dependent on others, and longing for 'happier days', as Charles phrased it.[147] Years before his death, Charles had written wryly to Catherine: 'I think I hear You say that this untill will lead us to the end of life without any thing being done; but You must not give way to such unpleasant thoughts.'[148] Alas, Catherine was right. Their lives hinged on a great 'untill', as they waited until the government compensated them for losses, until Charles sailed for Rhode Island an independent man, until their longed-for reunion, until life went back to normal. It never would. Unlike the happy fiction of Horatius and Flavilla, there were no 'blissful circumstances' between the reunited husband and wife. One husband never did return to his wife, and her sorrow at this fact must have exceeded even that of the grieving Flavilla.

[147] Charles Dudley to Catherine Dudley, 'London No 27 Suffolk Street 6 December 1785', Dudley Papers, NHS.
[148] Charles Dudley to Catherine Dudley, 'London 6th February 1785', ibid.

7

The Old Husband and the Young Wife: Scandal, Feeling, and Distance

> No more my heart domestic calm must know;
> Far from these joys, with sighs which memory traces,
> To sultry skies and distant climes I go.
>
> (M. G. Lewis, 1796)[1]

Would the old husband, smarting from her deceit, forgive his young wife (Fig. 7.1)? It would be hard to believe it, gazing upon him, so outrageously cuckolded. This rotund husband reclines in front of the fire, resting his aching foot on a gout-table, drowning his pained frustration in port, kept company only by his cat. The phallic objects around him—candle, picture pole, port bottle, and fire-poker—mock his flaccid form. In a classic early modern trope, the table legs form a set of horns, for the cuckold to wear. Also mocking him (and being scorned by his unfaithful wife) is the portrait behind him, of an ancestor, in a typical family portrait from an earlier era. Hand resting powerfully on his sword, this upright ancestor, fronting the vigorous copulation in the bedroom behind, underscores the subversion of the family name and family honor portrayed here. Such a satire, of the old husband, his young wife, and an interloper to the marriage bed, has timeless elements. But it is also as good a representation as we are likely to find of the cuckolding of John Tharp, an Anglo-Jamaican planter, and a gouty old husband himself. Family portraits and family trees do not dwell on episodes such as this one. In the chill of December 1800 John learned of the affair between his wife Ann and Richard Burton Burton Phillipson.[2] Like the protagonist of a magazine story, did he cry: 'Oh, d-mn matrimony! Why did I marry? Was it not evident I must be cuckolded?'[3] In fact, John's situation was worse than that of a fictional cuckold, because the interloper in his bed was his own son-in-law, married to his daughter Eliza, and an Anglican priest to boot.

---

[1] M. G. Lewis, *The Monk*, 3 vols. (London, 1796), ii. 166.
[2] John was well into his fifties, while Richard and Ann were around their late twenties/early thirties, a significant age disparity. See the Tharp Family Tree, CCRO.
[3] *Town and Country Magazine*, 18 (May 1785), 266.

Fig. 7.1. Thomas Rowlandson, 'The Old Husband' (*c.*1800), reprinted from Peter Wagner, *Eros Revived: Erotica of the Enlightenment in England and America* (London: Secker & Warburg, 1988). Bodleian Library, University of Oxford, M00.E 10035, p. 146.

The treachery was breathtaking. For Joseph Brissett, John Tharp's nephew and a fellow Anglo-Jamaican planter, the affair was further proof that 'it is an age, in which we are taught . . . not to wonder at any extravagance,—any unnatural & vicious crime that may come before us'.[4]

---

[4] Joseph Brissett to John Tharp, 'Barbary March 16th 1801', R55.7.128(c), CCRO.

The middle-aged cuckold, duped by his pretty young wife and her knavish partner, is an ageless trope of satirical culture.[5] Nevertheless, the husband's response to cuckoldry reveals a considerable amount about his age and its extravagances. The story of John Tharp's reactions to this sordid breach of family tranquillity exposes the little-charted terrain of Jamaican planter authority, as well as the agency of Anglo-Jamaican women in shaping not only their own lives but those of their husbands and fathers too. If in this era the cuckold was a favorite in a panoply of stock images, so too was the 'West-India tyrant', especially as the furor over the abolition of the slave trade gripped the British in the 1790s.[6] Writers and artists alike portrayed West Indian slave-holders as cruel and insensitive to the norms of a civilized culture. One abolitionist tract derided the planter: 'Whom every generous feeling hath defy'd | To whom, sweet, social love, is unally'd | . . . a greater tyrant is, than *Algier's* Chief.'[7] Refuting these charges as early as 1774, Edward Long, the well-known historian of Jamaica, admitted: 'Some alledge, that these slave-holders . . . are lawless bashaws [and] West-India tyrants.'[8] The word 'bashaw' (like the reference to '*Algier's* Chief') denoted another stereotype of this period: the 'Oriental despot', who maintained a harem of cowering wives along with his children and servants, and whose tyranny towards both his slaves and his family overrode the law.

The tale of John Tharp's reaction to the infidelity in his family undermines this conflation, made both by contemporaries and by later historians. One historian of eighteenth-century Jamaica has posited that 'white men found it difficult not to be tyrants in all their relationships'.[9] Nevertheless, while brutality characterized most master–slave relations in Jamaica, it did not necessarily define relations between Anglo-Jamaican husbands and wives, at least by the dawning of the nineteenth century.[10] Too often the historical image of Jamaican planters

---

[5] Thomas Rowlandson drew prints such as 'The Old Husband'. See Ronald Paulson, *Rowlandson: A New Interpretation* (London: Studio Vista, 1972). Isaac Cruikshank also took up this theme in his 'Folly of an Old Man Marrying a Young Wife'. Isaac Cruikshank, published 1 May, 1790 by Robert Sayer. Reprinted in The Fisher Gallery, University of Southern California and Huntington Library and Art Gallery, *Isaac Cruikshank and the Politics of Parody: Watercolors in the Huntington Collection* (San Marino, Calif.: Huntington Library Press, 1994).

[6] In his survey of the image of West Indians in eighteenth-century literature, Wylie Sypher has contended that: 'No anti-slavery novel or poem fails to inveigh against . . . the sugar-grower of St. Kitts, Neavis, or Jamaica.' Wylie Sypher, 'The West Indian as a "Character" in the Eighteenth Century', *Studies in Philology*, 36 (1939), 503–29, at 505.

[7] Timothy Touchstone, *Tea and Sugar, or the Nabob and the Creole* (London, 1792).

[8] Edward Long, *The History of Jamaica*, 2 vols. (London, 1774), ii. 267.

[9] Trevor Burnard, 'Theater of Terror: Domestic Violence in Thomas Thistlewood's Jamaica, 1750–1786', in Christine Daniels and Michael V. Kennedy (eds.), *Over the Threshold: Intimate Violence in Early America* (New York: Routledge, 1999), 237–53, at 244.

[10] Philip D. Morgan, for example, argues that 'Jamaican slavery . . . extended the bounds of severity inherent in patriarchalism to its very limits—and beyond'. Philip D. Morgan, 'Three Planters and Their Slaves: Perspectives on Slavery in Virginia, South Carolina, and Jamaica, 1750–1790', in Winthrop D. Jordan and Sheila L. Skemp (eds.), *Race and Family in the Colonial South* (Jackson, Miss.: University Press of Mississippi, 1987), 37–80, at 74. The diary of Thomas

remains that of men who ignored, or fought against, the British emphasis on sensibility. In this view, Jamaican planters epitomized the raw exercise of power and a blatant double standard in white sexuality.[11] John Tharp's tale traces out a different vision of Jamaican masculinity. It also offers a case study on British-Atlantic masculinity for an area, Jamaica, that has seen little such treatment. While various circumstances may have influenced John's handling of the affair, the most compelling explanation lies in changing languages of sentiment and their power in the family, especially when deployed by Anglo-Jamaican women. John was neither the laughably impotent husband of satire, nor the 'lawless bashaw' of popular interpretation. This narrative thus turns away from these dancing images of satire and polemics, and instead affords a keyhole view into shifting ideals of sensibility, even within a world once thought to be impenetrable to such impulses.

Born in 1744, John, a descendent of an established Jamaican family, was above all an ambitious man. By the time he was 10 John's grandfather and father had both died, leaving the bulk of their estates to him.[12] This inheritance, of two estates in Hanover parish, allowed him to be educated at Eton and Trinity College, Cambridge.[13] Yet John was not content to rest on the family laurels,

---

Thistlewood provides numerous examples of such brutality. See Douglas Hall, *In Miserable Slavery: Thomas Thistlewood in Jamaica, 1750–1786* (Basingstoke: Macmillan, 1989), and Trevor Burnard, *Mastery, Tyranny, and Desire: Thomas Thistlewood and His Slaves in the Anglo-Jamaican World* (Chapel Hill, NC: University of North Carolina Press, 2004). Trevor Burnard's 1991 claim that 'we know all too little about white family life in colonial Jamaica' continues to ring true. Philip D. Morgan has suggested that even amid its brutality, paternalism began to transform Jamaican life by the early nineteenth century. Morgan, 'Three Planters', 78. Useful as Morgan's insight here is, he does not develop it further. As yet there has been little work done on this transformation or its agents.

[11] In part, such an image might fit better earlier in the eighteenth century. For instance, Trevor Burnard, writing of an earlier period, maintains that many Jamaican men 'were rough, boorish men with few graces and minimal interest in the virtues of matrimony and monogamy'. Trevor Burnard, 'Inheritance and Independence: Women's Status in Early Colonial Jamaica', *William and Mary Quarterly*, 48 (1991), 93–114, at 110. Burnard further contends: 'The reality for white women in colonial Jamaica was that they were in fact irrelevant to male considerations. They exercised no power either sexually or economically'. Id., 'Family Continuity and Female Independence in Jamaica, 1665–1734', *Continuity and Change*, 7 (1992), 181–98, at 194. The work done on Thomas Thistlewood, a small planter, has tended to focus on the brutality of Jamaican plantation life. His story, however, should not obscure other trajectories of change in Jamaica, especially among richer planters more attuned to metropolitan norms and behavior.

[12] John Tharp was apparently born in 1744, according to the family tree at the Cambridgeshire County Record Office. He is mentioned in Venn as being aged 18 when admitted as fellow-commoner to Trinity College, Cambridge, on 19 January 1761. If this is correct, then he may have been born in 1743 or early 1744. He was certainly born prior to 25 February 1747, as he is mentioned in his father's will of that date. J. A. Venn, *Alumni Cantabrigienses* (Cambridge: Cambridge University Press, 1954), 146. See also Will of Joseph Tharp, 1747, R55.7.122(m).1, and Will of John Tharp, 1750, R55.7.122(m).2, CCRO. The two estates were Batchelor's Hall and Pedro. John's parents were Joseph Tharp and Margaret (Frost) Tharp.

[13] According to the *Eton College Register*, John Tharp was registered there from 1758 to 1760. According to the *Alumni Cantabrigiensis* and the *Trinity College Admissions* list, John was admitted as a fellow-commoner at Trinity in January 1761. Richard Arthur Austen-Leigh, *The Eton*

returning to Jamaica to parlay a decent inheritance into one of the greatest of Jamaican sugar fortunes.[14] He also acquired land and slaves in part through marriage. His first wife, Elizabeth Partridge, whom John married in 1765, was an heiress and survivor herself, attributes that surely increased her attractions. Elizabeth had inherited an estate in St James Parish, which passed to John at their marriage.[15] Nonetheless, John, unconvinced about the potential for growth in this area, sold that property in 1769 and purchased three adjoining estates in the relatively underdeveloped area that was to become Trelawney Parish.[16] Backed by a steady stream of capital from England, he continued to buy land, building up several thousand acres in Trelawney. Through purchasing, taking over, and 'improving' several estates, John labored for decades to amass his holdings in land, in cattle, and in human flesh. At the time of his death over 2,800 slaves worked in his fields, pens, wharves, and houses, placing John at the top of the Jamaican economic ladder.[17] He was an active entrepreneur, with an eye to increasing profits and prestige in Jamaica. Involved in political life, he was elected to the House of Assembly in 1772 and also served as a justice of the peace and as the custos of Trelawney, a position equivalent to the English lord-lieutenancy.[18]

Beyond his first wife's considerable landed assets, it is difficult to know much more about her, except that she bore children. Between 1766 and her death in 1780 Elizabeth had seven children, two of whom died young. The remaining five were educated in England: Joseph, John, William Blake, Thomas Partridge, and Elizabeth Partridge.[19] The first three became officers in the British military, in a

---

College Register: 1753–1790 (Eton: Spottiswoode, Ballantyne, & Co., 1921), 515; Venn, *Alumni Cantabrigienses*, 146; W. W. Rouse Ball and J. A. Venn, *Admissions to Trinity College, Cambridge*, 3 vols. (London: Macmillan, 1911), vol. 3 (*1701–1800*), 195.

[14] A. E. Furness, author of the only treatment of John's Jamaican estates, maintains that 'John Tharp's sugar plantations were the largest in Jamaica at the beginning of the nineteenth century'. A. E. Furness, 'The Tharp Estates in Jamaica,' unpublished essay (c.1961), I/1, CCRO. For John's many land transactions in Jamaica, see the numerous documents in R55.7.128, CCRO.

[15] Elizabeth was joint heiress to Potosi estate, taken over by John upon their marriage. Several deeds deal with the land transactions involved in this inheritance and the marriage of Elizabeth Partridge and John Tharp. See Items relating to Potosi, R55.7.122, Bundle 2, Items 1–9, 1763–76, CCRO.

[16] These three estates consisted of some 3,000 acres of land and nearly 500 slaves. Furness has found John Tharp's unceasing land acquisitions to be 'remarkable', as few planters continued to increase holdings in land universally recognized as uncertain. Moreover, John invested in water-mills at a time when few did so. Furness, 'The Tharp Estates' I/7, CCRO.

[17] Ibid. I/4, I/7, III/2, and III/3, CCRO. The major wharf in Martha Brae was known as Tharp's Wharf. For details of his will, see 'Will with 3 codicils of John Tharp Esqr, 1801–1804', R84/29, CCRO.

[18] Furness, 'The Tharp Estates', II–III, CCRO.

[19] Joseph Tharp was born on 11 June 1766. Like his father before him, he entered Trinity College, Cambridge, as a fellow-commoner, in 1785. Unlike his father, he was educated privately rather than at Eton. See Rouse-Ball and Venn, *Admissions to Trinity College, Cambridge*, 293, and Venn, *Alumni Cantabrigienses*, 147. William Blake followed his father's footsteps, enrolling at Eton and then at Cambridge (although at St John's College, not Trinity). See H. E. C. Stapylton, *The Eton School Lists: From 1791 to 1850*, 2nd edn. (London, 1864), 5; Robert Forsyth Scott, *Admissions*

period when Britain was engaged in almost continual war.[20] Elizabeth Partridge went on to marry the Revd Richard Burton Burton Phillipson.[21] All the children were Jamaican-born, but only Thomas and William returned to Jamaica in adulthood.

These children were not the only ones fathered by John Tharp. Between his two marriages, from 1780 to 1794, John appears to have engaged in some of the extramarital sexuality so characteristic of Jamaican planters of this period. In his will, he left his 'reputed daughter' Mary Hyde Tharp an annuity and a marriage settlement. Mary, most likely the child of John Tharp and a free woman of color, was born around 1785, five years after his wife's death.[22] This allocation of money suggests that John retained affection for his daughter. At the very least he took some responsibility for her.[23] John may have had other illegitimate children, but if he did, they leave no trace in the family records.

By 1794 John had decided to remarry. His bride was Ann Gallimore, a widow with one daughter named Sarah. John's old friend and fellow Jamaican planter, Simon Taylor, informed his cousin that John had chosen 'a very likely fine Young Woman about 20'. The reasons for John's decision to marry again are unclear. Simon felt that the decision had been 'sudden'.[24] Her ownership of two estates near John's own doubtless enhanced her appeal.[25] Just before the marriage, John and Ann settled a deed in which Ann gave up her estates in return

---

to the College of St. John the Evangelist, Part IV (1767–1802) (Cambridge: Cambridge University Press, 1931), 511; and Venn, *Alumni Cantabrigienses*, 147. John and Thomas Partridge appear to have been educated privately.

[20] According to Venn, *Alumni Cantabrigienses*, Joseph Tharp was a 'Sometime Captain' of the 1st Life Guards. Venn, *Alumni Cantabrigienses*, 147. John was a Captain in the Horse Guards Blue. L. G. Pine (ed.), *Burke's Genealogical and Heraldic History of the Landed Gentry*, 17th edn. (London: Burke's Peerage Ltd, 1952), 2488. William Blake served as lieutenant-colonel in St James' Regiment in Jamaica. Indeed, he died as a result, by being thrown from his horse while reviewing troops in Jamaica. Scott, *Admissions to . . . St. John*, 511.

[21] Marriage Agreement between Eliza Tharp and Richard Burton Burton Phillipson, 29 April 1797, R55.7.7.246, CCRO.

[22] Her mother was never named, but it seems likely she was not a slave, but a woman with her own last name of Hyde. Given the situation in Jamaica, it is far more likely that she was a woman of color than a white woman. The fact that Mary Hyde Tharp had two last names, and later married one Robert Hayward, further supports the idea that she was not the child of a slave, but this must remain speculation in the absence of further sources.

[23] In his will of 13 March 1801, John left Mary Hyde Tharp an annuity of £100 sterling, as well as £2,000 to be paid at age 21 or at her marriage, whichever came first. She was listed in the will as his 'reputed daughter', but this legacy suggests that John clearly recognized her as his daughter. In fact, Mary Tharp married in Jamaica in 1802, at about age 17, and thus John paid the £2,000 to her new husband, Robert Hayward and also settled another £1,000 on her. Codicil dated 6 May 1802. See 'Will with 3 codicils of John Tharp Esqr, 1801–1804', R84/29, CCRO.

[24] See Simon Taylor to John Taylor, 'Kingston Jamaica October. 11. 1794', XIV/B/2, Simon Taylor Papers, ICS. If she was about 20 when they married, she was 26 in 1800. Given that she was a widow with a child when she married John Tharp, she might in fact have been a little older than this estimation, and in fact in her early twenties, thus putting her at around 30 in 1800.

[25] These properties abutted John's estates of Wales, Potosi, and Good Hope.

for an annuity of £1,200 Jamaican currency in the event of John's death.²⁶ Ann Gallimore Tharp remains a much more elusive figure than her husband, although her few extant letters reveal much more about her than it is usually possible to discover about eighteenth-century Jamaican women. She was born Ann Virgo, into a middling Jamaican family.²⁷ She seems to have married up the social scale into the Gallimore family, thus inheriting estates from her first husband, who died young, leaving her with a daughter, Sarah. Joseph Brissett was certainly flattering his uncle when he described Ann, even after her 'lamentable fall', as 'so admired, & so much respected for the prudence of her Conduct, and the winning affability of her manners'.²⁸ She was apparently bright and charming, as later letters indicate. Historians have cited the work of Edward Long to argue for the passivity of Anglo-Jamaican women. Long noted: 'We may see . . . a very fine young woman aukwardly dangling her arms with the air of a Negroe-servant, lolling almost the whole day upon beds or settee . . . Her ideas are narrowed to the ordinary heights that pass before her, the business of the plantation, the tittle-tattle of the parish.'²⁹ Despite these stereotypes, Ann comes across in her letters as a literate and cosmopolitan woman, entirely at ease in London life. In 1803, when stories of Napoleon's plans to invade filled the newspapers and terrified England, Ann mocked: 'There is nothing talked of here but the French Invaders I expect that I shall be fraternised alamode Sans Culotte . . . no I have no fear of what may happen, and really am amused at all the 'Tale's of Terror' I read of in the papers on the Subject of the bold Corsicans intentions.'³⁰ Ann's familiarity with British politics extended into 1804, when she reported that: 'the King is quite Mad the Duke of Cambridge is the only Person who Can Manage him.'³¹ At the center of metropolitan events, surveying the scene with coolness, she belies the stereotypes of retiring West Indian women.

Nonetheless, Ann fits another West Indian trait well: an attenuated family life, made complicated by a system of debts and payments. In this respect, Ann was much like John Tharp, who ended up involved in lawsuits over the conduct of his brother-in-law. In 1802, for instance, Ann requested that William Green, John's attorney, sell several of her slaves in Jamaica, but further instructed him:

---

²⁶ Marriage Settlement between John Tharp and Ann Gallimore, 1794, R55.7.122(j).12, CCRO. John received the Lansquinet and Cheshire estates, which totaled 750 acres, along with their 375 slaves.

²⁷ In 1753 William Virgo, possibly Ann's father, held 173 acres in Hanover parish, a holding more on par with a yeoman than a great planter. 'A List of Landholders in the Island of Jamaica . . . taken from the Quitrent Book', CO 142/31/67, NA. Many thanks to Trevor Burnard for this reference.

²⁸ Joseph Brissett to John Tharp, 'Barbary March 16, 1801', R55.7.128(c)4, CCRO.

²⁹ Trevor Burnard, using Edward Long's remarks on white women, has argued: 'White women had little to do except bear small numbers of children and listlessly loll around the house, as the historian Edward Long complained.' Burnard, 'Family Continuity', 194. The full quotation is in Long, *History of Jamaica*, ii. 279. Ann Tharp does not fit this image very well.

³⁰ Ann Tharp to William Green, 'No 8 Lisson Grove New Road', undated but postmarked 25 Oct. 1803, R55.7.128(a), CCRO.

³¹ Ann Tharp to John Tharp, '4 June 1804', ibid.

'on no Consideration whatever to let any of my Family be purchasers as I am in immediate want of the Money... particularly as they are now owing me fourteen hundred pounds I wish not to have any more transactions with any of them... they will no more Consider it a debt & allow me to be just as I am without a Shilling.'³² In 1803 Ann asked Green to collect the £600 her uncle Montagu Virgo owed to her.³³ Ann also had problems with the family of her first husband. In 1803 she defended herself against the charge that she was spending her daughter's inheritance on her own needs: 'I cannot benefit from her Income in any Respect as her relations say.'³⁴ Connections between Ann and her immediate family were somewhat closer. In 1803 her brother Henry arrived in England as a military officer: 'My Brother has lately become one of the Red Coated Heroes... He is grown a very fine Young Man.'³⁵ Ann did not think her mother had provided him with enough money to pay for his expenses, and asked William Green: 'you must persuade my Mother to allow him at least two Hundred a Year... I was obliged to add the 20£ a Year.'³⁶ Beyond these few remarks, it is difficult to know a great deal more about her family situation, or indeed about her.

Her partner in crime, Richard Burton Burton Phillipson, remains an even more elusive figure, since none of his writings appear to survive. Richard was probably born around 1767.³⁷ Hailing from East Anglia, the site of John's English estate, Richard was the son of a prosperous clergyman and an heiress.³⁸ After attending Cambridge, Richard was ordained as a priest in 1791. In 1792 his great-uncle died, leaving his mother a substantial inheritance and thus ensuring his own future income (an inheritance that came to him at her death in 1803).³⁹ He became the rector for two East Anglian parishes in 1796, a year before his marriage to Eliza Tharp. Little is known of his character, except second-hand denunciations. Nonetheless, even the condemnations convey that Richard had

---

³² Ann Tharp to William Green, 'No 8 Lisson Grove New Rd 3 May 1802', R55.7.128(a), CCRO.

³³ Ann Tharp to William Green, '1 March 1802' (actually 1803), ibid.

³⁴ Ann Tharp to William Green, 'Lisson Grove 2 June 1803', ibid.

³⁵ Ann Tharp to William Green, 'No 8 Lisson Grove New Road,' undated but postmarked 25 Oct. 1803, ibid.

³⁶ Ann Tharp to William Green, '4 Jany 1804', ibid.

³⁷ Richard Burton Burton Phillipson was admitted as pensioner to St John's College, Cambridge University, on 17 July 1784. Most pensioners were around 17 when they began, thus putting the year of Richard's birth at something like 1767. He was thus about 33 in 1800. Venn, *Alumni Cantabrigienses*, pt. II, vol. VI, p. 597.

³⁸ Richard's peculiar name comes from the fact of his mother's inheritance. For although she married Charles Wright, becoming Susanna[h] Wright, and giving birth to Richard Burton Wright, an inheritance from a childless uncle, Richard Burton Phillipson, caused her, her husband, and family to alter their surname from Wright to Burton Phillipson. So he became Richard Burton Burton Phillipson. See Venn, *Alumni Cantabrigienses*, pt. II, vol. VI, p. 597. These sorts of renamings were not uncommon among the eighteenth-century landed gentry.

³⁹ The mention of Phillipson's mother's death and his improved circumstances comes in John Tharp (sr.) to John Tharp (jr.), 'Good Hope 19th July 1803', R55.7.22(a), CCRO.

captivated John, Eliza, and Ann. Joseph Brissett, John's nephew, remarked that before the affair John Tharp had spoken 'so highly in his favor' that Brissett had been afraid to criticize the Reverend. Eliza married him, and apparently Ann later fell in love with him: 'Mrs. Tharp's attachment to Phillipson appeared so great—that if she did not keep a strict guard over her passions... Phillipson would certainly make an attempt on her Virtue and probably succeed.'[40] Later, of course, the Tharp family roundly condemned him for his 'baseness and depravity of Heart' and his cruel treatment of Eliza.[41]

Eliza Tharp Phillipson is the most elusive figure of all, although ultimately a key player in this unfolding family drama. She was presumably taken to England in girlhood and educated there privately. How she and Richard met is unclear, but he held livings near her father's estate in Chippenham. They both represented elite families, and as such their marriage would probably have been seen as a good match. She and Richard married in 1797 and had three children in quick succession: John Tharp Phillipson, Richard Burton Phillipson, and Eliza Partridge Phillipson, names highlighting the strength of kinship (and the placating of rich relatives) for such gentry families. She and Richard continued to live near the Tharp family manse, a situation that may have led to the later state of affairs.

The perfidy of Ann and Richard was outrageous, but how had it begun? In a letter to John Tharp, Joseph Brissett denounced Richard in terms that would have done a contemporary novelist proud: 'that the wretch, who ought to have proved the adviser of every thing tending to support Mrs. Tharps honour, and your Happiness... that he above all others, should... act himself the base insidious villain,—appears altogether a character so much out of nature, that I sometimes conceive this Business more an offspring of the imagination, than a real and melancholy fact.'[42] In terms of obtaining information about how this affair started or proceeded, 'real and melancholy facts' are few. John Tharp himself apparently initially blamed his wife, although Joseph Brissett laid the blame squarely on Richard, declaring that his character was so debased that his own mother, 'if she had been handsome and desirable', would not have been safe

---

[40] Joseph Brissett to John Tharp, undated (1801), R55.7.128(c), CCRO.
[41] Joseph Brissett to John Tharp, undated (1801) and 'Barbary March 16th 1801', ibid. John Tharp condemned Richard as his 'blasted Son in Law', 'the infamous parson', 'the profligate Parson', and 'that beast'. He later castigated him for 'his indelicate conversation & abandoned familiarity towards the Servants in his house'. Eliza's brother Thomas, in Jamaica, informed his brother John in England that their brother-in-law was a 'wretch'. Thomas's wife, Mary, reported to her sister-in-law Maria in England: 'what a brute the Man must be, I am told he treats her [Eliza] cruelly.' Terms found in the following letters: 'blasted Son in Law' in John Tharp to Simon Taylor, 'No 41 Portland Place 1th March 1801', XIX/A/10, Simon Taylor Papers, ICS; 'infamous parson' in John Tharp (sr.) to John Tharp (jr.), 'Good Hope 19th July 1803', R55.7.22 (a); 'profligate Parson' in same to same, 'Chippenham Park 9t Augt 1801', ibid.; 'beast' in same to same, 'Chippenham Park 28th June 1801', ibid.; Thomas Partridge Tharp and Mary Basilia Tharp to John and Anna Maria Tharp, 'Westmoreland Chebucto 6th August 1801', R55.7.24.1. All in CCRO.
[42] Joseph Brissett to John Tharp, 'Barbary March 16th 1801', R55.7.128(c), CCRO.

with him.⁴³ Brissett informed John that, 'I fancy you will find yourself deceived in concluding that Mrs T seduced Phillipson'.⁴⁴ Initially, John also wrote Simon Taylor: 'my Wife . . . has defiled my Bed & Eloped from my house.'⁴⁵ Later, for reasons unclear, he was to place most of the blame on Richard. Who precisely was responsible for the affair is unknowable, but according to Brissett: 'From about April I perceived a sad and lamented forgetfulness of that singular and admired Prudence which used always to appear so conspicuous in her [Ann's] Conduct.' It is a further mystery how the liaison was discovered. Ann's pregnancy might well have been the catalyst, suggesting that John might have been impotent, or that the couple had not been together sexually due to John's infirmities. From 1794 to 1800 they had had no children.

Ann and Richard apparently both overcame the usual constraints of loyalty to kin, fear of scandal (or of the cuckolded husband), or religion. In fact, Ann may have harbored resentment against John. A small but vital clue about the relationship comes from an 1803 letter from Ann to William Green, in which she lamented John's latest attack of the gout: 'I was grieved to hear of his late indisposition . . . I feel much more for him than he ever did for me I fear when he is Ill than I can describe.'⁴⁶ Ann's 'mistake' reveals far more than the correction. Although she reconsidered this nugget of resentment, she nonetheless apparently harbored her own grudges. Had the Tharp marriage been troubled even before her decision to have an affair? Had John, eager to look after his extensive business concerns, ignored his young wife? This single line in her letter suggests this was possibly so. For whatever reason, Ann decided to turn to her stepson-in-law, and they apparently embarked on an affair in the spring of 1800. They may have sought to run away together, as John later noted that his wife had 'Eloped from my house'.⁴⁷ However, even this point is unclear.

What is clear is that, by December 1800, John had learned that Ann was pregnant with a child assumed by everyone to be Phillipson's. How did John respond? He could have stayed with Ann and raised the child as his own, a course of action quickly rejected.⁴⁸ He instead sought to end their marriage.⁴⁹ Dismantling a marriage in this era could be done in a variety of ways. Most easily, John could have abandoned his wife. Ann would have been left with no obvious English assets, but she could still have drawn on John's credit to pay bills. Therefore, it was not a satisfactory solution. Secondly, he could have drawn up

---

⁴³ Joseph Brissett to John Tharp, undated, R55.7.128(c)7, CCRO.   ⁴⁴ Ibid.
⁴⁵ John Tharp to Simon Taylor, 'No 41 Portland Place 1th March 1801', XIX/A/10, Simon Taylor Papers, ICS.
⁴⁶ Ann Tharp to William Green, 'Lisson Grove 2nd. June 1803', R55.7.128(a), CCRO.
⁴⁷ John Tharp to Simon Taylor, 'No 41 Portland Place 1th March 1801', XIX/A/10, Simon Taylor Papers, ICS.
⁴⁸ Apparently, he learned of the affair on 10 December 1800, and the deed for separation had already been signed and sealed by 20 December.
⁴⁹ John Tharp to Simon Taylor, 'No 41 Portland Place 1th March 1801', XIX/A/10, Simon Taylor Papers, ICS.

a private separation agreement, a popular route for many unhappy and well-off spouses. To receive a *legal* end to his marriage, John had two options: to take his wife to the ecclesiastical court, where he would most likely have received a separation (without permission to remarry) on the basis of adultery, or, since he was both rich and wronged by his wife's adultery, he might have pushed for a full divorce with permission to remarry by a private Act of Parliament.[50] Given the apparently damning evidence against Ann, John could presumably have won either an ecclesiastical or a civil case. In any event, Ann's maintenance settlement would have been meager, and she would probably have lost custody of her own daughter. Given her situation, Ann had little recourse if John chose to pursue one of these harsher actions.

Lady Mary Cadogan, a contemporaneous adulterous wife, suffered far more than Ann. Like John, the middle-aged Lord Cadogan was generous to a young clergyman, the Revd William Henry Cooper. In the 1790s the young Lady Cadogan and the Revd Cooper embarked on an illicit liaison. According to one historian, once Lord Cadogan learned of the adultery he 'acted with the swift purposefulness of a man determined both to get rid of his wife and to destroy her lover'. Lord Cadogan threw his wife out of the house, first winning an ecclesiastical suit before going to Parliament for a private divorce bill. Lord Cadogan was now free to remarry, while his wife lost her title, her jointure, and any access to her children.[51] Lady Cadogan's life was apparently 'irretrievably shattered'.[52] While Lord Cadogan represents a more extreme example of punishment, his story does trace out the parameters within which John could have acted.[53] After all, several historians have claimed that a critical power of patriarchy was the power to punish subordinates.[54] Of course such punishments were not without cost, as the salacious details of the affairs were then broadcast before a gossip-hungry audience.

John acted with far greater restraint—and far greater discretion—than the embittered Lord Cadogan. John and Ann ended their marriage by private separation agreement, with a surprisingly generous settlement.[55] John allowed Ann a lifetime annuity of £1,200, just that which was to have come to her at

---

[50] See Stone, *Road to Divorce*, 149.
[51] She was granted a small annuity. Stone, *Broken Lives*, 270–9.   [52] Ibid. 275, 278.
[53] Ibid. 270–9. Indeed, the reason why Stone was able to detail the case of *Cadogan* v. *Cadogan* so well is because Lord Cadogan pursued his wife and her lover through several different legal settings. Naturally, the divorce cases extant will reveal those who did choose the harsher options, as the rest relied on options which left fewer, if any, official sources: abandonment or private agreements.
[54] Rhys Isaac has argued that the patriarch 'had it in his power to punish or pardon'. Isaac, *The Transformation of Virginia*, 345. One of Kathleen M. Brown's central defining characteristics of patriarchy is his 'right to punish family members and laborers'. Brown, *Good Wives, Nasty Wenches, and Anxious Patriarchs*, 4. Philip D. Morgan has agreed, contending: 'The power to judge, rebuke, and inflict punishment was the most awesome trust placed in the hands of a patriarch.' Morgan, *Slave Counterpoint*, 277.
[55] Deed of Seperation [sic] between John Tharp Esqr. and Ux, 20 Dec. 1800, R55.7.7.246, CCRO.

his death.[56] Ann also kept her paraphernalia.[57] He even paid his wife's debts of approximately £2,000.[58] The separation deed was conventional in all respects but one: Ann was forbidden ever to contact Richard.[59] Although John was generous to his wife, he was determined to end the liaison. Still, he could have done much more. Beyond pressing his daughter to separate from Richard, John also had at his disposal the possibility of a suit of 'criminal conversation' that allowed a cuckolded husband to pursue a writ of trespass for the 'seducer's' damage to the husband's property (that is, his wife). To punish Richard was not only John's prerogative but nearly his duty. Indeed, the code of honor required that he either challenge Richard to a duel or launch a suit against him.[60]

In March 1801 John was still pondering whether or not to press a crim. con. action against Richard. John knew that such a move would have disastrous consequences for his son-in-law. Not only would John likely have won such a case, but he also suspected that as soon as he took action, the Church of England would remove Richard from his clerical livings.[61] Yet he did not pursue a suit against Richard, instead drafting a legal separation for Eliza and her husband which provided her with a means of living independently from Richard if she chose.[62] The trustees never signed the deed, indicating that it was drafted only in the event that Eliza decided to leave Richard, which she did not. This deed declared that, in the event of their separation, Eliza would have custody of the children and that Richard would be required to provide half his annual income to them. Like Ann, Eliza and Richard were also beneficiaries of John's largesse. John had granted the young Phillipsons £10,000 at their marriage (with 5 per cent interest the longer the principal went unpaid) and another £10,000

---

[56] Marriage Settlement between John Tharp and Ann Gallimore, 1 Oct. 1794, R55.7.122.(j).12, CCRO. Ann retained the annuity after John's death as well. His will, drawn up in 1801, states: 'And after reciting that he did previous to his Marriage with his then wife Ann Tharp execute a Settlement of £1200 per Annum Jamaica Currency on her during her life in the Event of her surviving him, in lieu of Dower, and she having by her conduct rendered herself unworthy of his regard He did not add in any manner to the said Settlement but merely confirmed the same.' See John Tharp, 'Abstract of the Will and Codicil of John Tharp Esqr.', R55.7.20.13, CCRO.

[57] Given her status, her personal effects would have been ample. Consider, for example, that in 1796 John Tharp paid £36. 8s. 0d. for her stockings alone (while, by comparison, the annual salary for their nursemaid for Sarah was £14. 14s. 0d.). See John Tharp's Account Book: Expenses in Cambs and London, Dec. 1795–July 1797, R55.7.8.7, CCRO.

[58] John Tharp (sr.) to John Tharp (jr.), 'Chippenham Park 28th June 1801', R55.7.22(a), CCRO.

[59] The deed declared that: 'if at any time...Ann Tharp...shall visit or permit the said Richard Burton Phillipson to visit her...the said Bond...shall immediately...become absolutely null and void...as if the said Ann Tharp had then actually departed this life.' 'Deed of Seperation [sic]'.

[60] Stone, *Road to Divorce*, 237–41.

[61] John Tharp to Simon Taylor, 'No 41 Portland Place 1th March 1801', XIX/A/10, Simon Taylor Papers, ICS.

[62] The marriage agreement for Eliza and Richard dates from 29 April 1797, although they were not married until 17 May 1797. Their separation agreement was signed on 28 April 1801. Deed of Separation for Eliza and Richard Phillipson, 28th Apr. 1801, R55.7.7.248, CCRO.

at his death.⁶³ John had been paying off the interest and part of the principal from 1797 to 1801, so that some £8,380 remained due to the Phillipsons. John could have tried to avoid paying the remainder, but he did not. Rather, in January 1801 John Tharp paid off the remaining £8,380; in fact, John, who was property-rich but sometimes cash-poor, had to borrow £7,000 to liquidate not only his wife's debts but also the money owed to the Phillipsons, along with a final payment for the house the Phillipsons had built.⁶⁴ John did revoke the £10,000 promised to the Phillipsons at his death.⁶⁵ In addition, apparently, John was not as generous to the couple as he had intended to be, but, as he wrote his son, 'there are certain situations when the innocent must suffer with the guilty, & hers, poor Woman, was one of these'.⁶⁶ Still, all told, John left the couple in fine financial form.

Therefore, although John held significant legal and financial leverage over both Ann and Richard, overall he chose not to exercise it. He drew up a private separation agreement with Ann and allowed her to retain a generous annuity. He even stayed in touch with her. Rather than taking Richard to court on a crim. con. action, John let him be. He drafted a legal separation for the couple, but, despite his own feelings about Richard, did not demand that his daughter leave him. John effectively did not punish either his wife or his son-in-law, allowing them both to live on his money, virtually unruffled by the scandal. How, then, to explain John's apparent clemency? What reasons did John himself give for his decisions? In 1801 he penned a remarkable letter to Simon Taylor, alerting him to the horror of his situation and detailing his course of action. He assured Taylor that: 'If Ever I wanted such a Friend as you are, it is upon so trying an occasion.' John felt that he faced two separate but related challenges: one concerning his wife, and another relating to his son-in-law.⁶⁷ That this affair so twisted his family authority, in that the interloper to his bed was his son-in-law

---

⁶³ Marriage Agreement between Eliza Tharp and Richard Burton Burton Phillipson, 29 Apr. 1797, R55.7.7.246, CCRO.

⁶⁴ Ibid. See also John Tharp (sr.) to John Tharp (jr.), 'Chippenham Park 28th June 1801', R55.7.22(a) CCRO. In this context, for this family, 'cash-poor' is a highly relative term; they were extremely rich. However, John Tharp was often forced to borrow money, as many West Indian planters were, to cover the exigencies that arose from Jamaican properties (and, in his case, from family catastrophe).

⁶⁵ His will states: 'And in Case his Daughter Eliza Partridge Phillipson should find it expedient to live separate and apart from her husband Richard Burton Burton Phillipson he gave and devised to her during such separation an Annuity of £300 Sterling ... not to be subject to the debts or controul of her said husband.' See John Tharp, 'Abstract of the Will and Codicil of John Tharp Esqr.', R55.7.20.13, CCRO.

⁶⁶ John Tharp (sr.) to John Tharp (jr.), 'Good Hope 19th July 1803', R55.7.22(a), CCRO.

⁶⁷ Both John Tharp and Simon Taylor were among the richest of Jamaican planters. Simon Taylor, for instance, was described by Lady Maria Nugent in her famous diary as 'the richest man in the island' (entry for 5 Mar. 1802). Frank Cundal (ed.), *Lady Nugent's Journal: Jamaica One Hundred Years Ago* (London: Adam & Charles Black for the Institute of Jamaica, 1907), 88. Historians have agreed with that assessment. See R. B. Sheridan, 'Simon Taylor, Sugar Tycoon of Jamaica, 1740–1813', *Agricultural History*, 45 (1971), 285–96.

and father to his grandchildren, left John in a deeply awkward position. So agonized was John that he declared that it had 'destroyed what little health I had', and threatened to annihilate his very 'Senses'. He dealt first with his wife. He acknowledged sheepishly that he had allowed Ann to retain her marital annuity, and gave his reasons for doing so: 'considering that I brought her to a strange Country that her disposition & manners had not secured one Single Friend, & feeling a pride that she should not be drawn to follow so infamous a practice for want of support'.[68] The last of these reasons was the most practical: John wanted her to avoid bringing further infamy on the Tharp name by turning to her former lover for assistance. Even the pragmatic Taylor approved of John's plan: 'When I first heard she had asked and you had . . . settled the £1200 p[er] ann[um] on her I thought it was infinitely more than she had merited but on cool reflection and Deliberation I think it is better that you have done so as she cannot plead that she was forced by Indigence to throw herself into his hands.'[69] Ann had evidently *asked* for the annuity—and had been successful in her request.

The other two reasons enumerated by John do not sit well with other evidence about Ann. For an elite Jamaican like Ann, England was not necessarily all that 'strange', particularly when many compatriots were educated there. Moreover, she remained in England after the demise of her marriage, indicating that she was not especially pining for Jamaica. Still, John apparently harbored some guilt at having brought her to England, or so he wanted Taylor to think. John's claim that Ann's disposition had not won her a single friend also seems incongruous, as later letters indicate a vibrant social circle. Nevertheless, John, either believing it to be so or trying to justify himself to his unsentimental, and unmarried, friend, emphasized her alienation and solitude. No such sympathy emanated from John about his errant son-in-law. He noted that his wife's annuity depended on her never again seeing 'my blasted Son in Law'. Moreover, he was evidently consulting his lawyers about how best to punish Richard's 'intricate . . . piece of Villainy'. To placate the outraged John, Richard had apparently offered to settle his church and family income on Eliza and the three children. John huffed that he would 'despise' this offer if only Eliza would leave Richard: 'but she is absorbed in this Man, notwithstanding his treatment . . . she declares to me if she leaves him she must die, & although I might provide for her & her Family again, yet upon her knee she Entreats I will take no steps against him, that my whole Fortune cannot make her happy, separated from him, & if I mean to kill her I must commence an action for CrimCon.'[70] Eliza, deploying the language of sympathy, thus attempted to avert a crim. con. suit against Richard. This

---

[68] John Tharp to Simon Taylor, 'No 41 Portland Place 1th March 1801', XIX/A/10, Simon Taylor Papers, ICS.
[69] Simon Taylor to John Tharp, 'Kingston Jamaica May 14. 1801', I/D/63, ibid.
[70] John Tharp to Simon Taylor, 'No 41 Portland Place 1th March 1801', XIX/A/10, ibid.

situation echoed a classic moment in which a distressed daughter fell to her knees to plead her cause to her father: that portrayed in Richardson's *Clarissa*. Clarissa reported to her friend Anna Howe the scene in which she attempted to appeal to her father not to force her into marriage: 'I trembled; I was ready to sink... Oh my papa!—my dear papa, said I, falling upon my knees, at the door—admit your child into your presence!—Let me but plead my cause at your feet!—Oh reprobate not thus your distressed daughter!'[71] Eliza was hardly the only daughter to follow suit, as Rhys Isaac has detailed.[72] Many fictional and historical daughters pleaded with fathers in similar ways, and they were, as in Eliza's case, more successful than Clarissa.

John summarized his dilemma thus: 'what a situation am I in, my honor in one side, & my poor Childs comfort & existence in the other.' Two visions of good fatherhood collided. In an older ideal, the good father protected the honor of his family in whatever ways he could. Reputation was vital, and punishment, whether duel or lawsuit, was requisite. In a different conception of fatherhood, the good father hearkened to his lovesick daughter and allowed his reputation to suffer to protect her, because it was more important to be a man of feeling than a man of honor. John also conveyed to Simon his concern for his grandchildren. In a decade in which damages in crim. con. suits were very high, John feared that his son-in-law might flee into exile and abandon his grandchildren: 'for if I press this rascal he is prepared to retire abroad by selling all he can, & leave not a trace but his villainy behind—I shall in that case... bring my Child & Grand Children in the ruins.'[73] John had to choose between two ways of sheltering his family. In the end, he opted for his 'poor Childs comfort & existence'. Enlightening as John's letter to Simon Taylor is, it cannot entirely explain why he acted as he did. What other reasons exist?

John was an 'old husband'.[74] As Rowlandson's print implies, there was a cultural trope of the old cuckold. John had breached unspoken norms in marrying Ann, and to many he had reaped what he had sown. Simon Taylor wrote to his sister-in-law with considerable smugness about the Tharp scandal: 'It must serve as a lesson to me never to think of marrying a young Girl for tho I am past one Period of my life when People fall in Love I am approaching another namely Sixty four when old Men marry their Cookmaids but I hope I

---

[71] Clarissa Harlowe to Anna Howe, 'Tuesday Evening; and continued thro' the night', letter XXXI (78), Richardson, *Clarissa*, ii. 197.
[72] See Isaac, *Landon Carter's Uneasy Kingdom*, ch 3.
[73] John Tharp to Simon Taylor, 'No 41 Portland Place 1th March 1801', XIX/A/10, Simon Taylor Papers, ICS. Stone elaborates on a trend in the 1790s in which accused men fled into exile on the continent before crim. con damages could be levied. See Stone, *Road to Divorce*, 284.
[74] Historians who have pursued a microhistorical focus have often emphasized the importance of life-cycle. Classic examples include Laurel Thatcher Ulrich, *A Midwife's Tale: The Life of Martha Ballard, Based on Her Diary, 1785–1812* (New York: Knopf, 1990), and Young, *The Shoemaker and the Tea Party*.

shall avoid that Piece of folly or rather Insanity.'[75] Taylor was using this 'lesson' as a warning to his sister-in-law, whose son was heir-apparent to Taylor's vast fortunes, that she should not be too complacent about the money going to her son. But Taylor never did marry his cookmaid; rather, he remained as a partner to his free Afro-Jamaican housekeeper, with whom he lived for twenty-seven years. John Tharp had also had at least one lover in between his two marriages. These two Jamaican planters had taken two different routes. Taylor was satisfied that in avoiding marriage he had chosen the right one; many Anglo-Jamaican men would have agreed. John, in going so far as to marry this young Anglo-Jamaican woman, had brought only grief to himself and his family: an old man's folly.

Joseph Brissett also blamed age for his uncle's troubles. Brissett insinuated that his uncle had lost the powers he had once possessed. In his time in England, Brissett claimed he had long suspected Richard's nature. Perhaps trying to justify his own complicity, Brissett marveled at his uncle's inability to discern Phillipson's true character: 'Your eyes used to be clear enough in penetrating the Conduct, and deciphering the actions of mankind—and I used to wonder how you could be so blind to all that which appeared as bright as day to others.'[76] How can a man have grown so blind as not to see his wife's dalliance with her own stepson-in-law? Had he, unlike those around him, not glimpsed the shared glances or heard the whispers in the corridors? Had John, unwilling to think ill of his daughter's choice of husband, overlooked Phillipson's 'impious witticisms & loose jests', which Brissett at least 'knew could come from nothing but a corrupt heart'? Brissett drew the lesson that his uncle had lost the power to read 'the actions of mankind.'

The self-serving and patronizing attitudes of both Simon Taylor and Joseph Brissett do not, of course, quite tell the whole story. It is not merely that the ageing husband had lost the power to retain his wife's affections or to discern the true character of her alleged seducer. His age might help to explain why he behaved as he did, once the affair came to light. In 1795 John Tharp had left Jamaica for England, to settle permanently in his new estate of Chippenham House, in Cambridgeshire. In 1797 John related to Simon Taylor: 'When I left Jamaica in 1795 I was in hopes that all my troubles were at an End, & that I was to set down at my Cambridgeshire Farm in peace & quiet for the rest of my days.' Such was his retirement plan, but events conspired against him. As he himself noted: 'but man appoints & God disappoints, for they were then beginning to cloud over my head, & I have had no peace or quiet since.'[77] John had left Jamaica in 1795 in order to escape the challenges of overseeing estates in Jamaica.

---

[75] Simon Taylor to Lady Taylor, 'Kingston Jamaica March 10. 1801', I/D/50, Simon Taylor Papers, ICS. John was probably born in 1744, Simon Taylor in 1740.
[76] Joseph Brissett to John Tharp, 'March 10th 1801 Lucia', R55.7.128(c), CCRO.
[77] John Tharp to Simon Taylor, 'Bath 8th June 1797', XIX/A/9, Simon Taylor Papers, ICS.

When his marriage crumbled, he continued to harbor a desire to relinquish his former control. When the affair between Ann and Richard first came to light, John had escaped to his London house in Portland Place.⁷⁸ But London was not far enough away for his tastes. John informed Taylor: 'I . . . am determined, as soon as I can get over this horrid business, to seek comfort & safety in Jamaica.'⁷⁹ Despite his retirement plan, then, John evidently felt that his native Jamaica ultimately offered the greatest possibility for 'comfort & safety'. Perhaps amid his slaves, and with the warm breezes wafting through the Palladian windows of Good Hope Estate, he could find the kind of succor for which he yearned.

So, in 1802 John Tharp returned permanently to Good Hope to nurse his gout and his grievances.⁸⁰ However, his own desire always to 'be doing something' meant that even his retirement was not exactly restful. Several months after his arrival, he ruefully reported to his son in England: 'my health continues mending, & if my anxiety to be seeing after my own concerns did not lead me too often into what I call Excess. I possibly would have less gout, but I do not . . . instead of indulging in bed & nursing my formidable Foe, I must crawl on Horseback & be doing something—The Negroes have a forcible expression for such zeal & Exertion, they say Mamma bring me so.'⁸¹ Deploying the Creole expression to describe his character, John was perhaps regretful that his own desire 'to be seeing after [his] own concerns' had in part spelled disaster for his marriage. Regardless, hoisting his gouty form onto the back of a horse, he could not stop himself from attempting to 'be doing something'. Yet, exhausted and ill, he could not do very much. In what seems a remarkable, if classic, statement of paternalist fiction-making, John, on his return to Good Hope in 1802, grumbled to his son: 'My Negroes have increased & are very happy, they kill me with their constant visits & attentions—it gives pleasure, though I am fatigued to death before the day is half gone, for I must talk & shake hands with Every one of them.'⁸² John was too infirm and tired even to shake hands with his slaves, let alone watch them, criticize them, or punish them as he surely once had. Notwithstanding his 'anxiety to be seeing after [his] own concerns', he was forced, by age and incapacity, to relinquish the careful control that he had long practised on his Jamaican estates. He basked instead in the belief that his slaves were happily flourishing.

Yet he felt he could not return to the quieter life of Chippenham Park in Cambridgeshire. He confessed to his son: 'I should return to England with some

---

⁷⁸ The Marylebone area was one of the many neighborhoods in London in which West Indians clustered. See O'Shaughnessy, *An Empire Divided*, 11.
⁷⁹ John Tharp to Simon Taylor, 'No 41 Portland Place 1th March 1801', XIX/A/10, Simon Taylor Papers, ICS.
⁸⁰ John Tharp arrived to Jamaica in July 1802. See John Tharp (sr.) to John Tharp (jr.), 'Good Hope 8t July 1802', R55.7.22(a), CCRO.
⁸¹ John Tharp (sr.) to John Tharp (jr.), 'Good Hope 3d Octr 1802', ibid.
⁸² John Tharp (sr.) to John Tharp (jr.), 'Good Hope 8t July 1802', ibid.

pleasure if that worthy p[arso]n was no more. I must confess whilst he is so near a Neighbour many joys would be dampted, & I trust his own mind & the disorder he labours under will soon drive him to feel those smarts he has inflicted upon others.'[83] Rather than making Richard quit the area, John was willing to step aside and leave the country. John did not want to exert the powers he had as a younger man; willing not to take direct responsibility for his slaves, he was also willing to leave Richard's life intact. His age thus helps to explain his behavior, although it is only one factor in a larger set of choices. In fact, John's health *was* failing, and he died a mere two years later, on the Good Hope Estate. He was the consummate old husband.

Another factor that may help to explain John's response is the particular sexual environment of Jamaica. Anglo-Jamaican male planters were notorious even at the time for their illicit relationships with the Afro-Jamaican women who surrounded them. Lacking sources, historians have generally said little about the sexuality of Anglo-Jamaican women.[84] One of the few historians to have addressed the issue has posited that these women were victims of a harsh double standard in which their own sexuality was repressed. Anglo-Jamaican men, preoccupied with sexual liaisons with Afro-Jamaican women, supposedly cast Anglo-Jamaican women as models of modest virtue who could safely be ignored.[85] Numerous contemporaries noted the ubiquity of relationships between Anglo-Jamaican men and Afro-Jamaican women.[86] Indeed, as early as 1760 the Jamaican assembly passed a law limiting the amount of property that could be bequeathed to Afro-Jamaican female partners and their offspring. Visitors to Jamaica were struck quickly and forcefully by the presence of such liaisons. Lady Maria Nugent wrote in her diary of men like Simon Taylor, who allegedly had numerous such children. For example, Nugent related being introduced to 'a little mulatto girl ... Mr. T[aylor]. appeared very anxious for me to dismiss her, and in the evening, the housekeeper told me she was his own daughter, and that he had a numerous family'.[87] Less well-known commentators, like

---

[83] John Tharp (sr.) to John Tharp (jr.), 'Good Hope 3d Octr 1802', R55.7.22(a), CCRO.

[84] Trevor Burnard, Douglas D. Hall, and Philip D. Morgan have all devoted attention to Thomas Thistlewood, a white planter whose sexual exploits with slave women were unceasing and numerous. See Hall, *In Miserable Slavery*, Burnard, *Mastery, Tyranny, and Desire*, and Philip D. Morgan, 'Interracial Sex in the Chesapeake and the British Atlantic World, c. 1700–1820', in Jan Ellen Lewis and Peter S. Onuf (eds.), *Sally Hemings and Thomas Jefferson: History, Memory, and Civic Culture* (Charlottesville, Va.: University Press of Virginia, 1999), 52–84.

[85] Trevor Burnard maintains: 'the sexuality of white women was fiercely protected ... Men actively employed a double standard of morality ... Safely fixed on their pedestals, [white] women could then be ignored by white men.' Burnard, 'Inheritance and Independence', 111–12.

[86] Indeed, surveying the literature of the eighteenth-century theater, Maaja A. Stewart has concluded: 'images of adultery, bigamy, incest, and illegitimacy appear compulsively in the eighteenth-century narratives about the West Indies.' Maaja A. Stewart, 'Inexhaustible Generosity: The Fictions of Eighteenth-Century British Imperialism in Richard Cumberland's *The West Indian*', *The Eighteenth Century*, 37 (1996), 42–55, at 46.

[87] Maria Nugent, *Lady Nugent's Journal*, 93. The entry was dated 10 Mar. 1802.

Christopher Ellery from Rhode Island, also remarked on his disgust at the way that Afro-Jamaican women were 'Furbelow'd of, and treated with . . . Fondness' by Anglo-Jamaican men.[88]

Even contemporary apologists for the West Indies and its slave system remarked on these unions. In his history of the West Indies, Bryan Edwards observed that the universal system of Anglo-Jamaican men taking mistresses of color was 'too notorious to be concealed or controverted'.[89] Edwards continued: 'the conduct of many of the Whites in this respect, is a violation of all decency.'[90] Of the general population of whites, Edwards conceded that: 'the climate undoubtedly encourages . . . early and habitual licentiousness.'[91] Despite lauding white Creole men in general, fellow historian Edward Long also shared this view: 'with a strong natural propensity to the other sex, they are not always the most chaste and faithful of husbands.'[92] Like Edwards, he also noted the general sexual licence, remarking that Jamaica was 'a place where, by custom, so little restraint is laid on the passions, the Europeans who at home have always been used to greater purity . . . are too easily led . . . to every kind of sensual delight'.[93] Yet Long also remarked on a feature of Jamaican life about which later historians have tended to remain silent: that Anglo-Jamaican women also transgressed sexually. After praising white Creole women, Long conceded: 'And, if we consider how forcibly the warmth of this climate must co-operate with natural instinct to rouze the passions, we ought to regard chastity here as no mean effort of female fortitude; or, at least, judge not too rigidly of those lapses which happen through the venial frailty and weakness of human nature.'[94] Perhaps John Tharp agreed with Long that sexual lapses by Creole women should be forgiven.

The less constrained sexual system of Jamaica, and John's own fathering of an illegitimate daughter, might have also persuaded John to forgive Ann for her own slips, as egregious as many might have believed them to be. While not forgiving the lapses of his son 'Colonel Tom', he nevertheless tolerated even more scandalous sexual behavior. Not only did Tom elope and run away to Jamaica, against his father's wishes, but once there he apparently was notorious for sexual activity with other men. John Tharp informed his other son: 'I do not hear a good account of him, it is said he tipples with low Company, & leaves? his bed hot with the perfumes of Arabia—If this be true you should try & correct such a disgraceful & most abominable practice.' This was a reference to Tobias Smollett's novel, *The Adventures of Roderick Random*, in which the foppish Captain Whiffle, who apparently engaged in a relationship with the ship's surgeon 'not fit to be named', appeared 'surrounded with a crowd of attendants, all of whom . . . seemed to be of their patron's disposition; and the air

---

[88] Christopher Ellery to Mary Ellery, 'Kingston Jamaica [1765?]', Folder 2, Box 62, NHS.
[89] Edwards, *The History*, ii. 22.   [90] Ibid.   [91] Ibid.
[92] Long, *History of Jamaica*, ii. 265.   [93] Ibid. ii. 328.
[94] Ibid. ii. 283. According to Wylie Sypher, this notion was echoed in eighteenth-century literary narratives about West Indians. Sypher, 'The West Indian as a "Character"', *passim*.

was so impregnated with perfumes, that one may venture to affirm the clime of Arabia'.[95] John's use of the word 'abominable' provides further evidence for the nature of Tom's activities. But John Tharp was as much, if not more, disturbed by the fact that Tom was squandering his fortune, and tippling in low company. He hardly condoned Tom's sexual dalliances. On the other hand, he did little to end them.

John's lenient response to Ann's own 'venial frailty', in conjunction with Long's remarks, undermines the traditional view of Jamaica's sexual milieu and suggests that Anglo-Jamaican women may have done more than just loll on their settees. Such a notion finds further support from the fact that Ann was able to survive this scandal with social networks intact. Her later letters make mention of considerable socializing, especially within colonial (both West Indian and Indian) circles. Although her separation from her husband was common knowledge, she nonetheless maintained connections with several acquaintances. In 1802 she mentioned her visit with Mr Shirley, whose house contained: 'a variety of Ladies... <u>Blacks</u>, <u>Browns</u>, <u>Straw Colour</u> & <u>White</u>.'[96] Ann visited Mr Barrett, a friend of her brother's and a member of the Anglo-Jamaican family depicted in Thomas Lawrence's portrait of 'Pinkie'.[97] She complained about the pompous young Barrett: 'I could not listen to his Conversation with any degree of patience to hear a <u>little</u> half grown lad of <u>Seventeen</u> telling of his intended Marriage with more ease & self Consequence than a <u>Man</u> would have done.'[98] In the summer of 1804 Ann wrote to John from the Hertfordshire home of her friends Major and Mrs Shaw, whose 'house is uncommonly agreeable & the Company genteel People mostly from India'.[99] Ann's continued social life, in conjunction with the statements of Long and Edwards, support the notion that Anglo-Jamaican women should not be dismissed so readily as passive victims of a double standard.

Ann's ability to remain part of English social circles shows, too, the benefits to all concerned of not having the case dragged through the courts. As John's remarks about his annuity settlement with Ann suggest, he was concerned

---

[95] Tobias George Smollett, *The Adventures of Roderick Random*, 2 vols. (London, 1748), i. 312, 306. I am grateful to Evan Davis for helping me with this reference. For a discussion of the circulation of this book in Philadelphia, see Clare A. Lyons, 'Mapping an Atlantic Sexual Culture: Homoeroticism in Eighteenth-Century Philadelphia', *William and Mary Quarterly*, 60 (2003), 119–54.

[96] Ann Tharp to William Green, 'Lisson Grove 2nd. June 1803', R55.7.128(a), CCRO.

[97] Edward Barrett was Pinkie's brother, and was later father to one Elizabeth Barrett Browning. Thomas Lawrence, *Sarah Barrett Moulton: Pinkie*, 1794. The painting is in the possession of HL.

[98] Ann Tharp to William Green, 'No 8 Lisson Grove New Road', undated but postmarked 25 Oct. 1803, R55.7.128(a), CCRO.

[99] Ann Tharp and Sarah Gallimore to John Tharp, 'South water July 6th. 1804', R55.7.128(a)*, CCRO. Indeed, evidence suggests that Ann Tharp remarried an Englishman, John Ratcliffe Parnell, on 3 September 1805 in Upton Helions, Devon, going on to live a rural domestic life, and giving birth to seven further children (seemingly never returning to Jamaica, although she bequeathed Jamaican estates to her sons). Many thanks to Graham Parnell for this information.

not to add to the 'infamy' that already attended the scandal. John probably did not pursue a public separation action, much less a parliamentary divorce, because he did not want to spill out the family secrets, his own possible failures as a husband and his own illegitimate child, before an audience of gossipmongers. John wanted to maintain some semblance of the life of an English gentleman and not provide greater fuel for the flames of infamy associated with Jamaican planters. In 1795 John had been eager to retire, perhaps, but he had wanted to retire not as a colonial upstart, but as a member of the English landed gentry.

John's ambitions in England were considerable. Or, as a contemporary poet wrote of West Indian planters who returned to Britain: 'He who has made an independence here, | At home in splendour hurries to appear.'[100] Like other West Indians before him, John wanted to live the life of the English elite.[101] In 1792 he paid £40,000 for the Chippenham estate and its lavish orchards and hunting grounds. In 1796–7 he paid another £3,000 to renovate his London home.[102] In 1799 he also began an extensive renovation project on Chippenham estate. This manor house was spacious and well furnished, containing thirty rooms, while a well-furnished 'Farm-House' (closer to a guest house than a barn) contained another fifteen. The main drawing-room contained '8 Japan'd Arm Chairs, with Cushions & printed Callico Covers lined', assorted mahogany tables, cabinets, bookstands, an 'elegant Time Piece of Stogarts', a 'Patent Grande Piano Forte', 'Three Silver . . . Urns', and assorted other furnishings. On the bookshelves of his estate were Hume's *History of England*, a ten-volume *Encyclopaedia*, and other books of an educated English gentleman. Hanging on his walls were 'a set of 4 small drawings of Raphael [of] Justice, Philosophy, Divinity, & Poetry', along with copies of paintings by Carlo Dolce and Guido, pictures that reflect a standard, if not especially adventurous, gentry aesthetic.[103] John Tharp did not obliterate his West Indian past: indeed, also hanging on his walls were 'a Negro dance' as well as plans for the Good Hope Estate and Windsor and Top Hill Pens in Jamaica. Nonetheless, he demonstrated to visitors that he had

---

[100] Captain Majoribank, *Slavery* (1792), as quoted in Sypher, 'The West-Indian as a "Character"', 519.

[101] O'Shaughnessy mentions that 'West Indians possessed impressive landed estates, which adorned the British countryside'. He cites such estates as Harwood House (Yorks.), Dodington Hall (Glos.), Standlynch (Wilts.), and Fonthill Splendens (Wilts.) as examples. O'Shaughnessy, *An Empire Divided*, 11.

[102] From 1796 to 1797 John carried out a complete overhaul of the Portman Square house. Some of the tasks completed included: 'Repairing Very rich Ornament Ceiling to Sattin Room & putting Sundry New Leaves &c Very Rich frieze & Cornice' and 'Gilding a Rich Glass frame in Burnish'd Gold in Music Room'. He paid £3036. 7s. 0d. altogether. See 'John Tharp Esqr to John Tasker For Sundry Business's Done at his House Portman Sqr. from May 1796 to Feby 1797', R55.7.101.1, CCRO.

[103] See 'Plans of extensions to Chippenham Hall and description of its surroundings', 1799, R55.14.1, CCRO. Many thanks to Kate Retford for her help on these questions of art history.

moved beyond the rough colonial world of Jamaica.[104] John wanted to succeed not only in Jamaica, but also in social circles of the metropolis. Why jeopardize these ambitions, for his children and for himself, by making a public case out of a private catastrophe? Even though John ended up returning to Jamaica, he did not want to endanger the chances for his children and grandchildren to become fully fledged members of the British elite. Indeed, John Tharp's oldest son had married Lady Susan Murray, daughter of the Earl of Dunmore.[105] John's grandson, John, would later marry a Scottish aristocrat. John's strategy, to protect the long-term reputation of the family by not dragging the case through court, overrode his worries about punishing his wife or his son-in-law.

John's leniency is surprising, especially when considered against the 'patriarchal anxiety' that historians have identified for the mainland colonies. They have attributed much of the anxiety of such patriarchs to their sense of colonial inferiority to the metropolis.[106] But for John, the way to gain metropolitan respectability was to keep the scandal quiet and to behave as befitted a man familiar with norms of metropolitan respectability. The era of John's decision to join the English landed gentry coincided exactly with a decade which witnessed the greatest concerns over Britain's participation in the slave trade: the 1790s. John did not want his family tarnished with the stereotypes of lawless bashaws and unbridled sexuality, especially during a period in which West Indian moralities were increasingly being scrutinized. The way to overcome his colonial vulnerability was not to exercise revenge and rage, but instead to minimize the shock of the scandal.

John's response and his ambitions trace out the useful distinctions that can be drawn between mainland, particularly Virginian, and West Indian ambitions and identities. Rich Anglo-Jamaicans were always closer than mainland colonials such as William Byrd to attaining the grandest heights of metropolitan society. The reasons for this situation are many, but two are worth highlighting. First, Jamaicans tended far to surpass mainland colonials in terms of wealth; after all, how many mainland planters died, as John did, with estates worth £362,262. 19*s*. 11*d*? Second, Jamaicans invested less in their home environment, especially by the later eighteenth century, and thereby remained more integrated in metropolitan society.[107] Anglo-Jamaicans invested far more in a British identity and ideals

---

[104] In this, John Tharp mirrors many of the merchants who sought the trappings of rich respectability as profiled in David Hancock, *Citizens of the World*, chs. 9–10, esp. the section on 'Art Collections', pp. 347–75.

[105] According to *Alumni Cantabrigienses*, Joseph Tharp, John's eldest son, married Lady Susan Murray, third daughter of the Earl of Dunmore, on 7 July 1788. Venn, *Alumni Cantabrigienses*, vi. 147.

[106] Brown, *Good Wives, Nasty Wenches, and Anxious Patriarchs*, 319 and Lockridge, *On the Sources of Patriarchal Rage*, 101.

[107] John Tharp's estate was valued at his death at £362,262. 19*s*. 11*d*. See 'Will with 3 codicils John Tharp Esqr, 1801–1804', R84/29, CCRO. O'Shaughnessy has fruitfully explored the contrast in wealth and in metropolitan education between the mainland and West Indian colonies, finding

than mainland Anglo-Americans. Thus, John's colonial fretfulness took the form of normalizing and quieting the affair, and keeping open the possibility of social advancement in English society for his descendants. Thus, his response to this private family scandal must be placed within a larger colonial context.

John wanted to demonstrate to the world that he was no 'West-India tyrant', but he was equally concerned to nurture a *self-image* as a forgiving and kind husband and father. Too few historians, especially those of the West Indies, have acknowledged the ways in which this newer discourse of sensibility offered opportunities for subordinates to temper the authority of the family master. Just as John was eager to believe that his slaves were 'very happy', so too was he concerned to live out a fiction of a happy family, even when evidence plainly declared otherwise.[108] John Tharp's response to these convoluted family affairs highlights the increasing prevalence of sensibility, even in Jamaica.[109] His wife and his daughter were both able to exploit his desire to be the good, sensible man, and they thus gained leverage in a situation in which they were legally and economically disadvantaged.

Men like John Tharp found new models for behavior in moral philosophy, in magazines, and in novels, even as older ways of acting remained in currency. In his fury at Richard, John invoked a more famous cleric gone wrong in a letter to his son: 'if the Devil had him on the precipice as he had Ambrosio in The Monk, it would be lenity to his deserts.'[110] John's familiarity with Matthew Lewis's *The Monk* provides insight into the way that this new language of sentiment, present in the novel, informed his behavior. Throughout the novel the refusal to forgive sins of the flesh signals the evil nature of certain characters.[111] In the world of

---

that, for example, far more West Indians than mainland Americans attended elite British schools, owned British estates, and generally involved themselves in British life. For instance, from 1753 to 1776 the number of Jamaicans at Eton was more than double that of all thirteen mainland colonies *combined*. The presence of these boys in these elite institutions suggests that they were far closer to achieving the metropolitan idea and more desirous of doing so. O'Shaughnessy, *An Empire Divided*, 19–27.

[108] John Tharp (sr.) to John Tharp (jr.), 'Good Hope 8t July 1802', R55.7.22(a), CCRO.

[109] Addressing a slightly earlier era, the mid- to late eighteenth century, Trevor Burnard has stressed that 'the paternalistic notions infusing planter-thinking in America were absent in the Caribbean'. Burnard, 'Family Continuity', 194. More recently, he has noted that 'this shift from patriarchy to paternalism had not occurred in Thistlewood's Jamaica'. Burnard, 'Theater of Terror', 241. These findings suggest that cultures of sensibility made their greatest inroads in Jamaica in the late eighteenth and early nineteenth centuries, and perhaps in part due to the movements of wealthier Anglo-Jamaicans such as John Tharp.

[110] John Tharp (sr.) to John Tharp (jr.), 'No. 41 Portland Place 13th Decbr 1801', R55.7.22(a), CCRO. John may have been remembering the scene in which the Devil taunts Ambrosio: 'Tremble, abandoned hypocrite! . . . incestuous ravisher! tremble at the extent of your offences!' Lewis, *The Monk*, iii. 310. 'Monk' Lewis was himself an Anglo-Jamaican planter. See D. L. MacDonald, *Monk Lewis: A Critical Biography* (Toronto, Ont.: University of Toronto Press, 2000).

[111] The most obvious examples are Ambrosio, the seemingly virtuous monk, who refused to forgive the nun Agnes for her trysts with her lover Raymond. His manifest failure of sympathy serves as an omen for the true, and depraved, nature of his character. Equally, Lewis paints the prioress of the St Clare's as desperately cruel for her refusal to forgive Agnes for her illicit pregnancy.

The Monk, truly good people exhibited forgiveness and sympathy. The novel, and John's awareness of it, gesture towards a newer mode of personal relations, in which sensibility and sentiment were paramount. That Anglo-Jamaicans wrote and read this book suggests that this cultural trend at least made an appearance in that most brutal of colonies.

This newer language of sensibility infused John's own writing, for example, even when he was most infuriated with his sons. John had ranted in a 1797 letter to Simon Taylor that the conduct of his son had almost driven him mad, yet he continued by referring to one son as 'my poor unfortunate youngest Son' and another as 'my Dear Joe', whom John claimed 'had a goodness of heart & honest principles'. Even his most willful son, Tom, was granted consideration. When Tom had proposed marrying a woman thought by his father to be unworthy, John had not forbidden the marriage outright. He recognized that his son had fallen 'in Love', and asked only that Tom wait to marry her until he had reached Jamaica. He thus 'told him if he continued in the same mind after he got to Jamaica, & coud not be happy without her, I woud then give my consent'. This declaration did not please the rebellious Tom, who 'married her privately in London' before embarking with her for Jamaica. What most irritated John was that he felt his son's disobedience demonstrated disrespect for his father, for 'a Child is dear when they behave properly, yet a parent ought in every case to be treated with respect'. To obtain the proper 'respect', while still treating those in his family as 'dear', was a delicate balancing act with which John was to become all too familiar.

In dealing with Ann after her manifest failure to show him 'respect', John continued in some regards to treat her as dear. In alerting Simon Taylor of Ann's behavior, he still noted that she was 'a Woman I doated on, & in whom my whole happiness centered'.[112] This statement is remarkable, especially considering that John was writing to a hard-hearted bachelor friend. John was well aware that a good, sympathetic husband doted on his wife and found his whole happiness in her. Even the tight-lipped Taylor acknowledged the force of Ann's power: 'she must have known that she was... wounding you in the most interesting feelings that a person can be susceptible off.'[113] Taylor later wrote to his own sister-in-law that: 'I am convinced it [the affair] must give Mr Tharp the highest uneasiness and Pain of Mind for I am convinced he was fond of her.'[114] Taylor was resolutely unromantic in all of his hundreds of surviving letters. For him to maintain that John was 'fond' of Ann was a considerable expression of feeling, although it sounds less dramatic than John's own.

John's continued fondness, along with a desire to play the sympathetic husband even when wounded, help to explain his clemency towards Ann, even after the

---

[112] John Tharp to Simon Taylor, 'No 41 Portland Place 1th March 1801', XIX/A/10, Simon Taylor Papers, ICS.
[113] Simon Taylor to John Tharp, 'Kingston Jamaica May 14. 1801', I/D/63, ibid.
[114] Simon Taylor to Lady Taylor, 'Kingston Jamaica March 10. 1801', I/D/50, ibid.

marriage fell apart. Far from casting Ann into darkness, John carried on a cordial epistolary relationship with her. She was aware of John's desire to play the good husband, and indeed even the good stepfather to her daughter. Examining Ann's letters provides a useful way to ascertain how women like her delicately negotiated within the constraints of their positions, pushing John into what might be termed more sensible modes of acting. For example, in her letters to William Green, Ann acknowledged friends and family frequently; she rarely brought them up in letters to John. Moreover, she explicitly lamented to John: 'I stand so Compleatly alone that I am obliged to act & think intirely for myself as yet I have Succeeded but in a few Years she [Sarah] will require an Abler head than mine to guide her properly.'[115] She was eager to convey how alone and needy she was, but she was equally eager to convey her endless sympathy towards him. To both William Green and John Tharp, Ann expressed her pity for John's unhealthy state. When Green was to see John again, Ann warned him: 'I daresay you will think Mr Tharp much altered he has had enough to torment him I feel more for his Situation than I can express.'[116] Ann skillfully combined an older language of deference (remarking on her need for an 'abler head', for example, and her helplessness) with the language of sensibility, in which appeals to affectionate ties were paramount.

Ann's concern for her daughter, Sarah Gallimore, explains her willingness to use vocabularies of sensibility herself, such as signing her 1804 letter to John with 'love [from] Your Most Affectionate Ann Tharp'.[117] In 1802 Ann advised William Green 'to advance a hundred more' beyond 'the 150 you allowed her to draw for yearly—as that Sum is not Sufficient to pay...expences'.[118] She instructed Green that all of Sarah's money should be placed in investment funds rather than in her Jamaican estate, as 'all Jamaica property is uncertain and as I have Educated my Girl to expectations'.[119] Ann also confided to Green: 'I shall require much more than my Income this year indeed I fear it will never be enough as my children Stands me in more than £150 P[e]r. Year.'[120] In 1803 she reminded Green that Sarah's 'Education is expensive & I expect as she grows older it will be the more so'.[121] Ann Tharp was a worried mother. She may also have been an extravagant one, but she consistently emphasized her maternal concerns in her letters to William Green and John Tharp. Despite the generous annuity, as well as her daughter's Jamaican properties inherited from Ann's first husband, Ann felt that she and her children would need more help in future. And

---

[115] Ann Tharp to John Tharp, '4 June 1804,' R55.7.128(a), CCRO.
[116] Ann Tharp to William Green, 'No 8 Lisson Grove New Road London, 5 May 1802,' ibid.
[117] Ann Tharp to John Tharp, '4 June 1804', ibid.
[118] Ann Tharp to William Green, 'No 8 Lisson Grove New Road 7 August 1802', ibid.
[119] Ann Tharp to William Green, 'No 8 Lisson Grove South 10th August 1804', ibid.
[120] Ann Tharp to William Green, 'No 8 Lisson Grove New Road 7 August 1802,' ibid.
[121] Ann Tharp to William Green, 'No 8 Lisson Grove New Road', undated but postmarked 25 Oct. 1803, ibid.

who better to provide it than the enormously wealthy and sympathetic husband and stepfather?

Another child was apparently also on Ann's mind. In her letters to Green she mentioned her 'Children'.[122] She also referred to Sarah as her 'Eldest Girl'.[123] Although no deed or Tharp family letter made mention of her illegitimate child, these guarded references in her letters indicate that she had given birth to a daughter by Richard.[124] Ann's hard bargaining and cautious attitude to Sarah's properties suggest that she was also working toward the future of this unmentionable daughter. Ann almost certainly received no support from Richard, but she was evidently hoping to raise this younger daughter to some sort of 'expectations' too. She hoped that her letters, and letters from Sarah to her stepfather, would play on John's self-image as the loving father and persuade him to offer assistance. In 1804, under her mother's watchful eye, Sarah Gallimore wrote to John Tharp, addressing her former stepfather as 'My dear Papa'. She prattled to him of her school holidays, of gossip, of the comings and goings of family friends. She signed the letter in the standard way of the time: from 'Your Affect[ionate] and Dutiful Daughter'. Ann Tharp added her own hand to this letter, assuring John that Sarah 'is grown a fine Genteel looking Girl'.[125] Ann pleaded that Sarah 'is just of an age that requires a constant watch . . . I shall feel greatly obliged & hope when you Come again to England you will be of service to her in many respects'.[126] It was Ann's fond hope that John would use his influence and money to launch Sarah Gallimore into life and an advantageous marriage. Such a hope was indeed a fond one, as John in fact left nothing to Sarah Gallimore (or Ann) in his will and seems to have provided no other assistance. Ann was not successful in this instance, but nonetheless her strategy in tying the older model of the ideal provider-father with that of the newer sensible father is clear.

Eliza Phillipson deployed this type of language with much greater success. John Tharp detested Richard. Yet he had left Richard alone—because of his daughter's appeal. If John was conversant with the language of novels, so too was Eliza. Going on her knees and simpering that without Richard she would die, she exploited the postures and language of sentiment for all they were worth.[127] Despite the separation agreement so carefully drafted for her and Richard, Eliza

---

[122] Ann Tharp to William Green, 'No 8 Lisson Grove New Road 7 August 1802', R55.7.128(a), CCRO.

[123] Ann Tharp to William Green, 'Lisson Grove 2nd. June 1803', ibid.

[124] An addendum to the Tharp family tree, constructed by the archivists at CCRO, suggests that Ann Tharp had an illegitimate son, but I believe she had a daughter, one possibly named Mary Ann Eliza (!) Tharp. This daughter is mentioned in a marriage announcement as 'youngest daughter of the late John Tharp, Esq. Of Chippenham Park, Cambridgeshire'. See 'Marriage Announcements', in the *Exeter Flying Post*, 19 Aug. 1824. Many thanks to James Evans for this reference.

[125] Ann Tharp and Sarah Gallimore to John Tharp, 'South water July 6th. 1804', R55.7.128(a)*, CCRO.

[126] Ibid.

[127] John Tharp to Simon Taylor, 'No 41 Portland Place 1th March 1801', XIX/A/10, Simon Taylor Papers, ICS.

never did leave her husband. When Richard died in 1826, she was an executrix to his will.[128] In the end, Richard benefited enormously from his wife's ability to persuade her father not to pursue his patriarchal privilege. In short, thanks to his doting wife and his father-in-law's clemency, the scoundrel got away with it.

Exactly why Eliza chose to advocate for and remain with her rakish husband will probably never be clear. Although in June 1801, her father reported that she did not seem especially happy with 'that beast her Husband', by August she had apparently improved in temper: 'Eliza is now with me, her spirits & looks are good, saying Every thing she can for her profligate Parson, & believes him no worse than Men in general.'[129] Whatever visions of masculinity Eliza had imbibed from her own family, her friends, and her reading, they were evidently not especially positive ones.[130] Perhaps that fact explains how she could bring herself to forgive her husband, who had not only slept with his stepmother-in-law, but who also apparently indulged in 'indelicate conversation & abandoned familiarity towards the Servants in his house'.[131] Part of the concerns about Richard arose from his illicit crossing of lines of familiarity. By December, John informed his son: 'when I left home your Sister was better than I have seen her since this time [last] year, the parson behaves tolerably well & they jog on as usual.'[132] It is possible that Eliza had a temporary revenge against Richard. According to John, Eliza refused to sleep with her husband: 'they have never yet bedded, & she declares she never will again, but the frailty of her Sex will, some day or other, unhinge those pious resolutions.'[133] Like Edward Long, John Tharp believed that women's 'frailty' meant that sexual desire could overcome piety. It is unclear how long Eliza's resolutions lasted, but the Phillipsons did have one more child, who must have been born after 1805.[134] Whatever her motives, Eliza had achieved what she wanted: to stay with her husband without subjecting him to a crim. con. suit brought by her father. She had successfully deployed the language of sentiment to obtain her wishes; Ann

---

[128] Will of Richard Burton Burton Phillipson, signed 7 July 1826, City of Bath, R84/44, CCRO.

[129] John Tharp (sr.) to John Tharp (jr.), 'Chippenham Park 28th June 1801', and same to same, 'Chippenham Park 9t Augt 1801', R55.7.22(a), CCRO.

[130] Many thanks to Michael Zuckerman, who vividly articulated this point in his comments on an earlier incarnation of this chapter.

[131] Or so Joseph Brissett claimed. Joseph Brissett to John Tharp, 'Barbary March 16th 1801', R55.7.128(c), CCRO.

[132] John Tharp (sr.) to John Tharp (jr.), 'No. 41 Portland Place 13th Decbr 1801', R55.7.22(a), CCRO.

[133] John Tharp (sr.) to John Tharp (jr.), 'Chippenham Park 9t Augt 1801', ibid.

[134] The daughter was named Mary Ann Burton Phillipson. In his July 1826 will, Richard Burton Burton Phillipson left a legacy to Mary Ann that was to be paid either when she married or reached the age of 21, thus suggesting that in 1826 she was not yet 21. Therefore, she has to have been born after July 1805, which was four-and-a-half years after the affair came to light. Will of Richard Burton Burton Phillipson, signed 7 July 1826, City of Bath, R84/44, CCRO. Considering that their first three children had been born in fairly rapid succession, it is possible that Eliza indeed maintained her resolutions for a few years at least.

Tharp tried to do the same. Their appeals to John's desire to play the sympathetic family man demonstrate one way Anglo-Jamaican women tempered the course of Anglo-Jamaican masculinity.

Was such use of this language of sensibility limited to the elite? Tantalizing clues from John Tharp's plantation, Good Hope, suggest that slaves too were able, at least very occasionally, to exploit new idioms of emotion.[135] Beyond the self-deception entailed in John's narrative about his happy slaves, was there perhaps something else? These slaves, adopting the genteel right of shaking hands, and pronouncing their delight to see their master again, seem to have been as canny as Ann Tharp in the speech of affection. While presumably they did not mean to kill him with kindness, the slaves certainly must have known that John Tharp considered himself a good, sympathetic master just as he considered himself a good, sympathetic father. 'Black Will' in particular managed to exploit this parlance of sympathy. Will worked on the Good Hope estate in Jamaica, while his wife was employed on the Chippenham estate in England. In John's last days, in 1804, Will, reminding his master of the pain of being separated from his wife, extracted a promise from the dying John that he would be allowed to join her in England.[136] Some months after John's death Will was anxiously awaiting passage to England. William Green declared that: 'I am under the necessity of Sending Will home, he would have gone Mad.'[137] Green, like John, recognized Will's tender feelings and overwhelming desire to see his wife again, and, as John had, Green honored these sentiments by sending Will 'home'. These glimpses of slave life suggest that it was not only elite women who exploited claims of sensibility to achieve their own ends.

These new languages, along with John's desire to see himself as a good master, provided occasional leverage even to slaves. Elite Anglo-Jamaican women like Ann Tharp and Eliza Phillipson held far greater advantages than Will and other slaves, but they too were in an inferior legal and financial position to their husbands and fathers. Still, both groups were at times able to exploit the resources of feeling, especially family feeling, to which elite Anglo-Jamaican women in particular had considerable access. Both Eliza and Black Will claimed their love for their spouse should override other considerations. Sensibility and family feeling thus entered family relations, but also, to a much lesser degree, master–slave relations, even among Anglo-Jamaicans. Subordinates were able at least occasionally to employ sentimental discourse to temper the power of the master. Changing languages and changing visions of ideal masculinity, and

---

135 John Tharp (sr.) to John Tharp (jr.), 'Good Hope 8t July 1802', R55.7.22(a), CCRO.
136 William Green wrote to John's son, John (jr.): 'Black Will is extremely anxious to go to England to see his Wife which your late Father promised that he should do, I can get him a passage home, and he may be usefull to you in the dairy, or otherwise during his stay, if you will say that you will take care of him, he shall go.' William Green to John Tharp (jr.), 'Good Hope Decembr. 6th. 1804', R55.7.128(h), CCRO.
137 William Green to John Tharp (jr.), 'Good Hope June 24th 1805', ibid.

the ability of Anglo-Jamaican women in particular to exploit them, provide the strongest reasons behind John's actions in the wake of the family scandal.

This tale, then, has revealed not only a family scandal, but also the difficult decisions made by a betrayed man and their larger cultural contexts. John's own letters make it clear that he agonized over what action to take. His personal circumstances, in particular his age, influenced his handling of the affair. His familial ambitions, so transparent in his accumulation of lands, slaves, and profits in Jamaica, led him to nurture hopes for his family that were best supported by the minimizing of a scandal, especially during an era of increased metropolitan scrutiny of West Indian moralities. When John decided against taking Richard to court, he informed Simon Taylor of the ruinous consequences such a public action might have had for his children and grandchildren: 'I shall in that case pull down the Fabrick I have been raising for them.'[138] John had spent his life raising the fabric for the future of his family, and he was not eager to rip it down on the basis of one ill-considered affair.

The story of one old husband allows, too, for the beginning of a reconsideration of old stories about colonial Jamaica, about its unmitigated masculine brutality and the powerlessness and sexlessness of its Anglo-American women. Such women were not necessarily relegated to ignorance and passivity by their violent, adulterous husbands. The sexual environment of Jamaica for all populations, including Anglo-American women, may have been looser than has been previously assumed. Even if Ann Tharp was an unusual woman in her boldness and her metropolitan *savoir faire*, the fact that such went unremarked suggests that women of her kind were not wholly novel for men like John Tharp, Simon Taylor, and Joseph Brissett. Moreover, the ability of women such as Ann Tharp and Eliza Phillipson to sway even one of Jamaica's most powerful men indicates the long-denied agency of such women, and the ways in which Jamaican women were able to exploit a variety of tools, including newer languages of sensibility and sympathy. John's mild treatment of the transgressors indicates that these vocabularies formed at least one, if hardly the only or even the predominant, strand in the web of Anglo-Jamaican social relations. Like other men in the British-Atlantic world, West Indian men could and did find roles beyond tyranny, especially at the prodding of canny—or desperate—subordinates. John's account of the heart-rending scene of Eliza on her knees, to explain himself and his actions to Simon Taylor—a man who fits much more neatly into classic understandings of hard-hearted Jamaican planters—is significant. That this language of feeling carried weight even with Taylor is evidence that such familial relations were not entirely unknown even in an Anglo-Jamaican experience.

In some senses, this narrative reflects an Anglo-Jamaican story. After all, John and his family, like most other elite Jamaicans of this era, were neither exclusively

---

[138] John Tharp to Simon Taylor, 'No 41 Portland Place 1th March 1801', XIX/A/10, Simon Taylor Papers, ICS.

British nor exclusively Jamaican. The ideal of the refined and gallant husband and father pervaded this British-Atlantic world, and John's desire to fit into this model indicates that even Anglo-Jamaicans had imbibed these newer notions by the end of the eighteenth century. This history thus provides an especially useful view of the ways in which transatlantic currents—in this case the emphasis on masculine politeness and sensibility—crossed oceans, sometimes with the people who themselves traversed the Atlantic repeatedly. While brutality swept much, if not most, of Jamaican plantation life, other winds also rustled amid the sugar canes. How else could John Tharp revel in the paternalist fiction that his slaves were 'very happy'? Contemporaries and historians have long considered Jamaicans, even the wealthiest and most metropolitan of them, to have been utterly out of step with the larger British-Atlantic culture of sentiment and sensibility, even by the end of the eighteenth century. John's story suggests otherwise. Certainly, it was a pleasing fiction for British metropolitan critics to dissociate themselves and their society from the British West India tyrants who ruled their households with the whip, and yet John's story makes it clear that this dichotomy between metropolis and colony is not quite so easily sustained. These worlds may have been closer than many have wanted to believe; for John, indeed, both were home.

In the end, John returned to his Jamaican home, left with the knowledge that all his energy, ambition, and success had not supplied the life—or the wife—that he wanted. A peep through the keyhole reveals neither the laughable old cuckold nor the West India tyrant. It exposes instead a weightier and more human form, saddled with a debilitating gout and with the anguish of a betrayal that would haunt him to the end of his life. In choosing his 'poor Childs comfort & existence' over his own 'honor', he was left with neither patriarchal rage nor with its potency, but he did make a set of decisions that allowed him also to experience some kind of 'comfort & safety'. Having weathered the contempt of being the old husband who ought to have known better, he could at least bask in his paternal abilities to raise the fabric for a family line in Britain. Even as he sat with fat bandaged legs on his Good Hope estate in Jamaica and ruminated on his own regrets, he could find some small comfort in these good hopes for his family.

Conclusion

Languages of family feeling could provide leverage to various people, including, as we have seen, wives and occasionally even slaves. They could also allow families to remain connected even across challenging distance, while also providing justification for a range of decisions, personal and political. Paying attention to families permits us to envision these processes with far greater clarity. Families were integral to building and sustaining Atlantic worlds, in ways sometimes impressive and sometimes pernicious. There was no public Atlantic world severed from the intimate worlds of family relations. People moving back and forth across the Atlantic did so for a variety of reasons; family ambitions were a powerful incentive for many. With its wars, its revolutions, and its enforced separations, the development of an Atlantic world, linked by communication, trade, and migrations, also increased anxieties about the nature of family life. Many on both sides of the Atlantic relied on similar rhetoric about family feeling, in all kinds of trying situations.

In order to remain connected, families told stories, in correspondence and other places, about their continued affections, and the ways that division would not alter family feelings. Investigating family letters elucidates what kinds of conventions were considered the most important in them, so that those languages that seem the most heartfelt and casual may be those most strongly influenced by conventions of sensibility and familiarity. Abigail and John Adams, among others, relied on such conventions. Letters sought to convey honesty and authenticity, even while acknowledging the possible inconsistencies between behavior and epistolary representation. This close attention to letters suggests that 'self-fashioning' worked in tandem with fashioning others, in ways both strategic and internalized. Individuals struggled to present themselves in particular ways (as, for example, a man of feeling) in order to influence, reassure, and change the behavior of others. They may also have themselves felt the power of their own self-presentations, choosing to alter their own behavior to conform to beliefs about themselves. The desire to display familiarity, sensibility, and credit, among other things, tugged certain individuals to act and to write accordingly.

Focusing on families and their self-presentations allows for a reconsideration not only of 'self-fashioning' but also of what has been termed the emergence of the modern self. The eighteenth century has received sustained attention as the time in which something like a modern notion of selfhood developed. One scholar has termed his history of the later eighteenth century 'the making of the modern self'.[1] Another has argued: 'it was in the hundred-year period between 1740 and 1840, the greater Revolutionary period, that many people in America first came to accept that they had an inner self that controlled their emotions and actions and to believe that they themselves might alter this self.'[2] In some claims, selfhood tends to take on a celebratory cast, since it often signals greater agency for populations who suffered legal, political, and economic disabilities. One scholar contends that novels such as *Pamela* and *Clarissa* 'told strong stories of self-realization and so contributed subtly but surely to the subversion of the ancient hierarchical order of ruling fathers'.[3]

Novels such as *Clarissa*, as well as tales about prodigal sons and separated spouses, among others, may have contributed to the subversion of patriarchy, but they also highlighted the problematic and often agonizing nature of 'self-realization'. A self making its way in the world, cut off from family, faced numerous obstacles, and many of these odysseys, including Clarissa's, did not end happily. Indeed, a laudatory view of the independent self and modern selfhood, largely inattentive to familiar attachments, would have perplexed many in the eighteenth century. Here is how John Adams, seeking independence for the American colonies in 1777, understood his independent selfhood: 'Poor, unhappy I! who have never an opportunity to share with my Family, their Distresses, nor to contribute in the least degree to relieve them! I suffer more in solitary silence, than I should if I were with them.'[4] One daughter of an exiled Loyalist crossed the Atlantic repeatedly, but this situation and the accompanying sense of dislocation did not please her: 'I do almost envy those people who live in the place which gave them birth, where they have grown, & strengthen'd every tie . . . their friends form'd by degrees & every dear association of childhood, youth, experience. not rudely torn asunder or weaken'd & shook so that doubts & discontent may arise without Supplying better things.'[5] Another woman lamented: 'The Cruel War to deprive me of my Sophia. I am sorry still to be left

---

[1] Dror Wahrman, *The Making of the Modern Self: Identity and Culture in Eighteenth-Century England* (New Haven: Yale University Press, 2004). Wahrman's stunning book offers many sources for the rise of 'selfhood', but family is not one of the categories upon which he spends time. See also the essays in Ronald Hoffman, Mechal Sobel, and Fredrika J. Teute (eds.), *Through a Glass Darkly: Reflections on Personal Identity in Early America* (Chapel Hill, NC: University of North Carolina Press for the Omohundro Institute for Early American History and Culture, 1997), and e.g. David Waldstreicher, 'Reading the Runaways: Self-Fashioning, Print Culture, and Confidence in Slavery in the Eighteenth-Century Mid-Atlantic', *William and Mary Quarterly*, 56 (1999), 243–72.

[2] Mechal Sobel, *Teach Me Dreams: The Search for Self in the Revolutionary Era* (Princeton: Princeton University Press, 2000), 3.

[3] Isaac, *Landon Carter's Uneasy Kingdom*, 47.

[4] John Adams to Abigail Adams, 'Philadelphia July 26. 1777', *Adams Family Correspondence*, ii. 289.

[5] Margaret Cowper to Eliza McQueen Mackay, 'Edinburgh Dec 4 1806', Mackay–Stiles Papers, SHC.

a poor solitary individual.'[6] 'Individual' was a word not used as often in this era, especially by letter-writers, and when it was used it tended, as in this example, to have negative connotations. Self-sufficiency did, too.[7] This 'poor, unhappy I', rudely torn asunder and wandering the world alone, was one side of independent selfhood in the eighteenth century, and it was a self to generate a host of anxieties about social connections of all sorts. To be left as a 'poor solitary individual' could be a deeply distressing experience, and, as the above examples suggest, many used letters to remain attached and to alleviate the painful uncertainties they faced.

Decades ago, historians placed communities and families at the forefront of their studies. Such studies increasingly came to seem limited, as historians focused much more closely on selves and on identities, weary, perhaps, of the demographic emphasis or debates about change that had come to dominate the field of family history. This move has been salutary in numerous respects. Nevertheless, we need to think critically about this headlong flight from family history, since we ignore family and community in the early modern world at our peril. It was an age when people were increasingly individualized, but it was nevertheless still a world in which individuals were deeply grounded in families and communities. These communities were not necessarily the New England towns or English parishes of old: they might have been enslaved Africans on a ship, Native Americans fleeing the depredations of war, families seeking to reconnect over oceans.[8] It is time to place the considerations of selves and identities, in all their complexities, in tandem with considerations of family and community.

After all, a process of profound alienation in households had to take place to reorient the individual to a selfhood, rather than a family and community. Perhaps, indeed, the eighteenth century created new forms of independence: independent selves, independent nations. But attendant on these exciting developments were pain, cruelty, and loneliness. What was for some the thrilling creation of the independent self and independent nation was for others 'indifference' and 'cruelty', and relationships, once nurtured, now upended, or ignored. They were 'aliens' and 'outcasts', 'loose fish' in the ocean of the world. Understanding the nebulous origins of the modern self requires first understanding

---

[6] Susanna Brown to Sophia Waterhouse Brown, '4th Sept 1797', John Brown Family Papers, NYHS.

[7] Indeed, in France Diderot famously lost the friendship of the irascible Jean-Jacques Rousseau by declaring: 'Only the evil man lives alone.' This episode receives attention in Darnton, *Great Cat Massacre*, 231. See also Ralph Wormeley to Warner Lewis Wormely, 'Rosegill 8th: Novr: 1803', Mss1/W8945/a-9, Wormeley Family Papers, 1791–1952, VHS, as discussed in Ch. 4.

[8] As Ned Landsman remarked about Scottish settlers in America, 'it appears that the patterned dispersal of the Scots, rather than isolating individual settlers from their homes and families, served instead to bind together the scattered settlements through a system of interlocking family networks. Rather than a deterrent, mobility was an essential component of community life.' The same might be said of family life. Landsman, *Scotland and its First American Colony*, 153.

what had to be stripped away, at least partially, to make room for that self: chief among these attenuated entities was the family. Families and household had grounded the early modern polity as well as early modern communities. They formed the basis for the nation, and they provoked considerable concern as a source of possible disorder. Patriarchal in orientation, they nevertheless depended on the actions and reputations of all of their members, even as they were ordered in a hierarchal manner, with the (usually male) household head at the top of that order. In earlier eras people felt less need to articulate the idea that families were important; it was widely understood that they were the foundation of the social and political order. As the basic political unit shifted from the household to the individual, people came to emphasize the sentimental, rather than the political, importance of the family. Families remained significant in all kinds of ways, of course, but other affiliations became equally so. Mobility continued, and individuals increasingly demanded their rights as individuals, not as members of households.

Letters helped to shape a self separate from a family; so did ideals of familiarity, sensibility, and credit. Without these privileges, an individual truly might be lost. Printed literature, as well as obscure family correspondence, told stories about ties and values that pointed both to the disorder attending families and to the ways by which a person might surmount them. Letters helped to forge these connections, and thus alleviated many of the pressures of distance and separation. Selfhood, if such a thing emerged in this period, relied first on such tales. In uncertain situations, narratives about affectionate attachments between family members, underpinned by recognition of prodigal sons, seduced daughters and wives, debts, war, revolution, and 'party-rage', provided reassurance. This is neither a cheering narrative of cold brutality melting into warm paternalism, nor a Whiggish rise of genuinely companionate or gentle or egalitarian family relations. Hierarchies and exclusions, conflicts and finances, remained central to Atlantic, as to other forms, of family life. Rather, the increase in those overblown representations of loving families, perpetuated not only in print culture but also in familiar letters, provided a powerfully compensatory ideology of family feeling, one that served to ameliorate the shocks and struggles of life in the eighteenth century.

Epilogue

These transatlantic letters continued to help ameliorate the struggles of life for some families, well beyond the eighteenth century. Like their authors, these letters have crossed the Atlantic and circulated; this process did not end with the death of their original authors. Eighteenth-century familiar letters speak about more than just their production and initial reception; they also speak about the choices of subsequent generations of those families. That we have these letters at all is a testament to the enduring power of family, across time as well as place. Just as familiar letters in the eighteenth century allowed many to surmount distance and to emphasize family feeling, so have they continued to function, in the generations that have followed. Their preservation, as much as their production and reception, makes claims about family affections and enduring relationships amid mobility and change. It also indicates privilege and resources of money, leisure, and literacy.

For eighteenth-century letters to be preserved and placed in twenty-first-century archives means that generations have had to take responsibility for guarding these papers, keeping them boxed up, and moving them to new houses. One Georgia family's letters were held in the 'superb Sheraton breakfront secretary (made by the Early American cabinetmaker, J. Barry of Philadelphia)', the same desk from which, a later editor claims, many of the letters were originally written.[1] It helps in the preservation of old letters to have antique furniture and a large manse in which to preserve them; few families are so fortunate. The later women of this particular line, the editor notes, preserved these papers even in the 'aftermath of the Confederacy'. The editor romantically proclaimed: 'It was in the atmosphere that the little girl [who had grown up and donated them to the Georgia Society of Colonial Dames] would be shown the numberless letters which the elderly sisters had so piously preserved through the troubled times.'[2] 'Troubled times' was a euphemism for a Civil War that ravaged the places mentioned in those letters. Members of families like these, often women, found comfort in old letters; they allowed access to a world that seemed nearly lost, or was already gone with the wind.

In acts of filial faithfulness, a lot of women 'piously preserved' letters. Many letters available for these researches were probably preserved by women who strove

---

[1] Hartridge (ed.), *The Letters of Robert Mackay to his Wife*, p. x. [2] Ibid., pp. xi–xii.

to make and maintain their own domestic histories. The following statement, in a modern edition of a family's letters, is typical: 'Certain old family documents were kept by each of his two wives, but the body of the papers pertains to the life of Charles Pettigrew.'[3] These wives, and other women, though often forgotten, acted as conservators and curators for the rich documentary evidence of their ancestors, and their husbands' ancestors. They placed value on the stories that these old letters could tell, and sought to make them available to later generations. Sometimes their handwritten family histories accompany the letters they saved.

For some people, especially women, correspondence from previous generations provided a solace in 'troubled times', provided entertainment on dull days, provided a link to a past that was felt to be worth keeping. One such woman, Eliza Ambler Brent Carrington, wrote a letter in the 1820s in which she ruminated on why she saved her family letters. She recalled when her first husband died after six weeks of marriage. In her grief, she had turned to 'an antiquated cabinet which I knew contained old letters and manuscripts of the family that had been accumulating for half a century, and having upon former occasions felt great pleasure in looking over them, I at least hoped to lose sight of myself in tracing the character of those who ought to be interesting to me'. Alone in her mourning, she found consolation in the 'old letters and manuscripts'. As a result of this experience, Carrington later chose to preserve her own letters for her descendants. Bolstered by these ancient heroics, Carrington was able to face the world. This experience 'determined me to put by letters and papers that were interesting... so as to make them useful to my young friends, who would probably be induced to read them, perhaps for no other reason but because they had been so preserved'.[4]

That Eliza Carrington could sit before a cabinet of family letters reminds us that she had the resources to save these letters. Their preservation was no accident. Nevertheless, many letters of hers as well as of most others have been lost, some probably because no one thought they merited saving. Older editions of collections reveal what was generally considered worth keeping: mention of political events, economic transactions, and high drama. One such family editor from 1827 announced: 'These letters I have selected as perhaps the most valuable of a very interesting collection.'[5] The original collection included letters from a father, a mother, and sisters. It is likely that the father's letters were considered 'most valuable', so that more letters from him survive.

White men wrote more than any other group, but their words were most often preserved, too. Letters of the enslaved, for example, rarely got saved. For

---

[3] Sarah McCulloh Lemmon (ed.), *The Pettigrew Papers*, 2 vols. (Raleigh, NC: State Department of Archives and History, 1971), *I (1685–1818)*, p. xx.

[4] Eliza Ambler Brent Carrington to Ann Fisher, 'October 10, 1796', Ambler–Brown Family Papers, DUL. Also in Eliza Jaquelin Ambler Brent Carrington Papers, LoC.

[5] Weeden Butler notation, 'Chelsea 24 Dec 1827', Pierce Butler Letter Collection, Add. Mss. 16603, BL.

instance, when Robert and Eliza Mackay took their enslaved nanny, Hannah, with them to England in the early nineteenth century, she wrote letters to her husband, left behind on the family estate in Georgia. Hannah's letters, mentioned in Mackay letters, do not seem to have survived. There are various possible explanations for their disappearance. Perhaps the letters remained within a slave family, who lacked the resources (an empty attic, a family house, and the like) or the interest to save them, or else (less likely) they remained within the Mackay family, who did not consider them worth keeping. They might have been destroyed during or after 'troubled times', or been left behind when families moved on. They may simply have rotted away in heat and humidity, or made a meal or a nest for insects or rodents. Whatever happened to them, their loss means that silences in the epistolary record haunt historians who seek to tell the stories of people who left little personal mark on the epistolary timeline. Letter collections also depend on who did the saving, so that one might end up with a full run of letters *to* a person with never a single letter from the recipient. For example, hundreds of Patrick Parker's letters to his father survive. However, of James's letters to Patrick, which once numbered in the hundreds, only a draft copy of a single letter survives. James Parker and his heirs in Britain saved incoming letters and later deposited them at a library; Patrick Parker's family in Virginia did not. This imbalance is the rule, not the exception.

Still, some families preserved their letters, and some later published them, or passed them on to individuals who sought to publish them. Occasionally, these printed versions may be the only remaining copy. The Dwarris family sent letters from Jamaica in the eighteenth century that seem to be preserved nowhere except in an edited version in a 1919 issue of a journal long ago discontinued.[6] The original set of correspondence has simply disappeared, perhaps stuffed in a cupboard of an old library building, perhaps, alas, left behind in a place where later finders simply carted it off as so much old trash. As anyone who has ever sorted out a messy attic will know, the line between treasured artifact and simple garbage can be a fine one. Other families passed their letters on to archives, where they remain still. They did so because the family wanted to preserve them publicly, and because an archive deemed them of sufficient interest to go to the considerable trouble of conserving, cataloguing, and making them available to the public. A researcher working in such repositories will probably jostle elbows with eager genealogists, searching for traces of their own ancestors. We historians like to feel that, unlike genealogists, we are professionals looking for the history of *the* family, or equally important topics. With no little smugness, we cherish this distinction. Still, we would do well to remember that many of our researches depend on those who sought to preserve the history of *a* family.

[6] Vere Langford, 'Dwarris of Jamaica', *Caribbeana*, 5 (1919), 19–32.

I have opened these family letters with good intentions, to make the dead still useful to the living. Still, hands grubby with dust, I know that every invasion has its costs. Descendants and public institutions have made these collections available, but I am the Pandora who has flung them open into print, floating family secrets out into the world. In the early years of the nineteenth century Margaret Cowper wrote to her cousin: 'Nothing but the golden rule of doing as I would be done by, induces me at present to take up my pen.'[7] I have felt the same, as I took up my laptop. The subjects of this study could no longer give or withhold consent for the use of their words, so I have tried to present their stories as accurately and as sympathetically as I could.

After all, you never know where that old love letter—or saucy email—might end up.

---

[7] Margaret and Mary Anne Cowper to Eliza McQueen Mackay, 'B. Hill 23[d] March', Mackay—Stiles Papers, SHC.

Bibliography

PRIMARY SOURCES

Unpublished Manuscripts

British Library, Manuscripts Division, London
Pierce Butler Letterbooks, Additional MS 16603.
Ricketts Family Papers, Additional MS 300001.

Cambridge University Library
Vannecke Papers.

Cambridgeshire County Record Office, Cambridge
Tharp Family Papers.

Columbia University Rare Books and Manuscript Library, New York City
Barrell Family Papers.
Ellison Family Papers.
Kent Family Papers.

Duke University Rare Books and Manuscript Library, Special Collections, Durham, North Carolina
John and Eliza Ambler Papers.
Ambler–Brown Family Papers.
Ballard's Valley Plantation Records.
William Bragg Papers.
James Iredell Sr. and Jr. Papers.
Louis Manigault Papers.
Eliza McQueen Mackay Papers.
Arthur Middleton Papers.
Edward Telfair Papers.

Historical Society of Pennsylvania, Philadelphia, Pennsylvania
Biddle Family Papers.
Thomas Coombe Papers/Coombe Family Papers.
Eliza Farmer Letterbook.
Elizabeth Graeme Ferguson Correspondence.
Galloway Family Papers.
Letters of Loyalist Ladies (bound volume).
Shippen Family Papers.
Shoemaker Family Papers.
Charles Steuart Letterbooks.
Warder Family Papers.

Huntington Library, San Marino, California
Elletson Collection, Brydges Correspondence, Stowe Collection.
Joseph Galloway Papers.
Norton–Savage–Dixon Papers, Brock Collection.
Nugent Letters, Grenville Correspondence, Stowe Collection.
West Indies Boxes, Brydges Correspondence, Stowe Collection.

Institute of Commonwealth Studies, University of London
Simon Taylor Papers.

Library of Congress, Washington, DC
John Leeds Bozman Papers.
Elizabeth Jaquelin Ambler Brent Carrington Papers.
Joseph Galloway Papers.
Hadwen-Bragg Family Papers.
Hannah Hobart Papers.
Nicholas Low Papers.
John Martin Papers.
The Pinckney Family Papers.
Thomas Pinckney Papers.
Thomas Ruston Papers.
Thomas Lee Shippen Papers.

Liverpool Record Office, Liverpool City Library
Parker Family Papers (PAR I–IV).

Massachusetts Historical Society, Boston, Massachusetts
Byles Family Papers.
Forbes Family Papers.

National Archives (of England), Kew, London
American Loyalist Claims Commission, Series I (1776–1831) and Series II (1780–1835) (especially AO 12/54, AO 13/68, 83, 134, and AO 12/84, 104, 109).
Colonial Office Papers (especially CO 142/31/67).

National Library of Scotland
Charles Steuart Papers.

Newport Historical Society, Rhode Island
Dudley Family Papers.
Ellery Family Papers.
Malbone–Brinley Family Papers.
Vernon Family Papers.
Wanton Family Papers.

New-York Historical Society, New York City
John Brown Family Papers.
Daniel Robert Letters.

Smith-Robert Family Letters.
Watts Family Papers.

Manuscripts and Archives Division, New York Public Library, Astor, Lenox, and Tilden Foundations, New York City
Edward and Ann Chandler Letters to Samuel Thorne.

Southern Historical Collection, Manuscripts Department, University of North Carolina, Chapel Hill, North Carolina
Brownrigg Family Papers.
McAllister Family Papers.
Mackay–Stiles Family Papers.

University of Virginia, Special Collections, Alderman Library, Charlottesville, Virginia
Robert H. Fisher, 'Narrative of a Voyage to the West Indies'.

Virginia Historical Society, Richmond, Virginia
Thomas Adams Papers.
Baylor Family Papers.
Beverly Family Papers.
Byrd Family Papers.
Carlyle Family Papers.
Cocke Family Papers.
DeButts Family Papers.
William Douglas Papers.
Downman Family Papers.
Durley Family Papers.
Edrington Family Papers.
Severn Eyre Letterbook.
Hunter Family Papers.
Jenings Family Papers.
Keane Family Papers.
Collection F, Lee Family Papers.
Mercer Family Papers.
Preston Family Papers.
Robertson Family Papers.
Skipwith Family Papers.
Spotswood Family Papers.
Stevens Family Papers.
Christopher Tompkins Papers.
Watson Family Papers.
Wickham Family Papers.
Wormeley Family Papers.

Microfilm

'Norfolk City Wills & Administration 1795/1796' (Library of Virginia).
'Virginia Publick Claims' (Library of Virginia).
'Bishop's Transcripts: Baptisms, Marriages, Burials for Staffordshire, 1673–1809', (Staffordshire: International Genealogical Institute).

'Trinity Parish Registers, 1709–1799' (Historical Society of Rhode Island).
'Parish Registers, 1573–1848' (Church of England, Parish Church of Eccleshall (Staffordshire): International Genealogical Institute).

Digital Resources

'Early American Newspapers, Series I, 1690–1876' (Readex).
'The Geography of Slavery in Virginia' (Virginia Center for Digital History, 2005).

Periodicals

Exeter Flying Post (1824).
The Gentleman's Magazine: And Historical Chronicle (1826).
The Times (London) (1797).
Town and Country Magazine, 1–26 (1769–95).

Epistolary Manuals

ANON, *The Accomplish'd Letter-Writer: Or, the Young Gentlemen and Ladies' Polite Guide to an Epistolary Correspondence in Business, Friendship, Love, and Marriage* (Newcastle upon Tyne, 1778).

―― *The Accomplished Letter-Writer: Or, Universal Correspondent* (London (and Kendal), 1779).

―― *The American Academy of Compliments; or, the Complete American Secretary* (Philadelphia, 1796).

―― *The American Letter-Writer, or, New Art of Polite Correspondence* (Hartford, Conn., 1814).

―― *The British Letter-Writer* (Gloucester, 1780?).

―― *The British Letter-Writer: Or Letter-Writer's Complete Instructor* (London, 1760?).

―― *The Columbian Letter-Writer, or, Young Lady and Gentleman's Guide to Epistolary Correspondence* (Alexandria, Va., 1811).

―― *The Complete American Letter-Writer, Containing Letters on Trade & Merchandize. Also, Letters on Familiar & Interesting Subjects* (Otsego, NY, 1807).

―― *The Complete Letter Writer* (Salem, Mass., 1802).

―― *The Complete Letter-Writer* (Falkirk, 1792).

―― *The Complete Letter-Writer, Containing a Great Variety of Plain, Easy, Entertaining & Familiar Letters* (London, 1808).

―― *The Complete Letter-Writer, Containing Familiar Letters on the Most Common Occasions in Life* (London, 1801).

―― *The Complete Letter-Writer, Containing Familiar Letters on the Most Common Occasions in Life* (Gainsborough, 1810).

―― *The Compleat [Complete] Letter-Writer: Or, New and Polite English Secretary*, 3rd edn. (London, 1756).

―― *The Complete Letter-Writer: Or, Polite English Secretary*, 4th edn. (London, 1757); 5th edn. (London, 1758); 6th edn. (London, 1759); 8th edn. (London, 1762); 10th edn. (London, 1765); 11th edn. (London, 1767); 12th edn. (London, 1768); 15th edn. (London, 1775); 16th edn. (London, 1778).

―― *The Complete Letter-Writer: Or, Polite English Secretary. Vol 2.* (London, 1789).

―― *The Complete Letter-Writer: Or, Polite English Secretary*, 19th edn. (London, 1800?).

―― *The Complete Letter-Writer. Containing Familiar Letters on the most common Occasions in Life*, 5th edn. (Edinburgh, 1776).

ANON, *The Complete Letter-Writer. Containing Familiar Letters on the most common Occasions in Life* (Edinburgh, 1778).
—— *The Court Letter Writer; Or the Complete English Secretary for Town and Country* (London, 1773).
—— *The Instructive Letter-Writer, and Entertaining Companion*, 2nd edn. (London, 1765).
—— *The Instructive Letter-Writer, and Entertaining Companion*, 3rd edn. (London, 1769).
—— *The Ladies Complete Letter-Writer; Teaching the Art of Inditing Letters on every Subject that can call for their Attention, as Daughters, Wives, Mothers, Relations, Friends, or Acquaintance* (London, 1763).
—— *The London Universal Letter-Writer; Or, Whole Art of Polite Correspondence*, rev. edn. (London, 1809?).
—— *The New Complete General Letter-Writer, And Universal Correspondent*, rev. edn. (London, 1803).
—— *The New Complete Letter Writer* (Glasgow, 1785).
—— *The New Complete Letter Writer* (Philadelphia, 1792).
—— *The New Complete Letter Writer* (Boston, Mass., 1798).
—— *The New Letter Writer; Or, The Art of Correspondence* (Whitehaven, 1775?).
—— *The New Universal Letter-Writer*, rev. edn. (Philadelphia, 1800).
—— *Newberry's Familiar Letter Writer* (London, 1788).
—— *[Scott's Cheap and Elegant Edition of] The Complete American Letter-Writer, and Best Companion for the Young Man of Business* (New York, 1807).
—— *The Secretary and Complete Letter Writer; Containing a Collection of Letters Upon Most Occasions and Situations in Life* (Birmingham, 1803).
—— *The Universal Letter-Writer*, rev. edn. (Boston, 1808).
—— *The Universal Letter-Writer*, rev. edn. (Philadelphia, 1810).
BROWN, GEORGE, *The English Letter-Writer* (London, 1779?).
—— *The [New and Complete] English Letter-Writer; Or, Whole Art of General Correspondence* (London, 1780?).
—— *The English Letter-Writer; Or, The Whole Art of General Correspondence* (London, 1785?).
BROWN, THOMAS, *The Lover's Secretary* (London, 1734).
BROWNE, JOHN, *The Marchants Avizo* [1589], ed. Patrick McGrath (Boston, Baker Library, Harvard Graduate School of Business Administration, 1957).
COOK(E), THOMAS, *The Universal Letter-Writer; Or, New Art of Polite Correspondence* (London, 1771).
—— *The Universal Letter-Writer; Or, New Art of Polite Correspondence* (London, 1775).
—— *The New and Complete Universal Letter-Writer; Or, Young Secretary's Instructor* (London, 1790).
—— *The Universal Letter-Writer; Or, New Art of Polite Correspondence* (London (and York), 1794).
—— *The Universal Letter-Writer; Or, New Art of Polite Correspondence* (London (and York), 1796).
—— *The Universal Letter-Writer; Or, New Art of Polite Correspondence* (London, 1801).
—— *The Universal Letter-Writer; Or, New Art of Polite Correspondence* (London, 1807).
—— *The Universal Letter-Writer; Or, New Art of Polite Correspondence* (Norwich, 1808).
—— *The Universal Letter-Writer; Or, New Art of Polite Correspondence* (London (and York), 1809).

Bibliography

DE LA SERRE, Monsieur, *The Secretary in Fashion: Or, An Elegant and Compendious Way of Writing All Manner of Letters* (London, 1654).

DILWORTH, H. W., *The Complete Letter-Writer: Or, Young Secretary's Instructor* (Glasgow, 1783).

―― *The Complete Letter-Writer: Or, Young Secretary's Instructor* (New-York, 1793).

DUBOIS, DOROTHEA, *The Lady's Polite Secretary, or New Female Letter Writer* (London, 1771).

―― *The Complete Letter-Writer; Or, Lady's Polite Secretary* (London, 1775?).

FORDYCE, DAVID, *The [New and Complete] British Letter-Writer; Or, Young Secretary's Instructor in Polite Modern Letter-Writing* (London, 1790?).

FULWOOD, WILLIAM, *The Enimie of Idlenesse* (London, 1568).

HAYWOOD, ELIZA, *Epistles for the Ladies* (London, 1749).

HOGG, HENRY, *The New and Complete Universal Letter-Writer: Or, Whole Art of General and Polite Correspondence* (London, 1790?).

HOGG, HENRY and BROWN, GEORGE, *The New and Complete Universal Letter-Writer: Or, Whole Art of General and Polite Correspondence*, rev. edn. (London, 1802).

JOHNSON, SAMUEL, *The New London Letter Writer, Containing the Compleat Art of Corresponding*, 7th edn. (London, 1800).

RICHARDSON, SAMUEL, *Letters to and from Particular Friends, on the Most Important Occasions* (London, 1741).

ROBERTS, P., *Art of Universal Correspondence* (Wrexham, 1802).

RULE, JOHN, *The English and French Letter-Writer, or, General Correspondent. [L'Ecrivain Anglois & François, Ou Le Correspondant General.]* (London, 1766).

SEYMOUR, GEORGE, *The Instructive Letter-Writer, and Entertaining Companion* (London, 1763).

SHEPARD, SYLVANUS, *The Natural Letter-Writer* (n.p., 1812).

TAVERNIER, JOHN, *The Entertaining Correspondent; Or, Newest and most Compleat Polite Letter Writer* (Berwick, 1759).

―― *[The Newest and most Compleat] Polite Familiar Letter-Writer*, 2nd edn. (Berwick, 1760).

―― *The Newest and Most Compleat Polite Familiar Letter-Writer*, 4th edn. (Berwick, 1768).

WALLACE, JAMES and TOWNSHEND, CHARLES, *Every Man his own Letter-Writer: Or, the New and Complete Art of Letter-Writing Made plain and familiar to every Capacity* (London, 1782).

Other primary printed material

Annals of Trinity Church, Newport, Rhode Island, 1698–1821 (Newport, RI, 1890).

'Documents: Travelers' Impressions of Slavery in America from 1750 to 1800', *Journal of Negro History*, 1 (1916), 399–435.

The Fatal Consequences of Domestick Divisions, especially in the Families of Princes (London, 1737).

THE REMEMBRANCER: *Addressed to Young Men in Business. Shewing How they may attain the Way to be* RICH *and* RESPECTABLE (London, 1793).

Trials for Adultery (London, 1790).

ABERCROMBIE, JANICE L., *Virginia Publick Claims: Princess Anne County* (Athens, Ga., n.d.).

APTHEKER, HERBERT (ed.), *A Documentary History of the Negro People in the United States* (New York: Citadel Press, 1951).

AUSTEN, JANE, *Persuasion* [1818], ed. Gillian Beer (London: Penguin Books, 1998).

AUSTEN-LEIGH, RICHARD ARTHUR, *The Eton College Register: 1753–1790* (Eton: Spottiswoode, Ballantyne, & Co., 1921).

BARTLETT, JOHN RUSSELL, *Records of the Colony of Rhode Island and Providence Plantations in New England*, 10 vols. (Providence, RI, 1861).

BEAWES, WYNDHAM, *Lex Mercatoria Rediviva: Or, the Merchant's Directory. Being a Complete Guide to all Men in Business* (London, 1771).

BLACKSTONE, WILLIAM, *Commentaries on the Laws of England*, ed. John Frederick Archbold, 4 vols. (London, 1811).

BOLINGBROKE, Viscount HENRY ST. JOHN, *Letters on the Study and Use of History*, 2nd edn. (London, 1752).

BURNEY, FANNY, *Evelina, or, A Young Lady's Entrance into the World, in a Series of Letters*, 3 vols. (London, 1779).

——— *Cecilia, Or Memoirs of an Heiress*, 5 vols. (London, 1782).

BUTTERFIELD, L. H., GARRETT, WENDELL D., and SPRAGUE, MARJORIE E. (eds.), *Adams Family Correspondence*, 6 vols. (Cambridge, Mass.: Harvard University Press, 1963).

CHESTERFIELD, PHILIP DORMER STANHOPE, Earl of, *Letters written by the late Right Honourable Philip Dormer Stanhope, Earl of Chesterfield, to his son, Philip Stanhope, Esq.*, 2 vols. (London, 1774).

CHEYNE, GEORGE, *The English Malady: or, A Treatise of Nervous Diseases of All Kinds* (London, 1733).

CHILD, JOSIAH, 'Brief Observations concerning trade, and interest of money' [1668], in William Letwin (ed.), *Sir Josiah Child, Merchant Economist* (Boston: Baker Library, Harvard Graduate School of Business Administration, 1959).

CLARK, STEPHEN, *A Catalogue of the Annapolis Circulating Library* (Annapolis, Md., 1786).

COBBET, THOMAS, *A Fruitfull and Usefull Discourse Touching the Honour Due from Children* (London, 1656).

COOKE, NICHOLAS, 'Revolutionary Correspondence of Governor Nicholas Cooke', ed. Matt B. Jones, *Proceedings of the American Antiquarian Society*, 36 (1926), 231–353.

CRÈVECOEUR, HECTOR ST. JOHN DE, *Letters from an American Farmer*, ed. Susan Manning (Oxford: Oxford University Press, 1997).

DAVENANT, CHARLES, *Two Manuscripts: 1. A Memorial Concerning the Coyn of England (November, 1695), and 2. A memoriall concerning Creditt (July 15, 1696)*, ed. Abbott Payson Usher (Baltimore: Johns Hopkins University Press, 1942).

——— *The Political and Commercial Works of that Celebrated Writer Charles D'Avenant, LL.D. Relating to the Trade and Revenue of England, The Plantation Trade, the East-India Trade, And African Trade* [1771], ed. Charles Whitworth, facs. reprint (Farnborough: Gregg, 1967).

DEFOE, DANIEL, *The Complete English Tradesman, in Familiar Letters* (London, 1726).

——— *The Family Instructor*, in *The Novels and Miscellaneous Works of Daniel Defoe*, 15 vols. (Oxford, 1841), Vol. 1 [1715].

DEWOLFE, BARBARA (ed.), *Discoveries of America: Personal Accounts of British Emigrants to North America during the Revolutionary Era* (Cambridge: Cambridge University Press, 1997).

DIBDIN, CHARLES, *Sea Songs and Ballads* (London, 1863).

DICKINSON, JOHN, *Letters from a Farmer in Pennsylvania, To the Inhabitants of the British Colonies* (Philadelphia, 1768).
DOUGLASS, FREDERICK, 'What to the Slave is the Fourth of July: An Address Delivered in Rochester, New York, on 5 July 1852', in John W. Blassingame (ed.), *The Frederick Douglass Papers, Series One: Speeches, Debates, and Interviews* (New Haven: Yale University Press, 1987), ii. 359–88.
EDWARDS, BRYAN, *The History, Civil and Commercial, of the British Colonies in the West Indies*, 2 vols., 2nd edn. (London, 1794).
EQUIANO, OLAUDAH, *The Interesting Narrative of the Life of Olaudah Equiano, Written by Himself*, ed. Robert J. Allison (Boston: Bedford Books of St Martin's Press, 1995).
FRANKLIN, BENJAMIN, *Advice to a Young Tradesman. Written by an Old One* (Boston, 1762).
FREIBERG, MALCOLM (ed.), *The Winthrop Papers*, 6 vols. (Boston: Massachusetts Historical Society, 1931).
GALLOWAY, GRACE GROWDEN, 'Diary of Grace Growden Galloway, 1778–1779', *Pennsylvania Magazine of History and Biography*, 55 (1931), 35–94; 58 (1934), 152–89.
[GALLOWAY, JOSEPH], *The Claim of the American Loyalists Reviewed and Maintained upon the Incontrovertible Principles of Law and Justice* (London, 1788).
GOETHE, JOHANN WOLFGANG VON, *The Sorrows of Werter: A German Story*, 2 vols. (London, 1779).
GOLDSMITH, OLIVER, *The Citizen of the World; or Letters from a Chinese Philosopher*, 2 vols. (London, 1762).
HALL, DOUGLAS (ed.), *In Miserable Slavery: Thomas Thistlewood in Jamaica, 1750–1786* (Basingstoke: Macmillan, 1989).
HANCOCK, DAVID (ed.), *The Letters of William Freeman, London Merchant, 1678–1685* (London: London Record Society, 2002).
HANNAY, DAVID (ed.), *Letters Written by Sir Samuel Hood (Viscount Hood) in 1781–2–3*, Publications of the Navy Records Society, 3 vols. (London, 1895).
HARTRIDGE, WALTER CHARLTON (ed.), *The Letters of Don Juan McQueen to His Family Written from Spanish East Florida, 1791–1807* (Columbia, SC: Bostick & Thornley for the Georgia Society of the Colonial Dames of America, 1943).
—— (ed.), *The Letters of Robert Mackay to His Wife, Written from Ports in America and England, 1795–1816* (Athens, Ga.: University of Georgia Press under the Auspices of the Georgia Society of Colonial Dames, 1949).
HENING, WILLIAM WALLER, *The Statutes at Large: Being a Collection of All the Laws of Virginia, From the First Session of the Legislature in the Year 1619*, 13 vols. (Richmond, Va., 1819–23).
HOFFMAN, RONALD, MASON, SALLY, and DARCY, ELEANOR S. (eds.), *Dear Papa, Dear Charley: The Peregrinations of a Revolutionary Aristocrat, as told by Charles Carroll of Carrollton and his father, Charles Carroll of Annapolis*, 3 vols. (Chapel Hill, NC: University of North Carolina Press for the Omohundro Institute of Early American History and Culture, 2001).
HOWARD, MARTIN, *A Letter from a Gentleman at Halifax, to his Friend in Rhode-Island, Containing Remarks upon a Pamphlet, Entitled, The Rights of Colonies Examined* (Newport, RI, 1765).
HULTON, ANNE, *Letters of a Loyalist Lady* (Cambridge, Mass.: Harvard University Press, 1927).

Hume, David, *A Treatise of Human Nature* [1739–40], ed. L. A. Selby-Bigge and P. H. Nidditch, 2nd edn. (Oxford: Clarendon Press, 1978).

―― *Essays Moral, Political, and Literary*, ed. Eugene F. Miller, rev. edn. (Indianapolis: Liberty Fund, 1987).

―― 'An Enquiry concerning Human Understanding' [1748], in Tom L. Beauchamp (ed.), *An Enquiry concerning Human Understanding*, Oxford Philosophical Texts (Oxford: Oxford University Press, 1999).

Hutcheson, Francis, *An Essay on the Nature and Conduct of the Passions and Affections with Illustrations on the Moral Sense* [1742], ed. Paul McReynolds, 3rd edn. (Gainesville, Fla.: Scholars' Facsimiles & Reprints, 1969).

―― *A System of Moral Philosophy* [1755], ed. Bernhard Fabian, 3rd edn. (facs. edn.), vol. 2 (Hildesheim: Georg Olms Verlag, 1990).

Johnson, Samuel, *A Dictionary of the English Language*, 2 vols. (London, 1755).

Karlsen, Carol F. and Crumpacker, Laurie (eds.), *The Journal of Esther Edwards Burr, 1754–1757* (New Haven: Yale University Press, 1984).

Kimball, Gertrude Selwyn (ed.), *The Correspondence of the Colonial Governors of Rhode Island, 1723–1775*, 2 vols. (Boston: Houghton, Mifflin & Co., 1903).

'A Lady', *Fatal Friendship. A Novel*, 2 vols. (Dublin, 1771).

Langford, Vere, 'Dwarris of Jamaica', *Caribbeana*, 5 (1919), 19–32.

Lemmon, Sarah McCulloh, *The Pettigrew Papers*, 2 vols. (Raleigh, NC: State Department of Archives and History, 1971).

Lewis, M. G., *The Monk*, 3 vols. (London, 1796).

Library Company of Philadelphia, *The Charter, Laws, and Catalogue of Books, of the Library Company of Philadelphia* (Philadelphia, 1770).

Long, Edward, *The History of Jamaica*, 2 vols. (London, 1774).

Macdonald, D. L., *Monk Lewis: A Critical Biography* (Toronto, Ontario: University of Toronto Press, 2000).

Mackenzie, Henry, *The Man of Feeling* (London, 1771).

Maling, Anne E., *Princess Anne County, Virginia: Land and Probate Records Abstracted from Deed Books Eight to Eighteen, 1755–1783* (Bowie, Md.: Heritage Books, 1993).

Malynes, Gerard, *Consuetudo, vel lex mercatoria, or the Ancient Law-merchant* (London, 1622).

Mason, Frances Norton (ed.), *John Norton and Sons, Merchants of London and Virginia, Being the Papers from their Counting House for the Years 1750 to 1795* (New York: Augustus M. Kelley, 1968).

Mason, George Carrington (ed.), *The Colonial Vestry Book of Lynnhaven Parish, Princess Anne County, Virginia, 1723–1786* (Newport News, Va.: State Archives/George Mason, 1949).

May, John, *A Declaration of the Estate of Clothing Now Used Within this Realme of England (London, 1613)* (*The English Experience: Its Record in Early Printed Books Published in Facsimile*; Amsterdam: Da Capo Press, 1971).

Mein, John, *A Catalogue of Mein's Circulating Library* (Boston, 1765).

Morgan, Edmund S., *Prologue to Revolution: Sources and Documents on the Stamp Act Crisis, 1764–1766* (Chapel Hill, NC: University of North Carolina Press for the Institute of Early American History and Culture, 1959).

Mozley, Geraldine (ed.), *Letters to Jane from Jamaica, 1788–1796* (London: The West India Committee, 1938).

MUNDY, GODFREY BASIL (ed.), *The Life and Correspondence of the Late Admiral Lord Rodney*, 2 vols. (London, 1830).

NUGENT, MARIA, *Lady Nugent's Journal: Jamaica One Hundred Years Ago*, ed. Frank Cundall, 1st edn. (London: Institute of Jamaica, 1906).

—— *Lady Nugent's Journal of her Residence in Jamaica from 1801 to 1805*, ed. Philip Wright (Kingston: University of West Indies Press, 1966).

PHELPS, HENRY P., *The Albany Rural Cemetery: Its Beauties, Its Memories* (Albany, NY, 1893).

PINCKNEY, ELISE (ed.), *The Letterbook of Eliza Lucas Pinckney, 1739–1762* (Chapel Hill, NC: University of North Carolina Press, 1972).

PLEASANTS, J. HALL, 'Letters of Molly and Hetty Tilghman', *Maryland Historical Magazine*, 21 (1926), 20–39, 123–49, 219–42.

POPE, ALEXANDER, *Letters of Mr. Alexander Pope, and Several of his Friends*, 2 vols. (London, 1737).

RICHARDSON, SAMUEL, *Pamela; or, Virtue Rewarded*, 2 vols., 2nd edn. (London, 1741).

—— *Clarissa; or, the History of a Young Lady*, 7 vols. (London, 1748).

ROUSE-BALL, W. W. and VENN, J. A., *Admissions to Trinity College, Cambridge: 1701–1800*, 3 vols. (London: Macmillan, 1911).

SANCHO, IGNATIUS, *Letters of the Late Ignatius Sancho, an African*, 2 vols. (London, 1782).

SHEBBEARE, JOHN, *Letters on the English Nation* (London, 1755).

SMITH, ADAM, *The Theory of Moral Sentiments* (London and Edinburgh, 1759).

SMOLLETT, TOBIAS GEORGE, *The Adventures of Roderick Random*, 2 vols. (London, 1748).

STAPYLTON, H. E. C., *The Eton School Lists: From 1791 to 1850*, 2nd edn. (London, 1864).

STERNE, LAURENCE, *Letters of the Late Rev. Laurence Sterne, To his most intimate Friends.*, 3 vols. (London, 1775).

STEUART, A. FRANCIS, 'Letters from the Nizam's Camp, 1791–1794', *The Imperial and Asiatic Quarterly Review*, 3rd ser. 34 (1912), 114–51.

—— 'Orkney News from the Letter-Bag of Mr. Charles Steuart', *Old-Lore Miscellany*, 6 (1913), 41–9, 101–9.

STILES, EZRA, *The Literary Diary of Ezra Stiles*, ed. Franklin Bowditch Dexter, 3 vols. (New York: Charles Scribner's Sons, 1901).

TIFFANY, NINA MOORE (ed.), *Letters of James Murray, Loyalist* (Boston: Griegg Press, 1972).

TILGHMAN, HARRISON, 'Letters Between the English and American Branches of the Tilghman Family', *Maryland Historical Magazine*, 33 (1938), 148–75.

TOUCHSTONE, TIMOTHY, *Tea and Sugar, or the Nabob and the Creole; A Poem, in Two Cantos* (London, 1792).

TRUXES, THOMAS M. (ed.), *Letterbook of Greg & Cunningham: Merchants of New York and Belfast* (Oxford: Oxford University Press for the British Academy, 2001).

TURELL, EBENEZER (ed.), *Memoirs of the Life and Death of the Pious and Ingenious Mrs. Jane Turell* (London, 1741).

VENN, J. A. (ed.), *Alumni Cantabrigienses* (Cambridge: Cambridge University Press, 1954), part II, vol. 6.

WATTS, I., 'Advice to a Young Man on His Entrance into the World', in *A Monitor for an Apprentice . . . Advice to a Young Man . . . and Two Essays by Dr. Benj. Franklin* (Boston, 1808), 105–33.

WEDD, A. F. (ed.), *The Love-Letters of Mary Hays (1779–1780)* (London: Methuen 1925).

WEDD, A. F. (ed.), *The Fate of the Fenwicks: Letters to Mary Hays (1798–1828)* (London: Methuen 1927).
WHEATLEY, PHILLIS, *Complete Writings*, ed. Vincent Carretta (New York: Penguin, 2001).
WINGO, ELIZABETH B., *Marriages of Princess Anne County, Virginia, 1749–1821* (Norfolk, Va.: Wingo, 1961).
—— *Marriages of Norfolk County, Virginia, 1706–1792* (Norfolk, Va.: Wingo, 1961).
—— *Norfolk County, Virginia, Tithables, 1751–1765* (Norfolk, Va.: Wingo, 1981).
—— and WINGO, W. BRUCE, *Norfolk County, Virginia, Tithables, 1730–1750* (Norfolk, Va.: Wingo, 1979).
—— —— *Norfolk County, Virginia, Tithables, 1766–1780* (Norfolk, Va.: Wingo, 1985).

SECONDARY SOURCES

AGNEW, JEAN-CHRISTOPHE, *Worlds Apart: The Market and the Theater in Anglo-American Thought, 1550–1750* (Cambridge: Cambridge University Press, 1986).
ALLISTON, APRIL, *Virtue's Faults: Correspondences in Eighteenth-Century British and French Women's Fiction* (Stanford, Calif.: Stanford University Press, 1996).
ALTMAN, JANET GURKIN, *Epistolarity: Approaches to a Form* (Columbus, Ohio: Ohio State University Press, 1982).
—— 'The Letter Book as a Literary Institution 1539–1789: Toward a Cultural History of Published Correspondence in France', *Yale French Studies*, 71 (1986), 17–62.
—— 'Political Ideology in the Letter Manual (France, England, New England)', *Studies in Eighteenth-Century Culture*, 18 (1988), 105–22.
—— 'Teaching the "People" to Write: The Formation of a Popular Civic Identity in the French Letter Manuals', *Studies in Eighteenth-Century Culture*, 22 (1992), 147–80.
—— 'Epistolary Conduct: The Evolution of the Letter Manual in France in the Eighteenth Century', *Studies on Voltaire and the Eighteenth Century*, 304 (1992), 866–70.
AMORY, HUGH and HALL, DAVID D. (eds.), *The History of the Book in America*, Vol. 1: *The Colonial Book in the Atlantic World*, ed. David D. Hall (Cambridge: Cambridge University Press, 2000).
ANDERSON, FRED, *Crucible of War: The Seven Years' War and the Fate of Empire in British North America, 1754–1766* (New York: Knopf, 2000).
ANDERSON, HOWARD, DAGHLIAN, PHILIP B., and EHRENPREIS, IRVIN (eds.), *The Familiar Letter in the Eighteenth Century* (Lawrence, Kan.: University of Kansas Press, 1966).
ANDREW, DONNA T., '"Adultery à-la-Mode": Privilege, the Law and Attitudes to Adultery 1770–1809', *History (The Journal of the Historical Association)*, 82 (1997), 5–23.
ARMITAGE, DAVID, *Greater Britain, 1516–1776: Essays in Atlantic History* (Aldershot: Ashgate, 2004).
—— and BRADDICK, MICHAEL J. (eds.), *The British Atlantic World, 1500–1800* (Basingstoke: Palgrave/Macmillan, 2002).
—— *et al.*, 'AHR Forum: The New British History in Atlantic Perspective', *American Historical Review*, 104 (1999), 426–500.
ARMSTRONG, NANCY, *Desire and Domestic Fiction: A Political History of the Novel* (Oxford: Oxford University Press, 1987).
ARNELL, J. C., *Transatlantic Mail to and from British North America from Early Days to U.P.U.*, Transatlantic Mail Study Group Handbook No. 4 (Oyama, British Columbia: British North America Philatelic Society, 1996).

ASHWORTH, JOHN, 'AHR Forum: The Relationship between Capitalism and Humanitarianism', *American Historical Review*, 92 (1987), 813–28.

BACKSHEIDER, PAULA R. and INGRASSIA, CATHERINE (eds.), *Blackwell Companion to the Eighteenth-Century English Novel and Culture* (Oxford: Blackwell, 2005).

BAILEY, JOANNE, *Unquiet Lives: Marriage and Marriage Breakdown in England, 1660–1800*, Anthony Fletcher, John Guy, and John Morrill, ed. Cambridge Studies in Early Modern British History (Cambridge: Cambridge University Press, 2003).

BAILYN, BERNARD, *Voyagers to the West: A Passage in the Peopling of America on the Eve of the Revolution* (New York: Knopf, 1986).

—— 'Introduction: Europeans on the Move, 1500–1800', in Nicholas Canny (ed.), *Europeans on the Move: Studies on European Migration* (Oxford: Clarendon Press, 1994), 1–8.

—— 'The Idea of Atlantic History', *Itinerario*, 20 (1996), 19–44.

—— *Atlantic History: Concept and Contours* (Cambridge, Mass.: Harvard University Press, 2005).

BANNET, EVE TAVOR, *The Domestic Revolution: Enlightenment Feminisms and the Novel* (Baltimore, Md.: Johns Hopkins University Press, 2000).

—— *Empire of Letters: Letter Manuals and Transatlantic Correspondence, 1680–1820* (Cambridge: Cambridge University Press, 2005).

BARKER, HANNAH, *The Business of Women: Female Enterprise and Urban Development in Northern England, 1760–1830* (Oxford: Oxford University Press, 2006).

BARKER-BENFIELD, G. J., *The Culture of Sensibility: Sex and Society in Eighteenth-Century Britain* (Chicago: University of Chicago Press, 1992).

BARRELL, JOHN, *The Spirit of Despotism: Invasions of Privacy in the 1790s* (Oxford: Oxford University Press, 2006).

BARTON, DAVID and HALL, NIGEL (eds.), *Letter Writing as a Social Practice* (Amsterdam: John Benjamins Publishing Co., 2000).

BASCH, NORMA, *Framing American Divorce: From the Revolutionary Generation to the Victorians* (Berkeley: University of California Press, 1999).

BAYLY, C. A., *Imperial Meridian: The British Empire and the World, 1780–1830* (London: Longman, 1989).

BEALES, ROSS W. and MONAGHAN, E. JENNIFER, 'Practices of Reading, Part One: Literacy and Schoolbooks', in Hugh Amory and David D. Hall (eds.), *The History of the Book in America*, Vol. 1: *The Colonial Book in the Atlantic World* (Cambridge: Cambridge University Press, 2000), 380–7.

BEEBEE, THOMAS O., *Epistolary Fiction in Europe, 1500–1850* (Cambridge: Cambridge University Press, 1999).

BELL, MALCOLM, Jr., *Major Butler's Legacy: Five Generations of a Slaveholding Family* (Athens, Ga.: University of Georgia Press, 1987).

BELLAMY, LIZ, *Commerce, Morality and the Eighteenth-Century Novel* (Cambridge: Cambridge University Press, 1998).

BENEDICT, BARBARA, *Framing Feeling: Sentiment and Style in English Prose Fiction, 1745–1800* (New York: AMS Press, 1994).

BENSTOCK, SHARI (ed.), *The Private Self: Theory and Practice of Women's Autobiographical Writings* (London: Routledge, 1988).

BERG, MAXINE, *Luxury and Pleasure in Eighteenth-Century Britain* (Oxford: Oxford University Press, 2005).

BERLIN, IRA, *Many Thousands Gone: The First Two Centuries of Slavery in North America* (Cambridge, Mass.: Harvard University Press, 1998).
BERRY, HELEN and FOYSTER, ELIZABETH (eds.), *The Family in Early Modern England* (Cambridge: Cambridge University Press, 2007).
BETTS, EDWIN MORRIS and BEAR, JAMES ADAM, Jr. (eds.), *The Family Letters of Thomas Jefferson* (Columbia, Miss.: University of Missouri Press, 1966).
BLACK, FRANK GEES, *The Epistolary Novel in the Late Eighteenth Century: A Descriptive and Bibliographical Study* (Eugene, Oreg.: University of Oregon Press, 1940).
BLAND, CAROLINE (ed.), *Gender and Politics in the Age of Letter-Writing, 1750–2000* (Aldershot: Ashgate, 2004).
BLOCH, RUTH H., 'The Gendered Meaning of Virtue in Revolutionary America', *Signs*, 13 (1987), 37–58.
──── *Gender and Morality in Anglo-American Culture, 1650–1800* (Berkeley: University of California Press, 2003).
──── 'Changing Conceptions of Sexuality and Romance in Eighteenth-Century America', *William and Mary Quarterly*, 60 (2003), 13–42.
BLOCK, SHARON, 'Rape Without Women: Print Culture and the Politicization of Rape, 1765–1815', *Journal of American History*, 89 (2002), 849–68.
──── *Rape and Sexual Power in Early America* (Chapel Hill, NC: University of North Carolina Press for the Omohundro Institute of Early American History and Culture, 2006).
BLOOM, HAROLD (ed.), *Fanny Burney's 'Evelina'* (New York: Chelsea House, 1988).
BOWEN, H. V., *Elites, Enterprise and the Making of the British Overseas Empire, 1688–1775* (Basingstoke: Macmillan, 1996).
BRANT, CLARE, *Eighteenth-Century Letters and British Culture* (Basingstoke: Palgrave Macmillan, 2006).
BRATHWAITE, EDWARD, *The Development of Creole Society in Jamaica, 1770–1820* (Oxford: Clarendon Press, 1971).
BRAY, JOE, *The Epistolary Novel: Representations of Consciousness* (London: Routledge, 2003).
BREEN, KENNETH, 'Sir George Rodney and St Eustatius in the American War: A Commercial and Naval Distraction, 1775–1781', *The Mariner's Mirror*, 84 (1998), 193–203.
BREEN, T. H., *Tobacco Culture: The Mentality of the Great Tidewater Planters on the Eve of Revolution* (Princeton: Princeton University Press, 1985).
──── 'An Empire of Goods: The Anglicization of Colonial America, 1690–1776', *Journal of British Studies*, 25 (1986), 467–99.
──── ' "Baubles of Britain": The American and Consumer Revolutions of the Eighteenth Century', *Past & Present*, 119 (1988), 73–104.
──── 'Narrative of Commercial Life: Consumption, Ideology, and Community on the Eve of the American Revolution', *William and Mary Quarterly*, 50 (1993), 471–501.
──── *The Marketplace of Revolution: How Consumer Politics Shaped American Independence* (Oxford: Oxford University Press, 2004).
BREWER, HOLLY, *By Birth or Consent: Children, Law, and the Anglo-American Revolution in Authority* (Chapel Hill, NC: University of North Carolina Press for the Omohundro Institute of Early American History and Culture, 2005).

BREWER, JOHN, *The Sinews of Power: War, Money and the English State, 1688–1783* (London: Unwin Hyman, 1994).
―― *The Pleasures of the Imagination: English Culture in the Eighteenth Century* (London: HarperCollins, 1997).
―― *A Sentimental Murder: Love and Madness in the Eighteenth Century* (London: HarperCollins, 2004).
BROWN, CHRISTOPHER LESLIE, *Moral Capital: Foundations of British Abolitionism* (Chapel Hill, NC: University of North Carolina Press for the Omohundro Institute of Early American History and Culture, 2006).
BROWN, KATHLEEN M., 'Brave New Worlds: Women's and Gender History', *William and Mary Quarterly*, 50 (1993), 311–27.
―― *Good Wives, Nasty Wenches, and Anxious Patriarchs: Gender, Race, and Power in Colonial Virginia* (Chapel Hill, NC: University of North Carolina Press for the Institute of Early American History and Culture, 1996).
―― 'Beyond the Great Debates: Gender and Race', *Reviews in American History*, 26 (1998), 96–123.
BROWN, RICHARD D., *Knowledge is Power: The Diffusion of Information in Early America, 1700–1865* (Oxford: Oxford University Press, 1989).
BROWN, WALLACE, *The King's Friends: The Composition and Motives of the American Loyalist Claimants* (Providence, RI: Brown University Press, 1965).
―― *The Good Americans: The Loyalists in the American Revolution* (New York: William Morrow and Co., 1969).
BRYSON, ANNA, *From Courtesy to Civility: Changing Codes of Conduct in Early Modern England* (Oxford: Clarendon Press, 1998).
BUEL, JOY DAY and BUEL, RICHARD Jr., *The Way of Duty: A Woman and her Family in Revolutionary America* (New York: Norton, 1984).
BUETTNER, ELIZABETH, *Empire Families: Britons and Late Imperial India* (Oxford: Oxford University Press, 2004).
BURCHELL, R. A. (ed.), *The End of Anglo-America: Historical Essays in the Study of Cultural Divergence* (Manchester: Manchester University Press, 1991).
BURNARD, TREVOR, 'Inheritance and Independence: Women's Status in Early Colonial Jamaica', *William and Mary Quarterly*, 48 (1991), 93–114.
―― 'Family Continuity and Female Independence in Jamaica, 1665–1734', *Continuity and Change*, 7 (1992), 181–98.
―― 'Theater of Terror: Domestic Violence in Thomas Thistlewood's Jamaica, 1750–1786', in Christine Daniels and Michael V. Kennedy (eds.), *Over the Threshold: Intimate Violence in Early America* (New York: Routledge, 1999), 237–53.
―― *Mastery, Tyranny, and Desire: Thomas Thistlewood and his Slaves in the Anglo-Jamaican World* (Chapel Hill, NC: University of North Carolina Press, 2004).
BURSTEIN, ANDREW, 'Jefferson and the Familiar Letter', *Journal of the Early Republic*, 14 (1994), 195–220.
―― *Sentimental Democracy: The Evolution of America's Romantic Self-Image* (New York: Hill & Wang, 1999).
BUSH, BARBARA, *Slave Women in Caribbean Society, 1650–1838* (London: James Currey, 1990).
BUSHMAN, RICHARD L., *The Refinement of America: Persons, Houses, Cities* (New York: Knopf, 1992).

CALHOON, ROBERT MCCLUER, *The Loyalists in Revolutionary America, 1760–1781* (New York: Harcourt Brace Jovanovich, 1973).
—— BARNES, TIMOTHY M., and RAWLYK, GEORGE A. (eds.), *Loyalists and Community in North America* (Westport, Conn.: Greenwood Press, 1994).
CANNY, NICHOLAS (ed.), *Europeans on the Move: Studies on European Migration, 1500–1800* (Oxford: Clarendon Press, 1994).
—— 'Writing Atlantic History; or, Reconfiguring the History of Colonial British America', *Journal of American History*, 86 (Dec. 1999), 1093–114.
—— and PAGDEN, ANTHONY (eds.), *Colonial Identity in the Atlantic World, 1500–1800* (Princeton: Princeton University Press, 1987).
CAPP, BERNARD, *When Gossips Meet: Women, Family, and Neighbourhood in Early Modern England* (Oxford: Oxford University Press, 2003).
CARSON, CARY, HOFFMAN, RONALD, and ALBERT, PETER J. (eds.), *Of Consuming Interests: The Style of Life in the Eighteenth Century* (Charlottesville, Va.: University Press of Virginia, 1994).
CARTER, PHILIP D., *Men and the Emergence of Polite Society, Britain, 1660–1800* (Harlow: Longman, 2001).
CHARTIER, ROGER, 'Introduction: An Ordinary Kind of Writing—Model Letters and Letter-Writing in Ancien Régime France', in Roger Chartier, Alain Boureau, and Cécile Dauphin (eds.), *Correspondence: Models of Letter-Writing from the Middle Ages to the Nineteenth Century* (Oxford: Polity Press, 1997), 1–23.
—— BOUREAU, ALAIN, and DAUPHIN, CÉCILE (eds.), *Correspondence: Models of Letter-Writing from the Middle Ages to the Nineteenth Century*, trans. Christopher Woodall (Oxford: Polity Press, 1997).
CLEARY, PATRICIA, *Elizabeth Murray: A Woman's Pursuit of Independence in Eighteenth-Century America* (Amherst, Mass.: University of Massachusetts Press, 2000).
COCLANIS, PETER A., '*Drang Nach Osten*: Bernard Bailyn, the World-Island, and the Idea of Atlantic History', *Journal of World History*, 13 (2002), 169–82.
—— (ed.), *The Atlantic Economy during the Seventeenth and Eighteenth Centuries: Organization, Operation, Practice, and Personnel* (Columbia, SC: University of South Carolina Press, 2005).
—— 'Atlantic World or Atlantic/World (Forum: Beyond the Atlantic)', *William and Mary Quarterly*, 63 (2006), 725–42.
COLLEY, LINDA, *Britons: Forging the Nation, 1707–1837* (New Haven: Yale University Press, 1992).
—— *Captives: Britain, Empire and the World, 1600–1850* (London: Verso, 2002).
CONWAY, STEPHEN, 'Britain and the Revolutionary Crisis, 1763–1791', in P. J. Marshall (ed.), *The Oxford History of the British Empire*, Vol. 2: *The Eighteenth Century* (Oxford: Oxford University Press, 1998), 325–46.
—— *The British Isles and the War of American Independence* (Oxford: Oxford University Press, 2000).
COOK, ELIZABETH HECKENDORN, *Epistolary Bodies: Gender and Genre in the Eighteenth-Century Republic of Letters* (Stanford, Calif.: Stanford University Press, 1996).
CORNELIUS, JANET DUITSMAN, *'When I Can Read My Title Clear': Literacy, Slavery, and Religion in the Antebellum South* (Columbia, SC: University of South Carolina, 1991).
COTT, NANCY F., *The Bonds of Womanhood: 'Woman's Sphere' in New England, 1780–1835* (New Haven: Yale University Press, 1977).

COTT, NANCY F., *Public Vows: A History of Marriage and the Nation* (Cambridge, Mass.: Harvard University Press, 2000).
COUCHMAN, JANE and CRABB, ANN (eds.), *Women's Letters Across Europe, 1400–1700: Form and Persuasion* (Aldershot: Ashgate, 2005).
COUNTRYMAN, EDWARD, *A People in Revolution: The American Revolution and Political Society in New York, 1760–1790* (New York: W. W. Norton & Co., 1989).
CRANE, ELAINE FORMAN, *A Dependent People: Newport, Rhode Island in the Revolutionary Era* (New York: Fordham University Press, 1985).
____ *Ebb Tide in New England: Women, Seaports, and Social Change, 1630–1800* (Boston: Northeastern University Press, 1998).
____ 'Political Dialogue and the Spring of Abigail's Discontent', *William and Mary Quarterly*, 56 (1999), 745–74.
CRATON, MICHAEL, *Empire, Enslavement and Freedom in the Caribbean* (Oxford: James Currey, 1997).
CREIGHTON, MARGARET S. and NORLING, LISA (eds.), *Iron Men, Wooden Women: Gender and Seafaring in the Atlantic World, 1700–1920*, Gender Relations in the American Experience (Baltimore, Md.: Johns Hopkins University Press, 1996).
CRESSY, DAVID, *Literacy and the Social Order: Reading and Writing in Tudor and Stuart England* (Cambridge: Cambridge University Press, 1980).
____ *Coming Over: Migration and Communication Between England and New England in the Seventeenth Century* (Cambridge: Cambridge University Press, 1987).
DANIELS, CHRISTINE and KENNEDY, MICHAEL V. (eds.), *Over the Threshold: Intimate Violence in Early America* (New York: Routledge, 1999).
DARNTON, ROBERT, *The Great Cat Massacre and Other Episodes in French Cultural History* (New York: Basic Books, 1984).
DAVIDOFF, LEONORE and HALL, CATHERINE, *Family Fortunes: Men and Women of the English Middle Class, 1780–1850*, Women in Culture and Society (Chicago: University of Chicago Press, 1987).
DAVIDSON, CATHY N., *Revolution and the Word: The Rise of the Novel in America* (Oxford: Oxford University Press, 1986).
____ (ed.), *Reading in America: Literature and Social History* (Baltimore, Md.: Johns Hopkins University Press, 1989).
DAVIES, KATE, *Catharine Macaulay and Mercy Otis Warren: The Revolutionary Atlantic and the Politics of Gender* (Oxford: Oxford University Press, 2005).
DAVIS, DAVID BRION, *The Problem of Slavery in the Age of Revolution* (Ithaca, NY: Cornell University Press, 1975).
____ 'AHR Forum: Reflections on Abolitionsim and Ideological Hegemony', *American Historical Review*, 92 (1987), 797–812.
DAVIS, RICHARD BEALE, *A Colonial Southern Bookshelf: Reading in the Eighteenth Century* (Athens, Ga.: University of Georgia Press, 1979).
DAYBELL, JAMES (ed.), *Early Modern Women's Letter Writing* (Basingstoke: Palgrave, 2001).
____ *Women Letter-Writers in Tudor England* (Oxford: Oxford University Press, 2006).
DAYTON, CORNELIA HUGHES, *Women Before the Bar: Gender, Law, and Society in Connecticut, 1639–1789* (Chapel Hill, NC: University of North Carolina Press for the Institute of Early History and Culture, 1995).
DECKER, WILLIAM MERRILL, *Epistolary Practices: Letter Writing in America Before Telecommunications* (Chapel Hill, NC: University of North Carolina Press, 1998).

DEMOS, JOHN, 'Digging Up Family History', in Anya Jabour (ed.), *Major Problems in the History of American Families and Children: Documents and Essays* (Boston: Houghton Mifflin, 2005), 1–18.

DESAN, SUZANNE, *The Family on Trial in Revolutionary France* (Berkeley: University of California Press, 2004).

DEVINE, T. M., *Scotland's Empire and the Shaping of the Americas, 1600–1815* (Washington, DC: Smithsonian Books, 2004).

DICKINSON, H. T., *Britain and the American Revolution* (London: Longman, 1998).

DIERKS, KONSTANTIN, ' "Let Me Chat a Little": Letter Writing in Rhode Island Before the Revolution', *Rhode Island History*, 53 (1995), 120–33.

—— 'Letter Writing, Masculinity, and American Men of Science, 1750–1800', *Pennsylvania History*, 65, Supplement (1998), 167–98.

—— 'Letter Writing, Gender, and Class in America, 1750–1800', Ph.D, Brown University (1999).

—— 'Letter Manuals, Literary Innovation, and the Problem of Defining Genre in Anglo-American Epistolary Instruction, 1568–1800', *Papers of the Bibliographical Society of America*, 94 (2000), 541–50.

—— 'Letter Writing, Stationery Supplies, and Consumer Modernity in the Eighteenth-Century Atlantic World', *Early American Literature*, 41 (2006), 473–94.

DITZ, TOBY L., 'Shipwrecked; or, Masculinity Imperiled: Mercantile Representations of Failure and the Gendered Self in Eighteenth-Century Philadelphia', *Journal of American History*, 81 (1994), 51–80.

—— 'Formative Ventures: Eighteenth-Century Commercial Letters and the Articulation of Experience', in Rebecca Earle (ed.), *Epistolary Selves: Letters and Letter-Writers, 1600–1945* (Aldershot: Ashgate, 1999), 59–78.

—— 'Secret Selves, Credible Personas: The Problematics of Trust and Public Display in the Writing of Eighteenth-Century Philadelphia Merchants', in Robert Blair St. George (ed.), *Possible Pasts: Becoming Colonial in Early America* (Ithaca, NY: Cornell University Press, 2000), 219–42.

DOERFLINGER, THOMAS A., *A Vigorous Spirit of Enterprise: Merchants and Economic Development in Revolutionary Philadelphia* (Chapel Hill, NC: University of North Carolina Press for the Institute of Early American History and Culture, 1986).

DOODY, MARGARET ANNE, 'Samuel Richardson: Fiction and Knowledge', in John Richetti (ed.), *The Cambridge Companion to the Eighteenth-Century Novel* (Cambridge: Cambridge University Press, 1996), 90–119.

DOUGLAS, ANN, *The Feminization of American Culture* (New York: Knopf, 1977).

DUBOIS, LAURENT, *Avengers of the New World: The Story of the Haitian Revolution* (Cambridge, Mass.: Belknap Press of Harvard University Press, 2004).

EARLE, REBECCA (ed.), *Epistolary Selves: Letters and Letter-Writers, 1600–1945* (Aldershot: Ashgate, 1999).

EKIRCH, A. ROGER, *Bound for America: The Transportation of British Convicts to the Colonies, 1718–1775* (Oxford: Clarendon Press, 1987).

ELLIOTT, J. H., 'Afterword: Atlantic History: A Circumnavigation', in David Armitage and Michael J. Braddick (eds.), *The British Atlantic World, 1500–1800* (Basingstoke: Palgrave/Macmillan, 2002), 233–49.

ELLIS, KENNETH, *The Post Office in the Eighteenth Century* (Oxford: Oxford University Press, 1958).

ELLIS, MARKMAN, *The Politics of Sensibility: Race, Gender and Commerce in the Sentimental Novel*, Cambridge Studies in Romanticism (Cambridge: Cambridge University Press, 1996).

ELLISON, JULIE, *Cato's Tears and the Making of Anglo-American Emotion* (Chicago: University of Chicago Press, 1999).

ELTIS, DAVID, *The Rise of African Slavery in the Americas* (Cambridge: Cambridge University Press, 2000).

――― LEWIS, FRANK D., and SOKOLOFF, KENNETH L. (eds.), *Slavery in the Development of the Americas* (Cambridge: Cambridge University Press, 2004).

ERICKSON, ROBERT A., *The Language of the Heart, 1600–1750* (Philadelphia: University of Pennsylvania Press, 1997).

EUSTACE, NICOLE, '"The Cornerstone of a Copious Work": Love and Power in Eighteenth-Century Courtship', *Journal of Social History*, 34 (2001), 517–46.

EUSTACE, NICOLE ELAINE, ' "Passion is the Gale": Emotion and Power on the Eve of the American Revolution', Ph.D, University of Pennsylvania (2001).

FAVRETT, MARY A., *Romantic Correspondence: Women, Politics and the Fiction of Letters* (Cambridge: Cambridge University Press, 1993).

FERGUSON, ROBERT A., *American Enlightenment, 1750–1820* (Cambridge, Mass.: Harvard University Press, 1997).

FERLING, JOHN E., *Loyalist Mind: Joseph Galloway and the American Revolution* (University Park, Penns.: Pennsylvania State University Press, 1977).

FINKELSTEIN, ANDREA, *Harmony and the Balance: An Intellectual History of Seventeenth-Century English Economic Thought* (Ann Arbor, Mich.: University of Michigan Press, 2000).

FINN, MARGOT C., *The Character of Credit: Personal Debt in English Culture, 1740–1914* (Cambridge: Cambridge University Press, 2003).

FISCHER, KIRSTEN, *Sex, Race, and Resistance in Colonial North Carolina* (Ithaca, NY: Cornell University Press, 2002).

Fisher Gallery, University of Southern California and Huntington Library and Art Gallery, *Isaac Cruikshank and the Politics of Parody: Watercolors in the Huntington Collection* (San Marino, Calif.: Huntington Library Press, 1994).

FLAVELL, JULIE M., 'The "School for Modesty and Humility": Colonial American Youth in London and Their Parents, 1755–1775', *Historical Journal*, 42 (1999), 377–403.

――― 'Government Interception of Letters from America and the Quest for Colonial Opinion in 1775', *William and Mary Quarterly*, 58 (2001), 403–30.

FLETCHER, ANTHONY, *Gender, Sex and Subordination in England, 1500–1800* (New Haven: Yale University Press, 1995).

FLIEGELMAN, JAY, *Prodigals and Pilgrims: The American Revolution Against Patriarchal Authority, 1750–1800* (Cambridge: Cambridge University Press, 1982).

――― *Declaring Independence: Jefferson, Natural Language, and the Culture of Performance* (Stanford, Calif.: Stanford University Press, 1993).

FLINT, CHRISTOPHER, *Family Fictions: Narrative and Domestic Relations in Britain, 1688–1798* (Stanford, Calif.: Stanford University Press, 1998).

FOSTER, THOMAS A., *Sex and the Eighteenth-Century Man: Massachusetts and the History of Sexuality in America* (Boston: Beacon Press, 2007).

FOYSTER, ELIZABETH, *Marital Violence: An English Family History, 1660–1857* (Cambridge: Cambridge University Press, 2005).

Foyster, Elizabeth A., *Manhood in Early Modern England: Honour, Sex and Marriage* (London: Longman, 1999).
Franklin, Colin, *Lord Chesterfield: His Character and Characters* (Aldershot: Scolar Press, 1993).
Froide, Amy M., *Never Married: Singlewomen in Early Modern England* (Oxford: Oxford University Press, 2005).
Games, Alison, *Migration and the Origins of the English Atlantic World* (Cambridge, Mass.: Harvard University Press, 1999).
—— 'Migration', in David Armitage and Michael J. Braddick (eds.), *The British Atlantic World, 1500–1800* (Basingstoke: Palgrave/Macmillan, 2002), 31–50.
—— 'Atlantic History: Definitions, Challenges, Opportunities', *American Historical Review*, 111: 3 (June 2006) 741–57.
—— 'Beyond the Atlantic: English Globetrotters and Transoceanic Connections (Forum: Beyond the Atlantic)', *William and Mary Quarterly*, 63 (2006), 675–92.
Games, Alison, et al., 'Forum: Beyond the Atlantic', *William and Mary Quarterly*, 63 (2006), 675–742.
Gauci, Perry, *The Overseas Merchant in State and Society, 1600–1720* (Oxford: Oxford University Press, 2001).
Geggus, David P. (ed.), *The Impact of the Haitian Revolution in the Atlantic World* (Columbia, SC: University of South Carolina Press, 2001).
Gelles, Edith B., *Portia: The World of Abigail Adams* (Bloomington, Ind.: Indiana University Press, 1992).
Genovese, Eugene D., *Roll, Jordan, Roll: The World the Slaves Made* (New York: Random House, 1972).
Gerlach, Larry R., 'Charles Dudley and the Customs Quandary in Pre-Revolutionary Rhode Island', *Rhode Island History*, 30 (1971), 52–9.
Gilje, Paul A., *Liberty on the Waterfront: American Maritime Culture in the Age of Revolution* (Philadelphia: University of Pennsylvania Press, 2004).
Gillis, Christina Marsden, *The Paradox of Privacy: Epistolary Form in Clarissa* (Gainesville, Fla.: University of Florida, 1984).
Gillis, John R., *For Better, For Worse: British Marriages, 1600 to the Present* (Oxford: Oxford University Press, 1985).
Gilroy, Amanda and Verhoeven, W. M. (eds.), *Epistolary Histories: Letters, Fiction, Culture* (Charlottesville, Va.: University Press of Virginia, 2000).
Glover, Lorri, *All Our Relations: Blood Ties and Emotional Bonds Among the Early South Carolina Gentry* (Baltimore, Md.: Johns Hopkins University Press, 2000).
Gobetti, Daniela, *Private and Public: Individuals, Households, and Body Politic in Locke and Hutcheson* (London: Routledge, 1992).
Goldsmith, Elizabeth C. (ed.), *Writing the Female Voice: Essays on Epistolary Literature* (Boston: Northeastern University Press, 1989).
Goodman, Dena, *The Republic of Letters: A Cultural History of the Enlightenment* (Ithaca, NY: Cornell University Press, 1994).
—— 'Furnishing Discourses: Readings of a Writing Desk in Eighteenth-Century France', in Maxine Berg and Elizabeth Eger (eds.), *Luxury in the Eighteenth Century: Debates, Desires, and Delectable Goods* (Basingstoke: Palgrave, 2003), 71–88.
—— 'Letter Writing and the Emergence of Gendered Subjectivity in Eighteenth-Century France', *Journal of Women's History*, 17 (2005), 9–37.

GOODMAN, DENA and NORBERG, KATHRYN (eds.), *Furnishing the Eighteenth Century: What Furniture Can Tell Us About the European and American Past* (New York: Routledge, 2007).

GOULD, ELIGA H., *The Persistence of Empire: British Political Culture in the Age of the American Revolution* (Chapel Hill, NC: University of North Carolina Press for the Omohundro Institute of Early American History and Culture, 2000).

GOWING, LAURA, *Domestic Dangers: Women, Words, and Sex in Early Modern London* (Oxford: Clarendon Press, 1996).

GRASSO, CHRISTOPHER, *A Speaking Aristocracy: Transforming Public Discourse in Eighteenth-Century Connecticut* (Chapel Hill, NC: University of North Carolina for the Omohundro Institute of Early American History and Culture, 1999).

GREENBLATT, STEPHEN, *Renaissance Self-Fashioning: From More to Shakespeare* (Chicago: University of Chicago Press, 1980).

GREENE, JACK P., *Pursuits of Happiness: The Social Development of Early Modern British Colonies and the Formation of American Culture* (Chapel Hill, NC: University of North Carolina Press, 1988).

―― BRANA-SHUTE, ROSEMARY, and SPARKS, RANDY J. (eds.), *Money, Trade, and Power: The Evolution of Colonial South Carolina's Plantation Society* (Columbia, SC: University of South Carolina Press, 2001).

GREVEN, PHILIP J., *The Protestant Temperament: Patterns of Child-Rearing, Religious Experience, and the Self in Early America* (New York: Knopf, 1977).

GUNDERSEN, JOAN R., 'Independence, Citizenship, and the American Revolution', *Signs*, 13 (1987), 59–77.

GUSTAFSON, SANDRA M., *Eloquence is Power: Oratory and Performance in Early America* (Chapel Hill, NC: University of North Carolina Press for the Omohundro Institute of Early American History and Culture, 2000).

HALL, DAVID D., 'The Atlantic World, Part One: The Atlantic Economy in the Eighteenth Century', in Hugh Amory and David D. Hall (eds.), *The History of the Book in America*, Vol. 1: *The Colonial Book in the Atlantic World* (Cambridge: Cambridge University Press, 2000), 152–62.

HAMILTON, DANIEL W., *The Limits of Sovereignty: Property Confiscation in the Union and the Confederacy During the Civil War* (Chicago: University of Chicago Press, 2007).

HAMILTON, DOUGLAS J., *Scotland, the Caribbean and the Atlantic World, 1750–1820*, ed. John M. Mackenzie, Studies in Imperialism (Manchester: Manchester University Press, 2005).

HANCOCK, DAVID, *Citizens of the World: London Merchants and the Integration of the British Atlantic Community, 1735–1785* (Cambridge: Cambridge University Press, 1995).

―― 'Self-Organized Complexity and the Emergence of an Atlantic Market Economy, 1651–1815', in Peter A. Coclanis (ed.), *The Atlantic Economy During the Seventeenth and Eighteenth Centuries: Organization, Operation, Practice, and Personnel* (Columbia, SC: University of South Carolina Press, 2005), 30–71.

HAREVAN, TAMARA K., 'The History of the Family and the Complexity of Social Change', *American Historical Review*, 96 (1991), 95–124.

―― and PLAKANS, ANDREJS (eds.), *Family History at the Crossroads: A Journal of Family History Reader* (Princeton: Princeton University Press, 1987).

HARRIS, SHARON M., 'Early American Women's Self-Creating Acts', *Resources for American Literary Study*, 19: 2 (1993), 223–45.

HARROW, SHARON, *Adventures in Domesticity: Gender and Colonial Adulteration in Eighteenth-Century British Literature* (Brooklyn, New York: AMS Press, 2004).
HARVEY, KAREN, *Reading Sex in the Eighteenth Century: Bodies and Gender in English Erotic Culture* (Cambridge: Cambridge University Press, 2004).
HASKELL, THOMAS L., 'Capitalism and the Origins of Humanitarian Sensibility, Part 1', *American Historical Review*, 90 (1985), 339–61.
—— 'Capitalism and the Origins of Humanitarian Sensibility, Part 2', *American Historical Review*, 90 (1985), 547–66.
—— 'AHR Forum: Convention and the Hegemonic Interest in the Debate over Anti-slavery: A Reply to Davis and Ashworth', *American Historical Review*, 92 (1987), 829–78.
HAST, ADELE, *Loyalism in Revolutionary Virginia: The Norfolk Area and the Eastern Shore*, ed. Robert Berkhofer, Studies in American History and Culture (Ann Arbor, Mich.: UMI Research Press, 1979).
HAYES, EDMUND M., 'Notes and Documents: Mercy Otis Warren versus Lord Chesterfield 1779', *William and Mary Quarterly*, 40 (1983), 616–21.
HEMPHILL, C. DALLETT, 'Women in Court: Sex-Role Differentiation in Salem, Massachusetts, 1636 to 1683', *William and Mary Quarterly*, 39 (1982), 164–75.
—— 'Middle Class Rising in Revolutionary America: The Evidence from Manners', *Journal of Social History*, 30 (1996), 317–44.
—— *Bowing to Necessities: A History of Manners in America, 1620–1860* (Oxford: Oxford University Press, 1999).
HERNDON, RUTH WALLIS, 'The Domestic Cost of Seafaring: Town Leaders and Seamen's Families in Eighteenth-Century Rhode Island', in Margaret S. Creighton and Lisa Norling (eds.), *Iron Men, Wooden Women: Gender and Seafaring in the Atlantic World, 1700–1920*, Gender Relations in the American Experience (Baltimore, Md.: Johns Hopkins University Press, 1996), 55–69.
HILL, BRIDGET, *Women Alone: Spinsters in England, 1660–1850* (New Haven: Yale University Press, 2001).
HILL, CHRISTOPHER, *A Tinker and a Poor Man: John Bunyan and his Church, 1628–1688* (New York: W. W. Norton & Co., 1988).
HITCHCOCK, TIM, *English Sexualities, 1700–1800* (New York: St Martin's Press, 1997).
—— and COHEN, MICHELE (eds.), *English Masculinities, 1660–1800* (London: Addison Wesley, 1999).
HODES, MARTHA (ed.), *Sex, Love, Race: Crossing Boundaries in North American History* (New York: New York University Press, 1999).
HOFFMAN, LEONORE and CULLEY, MARGO (eds.), *Women's Personal Narratives: Essays in Criticism and Pedagogy* (New York: Modern Language Association of America, 1985).
HOFFMAN, RONALD with MASON, SALLY D., *Princes of Ireland, Planters of Maryland: A Carroll Saga* (Chapel Hill, NC: University of North Carolina Press for the Omohundro Institute of Early American History and Culture, 2000).
—— SOBEL, MECHAL, and TEUTE, FREDRIKA J. (eds.), *Through a Glass Darkly: Reflections on Personal Identity in Early America* (Chapel Hill, NC: University of North Carolina Press for the Omohundro Institute of Early American History and Culture, 1997).
HOLTON, WOODY, *Forced Founders: Indians, Debtors, Slaves, and the Making of the American Revolution in Virginia* (Chapel Hill, NC: University of North Carolina Press for the Omohundro Institute of Early American History and Culture, 1999).

HOPPIT, JULIAN, *Risk and Failure in English Business, 1700–1800* (Cambridge: Cambridge University Press, 1987).
―― *A Land of Liberty? England, 1689–1727* (Oxford: Oxford University Press, 2000).
HORN, JAMES and MORGAN, PHILIP D., 'Settlers and Slaves: European and African Migrations to Early Modern British America', in Elizabeth Mancke and Carole Shammas (eds.), *The Creation of the British Atlantic World* (Baltimore, Md.: Johns Hopkins University Press, 2005), 19–44.
HORNBEAK, KATHERINE GEE, 'The Complete Letter Writer in English, 1568–1800', *Smith College Studies in Modern Languages*, 15 (1934), pp. iii–150.
HORNBLOWER, SIMON and SPAWFORTH, ANTONY, *The Oxford Classical Dictionary*, 3rd edn. (Oxford: Oxford University Press, 1996).
HOULBROOKE, RALPH A., *The English Family, 1450–1700*, ed. J. Stevenson, Themes in British Social History (London: Longman, 1984).
HOUSTON, R. A., *Literacy in Early Modern Europe: Culture and Education, 1500–1800*, 2nd edn. (Harlow: Longman, 2002).
HOW, JAMES, *Epistolary Spaces: English Letter Writing from the Foundation of the Post Office to Richardson's Clarissa* (Aldershot: Ashgate, 2003).
HUDSON, PAT, *The Genesis of Industrial Capital* (Cambridge: Cambridge University Press, 1986).
HUNT, LYNN AVERY, *The Family Romance of the French Revolution* (Berkeley: University of California Press, 1992).
HUNT, MARGARET R., *The Middling Sort: Commerce, Gender, and the Family in England, 1680–1780* (Berkeley: University of California Press, 1996).
HUNTER, J. PAUL, *Before Novels: The Cultural Contexts of Eighteenth-Century English Fiction* (New York: W. W. Norton & Co., 1990).
INGRAM, MARTIN, *Church Courts, Sex and Marriage in England, 1570–1640* (Cambridge: Cambridge University Press, 1987).
IRVIN, BENJAMIN H., 'Tar, Feathers, and the Enemies of American Liberties, 1768–1776', *New England Quarterly*, 76 (2003), 197–238.
ISAAC, RHYS, *The Transformation of Virginia, 1740–1790* (Chapel Hill, NC: University of North Carolina for the Institute of Early American History and Culture, 1982).
―― 'Communication and Control: Authority Metaphors and Power Contests on Colonel Landon Carter's Virginia Plantation, 1752–1778', in Sean Wilentz (ed.), *Rites of Power: Symbolism, Ritual, and Politics Since the Middle Ages* (Philadelphia: University of Pennsylvania Press, 1985), 275–302.
―― *Landon Carter's Uneasy Kingdom: Revolution and Rebellion on a Virginia Plantation* (Oxford: Oxford University Press, 2004).
JABOUR, ANYA, ' "No Fetters But Such As Love Shall Forge": Elizabeth and William Wirt and Marriage in the Early Republic', *Virginia Magazine of History and Biography*, 104 (1996), 211–50.
―― *Marriage in the Early Republic: Elizabeth and William Wirt and the Companionate Ideal* (Baltimore, Md.: Johns Hopkins University Press, 1998).
―― (ed.), *Major Problems in the History of American Families and Children: Documents and Essays* (Boston: Houghton Mifflin, 2005).
JANZEN, OLAF UWE (ed.), *Merchant Organization and Maritime Trade in the North Atlantic, 1660–1815* (St John's, Newfoundland: International Maritime Economic History Association, 1998).

JOHN, RICHARD R., *Spreading the News: The American Postal System from Franklin to Morse* (Cambridge, Mass.: Harvard University Press, 1995).

JOHNSON, ALLEN and MALONE, DUMAS, *Dictionary of American Biography*, 20 vols. (New York: Charles Scribner's Sons, 1937).

JONES, COLIN and WAHRMAN, DROR (eds.), *The Age of Cultural Revolutions: Britain and France, 1750–1820* (Berkeley: University of California Press, 2002).

KAMENSKY, JANE, *Governing the Tongue: The Politics of Speech in Early New England* (Oxford: Oxford University Press, 1997).

KAPLAN, DEBORAH, 'Representing Two Cultures: Jane Austen's Letters', in Shari Benstock (ed.), *The Private Self: Theory and Practice of Women's Autobiographical Writings* (London: Routledge, 1988), 211–29.

KARRAS, ALAN L., *Sojourners in the Sun: Scottish Migrants in Jamaica and the Chesapeake, 1740–1800* (Ithaca, NY: Cornell University Press, 1992).

KELLEY, MARY, 'Reading Women/Women Reading: The Making of Learned Women in Antebellum America', *Journal of American History*, 83 (1996), 401–24.

KERBER, LINDA K., 'Daughters of Columbia: Educating Women for the Republic, 1787–1805', in Jean E. Friedman and William G. Shade (eds.), *Our American Sisters: Women in American Life and Thought*, 2nd edn. (Boston: Allyn and Bacon, 1976), 76–92.

—— *Women of the Republic: Intellect and Ideology in Revolutionary America* (New York: W. W. Norton & Co., 1980).

—— 'Separate Spheres, Female Worlds, Woman's Place: The Rhetoric of Women's History', *Journal of American History*, 75 (1988), 9–39.

—— ' "Beyond Roles, Beyond Spheres": Thinking about Gender in the Early Republic', *William and Mary Quarterly*, 46 (1989), 565–85.

—— *Toward an Intellectual History of Women* (Chapel Hill, NC: University of North Carolina Press, 1997).

—— 'The Paradox of Women's Citizenship in the Early Republic: The Case of *Martin vs. Massachusetts*, 1805', in *Toward an Intellectual History of Women* (Chapel Hill, NC: University of North Carolina Press, 1997), 261–302.

KERRISON, CATHERINE, 'By the Book: Eliza Ambler Brent Carrington and Conduct Literature in Late Eighteenth-Century Virginia', *Virginia Magazine of History and Biography*, 105 (1997), 27–52.

—— *Claiming the Pen: Women and Intellectual Life in the Early American South* (Ithaca, NY: Cornell University Press, 2006).

KLEIN, HERBERT S., *The Atlantic Slave Trade* (Cambridge: Cambridge University Press, 1999).

KLEIN, LAWRENCE E., *Shaftesbury and the Culture of Politeness: Moral Discourse and Cultural Politics in Early Eighteenth-Century England* (Cambridge: Cambridge University Press, 1994).

—— 'Gender and the Public/Private Distinction in the Eighteenth Century: Some Questions About Evidence and Analytic Procedure', *Eighteenth-Century Studies*, 29 (1995), 97–109.

KLEPP, SUSAN E. and MCDONALD, RODERICK A., 'Inscribing Experience: An American Working Woman and and English Gentlewoman Encounter Jamaica's Slave Society, 1801–1805', *William and Mary Quarterly*, 58 (2001), 637–60.

KLOOSTER, WIM and PADULA, ALFRED (eds.), *The Atlantic World: Essays on Slavery, Migration, and Imagination* (Upper Saddle River, NJ: Pearson/Prentice, 2005).

KNOTT, SARAH, 'A Cultural History of Sensibility in the Era of the American Revolution', D.Phil., Oxford University (1999).

―― 'Sensibility and the American War for Independence', *American Historical Review*, 109 (2004), 19–39.

―― and TAYLOR, BARBARA (eds.), *Women, Gender and Enlightenment* (Basingstoke: Palgrave/Macmillan, 2005).

KULIKOFF, ALLAN, *Tobacco and Slaves: The Development of Southern Cultures in the Chesapeake, 1680–1800* (Chapel Hill, NC: University of North Carolina Press for the Institute of Early American History and Culture, 1986).

LANDES, JOAN B., *Women and the Public Sphere in the Age of the French Revolution* (Ithaca, NY: Cornell University Press, 1988).

LANDSMAN, NED C., *Scotland and Its First American Colony, 1683–1765* (Princeton: Princeton University Press, 1985).

―― *From Colonials to Provincials: American Thought and Culture, 1680–1760* (New York: Twayne, 1997).

―― 'Presbyterians, Evangelicals, and the Education Culture of the Middle Colonies', *Pennsylvania History*, 64 (1997), 168–82.

LANGFORD, PAUL, *A Polite and Commercial People, England, 1727–1783* (Oxford: Oxford University Press, 1989).

LAQUEUR, THOMAS, *Making Sex: Body and Gender from the Greeks to Freud* (Cambridge, Mass.: Harvard University Press, 1990).

LAW, ALEXANDER, *Education in Edinburgh in the Eighteenth Century* (London: University of London Press, 1965).

LENMAN, BRUCE, 'Colonial Wars and Imperial Instability, 1688–1793', in P. J. Marshall (ed.), *The Oxford History of the British Empire*, Vol. 2: *The Eighteenth Century* (Oxford: Oxford University Press, 1998), 151–68.

LEPORE, JILL, *The Name of War: King Philip's War and the Origins of American Identity* (New York: Knopf, 1998).

LERNER, GERDA, *The Creation of Patriarchy* (Oxford: Oxford University Press, 1986).

LEVY, BARRY, *Quakers and the American Family: British Settlement in the Delaware Valley* (Oxford: Oxford University Press, 1988).

LEWIS, JAN, 'Domestic Tranquillity and the Management of Emotion Among the Gentry of Pre-Revolutionary Virginia', *William and Mary Quarterly*, 39 (1982), 135–49.

―― *The Pursuit of Happiness: Family and Values in Jefferson's Virginia* (Cambridge: Cambridge University Press, 1983).

―― 'The Republican Wife: Virtue and Seduction in the Early Republic', *William and Mary Quarterly*, 44 (1987), 689–721.

LEWIS, JAN ELLEN, 'The White Jeffersons', in Jan Ellen Lewis and Peter S. Onuf (eds.), *Sally Hemings and Thomas Jefferson: History, Memory, and Civic Culture* (Charlottesville, Va. University Press of Virginia, 1999), 127–60.

―― and ONUF, PETER S. (eds.), *Sally Hemings and Thomas Jefferson: History, Memory, and Civic Culture* (Charlottesville, Va.: University Press of Virginia, 1999).

LINEBAUGH, PETER and REDIKER, MARCUS, *The Many-Headed Hydra: Sailors, Slaves, Commoners, and the Hidden History of the Revolutionary Atlantic* (Boston: Beacon Press, 2000).

LIVELY, SUSAN LINDSEY, 'Going Home: Americans in Britain, 1740–1776', Ph.D, Harvard University (1996).
LLOYD, CHRISTOPHER, *The British Seaman, 1200–1860: A Social Survey* (Rutherford, NJ: Fairleigh Dickinson University Press, 1968).
LOCKRIDGE, KENNETH A., *On the Sources of Patriarchal Rage: The Commonplace Books of William Byrd and Thomas Jefferson and the Gendering of Power in the Eighteenth Century*, The History of Emotions Series (New York: New York University Press, 1992).
LOMBARD, ANNE S., *Making Manhood: Growing Up Male in Colonial New England* (Cambridge, Mass.: Harvard University Press, 2003).
LOVEJOY, DAVID S., *Rhode Island Politics and the American Revolution, 1760–1776* (Providence, RI: Brown University Press, 1958).
LOVELL, MARGARETTA M., *Art in a Season of Revolution: Painters, Artisans, and Patrons in Early America* (Philadelphia: University of Pennsylvania Press, 2005).
LYONS, CLARE A., 'Mapping an Atlantic Sexual Culture: Homoeroticism in Eighteenth-Century Philadelphia', *William and Mary Quarterly*, 60 (2003), 119–54.
──── *Sex among the Rabble: An Intimate History of Gender and Power in the Age of Revolution, Philadelphia, 1730–1830* (Chapel Hill, NC: University of North Carolina Press for the Omohundro Institute of Early American History and Culture, 2006).
MAAS, D. E., *The Return of the Massachusetts Loyalists* (New York: Garland Publishing, 1989).
MCCALL, LAURA and YACAVONE, DONALD (eds.), *A Shared Experience: Men, Women, and the History of Gender* (New York: New York University Press, 1998).
MCCORMACK, MATTHEW, *The Independent Man: Citizenship and Gender Politics in Georgian England* (Manchester: Manchester University Press, 2005).
MCCURRY, STEPHANIE, *Masters of Small Worlds: Yeoman Households, Gender Relations, and the Political Culture of the Antebellum South Carolina Low Country* (Oxford: Oxford University Press, 1995).
MCCUSKER, JOHN J., *Money and Exchange in Europe and America, 1600–1775: A Handbook* (Chapel Hill, NC: University of North Carolina Press for the Institute of Early American History and Culture, 1978).
MCCUSKER, JOHN J. and MORGAN, KENNETH (eds.), *The Early Modern Atlantic Economy* (Cambridge: Cambridge University Press, 2000).
MACDONALD, D. L., *Monk Lewis: A Critical Biography* (Toronto, Ont.: University of Toronto Press, 2000).
MACFARLANE, ALAN, *Marriage and Love in England: Modes of Reproduction, 1300–1840* (Oxford: Blackwell, 1986).
MCGANN, JEROME, *The Poetics of Sensibility: A Revolution in Literary Style* (Oxford: Clarendon Press, 1996).
MCGIFFERT, MICHAEL, et al., 'Forum: How Revolutionary Was the Revolution? A Discussion of Gordon S. Wood's *The Radicalism of the American Revolution*', *William and Mary Quarterly*, 51 (1994), 677–716.
MCINTOSH, CAREY, *Common and Courtly Language: The Stylistics of Social Class in Eighteenth-Century English Literature* (Philadelphia: University of Pennsylvania Press, 1986).
──── *The Evolution of English Prose, 1700–1800: Style, Politeness, and Print Culture* (Cambridge: Cambridge University Press, 1998).

McIntyre, Sheila McCall, ' "This Loving Correspondency": New England Ministerial Communication and Association, 1670–1730', Ph.D, Boston University (1996).

McKenzie, Alan T. (ed.), *Sent as a Gift: Eight Correspondences from the Eighteenth Century* (Athens, Ga.: University of Georgia Press, 1993).

Mancke, Elizabeth and Shammas, Carole (eds.), *The Creation of the British Atlantic World* (Baltimore, Md.: Johns Hopkins University Press, 2005).

Mann, Bruce H., *Republic of Debtors: Bankruptcy in the Age of American Independence* (Cambridge, Mass.: Harvard University Press, 2002).

Mapp, Paul W., 'Atlantic History from Imperial, Continental, and Pacific Perspectives (Forum: Beyond the Atlantic)', *William and Mary Quarterly*, 63 (Oct. 2006), 713–24.

Marshall, David, *The Surprising Effects of Sympathy: Marivaux, Diderot, Rousseau, and Mary Shelley* (Chicago: University of Chicago Press, 1988).

Marshall, P. J. (ed.), *The Oxford History of the British Empire*, Vol. 2: *The Eighteenth Century* (Oxford: Oxford University Press, 1998).

____ *'A Free Though Conquering People': Eighteenth-Century Britain and its Empire* (Aldershot: Ashgate, 2003).

____ *The Making and Unmaking of Empires: Britain, India, and America, c.1750–1783* (Oxford: Oxford University Press, 2005).

Mason, Keith, 'A Loyalist's Journey: James Parker's Response to the Revolutionary Crisis', *Virginia Magazine of History and Biography*, 102 (1994), 139–66.

Mathias, Peter, 'Risk, Credit and Kinship in Early Modern Enterprise', in John J. McCusker and Kenneth Morgan (eds.), *The Early Modern Atlantic Economy* (Cambridge: Cambridge University Press, 2000), 15–35.

Maza, Sarah, 'Domestic Melodrama as Political Ideology: The Case of the Comte de Sanois', *American Historical Review*, 94 (1989), 1249–64.

____ *Private Lives and Public Affairs: The Causes Célèbres of Pre-Revolutionary France* (Berkeley: University of California Press, 1993).

____ 'Review Essay: Stories in History: Cultural Narratives in Recent Works in European History', *American Historical Review*, 101 (1996), 1493–515.

____ 'Only Connect: Family Values in the Age of Sentiment: Introduction', *Eighteenth-Century Studies*, 30 (1997), 207–12.

Morgan, Edmund, *The Puritan Family: Religion and Domestic Relations in Seventeenth-Century New England*, rev. edn. (New York: Harper & Row, 1966).

____ and Morgan, Helen M., *The Stamp Act Crisis: Prologue to Revolution* (Chapel Hill, NC: University of North Carolina Press for the Institute of Early American History and Culture, 1953).

Morgan, Gwenda and Rushton, Peter, *Eighteenth-Century Criminal Transportation: The Formation of the Criminal Atlantic* (Basingstoke: Palgrave/Macmillan, 2004).

Morgan, Jennifer, *Laboring Women: Reproduction and Gender in New World Slavery*, Early American Studies (Philadelphia: University of Pennsylvania Press, 2004).

Morgan, Kenneth, 'Business Networks in the British Export Trade to North America, 1750–1800', in John J. McCusker and Kenneth Morgan (eds.), *The Early Modern Atlantic Economy* (Cambridge: Cambridge University Press, 2000), 36–62.

Morgan, Philip D., 'Three Planters and Their Slaves: Perspectives on Slavery in Virginia, South Carolina, and Jamaica, 1750–1790', in Winthrop D. Jordan and Sheila L. Skemp (eds.), *Race and Family in the Colonial South* (Jackson, Miss.: University Press of Mississippi, 1987), 37–80.

MORGAN, PHILIP D., *Slave Counterpoint: Black Culture in the Eighteenth-Century Chesapeake and Lowcountry* (Chapel Hill, NC: University of North Carolina Press, 1998).

—— 'The Black Experience in the British Empire, 1680–1810', in P. J. Marshall (ed.), *The Oxford History of the British Empire*, Vol. 2: *The Eighteenth Century* (Oxford: Oxford University Press, 1998), 465–86.

—— 'Interracial Sex in the Chesapeake and the British Atlantic World, c. 1700–1820', in Jan Ellen Lewis and Peter S. Onuf (eds.), *Sally Hemings and Thomas Jefferson: History, Memory, and Civic Culture* (Charlottesville, Va.: University Press of Virginia, 1999), 52–84.

MUIR, EDWARD and RUGGIERO, GUIDO (eds.), *Microhistory and the Lost Peoples of Europe* (Baltimore, Md.: Johns Hopkins University Press, 1991).

MULCAHY, MATTHEW, *Hurricanes and Society in the British Greater Caribbean, 1624–1783* (Baltimore, Md.: Johns Hopkins University Press, 2006).

MULDREW, CRAIG, *The Economy of Obligation: The Culture of Credit and Social Relations in Early Modern England*, Early Modern History: Society and Culture (Basingstoke: Macmillan, 1998).

MULLAN, JOHN, 'The Language of Sentiment: Hume, Smith, and Henry Mackenzie', in Andrew Hook (ed.), *The History of Scottish Literature* (Aberdeen: Aberdeen University Press, 1987), ii. 273–90.

—— *Sentiment and Sociability: The Language of Feeling in the Eighteenth Century* (Oxford: Clarendon Press, 1988).

MULLIN, MICHAEL, *Africa in America: Slave Acculturation and Resistance in the American South and the British Caribbean, 1736–1831* (Urbana, Ill.: University of Illinois Press, 1992).

NASH, R. C., 'The Organization of Trade and Finance in the British Atlantic Economy, 1600–1830', in Peter A. Coclanis (ed.), *The Atlantic Economy During the Seventeenth and Eighteenth Centuries: Organization, Operation, Practice, and Personnel* (Columbia, SC: University of South Carolina Press, 2005), 95–151.

NEESER, ROBERT W. (ed.), *American Naval Songs and Ballads* (New Haven: Yale University Press, 1938).

NEW, M. CHRISTOPHER, *Maryland Loyalists in the American Revolution* (Centreville, Md.: Tidewater Publishing, 1996).

NICHOLS, ELISABETH B., '"Pray Don't Tell Anybody that I Write Politics": Private Expressions and Public Admonitions in the Early Republic', Ph.D, (University of New Hampshire (1997).

NORLING, LISA, *Captain Ahab Had a Wife: New England Women and the Whalefishery, 1720–1870*, Gender and American Culture (Chapel Hill, NC: University of North Carolina Press, 2000).

NORTON, MARY BETH, *The British-Americans: The Loyalist Exiles in England, 1774–1789* (Boston: Little, Brown and Company, 1972).

—— 'Eighteenth-Century American Women in Peace and War: The Case of the Loyalists', *William and Mary Quarterly*, 33 (1976), 386–409.

—— *Liberty's Daughters; The Revolutionary Experience of American Women, 1750–1800* (Boston: Little, Brown & Co., 1980).

—— 'Gender and Defamation in Seventeenth-Century Maryland', *William and Mary Quarterly*, 44 (1987), 3–39.

Nussbaum, Felicity A., 'Eighteenth-Century Women's Autobiographical Commonplaces', in Shari Benstock (ed.), *The Private Self: Theory and Practice of Women's Autobiographical Writings* (London: Routledge, 1988), 147–71.

O'Brien, Patrick K., 'Inseparable Connections: Trade, Economy, Fiscal State, and the Expansion of Empire, 1688–1815', in P. J. Marshall (ed.), *The Oxford History of the British Empire*, Vol. 2: *The Eighteenth Century* (Oxford: Oxford University Press, 1998), 53–77.

——— 'Merchants and Bankers as Patriots or Speculators? Foreign Commerce and Monetary Policy in Wartime, 1793–1815', in John J. McCusker and Kenneth Morgan (eds.), *The Early Modern Atlantic Economy* (Cambridge: Cambridge University Press, 2000), 250–77.

O'Day, Rosemary, *The Family and Family Relationships, 1500–1900: England, France and the United States of America* (New York: St Martin's Press, 1994).

O'Shaughnessy, Andrew Jackson, *An Empire Divided: The American Revolution and the British Caribbean* (Philadelphia: University of Pennsylvania Press, 2000).

Outhwaite, R. B. (ed.), *Marriage and Society: Studies in the Social History of Marriage* (New York: St Martin's Press, 1982).

'Oxford English Dictionary Online (2nd edn.)' (Oxford University Press, 1989).

Paulson, Ronald, *Rowlandson: A New Interpretation* (London: Studio Vista, 1972).

Pearsall, Sarah M. S., ' "After All These Revolutions": Epistolary Identities in an Atlantic World, 1760–1815 ', Ph.D, Harvard University (2001).

——— 'Hume—and Others—on Marriage', in Marina Frasca-Spada and P. J. E. Kail (eds.), *Impressions of Hume* (Oxford: Clarendon Press, 2005), 269–291.

Peck, John, *Maritime Fiction: Sailors and the Sea in British and American Novels, 1719–1917* (Basingstoke: Palgrave, 2001).

Penningroth, Dylan, *The Claims of Kinfolk: African American Property and Community in the Nineteenth-Century South* (Chapel Hill, NC: University of North Carolina Press, 2003).

Perry, Ruth, 'Colonizing the Breast: Sexuality and Maternity in Eighteenth-Century England', *Journal of the History of Sexuality*, 2 (1991), 204–23.

——— *Novel Relations: The Transformation of Kinship in English Literature and Culture, 1748–1818* (Cambridge: Cambridge University Press, 2004).

Pettengill, Claire C., 'Sisterhood in a Separate Sphere: Female Friendship in Hannah Webster Foster's *The Coquette* and *The Boarding School*', *Early American Literature*, 27 (1992), 185–203.

Phillips, Roderick, *Untying the Knot: A Short History of Divorce* (Cambridge: Cambridge University Press, 1991).

Pine, L. G. (ed.), *Burke's Genealogical and Heraldic History of the Landed Gentry*, 17th edn. (London: Burke's Peerage, 1952).

Pollock Linda A., *Forgotten Children: Parent–Child Relations from 1500 to 1900* (Cambridge: Cambridge University Press, 1983).

Polly, Gregory Paul, 'Private and Public Letters: Epistolary Negotiations in the Early Republic', Ph.D, Harvard University (1997).

Porter, Charles, 'Foreword: Men/Women of Letters', *Yale French Studies*, 71 (1986), 1–14.

Porter, Roy and Rousseau, G. S., *Gout: The Patrician Malady* (New Haven: Yale University Press, 1998).

POTTER, JANICE, *The Liberty We Seek: Loyalist Ideology in New York and Massachusetts* (Cambridge, Mass.: Harvard University Press, 1983).

POTTER-MACKINNON, JANICE, *While the Women Only Wept: Loyalist Refugee Women* (Montreal: McGill-Queen's University Press, 1993).

PRICE, JACOB, *Capital and Credit in British Overseas Trade* (Cambridge, Mass.: Harvard University Press, 1980).

Price, Jacob M., 'What Did Merchants Do? Reflections on British Overseas Trade, 1660–1790', *Journal of Economic History*, 49 (1989), 267–84.

―― 'The Imperial Economy, 1700–1776', in P. J. Marshall (ed.), *The Oxford History of the British Empire*, Vol. 2: *The Eighteenth Century* (Oxford: Oxford University Press, 1998), 78–104.

PRIEST, CLAIRE, 'Creating an American Property Law: Alienability and its Limits in American History', *Harvard Law Review*, 120 (2006), 385–459.

PYBUS, CASSANDRA, *Epic Journeys of Freedom: Runaway Slaves of the American Revolution and Their Global Quest for Liberty* (Boston: Beacon Press, 2004).

RANLET, PHILIP, *The New York Loyalists* (Knoxville, Tenn.: University of Tennessee Press, 1986).

RAVEN, JAMES, 'The Atlantic World, Part 3: The Importation of Books in the Eighteenth Century', in *The History of the Book in America*, Vol. 1: *The Colonial Book in the Atlantic World* (Cambridge: Cambridge University Press, 2000), 183–97.

―― *London Booksellers and American Customers: Transatlantic Literary Community and the Charleston Library Society, 1748–1811* (Columbia, SC: University of South Carolina Press, 2002).

―― SMALL, HELEN, and TADMOR, NAOMI (eds.), *The Practice and Representation of Reading in England* (Cambridge: Cambridge University Press, 2006).

REDFORD, BRUCE, *The Converse of the Pen: Acts of Intimacy in the Eighteenth-Century Familiar Letter* (Chicago: University of Chicago Press, 1986).

REDIKER, MARCUS, *Between the Devil and the Deep Blue Sea: Merchant Seamen, Pirates, and the Anglo-American Maritime World, 1700–1750* (Cambridge: Cambridge University Press, 1987).

RETFORD, KATE, *The Art of Domestic Life: Family Portraiture in Eighteenth-Century England* (New Haven: Yale University Press, 2006).

REVEL, JACQUES (ed.), *Jeux d'échelles: la micro-analyse à l'expérience* (Paris: Gallimard/Le Seuil, 1996).

―― 'Micro-analyse et construction du social', in Jacques Revel (ed.), *Jeux d'échelles: la micro-analyse à l'expérience* (Paris: Gallimard/Le Seuil, 1996), 15–36.

RHODEN, NANCY L., *Revolutionary Anglicanism: The Colonial Church of England Clergy During the American Revolution* (New York: New York University Press, 1999).

RISKIN, JESSICA, *Science in the Age of Sensibility: The Sentimental Empiricists of the French Enlightenment* (Chicago: University of Chicago Press, 2002).

ROACH, JOSEPH, *Cities of the Dead: Circum-Atlantic Performance* (New York: Columbia University Press, 1996).

ROBERTSON, JEAN, *The Art of Letter Writing: An Essay on the Handbooks Published in England During the Sixteenth and Seventeenth Centuries* (Liverpool: University Press of Liverpool, 1942).

ROBINSON, HOWARD, *The British Post-Office: A History* (Princeton: Princeton University Press, 1948).

RYAN, MARY P., *Cradle of the Middle Class: The Family in Oneida County, New York, 1790–1865*, Interdisciplinary Perspectives on Modern History (Cambridge: Cambridge University Press, 1981).

SAUNDERS, GAIL, *Bahamian Loyalists and their Slaves* (London: Macmillan Caribbean, 1983).

SCHIEBINGER, LONDA, 'Why Mammals Are Called Mammals: Gender Politics in Eighteenth-Century Natural History', *American Historical Review*, 98 (1993), 382–411.

SCOTT, ROBERT FORSYTH (ed.), *Admissions to the College of St. John the Evangelist in the University of Cambridge*, Part 4: *1767–1802*, (Cambridge: Deighton, Bell & Co, 1931).

SEAVER, PAUL, *Wallington's World: A Puritan Artisan in Seventeenth-Century London* (Stanford, Calif.: Stanford University Press, 1985).

SHAMMAS, CAROLE, 'Anglo-American Household Government in Comparative Perspective', *William and Mary Quarterly*, 52 (1995), 104–44.

——— *A History of Household Government in America* (Charlottesville, Va.: University of Virginia Press, 2000).

SHEPARD, ALEXANDRA, *Meanings of Manhood in Early Modern England* (Oxford: Oxford University Press, 2003).

SHERIDAN, RICHARD, *Sugar and Slavery: An Economic History of the British West Indies, 1632–1775* (Baltimore, Md.: Johns Hopkins University Press, 1974).

SHERIDAN, R. B., 'Simon Taylor, Sugar Tycoon of Jamaica, 1740–1813', *Agricultural History*, 45 (1971), 285–96.

SHIELDS, DAVID S., *Civil Tongues and Polite Letters in British America* (Chapel Hill, NC: University of North Carolina Press for the Institute of Early American History and Culture, 1997).

SHOEMAKER, ROBERT B., *Gender in English Society, 1650–1850: The Emergence of Separate Spheres?* (London: Longman, 1998).

SHUFFLETON, FRANK, 'In Different Voices: Gender in the American Republic of Letters', *Early American Literature*, 25 (1990), 289–304.

SHY, JOHN, *A People Numerous and Armed: Reflections on the Miltary Struggle for American Independence*, rev. edn. (Ann Arbor, Mich.: University of Michigan Press, 1990).

SIEVENS, MARY BETH, *Stray Wives: Marital Conflict in Early National New England* (New York: New York University Press, 2005).

SIMISTER, FLORENCE PARKER, *The Fire's Center: Rhode Island in the Revolutionary Era, 1763–1790*, Rhode Island Bicentennial Foundation (Providence, RI: 1979).

SKINNER, GILLIAN, *Sensibility and Economics in the Novel, 1740–1800* (Basingstoke: Macmillan, 1999).

SMAIL, JOHN, 'Credit, Risk, and Honor in Eighteenth-Century Commerce', *Journal of British Studies*, 44 (July 2005), 439–56.

SMITH, DANIEL BLAKE, *Inside the Great House: Planter Family Life in Eighteenth-Century Chesapeake Society* (Ithaca, NY: Cornell University Press, 1980).

——— 'The Study of the Family in Early America: Trends, Problems, and Prospects', *William and Mary Quarterly*, 39 (1982), 3–28.

SMITH, MERRIL D., *Breaking the Bonds: Marital Discord in Pennsylvania, 1730–1830* (New York: New York University Press, 1991).

SMITH, MERRIL D., (ed.), *Sex and Sexuality in Early America* (New York: New York University Press, 1998).
SMITH, PAUL H., *Loyalists and Redcoats: A Study in British Revolutionary Policy* (Chapel Hill, NC: University of North Carolina Press for the Institute for Early American History and Culture, 1964).
SMITH, SIMON, 'British Exports to Colonial North America and the Mercantilist Fallacy', *Business History*, 37 (1995), 45–63.
SMITH, S. D., *Slavery, Family, and Gentry Capitalism in the British Atlantic: The World of the Lascelles, 1648–1834* (Cambridge: Cambridge University Press, 2006).
SMITH-ROSENBERG, CARROLL, 'The Female World of Love and Ritual: Relations Between Women in Nineteenth-Century America', *Signs*, 1 (1975), 1–29.
―― 'Domesticating Virtue: Coquettes and Revolutionaries in Young America', in Elaine Scarry (ed.), *Literature and the Body: Essays on Populations and Persons* (Baltimore, Md.: Johns Hopkins University Press, 1988), 160–84.
SMOUT, T. C., LANDSMAN, N. C., and DEVINE, T. M., 'Scottish Emigration in the Seventeenth and Eighteenth Centuries', in Nicholas Canny (ed.), *Europeans on the Move: Studies on European Migration, 1500–1800* (Oxford: Clarendon Press, 1994), 76–112.
SNYDER, HOLLY, 'A Sense of Place: Jews, Identity, and Social Status in Colonial British America, 1654–1831', Ph.D, Brandeis University (2000).
SNYDER, TERRI L., *Brabbling Women: Disorderly Speech and the Law in Early Virginia* (Ithaca, NY: Cornell University Press, 2003).
SOBEL, MECHAL, *The World They Made Together: Black and White Values in Eighteenth-Century Virginia* (Princeton: Princeton University Press, 1982).
―― *Teach Me Dreams: The Search for Self in the Revolutionary Era* (Princeton: Princeton University Press, 2000).
ST GEORGE, ROBERT BLAIR, *Conversing by Signs: Poetics of Implication in Colonial New England Culture* (Chapel Hill, NC: University of North Carolina Press, 1998).
―― (ed.), *Possible Pasts: Becoming Colonial in Early America* (Ithaca, NY: Cornell University Press, 2000).
STEELE, IAN K., *The English Atlantic, 1675–1740; An Exploration in Communication and Community* (Oxford: Oxford University Press, 1986).
STERN, JULIA A., *The Plight of Feeling: Sympathy and Dissent in the Early American Novel* (Chicago: University of Chicago Press, 1997).
STERN, PHILIP J., 'British Asia and British Atlantic: Comparisons and Connections (Forum: Beyond the Atlantic)', *William and Mary Quarterly*, 63 (Oct. 2006), 693–712.
STEVENSON, BRENDA E., *Life in Black and White: Family and Community in the Slave South* (New York: Oxford University Press, 1996).
STEWART, MAAJA A., 'Inexhaustible Generosity: The Fictions of Eighteenth-Century British Imperialism in Richard Cumberland's *The West Indian*', *The Eighteenth Century*, 37 (1996), 42–55.
STEWART, VIRGINIA ELSIE RADATZ, 'The Intercourse of Letters: Familiar Correspondence and the Transformation of American Identity in the Eighteenth Century', Ph.D, Northwestern University (1997).
STONE, LAWRENCE, *The Family, Sex and Marriage in England, 1500–1800* (New York: Harper & Row, 1977).

STONE, LAWRENCE, *Road to Divorce: England, 1530–1987* (Oxford: Oxford University Press, 1990).
―― *Broken Lives: Separation and Divorce in England, 1660–1857* (Oxford: Oxford University Press, 1993).
―― *Uncertain Unions and Broken Lives: Marriage and Divorce in England, 1660–1857*, abridged edn. (Oxford: Oxford University Press, 1995).
―― (ed.), *An Imperial State at War: Britain from 1689 to 1815* (London: Routledge, 1994).
STOWE, STEVEN M., 'The Rhetoric of Authority: The Making of Social Values in Planter Family Correspondence', *Journal of American History*, 73 (1987), 916–33.
―― *Intimacy and Power in the Old South: Ritual in the Lives of the Planters* (Baltimore, Md.: Johns Hopkins University Press, 1987).
STURTZ, LINDA L., *Propertied Women in Colonial Virginia* (New York: Routledge, 2002).
SULLIVAN, CERI, *The Rhetoric of Credit: Merchants in Early Modern Writing* (Madison, Wisc.: Fairleigh Dickinson University Press, 2002).
SYPHER, WYLIE, 'The West Indian as a "Character" in the Eighteenth Century', *Studies in Philology*, 36 (1939), 503–29.
TADMOR, NAOMI, ' "Family" and "Friend" in Richardson's *Pamela*: A Case Study in the History of the Family in Eighteenth-Century England', *Social History*, 13 (1989), 289–306.
―― 'The Concept of the Household-Family in Eighteenth-Century England', *Past & Present*, 151 (1996), 111–40.
―― *Family and Friends in Eighteenth-Century England: Household, Kinship, and Patronage* (Cambridge: Cambridge University Press, 2001).
THOMPSON, E. P., 'Patrician Society, Plebeian Culture', *Journal of Social History*, 7(1974), 382–405.
THORNTON, TAMARA PLAKINS, *Handwriting in America: A Cultural History* (New Haven, Conn.: Yale University Press, 1996).
TODD, JANET, *Sensibility: An Introduction* (London: Methuen, 1986).
TOSH, JOHN, *A Man's Place: Masculinity and the Middle-Class Home in Victorian England* (New Haven, Conn.: Yale University Press, 1999).
TURNER, DAVID M., *Fashioning Adultery: Gender, Sex and Civility in England, 1660–1740*, ed. Lyndal Roper, Past & Present Publications (Cambridge: Cambridge University Press, 2002).
TURNER, VICTOR W., *The Ritual Process: Structure and Anti-Structure* (Hawthorne, NY: Aldine Publishing Co., 1969).
ULRICH, LAUREL THATCHER, *Good Wives: Image and Reality in the Lives of Women in Northern New England, 1650–1750* (New York: Knopf, 1980).
―― *A Midwife's Tale: The Life of Martha Ballard, Based on Her Diary, 1785–1812* (New York: Knopf, 1990).
―― *The Age of Homespun: Objects and Stories in the Creation of an American Myth* (New York: Knopf, 2001).
―― *Well-Behaved Women Seldom Make History* (New York: Knopf, 2007).
VAN SANT, ANN JESSIE, *Eighteenth-Century Sensibility and the Novel: The Senses in Social Context* (Cambridge: Cambridge University Press, 1993).
VICKERY, AMANDA, *The Gentleman's Daughter: Women's Lives in Georgian England* (New Haven, Conn.: Yale University Press, 1998).

VICKERY, AMANDA J., 'Golden Age to Separate Spheres: A Review of the Categories and Chronology of English Women's History', *Historical Journal*, 36 (1993), 383–414.

VINCENT, DAVID, *Literacy and Popular Culture: England, 1750–1914*, Cambridge Studies in Oral and Literate Cultures (Cambridge: Cambridge University Press, 1989).

VINCENT-BUFFAULT, ANNE, *The History of Tears: Sensibility and Sentimentality in France* (Basingstoke: Macmillan, 1991).

WAGNER, JENNIFER A., 'Privacy and Anonymity in *Evelina*', in Harold Bloom (ed.), *Fanny Burney's 'Evelina'* (New York: Chelsea House, 1988), 99–110.

WAGNER, PETER, *Eros Revived: Erotica of the Enlightenment in England and America* (London: Paladin, 1988).

WAHRMAN, DROR, *The Making of the Modern Self: Identity and Culture in Eighteenth-Century England* (New Haven, Conn.: Yale University Press, 2004).

WALDSTREICHER, DAVID, 'Reading the Runaways: Self-Fashioning, Print Culture, and Confidence in Slavery in the Eighteenth-Century Mid-Atlantic', *William and Mary Quarterly*, 56 (1999), 243–72.

WALKER, JAMES W. ST G., *The Black Loyalists: The Search for the Promised Land in Nova Scotia and Sierra Leone, 1783–1870* (Halifax, Nova Scotia: Dalhousie University Press, 1976).

WALL, HELENA M., *Fierce Communion: Family and Community in Early America* (Cambridge, Mass.: Harvard University Press, 1990).

WALL, RICHARD, *et al.*(eds.), *Family History Revisited: Comparative Perspectives* (Newark, Del.: University of Delaware Press, 2001).

WATSON, NICOLA J., *Revolution and the Form of the British Novel, 1790–1825: Intercepted Letters, Interrupted Seductions* (Oxford: Clarendon Press, 1994).

WATT, IAN, *The Rise of the Novel: Studies in Defoe, Richardson, and Fielding* (Harmondsworth: Penguin, 1957).

WEBER, MAX, *The Protestant Ethic and the Spirit of Capitalism*, trans. Talcott Parsons (London: George Allen & Unwin, 1930).

WEISS, HARRY, *American Letter-Writers, 1698–1943* (New York: New York Public Library, 1945).

WHYMAN, SUSAN E., *Sociability and Power in Late-Stuart England: The Cultural Worlds of the Verneys, 1660–1720* (Oxford: Oxford University Press, 1999).

WHYTE, IAN D., *Migration and Society in Britain, 1550–1830*, ed. Jeremy Black, Social History in Perspective (Basingstoke, Hampshire: Macmillan, 2000).

WILENTZ, SEAN (ed.), *Rites of Power: Symbolism, Ritual, and Politics Since the Middle Ages* (Philadelphia: University of Pennsylvania Press, 1985).

WILSON, KATHLEEN, *The Island Race: Englishness, Empire and Gender in the Eighteenth Century* (London: Routledge, 2003).

—— (ed.), *A New Imperial History: Culture, Identity, and Modernity in Britain and the Empire, 1660–1840* (Cambridge: Cambridge University Press, 2004).

WILSON, LISA, *Ye Heart of a Man: The Domestic Life of Men in Colonial New England* (New Haven, Conn.: Yale University Press, 1999).

WOOD, GORDON S., *The Radicalism of the American Revolution* (New York: Knopf, 1991).

WOOLF, VIRGINIA, *A Room of One's Own* [1929], ed. Jennifer Smith (Cambridge: Cambridge University Press, 1995).

WRIGHT, ESMOND, 'The New York Loyalists: A Cross-Section of Colonial Society', in Robert A. East and Jacob Judd (eds.), *The Loyalist Americans: A Focus on Greater New York* (Tarrytown, NY: Sleepy Hollow Restorations, 1975).

WRIGHTSON, KEITH, 'The Family in Early Modern England: Continuity and Change', in Stephen Taylor, Richard Connors, and Clyve Jones (eds.), *Hanoverian Britain and Empire: Essays in Memory of Philip Lawson* (London: Boydell Press, 1998), 1–22.

WRIGLEY, E. A. and SCHOFIELD, R. S., *The Population History of England, 1541–1871: A Reconstruction*, Studies in Social and Demographic History (Cambridge, Mass.: Harvard University Press, 1981).

WULF, KARIN, *'Not All Wives': Women of Colonial Philadelphia* (Ithaca, NY: Cornell University Press, 2000).

YAZAWA, MELVIN, *From Colonies to Commonwealth: Familial Ideology and the Beginnings of the American Republic* (Baltimore, Md.: Johns Hopkins University Press, 1985).

YOKOTA, KARIANN, 'A Culture of Insecurity: The United States as a Post-Colonial Nation', Ph.D., University of California, Los Angeles (2002).

YOUNG, ALFRED F., *The Shoemaker and the Tea Party: Memory and the American Revolution* (Boston: Beacon Press, 1999).

──── *Masquerade: The Life and Times of Deborah Sampson, Continental Soldier* (New York: Knopf, 2004).

──── *Liberty Tree: Ordinary People and the American Revolution* (New York: New York University Press, 2006).

ZACZEK, BARBARA MARIA, *Censored Sentiments: Letters and Censorship in Epistolary Novels and Conduct Material* (Newark, Del.: University of Delaware Press, 1997).

ZAGARRI, ROSEMARIE, 'Morals, Manners, and the Republican Mother', *American Quarterly*, 44 (1992), 192–215.

──── 'The Rights of Man and Woman in Post-Revolutionary America', *William and Mary Quarterly*, 55 (1998), 203–30.

ZAHEDIEH, NUALA, 'Economy', in David Armitage and Michael J. Braddick (eds.), *The British Atlantic World, 1500–1800* (Basingstoke: Palgrave/Macmillan, 2002), 51–68.

ZUCKERMAN, MICHAEL, 'The Fabrication of Identity in Early America', *William and Mary Quarterly*, 34 (1977), 183–214.

Index

Adams Family 5, 240
   see also Adams, Abigail and Adams, John
Adams, Abigail
   and 'Remember the Ladies' letter 4–5, 9, 16–18, 109
   and sensible letters 80–83, 85
Adams, John 4–5, 9–10, 15–16, 102, 125, 241
adultery 49
   and 'criminal conversation' 48, 52, 66, 221–3
   and cuckoldry 146, 210–239
   and familiarity 66, 236
   and family 210–239
affection
   and gender 124
African-Americans
   and claims of insensibility 88, 95–6, 105
   and images of 230
   and Jamaica 226
   and letters 42–3
   and sensible letters 94–6
age of consent, *see* marriage and age of consent
Aitchison, Mary (Molly), *see* Parker, Mary Aitchison (Molly)
Aitchison, Rebecca 153–4, 164–5
   relations with Steuart Family 64
Aitchison, William 153–4, 158–160
alienation 168, 223, 242
ambition, *see* family and ambition
Ambler, Eliza 32, 42
Ambler, John 32
American Revolution
   and Adams' letters 4–5
   and 'Boston Tea Party' 202
   and coming of 96
   and confiscation of property 160
   and connections 205
   and credit 192–3
   and cruelty 191, 195–8, 202–3, 206–7
   and Customs 186–7
   and deference 160
   and dependence 161–2, 177–178, 209
   and end of harmony 159–160
   and exiles 44–5, 63
   and familiarity 187
   and 'family feeling' 205
   and family life 16, 243
   and father-child relations 63, 203–4, 206–7
   and financial problems 171
   and imprisonment 160–1
   and independence 183
   and 'man of feeling' 195–6, 205, 208
   and marriage 181
   and mother-child relations 63, 154–5, 202
   and Non-Importation Acts 202
   and propaganda 201–4
   and resentment 189, 197, 204
   and rhetoric 16
   and ruin 205
   and sensibility 182–3, 194–205, 208–9
   and sensible letters 109–110
   and tenderness 204–5
   and tyranny 204
   see also American Revolutionary War; 'rights talk'; Loyalists
American Revolutionary War 44–5, 179–183
   and Battle of Lexington and Concord 184, 202
   and debt 190–3, 206–7
   and family separations 241–2
   and home 195–6, 197, 199, 202
   and soldiers 179, 182, 195–6
   and tears 196, 203–4
   and violation of women 202–3
   and women 195–7, 201–3
   see also exiles
'anxious patriarchs' 146
   and images of 147, 152, 155, 183, 231–2
   in Virginia 162
apologies for letter writing 75–8
art 230
assault 185
Atlantic economy
   and agency of the family 112–113, 114
   and family 146, 166
   and growth 32–34
   and importance of credit 115–123
   and its perils 118–120
   and sensibility 87, 127
   and trust 118
   as 'empire of goods' 33
   see also credit; bill of exchange
Atlantic history
   as analytical category 10–11, 12
   definition 12
Atlantic Ocean 30, 55
Atlantic separations
   and credit 145

Atlantic separations (*cont.*)
  and familiarity 145
  and family 1, 29–31, 45, 145, 163–4, 240
  and marriage 146
  and sensibility 145
Ambler Family 32
Arnold, Benedict 196
Austen, Jane 179
authenticity 24–5, 133, 169, 174–6, 178

Ballard, Martha 29
barbarism 173, 202–3
Barrell, Abigail 37
Barrett Family 229
Barry, J. (cabinetmaker) 244
benevolence (moral)
  and family 6
  and humanitarianism 127
  and sensibility 85–6
Bennet, Jean 128
bill of exchange 120, 126, 166, 171
Blackstone, William 140
'Black Will' 237–8
body, *see* sensibility and the body
Bolingbroke, Viscount Henry St John 145, 148
Bon Ton Magazine 48
books, *see* communications infrastructure
Boston 130, 160
'Boston Tea Party', *see* American Revolution
breastfeeding 108
bridal pregnancy 47–8
Brissett, Joseph 211, 216, 218–219, 238
brothels 123
Brown, Alexander 78
Brown, Caesar 107
Brown Family 77–8, 107
Brown, Patrick 77, 102
Brown, Sophia Waterhouse 62, 100, 102
Brown, Susanna 77, 241–2
Brownrigg, John 38, 62, 101
Burney, Frances
  and *Cecilia* 90, 168, 170
  and *Evelina* 74, 91–2, 99, 103–4
Butler Family
  and tutor 62–3
Butler, Harriet 129
Butler, Mary 101
  death of 104–5
Butler, Pierce
  and concerns over familiarity 60
  and concerns over letter-writing 78
  and debt language 129–130
  and rhythms of letter writing 39
  and sensibility 103–5
  and 'strict scrutiny' 135–8, 141–2

Butler, Sarah 136–7
Butler, Thomas 62–3, 103–5, 135–8, 141–2
Butler, Weeden 63, 103–5
Byrd, William 36, 231

Cadogan v. Cadogan 220
Cambridge University 59, 134, 213, 217
Caribbean Sea 30
Carrington, Eliza Ambler Brent 62, 245
Carroll, Charles 47, 132–3
Cecilia, *see* Burney, Frances
Cely, Margaret 60 n. 14
censorship, *see* letter writing
Chandler, Ann 42, 187 n. 34
Chandler, Edward 42, 189
character 117, 167, 171, 173–5, 208
  of Britain 204–5
Charles 154
Chesterfield, Philip Dormer Stanhope, Earl of,
  and business letters 132
  and friendship 124
  and Madame de Sevigné 78–9
  and 'strict scrutiny' 124–5
  comparisons with 78, 133, 134
  letter collection 73, 78–9, 194
  letters in letter-writing manuals 71
Cheyne, George 83, 87, 89, 91
Chesapeake, *see* Virginia
child rearing 8
  and credit 123–6, 193–4
  and familiarity 60–1
  and patrimony 207–8
  and 'performing a parents duty' 62–5
  and letter writing 72
  styles of 156–7
Chippenham Park estate
  (Cambridgeshire) 218, 225–6, 230, 237
Chloe 154
'citizen of the world' 114
Civil War 244
Clarissa, *see* Richardson, Samuel
Clark, Eliza 127–8
clergy 46, 77, 210, 217, 221
Cobbet, Thomas 60–1
coffeehouses 38
communications infrastructure 34–5
  and books 35
  and newspapers 35
  and packet services 35
  and postal services 35–6, 42, 102
communities 12, 242–3
Complete Letter-Writer, The 67, 70, 145
  and alternative title 72
  and inscriptions 71
  and letters of Ignatius Sancho 94–5

conduct literature, *see* letter-writing manuals
confiscation, *see* American Revolution and confiscation of property
Constitutional Convention 103, 141
conversation, *see* letter writing
connections ('connexions') 145
  and American Revolution 46, 205
  between nerves 83
  sympathetic 83
'consumer revolution' 89
Coombe, Sally 99–100, 128
Coombe, Thomas 38, 39, 77–8, 99–100, 128
  and 'ocean of the world' metaphor 46
Court Letter-Writer, The 26–7, 29
Court Letter-Writer, The (frontispiece) 27
courtship
  and sensibility 194–5
Cowper, Margaret 59, 100, 241, 247
credit
  and American Revolution 192–3
  and Atlantic economy 115–123
  and authority 116
  and Charles S. Parker 165
  and child rearing 123–6, 146
  and the family 113, 167–8, 173, 240
  and gender 116
  and independence 183
  and letter writing 125–132
  and mother-child relations 128
  and selfhood 243
  and sensibility 172–5, 177
  and sibling relations 128–130
  and 'strict scrutiny' 171
  and tears 167
  and tenderness 171–2, 177
  and women 116, 219
  definition of 115–116
  importance of 114–123
  see also 'man of credit'
Crèvecoeur, Hector St John de 161
'criminal conversation', *see* adultery
Crooke, Ann (Wickham) 185
Crooke, Catherine, *see* Dudley, Catherine (Crooke)
Crooke, Robert 185–6
cruelty 191
  and American Revolution 191, 195–8, 202–4, 206–7
  and family 172, 218
  and independence 242
  and sensibility 195–6, 197–8
  and slavery 162–3
courtly styles, *see* letter writing
courtship 65–6
Cumberland, Richard
  and *The West Indian* 50–1

Customs 183–5
  and American Revolution 186–7, 190, 202

daughters pleading with fathers 203–4, 223–4
debt
  and American Revolutionary War 190–3, 206–7
  and family 128–130, 176, 217, 221, 243
  and magazine stories 149
  and sensibility 151
  culture of, in Virginia 158
  desire to avoid 190–3
  national 123
debtors
  and lawsuits against 158
  and treatment of 155
  and Patriots 159, 161, 175
debtors' prison 173, 192
Declaration of Independence 16, 173
deference 97, 160, 162
  see also letter writing and deferential styles
deferential styles, *see* letter writing and deferential styles
Defoe, Daniel
  and *The Complete English Tradesman* 117, 121, 125, 131, 169, 176
demography 242
dependence
  and American Revolution 161–2, 177–178, 209
  and ruin 121
desks/secretaries 38, 244
Dickinson, John 109
Dictionary, see Johnson, Samuel
Diderot 242 n. 7
Dinah 154
disinheritance 111, 137, 140, 225
distress 172–4, 199, 241
  and Loyalism 46, 173, 192, 193, 203–5
  and tyranny 173–4
divorce, *see* marriage and separation/divorce
'Doctor' 154
Douglass, Frederick 23
drafts, *see* letter writing
Dudley, Catherine (Crooke) 181–209
Dudley, Charles 35, 181–209
Dudley, Charles (jr) 187
Dudley, Mary-Ann 187
Dunmore, Earl of, *see* Murray, John
Dwarris Family 246
dunning 115, 120, 141, 172
Durrell, William 70

earthquakes, *see* natural disasters
Eastwood 154
ecclesiastical court 220

economy, *see* Atlantic economy
Eden 153
Edinburgh 152, 154
education
  English 47, 214–5
  Scottish 149, 152–4
  women's 186, 234
Edwards, Bryan 49, 228
effeminacy 49
  and foppish letter-writing 67
  and 'macaroni' 50, 55
Ellery, Christopher 45, 96–7, 102–3, 228
Ellery, Mary 45, 102–103
Elletson, Roger Hope 106
email 1, 247
emancipation scheme 162–3
empire 11, 207
England 38, 62, 106–7, 112, 134
  and Dudley family 146, 187, 200
  and Taylor family 137–141
  and Tharp family 146, 214, 226–7
English Channel 30
English Letter-Writer, The 39, 69
English Letter-Writer, The (frontispiece) 40
Enimie of Idlenesse, The 130–1, 207
epistolary novels 6
  and authenticity 25
  and circulation 75, 190, 194
  and familiarity 74
  and father-child relations 56, 74, 203–4
  and kin relations 74
  and mobility 29, 56
  and mother-child relations 56, 92
  and patriarchy 241
  and sensibility 235–6
  and sensible letters 90–2
  and sibling relations 74
Equiano, Olaudah 89
Esten v. the Duke of Hamilton 50–4
Erskine, Thomas 52–3
Eton 213
Evelina, see Burney, Frances
exiles 44–5, 63, 241
exports, *see* trade
Eyre, Severn 76–7, 102

familiarity
  and adultery 66, 236
  and American Revolution 187
  and apologies for letter-writing 75–8
  and 'being under the same roof' 63
  and courtship 65
  and family 240
  and father-child relations 59–60, 62–3
  and 'fictive families' 56
  and gift-giving 65
  and kin relations 62, 64–5
  and letter-writing 66–79
  and mother-child relations 60–1
  and Parker family 151
  and selfhood 243
  and sibling relations 62, 64
  as tone 66–8
  contrasted with formality 60–1
  contrasted with intimacy 57–8, 68
  contrasted with politeness 57–9, 68–9
  definitions 57–8
  denied to servants and slaves 58
  see also child rearing, friendship, marriage,
'familiar letters' 66–79
  and letter-writing manuals 67–8
  and marriage 182
  and Parker family 151
family
  and adultery 210–239
  and ambition 145, 230–2, 238
  and artifact of letters 1–3, 244–7
  and Atlantic economy 114
  and Atlantic separations 1, 29–31, 45, 145, 163–4, 240
  and credit 113
  and debt 217, 221
  and debt language 128–130
  and lawsuits 216–217
  and rivalries 86
  and ruin 122–3
  and sensibility 85–86, 209
  definitions of 28–9
  see also friendship
'family feeling' 7–8, 9, 11, 16, 146, 240
  and agitation to end slavery 107–8
  and American Revolution 205
  and *Esten v. the Duke of Hamilton* 53
  and letters 54, 182, 243
  as political tool 17, 182, 205
family networks
  and Jews 33
  and Quakers 33
  and Scots 33, 64
family portraits 6, 179
  and letter-writing manuals 26, 39, 69, 179
Farewell, The 180
father-child relations
  and American Revolution 63, 203–4, 206–7
  and Chesterfield, Philip Dormer Stanhope, Earl of 73, 78–9, 124–5, 132
  and concerns over imperial ventures 50
  and courtship 65
  and credit 24, 114–115, 123–6, 128–130
  and deference 97
  and definition of family 28
  and dependence 161

and Dudley family 187–8, 191–3
and duties 49
and epistolary novels 56, 74, 203–4
and *Esten v. the Duke of Hamilton* 52
and familiarity 59–61, 62–3
and frontispieces 26, 40, 69
and illegitimacy 215, 227–8
and justifications of behavior 16
and letter-writing manuals 70, 71, 93
and letters 77, 78
and Parker family 146, 149–178
and patriarchy/paternalism 111–112, 156–7, 165
and sending of letters 39, 89
and sensibility 10, 101, 102–4
and separations from children 29–31, 32, 45, 46–7, 64
and silences 37–8
and slavery 106, 108
and 'strict scrutiny' 132–142
and Tharp family 214–215, 218, 221–4, 228–9, 231–9
see also patriarchy; child rearing; daughters pleading with fathers
Fenwick, Eliza 88–9
flotsam 119
Forbes, Bennet 39
Forbes, Dorothy 127–8
Forbes, John M. 39
Force, John B. 43 n. 64
France 160–1
Franklin, Benjamin 115, 117–118, 125
French Revolution
  and 'moral panic' 48
  and ruin 123
  and sensibility 105
friendship 108, 222–3
  and business relations 34, 175
  and Chesterfield, Philip Dormer Stanhope (Earl of) 124
  and connections 45
  and Dudley family 190, 194
  and familiarity 59, 62
  and letter writing 46, 69, 78, 93–4
  as synonym for family 28, 192
  in marriage 81–2, 163–4, 198–201, 205
  related to humanity 82

gambling 123, 125
Gallimore, Sarah 215, 234–5
Galloway, Elizabeth 37, 59, 63
Galloway Family 37, 63
Galloway, Grace 37, 63, 196
Galloway, Joseph 63, 196

gender
  and affection 124
  and ruin 121
  and sensibility 87–8, 194–203
  see also women, men
genealogy 246
George III 173–4, 216
Georgia 38, 100, 246
gift-giving 65
Glasgow 152
Goethe, Johann Wolfgang von 149, 168, 190
Goldsmith, Oliver 23
Good Hope (estate) 226, 230, 237, 239
gout 226, 239
Green, William 216–217, 234–5, 237
Greg Family 59–60

Hadwen, Elizabeth 39, 128
Haiti 52, 53, 160
  and Revolution 44–5
Hannah 246
Hanover Parish (Jamaica) 213–214
harpsichord 195
Harrow 134
hearts, as literary motif
  and corruption 225
  and courtship 194
  and finances 191–2
  and Goethe, Johann Wolfgang von 149
  and letter collections 93
  and sensibility 9, 84, 88, 167, 181, 204
  and slavery 94–5
  in letter-writing manuals 69, 93–4
  in letters 82, 86, 99–105, 152
hero 151, 167–8, 178
Hessian troops 201
History of Miss Betsy Thoughtless, The 194
home
  and American Revolutionary War 195–6, 197, 199, 202
honesty 173, 178
honor 168
Hopkins, Esek (General) 186, 195–6
'household-family' 13, 28, 29, 49, 58 n. 5, 243
Howard, Martin 184
Hulton, Ann 130, 202–3
Hume, David 6–7, 83, 85, 230
hurricanes, *see* natural disasters
husbands, *see* marriage
Hutcheson, Francis 85, 200
Hutchinson Family 202

idleness, 111–112, 124, 129, 132–3, 139
  and letter-writing manuals 130–1
  and letters 136

illegitimacy 47–8, 235
   and father-child relations 215, 227–8
   and luxury 49
   in West Indies 49, 228
immigrants
   voluntary 32
imports, see trade
imprisonment 160–1, 176
independence 149
   and American Revolution 16, 183, 190–3, 207–8
   and credit 183
   and West Indies 230
   as ideal 168, 177–8, 183, 242
India 229
Indian Ocean 30
individuals 242–3
ink 1, 24, 38
Inns of Court 134
inoculations (smallpox) 157–8
insensibility
   alleged, in African-Americans 95–6, 105
   and slavery 88–9, 105
   as political claim 95–6, 105, 146, 201–4, 208
insurance 119–120
intimacy
   contrasted with familiarity 57–8
Ireland 38, 62, 101, 134
Irish Sea 30
Italy 50, 54

Jamaica 100
   and African-Americans 226
   and custos position 214
   and House of Assembly 214, 227
   and letters 246
   and marriage 212–213, 225
   and masculinity 212–213, 238–9
   and sensibility 212–213, 238
   and slave letters 106–7
   and Simon Taylor letters 137–141
   and Tharp family 146, 212–239
   and women 227–9, 238
   see also West Indies
Jefferson, Thomas 102
Jenings Family 42 n. 61
jetsam 119
Jews, see family networks
Johnson, Samuel
   and *Dictionary* 28, 57, 115–116, 118
Juba 154
justice 158, 186, 190–1, 207

Keane Family 59
Keane, Michael 59–60, 134–5

Keane, Hugh P. 59–60, 134–5
Kennedy, Ann Watts 129
kin relations
   and epistolary novels 74
   and familiarity 62, 64–5
   and letter-writing manuals 70
   and letters 39, 77, 90
   and Parker family 153, 154, 166
   and sensibility 100, 241
   and 'strict scrutiny' 137–141
   and Tharp family 217
kisses 101

Lady's Polite Secretary 39
Lady's Polite Secretary (frontispiece) 41
lawsuits 50–4, 158, 216–217, 220
Lee Family 42 n. 61
letter collections 73
   and editing 245–6
   and Jamaica 246
   and letter-writing manuals 72–3
   see also Chesterfield, Philip Dormer Stanhope, Earl of; Pope, Alexander; Richardson, Samuel; Sancho, Ignatius; Sterne, Laurence
letter writing
   and apologies 75–8
   and audience 76
   and business 75
   and censorship 37
   and conventions 240
   and conversational style 92
   and courtly styles 96–7
   and credit 125–132
   and deferential styles 96, 97–9, 106–8, 234
   and education 75
   and familiarity 66–79
   and friendship 46, 69, 78, 93–4
   and idleness 136
   and marriage 207–8
   and Protestantism 69, 75, 81
   and reading of letters 36
   and religious styles 96–7
   and rhythms 38
   and selfhood 243
   and sensibility 89–110, 234–5
   and servants 97, 131
   and slaves 97, 106–107, 245–6
   and spelling 133–4, 138
   and 'strict scrutiny' 125–6, 132–142
   and tools needed 38
   and use of clerks/scribes 68
   as conversation 67–8, 72–3, 77
   as subject of letters 36
   see also letter collections; letter-writing manuals; letters

letter-writing manuals
   and American editions 70–1
   and circulation 71–2, 75
   and 'familiar letter' 67–8
   and family letters 70
   and father-child relations 70, 71, 93
   and gender 71
   and heart motif 69
   and idleness 130–1
   and kin relations 70
   and letter collections 72–3
   and moral instruction 72
   and mother-child relations 70
   and sensible letters 93–5
   as pedagogical tools 72
letters
   and concern over non-receipt 37–8, 174
   and drafts 42
   and physical appearance 1–2, 132, 136–8
   and preservation 244–7
   and styles of production 39
   and styles of writing 39
   see also love letters
Letters to and from Particular Friends, see Richardson, Samuel
Lewis, Matthew ('Monk')
   The Monk 210, 232–3
Lex Mercatoria Rediviva 119, 121, 131
Library Company of Philadelphia 75 n. 82
liminality 54
literacy 34–5
London 111, 151, 154–5
   and the Dudleys 183, 190, 193, 208
Long, Edward 49, 212, 216, 228
Lord Hardwicke's Marriage Act (1753), *see* marriage
'loose fish' (metaphor) 53, 54–5, 91, 242
love letters 65, 93, 203
Low, Isaac 46, 128
Loyalism
   and conservatism 156–7, 183, 189–190
   and distress 173, 202–4
   and explanatory force 155–6
   and Newport 189, 197
   and propaganda 201–4
   and resentment 189
   and transatlantic perspective 157–8
   and women 154, 202–4, 241
   see also Loyalists
Loyalists 46, 129, 146
   and images of 147, 152
   and losses 153, 161, 188, 190–3, 205
   and opposition to Stamp Act 186
   and service 153
   motivated by ideal of independence 168, 177

luxury 49
   see also illegitimacy, effeminacy
Lynnhaven Parish (Princess Anne County, Virginia) 153

'macaroni', *see* effeminacy
Mackay, Eliza (McQueen) 102
Mackay Family 244, 246
Mackay, Robert 38, 101, 102
Mackenzie, Henry
   and *The Man of Feeling* 99, 194
Maintenon, Madame de 194
Malbone, Mary 100–1
Malcolm, John 202–3
'man of business' *see* 'man of credit'
'man of credit' 114–117, 123, 130
   and ideal of independence 191–3
   and 'man of business' 131–3, 135, 138
   and Parker family 155, 162, 166–8, 170, 175, 177–8
   and writing style 131–2
'man of fashion' 139
'man of feeling' 86–7, 189–190
   and American Revolution 205, 208
   and *Esten v. the Duke of Hamilton* 52
   and marriage 164, 167–8, 194–201
   and 'self-fashioning' 240
   and Tharp family 224
   opposed to tyranny 196
   see also Mackenzie, Henry
'man of honor' 224
Marchant's Avizo, The 131
marriage 47–8
   and age of consent 169
   and ambition 235
   and Atlantic separations 146
   and 'familiar letters' 182
   and familiarity 60, 65–6
   and Jamaica 212–213, 225
   and letters 207–8
   and Lord Hardwicke's Marriage Act (1753) 48
   and 'man of feeling' 164
   and marrying too early 169–170, 176–7
   and 'old husband' image 224–7
   and resentment 219
   and sensibility 179–183, 193–201, 208
   and separation/divorce 219–222
   and tenderness 201
   and West Indies 198–9
   as 'companionate marriage' 8
   as friendship 81–2, 163–4, 198–201, 205
   as submission for women 198–9, 200–1
   case study of the Dudleys 181–209
   clandestine marriage 149

marriage (cont.)
    disputes over 140, 155, 167–170, 233
    see also adultery
Martin, John 62
masculinity
    and Jamaica 213, 236, 238–9
    see also 'man of credit'; 'man of fashion'; 'man of feeling'; 'man of honor'
Massachusetts Assembly, 106–7
Maunsell, Betsy Brown 187 n. 34, 198–9
Maunsell, Sewell 198–9
Mein, William 101
men
    and sensible letters 101–3
see also masculinity
mercantile language of affection 126–132
Middle Temple Macaroni, The 51
migration
    and family 29–30
    internal 30
mobility 243
Monk, The, see Lewis, Matthew ('Monk')
mother-child relations
    and American Revolution 63, 154–5, 202
    and concerns over imperial ventures 50
    and credit 128
    and definition of family 28
    and Dudley family 187–8
    and epistolary novels/stories 56, 92
    and familiarity 60–1
    and frontispieces 26, 40, 69
    and letters 37, 77, 96–7
    and letter-writing manuals 70
    and Parker family 164–5
    and sensibility 9, 100–1, 102
    and separations from children 29–31, 32, 45, 46
    and slavery 88, 106–7, 108
    and Tharp family 214, 218, 234–5
    see also child rearing
Murray, John, Earl of Dunmore 158–9, 231
Murray, Lady Susan 231

Napoleonic invasion scare 216
Nanny 154
natural disasters 118–119
Ned 43 n. 64, 160
New Complete General Letter Writer 1
New England 112, 146
New Jersey 62, 100
New York 151, 172
Newport (Rhode Island) *see* Rhode Island
Newport Mercury 197

Newberry's Familiar Letter Writer 69
newspapers, *see* communications infrastructure
Non-Importation Acts, *see*, American Revolution
Norfolk (Virginia) 154, 158–160
Norris, Isaac 78, 128–9
North Sea 30
Nova Scotia 172
Nova Zembla 53
'normal exception' 10
North Carolina 38, 62, 101
Nugent, Lady Mary 227

'ocean of the world' (metaphor) 46–7, 54–5, 242
oceanic metaphors of destruction 121, 138–9
'Old Husband, The' 211
outcast 172, 174, 242
Oxford University 47

Pacific Ocean 30
packets, *see* communications infrastructure
Pamela, see Richardson, Samuel
paper 1, 38
parent-child relations, *see* father-child relations; mother-child relations; child rearing
Parker Family 151–178
    and slaves 162–3
    and Steuart Family 64, 66
Parker, Charles S. 129, 162
    and American Revolution 153–154
    and childhood 156–7
    and credit 165
    and relationship with father 165
    and views on marrying too early 169–170
    and West Indies 165
Parker, James 151–178, 198, 246
    relations with Steuart Family 64
Parker, Margaret
    and American Revolution 153–4, 187 n. 34
    and slaves 162–3
    and Virginia 164
    death of 154–5
    relations with husband 156, 162–5, 198
    relations with Steuart Family 64
Parker, Mary Aitchison (Molly) 90, 155, 176
    and marriage with Patrick Parker 166–170
Parker, Patrick 38, 151–178, 246
Parker, Susan 129, 153–5, 156, 162
    and relationship with father 165
paternalism, *see* patriarchy
patriarchal authority 151, 166, 177–8
    and punishment 220
patriarchal styles of child rearing 157
patriarchy

Index

and conservativism 189–190
and paternalism, 8, 15, 111–112, 114, 135, 141
and paternalism and slavery 162–4
and paternalist families 243
and rage 239
and subversion by novels 241
as structure 189, 243
in Virginia 152, 177–8
see also 'anxious patriarchs'
Patriots 152, 157
and debtors 159, 161, 175
Pease, Simon 197
Penitent Son, The 150
Pennsylvania Gazette 117, 122
petitions 97–8, 173
to end slavery 107–8
see also letter writing, and deferential styles
Petrarch 97
Pettigrew Family 245
Phelps, Elizabeth 62
Phibbah 58
Philadelphia 196
Phillipson, Eliza Partridge 218
Phillipson, Eliza Tharp 210, 214–215, 217–218, 221–5, 235–6, 238
Phillipson, John Tharp 218
Phillipson, Richard Burton 218
Phillipson, Richard Burton Burton 210, 217–219, 221–5, 227, 235–6, 238
and *The Monk* 232–3
Pierce, Nathaniel 106–7
Pierce, Diana 106–7
Pinckney, Thomas 129, 130
pirates 119, 120
planting 118–119
politeness
and letters 68
contrasted with familiarity 57–9
Polydore 189
Pope, Alexander
letter collection 73, 92
population growth in England and colonies, 31–32
Portland Place 226
postal services, *see* communications infrastructure
Potter, Simon 188, 192
pregnancy 47–8, 158, 187, 219
privacy 37
see also public
privateers 119
prodigal son image 149–152, 167, 172, 178, 243
Protestantism
and letter-writing 69, 75, 81

public
and private distinctions 15–6, 26–7, 54, 113–114

Quakers (Society of Friends) 76
and letters 96
see also family networks
quills 38

race
and sensibility 88–9
rascal 172
reason 195, 198
Redwood, Abigail 37
religious styles, *see* letter writing
remittance 128
representation 151, 169, 174–6
resentment
and American Revolution 189, 197, 204
and marriage 219
retirement 226
'revolution against patriarchal authority' 124
Rhode Island 96–7, 102–3, 160
Newport 183–209
Rhode Island Assembly 186
Richardson, Samuel 83
and *Clarissa* 74–5, 90–1, 224, 241
and *Letters to and from Particular Friends* 73–4
and *Pamela* 30, 56, 65–6, 73–4, 90, 200, 241
Richmond, Colonel 195
'rights talk' 16, 17, 107–8
Robert, Daniel 46
Robertson, Elizabeth 42
Rodney, George (Admiral) 181, 206–7, 209
Roger 154
Romeo-and-Juliet tale 203
Rose, The (ship) 186, 194, 196, 202
Rousseau, Jean-Jacques 157, 190, 242 n. 7
Rowlandson, Thomas 211
ruin
and American Revolution 205
and anxiety 115, 120, 170–1
and dependence 121
and families 122–3, 172–4, 177–8
and female virtue 121
and French Revolution 123
and gender 121–2
and idleness 132–3
and marriage 167–170, 176–7
and slander 122
and tears 121
as domestic issue 113–114
as national issue 113–115, 123
as rhetorical claim 121–3

runaways 43, 160–1
Ruscoe, John 71
Ruscoe, Joseph 71
Rush, Benjamin 88
Ruston, Thomas 37, 89, 128

sailors 43, 102, 185
'sailors' lament' 43
St Eustatius 181, 206–7, 208
St James Parish (Jamaica) 214
Sancho, Ignatius
   and letters with Laurence Sterne 94–5
   letter collection 73, 89, 94–6, 107
San Domingue (San Domingo), *see* Haiti
Sarah 154
Scotland 86, 112
Scots
   and medicine 157
   and migration 30
   and Virginia 157–9, 161
   antipathy towards 157–9
   see also education, family networks
'self-fashioning' 14, 240
self-sufficiency 134, 242
selfhood 240–2, 243
sensible letters
   and African-Americans 94–6
   and age 94
   and American Revolution 109–110
   and class 94
   and epistolary novels 90–2
   and family 96–106
   and gender 94, 97, 101–2
   and letter collections 92–3
   and letter-writing manuals 93–5
   and magazines 92
   and race 94–6
   and slavery 94–6
   as compensatory 193–4, 234–5
sensible suffering 199–200, 204, 208
sensibility
   and American Revolution 182–3, 194–205, 208–9
   and Atlantic economy 87, 127
   and benevolence 85–6
   and the body 84–5, 89, 149, 199
   and 'consumer revolution' 89
   and courtship 194–5
   and credit 172–5, 177
   and cruelty 195–6, 197–8
   and debt 151
   and *Esten v. the Duke of Hamilton* 53
   and family 8, 85–6, 240
   and farewells 179–181
   and father-child relations 10, 101, 102–4
   and French Revolution 105
   and gender 87–8, 194–203
   and the heart 84
   and inclusions/exclusions 87–8
   and Jamaica 212–213, 238
   and kin relations 100, 241
   and letter writing 89–110
   and marriage 179–183, 193–201, 208
   and mother-child relations 9, 100–1, 102
   and Parker family 162
   and race 87–8
   and reading 189–190
   and selfhood 243
   and sibling relations 99–100, 101
   and slavery 88–9, 237–8
   and sympathy 83–4, 181
   and war 182–3, 194–8
   and West Indies 232–9
   as compensatory 86–7, 243
   as political tool 201–5
   definitions of 84
   origins in the family 87
   see also insensibility; sensible letters; sensible suffering; tears
'separate spheres' 102
servants
   and letter-writing 69–70, 94, 97, 131
   denied familiarity 58
Sevigné, Madame de, *see* Chesterfield, Philip Dormer Stanhope, Earl of
sexual relations
   between men 228–9
   in West Indies 49, 137, 215, 225, 227–9, 231, 236
Shebbeare, John 81
shipwrecks 119–120, 159
shoes 165
slander 122
Shaw, Major and Mrs 229
Shoemaker Family 76
Shoemaker, Rebecca 55, 76, 77, 128, 189
sibling relations
   and credit 128–130
   and epistolary novels 74
   and familiarity 62, 64
   and frontispieces 26
   and letters 37, 42, 46, 78
   and Parker family 153, 154, 169–170, 172
   and sensibility 99–100, 101
   and separations 55
   and Tharp family 217, 228
'silken cords' 43, 111, 146
sincerity 68, 104, 129–130
   see also authenticity
slavery
   and cruelty 162–3
   and economic growth 34

and father-child relations 106, 108
and mother-child relations 88, 106–7, 108
and paternalism 162–3, 226
and sensibility/insensibility 88–9, 105, 237–8
and sensible letters 94–6
and slave trade 185, 231
and tears 95
and tyranny 95, 163
petitions to end 107–8
see also slaves
slaves 55
and arguments for freedom 17
and Atlantic economy 119
and family 43
and letter writing 42–3, 97, 106–7, 245–6
and Parker family 153–4, 162–3
and patriarchy and paternalism 162–4
and sensible letters 94–6
and Tharp family 214, 226, 237–8
as runaways 43, 160
denied familiarity 58
smallpox, *see* inoculations
Smith, Adam 6–7, 83, 85, 93
Smollett, Tobias
  The Adventures of Roderick Random 228–9
smugglers 183–4
soldiers 179–180, 182, 217
Sons of Liberty 184, 185
The Sorrows of Young Werther, *see* Goethe, Johann Wolfgang von
South Carolina 103, 172, 175, 183
spelling 133, 138
Stamp Act 184
  and Loyalists 186
  and protests 184, 185–6
Sterne, Laurence
  and letters with Ignatius Sancho 94–5
  letter collection 73, 92–3
stereotypes 147–8
Steuart Family 64
Steuart, Charles 64, 66, 152, 170
Steuart, Jennie (Jeannie) 64, 166
Stevens, James 86, 102
Stevens, Martha 86
Stiles, Ezra 184–5
Story, Mary 39
stratification 47
'strict scrutiny' 114–115, 141
  and Chesterfield, Philip Dormer Stanhope, Earl of 124–5
  and credit 171
  and gender pressures 136–138
  and kin relations 137–141
  and letters 125–6, 132–142, 135–6
  and Parker family 155
  and status pressures 136–138

Swift, Jonathan 136
sympathy 167
  and distress 193
  and family 223–4
  and tyranny 165, 190
  as 'fellow-feeling' 84
  see also sensibility

tarrings-and-featherings 158, 202
Tavernier, John 67
taverns 122, 123
Taylor, Simon 137–141, 227
  and cousin 63
  and familiar letters 39, 42 n. 60, 62
  and 'strict scrutiny' 125
  and Tharp marriage 215, 219, 222–5, 225–6, 233, 238
Taylor, Sir Simon Richard Brissett 137–141
tears 80
  and American Revolutionary War 195–6, 203–4
  and credit 167
  and family letters 100–1, 102, 104
  and men 196
  and reading 92, 197
  and ruin 121
  and sensibility 199
  and slavery 95
  and writing 201
tenderness
  and American Revolution 204–5
  and credit 171–2, 177
  and marriage 201
Tharp, Ann Virgo Gallimore 37, 210, 215–239
Tharp, Eliza *see* Phillipson, Eliza Tharp
Tharp, Elizabeth Partridge 214
Tharp, John 210–239
Tharp, John (jr) 214–215
Tharp, Joseph 214–215, 233
Tharp, Mary Hyde 215
Tharp, Thomas Partridge 214–215, 228–9, 233
Tharp, William Blake 214–215
Thistlewood, Thomas 58
thrift 170
Times, The 50
Town and Country Magazine 3, 48, 50, 179
  and 'The Repentant Son' 149
  and sensibility 83, 92, 203–4
trade 172
  and imports 32
  and exports 33
  and traders 183–4
Trelawney Parish (Jamaica) 214
trust 118, 171, 204

Turell, Jane Colman 61
Turner, Thomas 200
tyranny
  and Abigail Adams 4, 16, 81
  and American Revolution 204
  and distress 173–4
  and epistolary novels/stories 92
  and family 173–4
  and slavery 95, 163
  and sympathy 165, 190
  and West Indies 147, 212–213, 232, 239
  opposed to 'man of feeling' 196

Universal Letter-Writer, The 98
urbanization 47

Virginia 62, 86, 90, 102
  and fatherly letters 111–112
  and Parker family 146, 151–178, 246
Virgo, Ann *see* Tharp, Ann Gallimore Tharp
Virgo, Henry 217
Virgo, Montagu 217
virtue
  and family 49
  and ruin 121
  female 52, 116, 121, 218
Voltaire 157

Wallington, Nehemiah 29
Wanton, Edward 96–7
Wanton, Joseph (Governor of Rhode Island) 185, 186
Wanton, Mary 96–7
Warren, Mercy Otis 128
wars
  and family separations 44, 241–3
  and sensibility 182–3, 194–8
  and trade 119
see also exiles
Washington, George 141–2
Weber, Max 114–115
Werther, *see* Goethe, Johann Wolfgang von

West Indies 62
  and ambitions 213–214, 230–2
  and American Revolution 181
  and Brown Family 78
  and *Esten v. the Duke of Hamilton* 52, 53
  and image of 'bashaw' 212, 231
  and independence 230
  and Keane Family 59, 134
  and letters 46, 96–7, 102–3, 107, 112
  and 'macaroni' 50–1
  and marriage 198–9
  and Parker Family 165, 169–170, 175
  and ruin 122
  and sensibility 232–9
  and sexual relations 49, 137, 215, 225, 227–9, 231, 236
  and slavery 94–5
  and Steuart Family 64
  and trade 32–3
  and tyranny 147, 212–213, 232, 239
  and women 216
  property in 139–140
  see also Jamaica; St. Eustatius
Whiskey Rebellion 105
wine 194
Winthrop, Margaret and John 80–2
wives, *see* marriage
women
  and American Revolutionary War 195–7, 201–3
  and credit 116, 219
  and 'delicate sensations' 81–2, 87–8, 97
  and Jamaica 227–9, 238
  and letter preservation 244–5
  and sensible letters 100–3
  domestic leverage 164–5
  in West Indies 216
  left alone 43, 63, 181–2, 191, 198
  violated in American Revolution 202–3
Woolf, Virginia 18, 19
Wormeley Family 62
Wormeley, Ralph 59, 62, 111–112, 132–4
Wormeley, Warner Lewis 62, 111–112, 132–4